The New Political Culture

EDITED BY

Terry Nichols Clark
and Vincent Hoffmann-Martinot

WITH ASSISTANCE FROM

Mark Gromala

WestviewPress

A Division of HarperCollins*Publishers*

Urban Policy Challenges

Copyright © 1998 by Westview Press, A Member of the Perseus Books Group

Published in 1998 in the United States of America by Westview Press, 5500 Central Avenue, Boulder, Colorado 80301-2877, and in the United Kingdom by Westview Press, 12 Hid's Copse Road, Cumnor Hill, Oxford OX2 9JJ

A CIP catalog record for this book is available from the Library of Congress.
ISBN 0-8133-6694-1

The paper used in this publication meets the requirements of the American National Standard for Permanence of Paper for Printed Library Materials Z39.48-1984.

10   9   8   7   6   5   4   3   2   1

The New Political Culture

URBAN POLICY CHALLENGES

Terry Nichols Clark
SERIES EDITOR

Cities are critical. From the Los Angeles riots of 1992 to the Hong Kong reversion of 1997, cities represent in microcosm the problems and potentials we face at all governmental levels.

Focusing on cities can help clarify our most challenging issues. Most key decisions affecting our lives are made locally. Although national governments collect the majority of funds, most welfare state programs around the world are provided by local governments. Urban leaders play key roles in encouraging economic development, maintaining quality public services, and mandating reasonable taxes.

And they are pressed to do more: provide attractive physical environments, improve amenities such as bike paths, help encourage recycling, assist disadvantaged groups to achieve broader acceptance and access to public facilities, keep streets safe, and fill the gaps in health and social services.

Books in the *Urban Policy Challenges* series will explore the range of urban policy problems and will detail solutions that have been sought and implemented in cities from around the world. They will build on studies of leadership, public management, organizational culture, community power, intergovernmental relations, public finance, citizen responsiveness, and related elements of urban public decisionmaking.

These approaches to urban challenges will range from case studies to quantitative modeling. The series will include monographs, texts, as well as edited volumes. While some works will target professional and student audiences, many books will elicit attention from thoughtful public leaders and informed citizens as well

Books in the Series

The Los Angeles Riots: Lessons for the Urban Future,
    edited by Mark Baldasarre
Local Elites in Western Democracy: A Comparative Analysis of Urban Political Leaders in the United States, Sweden and The Netherlands,
    Samuel J. Eldersveld, Lars Stromberg, and Wim Derksen
Local Economic Development: Incentives and International Trends,
    edited by Norman Walzer
Local Democracy and the Processes of Transformation in East-Central Europe,
    edited by Harald Baldersheim, Michael Illner, Audun Offerdal,
    Lawrence Rose, and Pawel Swianiewicz
Politics and Plutocracy in New York City,
    by Gabriel Almond.
Citizen Politics in Post-Industrial Societies,
    edited by Terry Nichols Clark and Michael Rempel

Contents

Part 1—The New Political Culture: An Analytical Framework to Interpret What Has Changed, Where, and Why

Part 2—Where Has the New Political Culture Emerged and Why?

Part 3—How Hierarchies and Parties Specifically Redirect Politics and Policy Priorities

Contributors to the Volume

Zhiyue Bo completed a Ph.D. at the University of Chicago and has taught at Roosevelt University and the University of Chicago. He is research director of the Fiscal Austerity and Urban Innovation (FAUI) Project.

Terry Nichols Clark is professor of sociology at the University of Chicago and coordinator of the FAUI Project.

Ronald Inglehart is well-known for his work on postmaterialism in *The Silent Revolution* and *Culture Shift*; he is professor of political science at the University of Michigan.

Vincent Hoffmann-Martinot is a political scientist at the French Urban Center, Cervel, and the CNRS in Bordeaux. He is editor of Logopol, the urban research journal of the European Consortium for Political Research and coordinator of urban programs for Minitel, the French home-TV network.

Jerzy Bartkowski is a political sociologist who teaches at the University of Warsaw; he has published two books on polish local government and visited the University of Chicago several times.

Eric Fong, Mark Gromala, Doug Huffer, Dennis Merritt, Ziad Munson, Yun-Ji-Qian, and Michael Rempel are recent graduates of the University of Chicago and worked with the FAUI project as student research assistants for several years.

Lincoln Quillian worked on the FAUI project as a student at the University of Chicago, for much of a year in France, and as a graduate student at Harvard. He is now assistant professor at the University of Wisconsin, Madison.

Oscar Gabriel is professor of political science and director of the Institute of Politics at the University of Stuttgart. His coauthors, Katja Ahlstich, Frank Brettschneider, and Volker Kunz, are assistants at the institute.

Mark Baldassare is professor and chairman of the school of social ecology, University of California, Irvine.

Hans Geser is professor of sociology at the University of Zurich and has conducted a major study of local political parties in Switzerland.

Preface

What is the New Political Culture (NPC)? Many interpreters misunderstand the NPC by labeling it as "Right" or "Left." The NPC joins elements of both the traditional right and left to make it more than either, and it adds new concerns—like making government more efficient and helping average citizens understand and genuinely participate in policymaking. It is a major new force on the political scene around the world. We do not suggest that traditional right or left parties have disappeared, or that class politics and clientelism are dead. The NPC competes with these past types of politics; indeed, much of politics is debate over whose rules to follow. Our main attention to the NPC in this book, rather than other patterns, follows from the importance of understanding what is new in order to contrast it with the old. When we first began these efforts, many felt that the NPC simply did not exist; some people still ignore it, but more are fighting against it. We do not defend it as morally good; the book attempts positive analysis, not normative assessment. Yet it is clear that the NPC brings many things widely seen as "bad," such as volatile leadership, fragile policy commitments, loose linkages to enduring social groups (like unions, classes, or ethnic groups), and more. Many are detailed below along with traits widely appreciated. In a word, however, average citizens in many countries often support candidates and programs of the NPC, whereas professional politicians, certain interest groups, and traditional party officials often do not. As citizens have grown more important, so has the NPC.

Labeling is a common problem. For instance, new leaders in Italy, Eastern Europe, and Latin America are often labeled "capitalists" or "the New Right." Such labels reflect the observer's (old) ideologies as much as the new leaders they describe. NPC leaders disagree as much with the views of Ronald Reagan and Margaret Thatcher as they do with Karl Marx and Franklin Roosevelt. It is human nature to pour new wine into old bottles, but the labels are now often wrong. The main conflicts today are not about socialism versus capitalism or more versus less government, but about hierarchy versus egalitarianism. The

U.S. Postal Service, General Motors, and armies in every country are all hierarchies that egalitarians seek to level.

Chapter 2 outlines the theory in most detail. Subsequent chapters assess the Chapter 2 propositions with evidence from citizen surveys, census data, and ethnographic work—but especially from 7,000 cities around the world. These comparative urban data were assembled in the Fiscal Austerity and Urban Innovation (FAUI) Project over 14 years, representing a huge investment of time and money by over 500 persons. Some twenty books and more than 200 articles have emerged from the FAUI Project to date, but this is the first on political processes in international perspective. It has been exciting to see how many theories of politics that work in one country must be recast to interpret different countries. Observing such contextual variation both strengthens our theories and chastens our nationalist impulses. Examples are in the Overview.

The book is written for social scientists as well as more general readers, including college students, elected officials, civic leaders, and interested citizens. Most technical points are relegated to notes and appendices to keep the reading clear. But we have not sought to simplify complex ideas when the phenomena themselves are complex, as is the case with the main topic of the book—the New Political Culture.

This is number three of a trilogy of books about the NPC, the last and most comprehensive. The conceptual origin of all three books was an early draft of Chapter 2, "The New Political Culture" (Clark and Inglehart 1989, 1990). It contrasted class politics and the New Political Culture and formulated 22 propositions about where the NPC is important. The second volume is Clark and Rempel (1997), which tests NPC propositions using primarily citizen survey data. Such citizen data are useful to probe individual characteristics like occupation, age, and gender, which are associated with other characteristics in urban data. The first volume is Clark (1994), which tests propositions about the NPC with American urban data, and analyzes policies like growth control and new management techniques as implementing this political culture. The NPC propositions have been adapted to several contexts, such as Western and Eastern Europe, Australia, Japan (in this volume), and, in more detail, in postcommunist Eastern Europe. The NPC paper was translated into Polish and Hungarian and recast for Eastern Europe (in Clark 1993; see also Peteri 1991; Surazska 1995), Spain (Rojo 1990), and Latin America (Landa 1995, 1996). The propositions also helped spark an ongoing exchange about whether "social class is dying" or yielding to postindustrial politics (Clark and Lipset 1991; Clark, Lipset and Rempel 1993; Hout et al. 1995; see Chapter 4 in this volume).

The propositions suggest several processes. Some concern *individual citizens* (e.g., more highly educated persons should be more socially liberal), whereas others concern *social/political system characteristics* (e.g., the more ideologically coherent are political parties, the less likely is the emergence of NPC). The propositions are sufficiently complex that several sub-projects were pursued to address them with overlapping teams and different types of data. Although some ideas have been presented to professional meetings and in journal articles, these three volumes report the main results. Each volume pursues those propositions most appropriate to test with a particular type of data or national context.

The three volumes are team efforts. Some initial propositions were sparked by discussions of postindustrial developments in conferences of the FAUI Project. As we compared interpretations, we might hear that "bureaucrats are more important in Oslo," "Japan has few new social movements," and so on. Dozens of such observed differences challenged us to build an analytical framework to interpret them. Our goal throughout has been to explain cases and exceptions by articulating a general theory, which we understand as a set of propositions and assumptions about conditions where the propositions hold. For example, rather than just stating that class politics is important in France and postindustrial politics more important in the United States, we formulate more abstract propositions, such as more education for citizens and weak political parties should promote postindustrial politics. These propositions should in turn capture key processes to explain differences between France and the United States but also differences elsewhere.

Much past research is on one or a few nation-states. Results often differ from one country to the next. This is inherent in "small N" studies: Nations are scarce animals and distinct in part for idiosyncratic reasons. What then? Some suggest in depth case studies of one or two nations (e.g., Skocpol 1979) or comparing a few nations using procedures like "Boolean analysis" (e.g., Ragin 1987). Although each such approach can add insight, we find it useful to conduct case studies of nations or cities identified as theoretically critical and thus interesting to build on for generalizing (such as the rise of new leaders in Eastern Europe, Italy, and France.) We simultaneously try to join case studies with comparative work. The comparative work locates the cases and indicates the generality or distinctiveness of each case. For comparative work we find it methodologically compelling to increase the N and then undertake conceptually-informed comparisons via testing propositions. Put differently, can we build a science better using a handful of scarce dinosaurs—or with thousands of fruit flies? Our approach builds on the methodological innovations in crossnational comparative research of persons like Stein Rokkan in the 1960s. Alas, there has not been substantial methodological progress since. Our assessment is shared by others, for example, recent reviews by Erwin Scheuch and Henry Teune (in Oyen 1990) and Kaase and Newton (1995).

General methodological discussions repeatedly stress the value of a large number of cases to permit unraveling causal processes. A large N can reduce idiosyncrasies of individual cases to "noise." We have sought to achieve this by analyzing either (1) citizens in different countries to assess the importance of individual characteristics like education or age, or (2) local governments to analyze political system characteristics, like income inequalities or party strength. We have correspondingly spent more than a decade assembling and analyzing data for more than 60,000 citizens and 7,000 cities around the world, reported in these three volumes. Thus we study localities and citizens to generalize more precisely about political systems. It is gratifying to be able to report how well many general propositions hold.

We often build on the FAUI Project. Initiated in 1983, the FAUI project has become the most extensive study of local government in the world. It includes more than 550 persons in 35 countries. Participants meet in conferences, via the Internet, and analyze a core of comparable data. Participants have collected and shared data concerning citizens, local public officials, and socioeconomic characteristics of localities, regions, and nations. Many items have been included specifically to map postindustrial politics. Most of these data can now be made available to researchers via the Internet. Contact tnc@spc.uchicago.edu.

The wonderful colleagues who participated in the FAUI Project for more than a decade deserve first acknowledgment; many are listed in the Appendix. Vincent Hoffmann-Martinot helped launch the book when he spent a year visiting Chicago, Michigan, and Harvard and helped organize a Paris conference of FAUI colleagues (published as Baldersheim et al. 1989). The FAUI Project is remarkable in doing so much with so little funding; the secret is generous contributions of time and resources from many, many persons. We created a non-profit organization to pursue several overlapping activities, Urban Innovation Analysis, Inc., whose board members have been unusually wise and helpful, especially Sydney Stein Jr., Ferdinand Kramer, Marshall Holleb, Melvin Mister, Burton Ditkowsky, and Mayor William Morris, who serves as chairman. Lorna Ferguson graciously encouraged FAUI activities from Tokyo to Florence. Rowan Miranda and Richard Balme helped us launch the pooling effort. Mark Gromala closely critiqued all manuscripts. Edward Vytlatcil managed people and data. Pawel Swianiewicz, Ewa Jurczynska, and Janet Stametal enlightened us on Eastern Europe. Kevin Sahl stalked the library. Carlen Rader coded educational data from a huge stack of reports for every prefecture in Japan. Howard Runyan and Jon Howard edited skillfully. George Rumsey produced camera-ready graphics and text.

We gratefully acknowledge financial and institutional support from the U.S. Department of Housing and Urban Development, The Ford Foundation, The Joyce Foundation, the University of Chicago, University of Florence, Burton Ditkowsky, Urban Innovation Analysis, and the Center for the Study of Urban Inequality through funds made available by the Ford, MacArthur, and Rockefeller Foundations.

Most data used in this volume are available to others. Please address inquiries to: Terry Nichols Clark, 1126 East 59th Street, Suite 322, The University of Chicago, Chicago, Illinois 60637, USA, Tel: 773-702-8686; fax: 773-702-9673; tnc@spc.uchicago.edu.

Terry Nichols Clark
Chicago, August 1997

For Mayor William Morris, who shaped the New Political Culture

In 1983 we organized a conference entitled "Questioning the Welfare State and the Rise of the City" at the University of Paris, Nanterre, with help from the new Mitterand government. It was clear that old Socialist ideas were being questioned inside and outside the Socialist Party and government, especially in the important decentralization reforms. Similar problems have faced most parties of the left around the world. Various managerial solutions are emerging. These are often linked to changes in political leadership and the political culture of citizens and organized groups. One, which we here seek to clarify, has been termed "New Fiscal Populism" in the United States. To illustrate it, a particularly forceful and articulate mayor was invited to Nanterre: Bill Morris, mayor of Waukegan, Illinois, a city of 67,000 north of Chicago. He was a leftist Democrat in background but had grown conservative on fiscal issues while remaining progressive on social issues concerning race, women, and the like. He appealed in populist manner to individual citizens over the heads of traditional parties and organized group leaders. He stressed productivity and improved service delivery to respond to the disadvantaged while reducing costs to the taxpayer.

In Nanterre, Bill Morris was politely treated as an alien visitor. He might have come from Mars. The French and other European participants clearly felt there was nothing like this on European soil. One said, "we have a Left and a Right which are far more explicitly defined and consistent with our history." Still, one participant, Milan political sociologist Guido Martinotti, thought there might be lessons here for Italian mayors, and so he published an article to that effect in *Corriera della Serra*. A curious phenomenon—but clearly non-European.

Things changed just a year later. A small number of French mayors and younger politicians with national ambitions were making waves. One press account even referred to them as "the New Mayors." (Excerpted from Balme, Clark, Becquart-Leclercq, Hoffmann-Martinot, and Nevers, 1987: 263).

Part 1

The New
Political Culture:

An Analytical Framework to Interpret
What Has Changed, Where, and Why

1

Overview of the Book

Terry Nichols Clark

This volume introduces a new style of politics, the New Political Culture (NPC), which began in many countries in the 1970s. It has become dominant in some locations. It defines new rules of the game for politics, challenging two older traditions: class politics and clientelism. Advocates of the New Political Culture include Bill Clinton, Tony Blair, and Francois Mitterand. They revolutionized the politics of their countries by embracing NPC issues. These include citizen democracy, environmentalism, gay rights, and abortion—generally consumption and lifestyle issues, with less emphasis on workplace and jobs than in the past. Leadership comes less from parties, unions, and ethnic groups in coalitions of rich versus poor, or high- versus low-status persons. Rather, leadership shifts from issue to issue; leaders on abortion are distinct from leaders on environmental issues. Issue-specific leaders are thus more active, as are citizens and the media. This NPC emerges more fully and forcefully in cities and countries with more highly educated citizens, higher incomes, and high-tech service occupations.

This book is distinctive in clarifying changes in these basic rules of the game by which politics is played. Seven key elements defining the NPC are introduced; propositions then specify where and why the NPC emerges. Global political transformations related to NPC developments include the collapse of traditional political hierarchies, such as Soviet communism, the Italian political system in 1993, and socialist parties in many countries that shifted from state centralism toward citizen participation and market individualism. Parallel shifts away from authoritarian hierarchy are found in corporate cultures embracing collegial staff relations as well as in families giving wives and children more autonomy. These declines in social and economic hierarchies undermine traditional class politics, coherent political parties, and authoritarian political leaders. They open the door to the NPC.

Our sources include citizen surveys, case studies by actual participants, national statistical reports, and reviews of past research. Several chapters use data of the Fiscal Austerity and Urban Innovation (FAUI) Project from some 7,000 cities in 20 countries. These data permit more precise and comprehensive international comparisons of political processes than any past urban study. This is the first book on political processes using the international FAUI data.

In Part 1, we look at fundamental ideas behind the NPC, which includes seven core elements. It (1) redefines the classic left-right continuum; (2) distinguishes fiscal from social issues; (3) stresses social issues; (4) emphasizes market and social individualism; (5) reassesses the welfare state; (6) focuses political debate on issues more than party loyalty; and (7) is supported by younger, more educated, affluent individuals and societies. Elements of this NPC have been termed New Fiscal Populist, Postmaterialist, green, neo-liberal, Yuppie politics, postindustrial politics, and new politics.

A framework to interpret these changes includes three general ideas: declining hierarchy, democratization of resources, and shifting structural conditions. These are detailed by identifying their operation in twenty-two specific propositions about shifting political party appeals, new social movements, transformation of economic and family structures, rising income and education, and enhanced communications via television, fax, and computers. For instance: *16. Younger, more highly educated persons support more socially liberal issues. Although they support the output of many welfare state programs, they also prefer increased efficiency in service delivery and correspondingly lower costs and taxes. These changes in fiscal/administrative preferences are largest (a) among more affluent persons, (b) in affluent societies with extensive welfare state programs, and (c) among younger persons.*

More enduring patterns like Protestantism, national welfare states, and population homogeneity shift effects of these recent changes. Selected propositions are tested in Chapter 2, but the main evidence is in later chapters. Chapter 2 combines the social-psychological dynamics identified by Ronald Inglehart with social and political structural transformations elaborated by Terry Clark. Past studies have discussed several of these elements separately, but no one has identified the NPC with this specificity. The NPC theory identifies a new form of politics, a paradigm change emerging around the world. But the NPC theory itself consists of distinct propositions which permits their testing one by one; indeed we find some propositions clearly supported and others far less.

In Part 2, Chapter 3 considers critical cases of political transformations in recent decades, asking how they square with NPC concepts.

- The decline of Communism in Eastern Europe is examined via biographies of the first new mayors chosen in democratic elections in 1990, and an assessment of these by Wisla Surazska.
- Almost simultaneous with the East European developments, in Italy national party leaders, parliamentarians, and mayors of many cities were removed in scandals, followed by elections of hundreds of new leaders. Enrico Ercole interprets these.
- Socialist parties around the world, from the late 1970s through the 1990s, largely

abandoned their support of central state planning of the economy and embraced market-linked programs. We draw on Seymour Martin Lipset's review of this shift based on socialist policy statements from Europe, Asia, and Latin America.

- The rise of NPC elements in Japan is charted via studies of citizens and leaders by Wonho Jang.
- Intriguing reports also come from a French Communist city, resistance to New Labour in a British working class town, and reform efforts of the U.S. federal and local governments.

That these diverse locales, interpreters, and methods all suggest converging views provide powerful evidence of global trends moving broadly toward the NPC.

Chapter 4 investigates NPC ideas using the most extensive study of local government in the world to date, the FAUI Project. It includes surveys of local officials in the United States, Canada, Japan, Australia, Argentina, much of Western Europe, and four East European countries, totaling some 7,000 cities. The NPC is measured by percentages of women mayors and council members, mayors' age and education, importance of organized groups and mass media, and mayors' preferences about fiscal policy, abortion, sex education, and citizen responsiveness. Often, those cities with more such NPC characteristics have more citizens who are professionals and more highly educated, and fewer blue-collar workers. But inequality of education and income, outside the United States, does not affect leaders' policy preferences. Why not? Parties buffer leaders from such cleavages, as well as from NPC transformations in many counties. Indeed, parties dramatically redirect activities of other participants, leading supporters of new issues like ecology to work inside existing parties in some locations but forcing them in others to start new parties or create new organized groups. Yet parties can change too. Parties have not been incorporated adequately into past work on class politics, which is reinterpreted here by analyzing 250 national party programs for changes from 1945 through the 1980s; many move toward NPC themes.

Chapter 4 succeeds at testing general propositions using data from up to 20 countries. A few patterns in the chapter are country-specific, but a distinctive contribution is its success at transcending country-specific explanations. Moving back and forth between local, national, and pooled international results permits us to identify precisely how unique some countries are, as well as, often, how most national patterns are successfully explained by more general propositions. Our success is due in good part to the larger number of cases than available to analysts of just nations. The chapter shows how a multi-level analysis can generate more powerful answers to many of the same questions that have previously been considered with mainly national data. For instance, when and where class politics persists, and how parties play critical roles in shifting policy are questions answered with far more precision than past studies.

In Part 3, Chapter 5 probes further into political parties, as they critically constrain elected officials who take positions and act. Vincent Hoffmann-Martinot here presents the most comprehensive synthesis to date of past research on local party structures around the world. He documents major differences in party penetration of government: minimal in Australia and Canada, deep in France and Italy. Parties also substantially vary in their openness to citizens and organized groups—of business, labor, and others, as well as to new social movements concerning ecology and women. Parties founded on traditional class cleavages and unions, or clientelism and patronage by *padrone*, resist NPC developments—which can drive citizens to alienation, to protest, or to embrace new parties or organized groups.

Chapter 6 contrasts old and new politics orientations among local officials in Germany. Generally, traditional "bread and butter" issues (e.g., social security, economic development, street construction) lost salience in favor of new-politics issues (e.g., environmental protection, political participation, minority rights). But party representatives differ in their sensitivities to new issues. The new politics is strongest among Social Democrats and Greens, who take these concerns into account when reshaping local spending. The Greens also include a strong concern for social welfare. This contrasts sharply with the preference for economy-related spending on the right/materialist end of the ideological spectrum, of the Christian Democrats, CDU/CSU, and FDP parties. No ideologically neutral, nonpartisan style politics was found in any city studied. Members of the CDU/CSU are most responsive to the electorate (Pearson r = .43), the Greens least so (.26), and the Social Democrats (.33) are in between. The Greens see themselves as representing demands of particular minorities among the electorate— *not* the majority.

In Chapter 7, Hans Geser criticizes certain NPC propositions. He presents evidence from Switzerland that issue positions on "old politics" (fiscal liberalism) and "new politics" (social and ecological liberalism) are strongly interrelated. These positive correlations are consistently highest when community affluence is high and party members are young. He suggests this implies that a single-dimensional, generalized, new ideological polarization is emerging in Switzerland. New political issues are "coded" into the traditional left-right paradigm. Does this contradict the NPC propositions? Perhaps. Reservations: The study is based on 2,638 local party leaders, not citizens, so one would expect them to be more ideologically consistent. Such consistency in more urban and wealthier contexts may reflect the general tendency of higher-educated social strata and political elites to hold more coherent political attitudes (e.g., to show higher correlations between their general left-right views and specific political issues). Indeed, this same pattern is found in Inglehart (1990) and Rempel (1992) in other countries. Considered in cross-national context, these Swiss findings document powerfully how responsive the Swiss parties are in incorporating new young activists, especially women, successfully joining their energies with traditional party programs. Such success at co-optation of new politics activists stands in sharp contrast with the French or Italian cases, where in the same years traditional parties remained generally unresponsive. This illustrates the general responsiveness of Swiss political leaders and parties to new issues and citizen concerns, heightened by Swiss localism and commitment to popular democracy: Switzerland has no "national" government at all but is a weak confederation of cantons; parties are similarly based in cantons (Clark and Jeanrenaud 1989).

Chapter 8 explores politics in a locale typical of many citizens in postindustrial

societies but one seldom studied by social scientists: middle- and upper-income suburbs. Indeed, a majority of American citizens lives not in central cities or rural towns
but in suburbs. Suburbs are growing in much of Western Europe and some Asian
countries. Mark Baldassare conducted surveys for more than a decade of citizens and
local officials in the thirty-one municipalities of Orange County, California, just south
of Los Angeles. He also directed the FAUI survey throughout California. These rich
data permit him to map changes with unprecedented detail. He asked a range of
questions, including some about local controls on economic and population growth,
whose salience in Orange County is near unique in the United States. The profile of
Orange County residents—young, affluent, educated, and with rising incomes—should
make them, per the Chapter 2 propositions, supporters of the NPC. Baldassare finds
this generally to be the case. This contradicts the traditional image of such suburbanites
as classic conservatives; Baldassare maps their rising social liberalism. Focusing specifically on growth controls, he finds that support increased while incomes rose in the
1980s; support decreased during the economic recession of the 1990s. As evidence of
the "issue-oriented" nature of the anti-growth movement, community attitudes consistently predict suburban support for local growth controls, whereas political party
affiliation and political orientation do not (nor do demographic factors). These fluctuations in policy preferences illustrate the volatility and fragility of politics in the New
Political Culture.

2

The New Political Culture: Changing Dynamics of Support for the Welfare State and other Policies in Postindustrial Societies[1]

Terry Nichols Clark
and
Ronald Inglehart

A specter is haunting Industrial Society—a specter of new political fault lines and a new political culture. When a new class or issue first surfaces, it is labeled an exception—to the old. But as exceptions grow in number, they weaken the old categories to the breaking point. We are now there. In the past two decades, exceptions to the traditional model of class politics have mounted in number and importance. The traditional left-right issues have lost their dynamic force: Polarization of parties around class conflict explains less and less. Different fault lines and issues are emerging, some new, some not. They combine in a New Political Culture (NPC). Consider:

- The percent of voters who do not identify with established political parties has been rising. For example, in the United States in the 1980s Independents rose to about one-third of the electorate. (Specific percentages vary with how party identification is asked.)
- Ecology movements and green parties emerged after 1982 when the West German Greens became a political force. In the 1989 European Community elections, Green parties won about 15 percent of the seats, more than the Liberal Party in Britain, or the Communist Party in France.
- New style candidates are coming to office who break with established parties and programs. Some are national leaders (Francois Mitterand, Bill Clinton, Tony Blair), but since cities vary more than nations, local leaders

are often clearer examples of the new, and more able to implement their policies—from Mayors Diane Feinstein in San Francisco, to Alain Carignon in Grenoble, to Guy-Olivier Segond in Geneva. Their numbers are growing in our surveys of mayors and council members.

- The heightened, sometimes heated, importance of ethnic, linguistic, and regional cleavages—new in many European countries—including persistent guerrilla activities in Basque/Spain and Ireland.
- Highly visible immigrants in most European countries and North America, who increasingly press for political rights and assistance.
- New anti-immigrant elements in many European parties in response to immigrant demands, such as the National Front in France since 1984, and xenophobic Republicans in West Germany.
- The rise of religious fundamentalism, from electronic ministers in the United States, to cults in Europe, to Muslim fundamentalism in Iran—often with open and active political involvement.
- New social movements for more democracy, decentralization, individual freedom, and other non-economic issues in China, the former Soviet Union, and Eastern Europe.

A Framework for Analysis of the New Political Culture (NPC): Seven Defining Elements

A New Political Culture is emerging, but its recognition is long overdue—largely because many intelligent persons wear analytical lenses that do not focus on it. Class politics is not dead, but increasingly inadequate. Clientelism is also weakening in many locations. Social stratification is expressed in new ways. Class never explained all the variance, yet was often the "best tool in the tool box" and seemed adequate from the late nineteenth to mid-twentieth century. Since the 1970s, new nonclass cleavages have emerged concerning gender, race, regional loyalty, sexual preference, ecological concern, and broader citizen participation. These social issues are distinct from fiscal/economic issues. They may even cost government nothing; they concern new social patterns, lifestyles—cultural norms about how people should live. Most social issues began earlier, but their cumulative combination brings a fundamental change, a New Political Culture. While the broader sources and dynamics of change encompass many social institutions, key actors in changing specific political cultures are often elected officials, and especially candidates for office. They tend to crystallize fundamental disagreements, state alternatives more forcefully and completely than individual citizens, and yet rise and fall only with support of citizens qua voters. While broader socio-economic changes are captured in propositions in this chapter, they operate through concrete actors. Our examples in the text and still more in chapters 3 and 4 show how candidates for elective office are often critical actors, "carriers" as Max Weber termed them, driving change.

The New Political Culture is distinct in seven key respects:

1. The classic left-right dimension has been transformed People still speak of left and right, but definitions are changing. *Left* increasingly means social issues, less often traditional class politics issues. In Eastern Europe the polarity of left and right so changed that in the late 1980s the political left sometimes referred to those who support increasing private ownership and *less* state intervention in the economy. The change is less dramatic in the West, but increasing the role of government is no longer automatically equated with progress, even on the left; and the most intensely disputed issues no longer deal with ownership and control of the means of production. Many leaders, and citizens, feel disoriented by the shifting meaning of the left-right map.

2. Social and fiscal/economic issues are explicitly distinguished. Social issues demand analysis in their own terms. They are not just "ideological superstructure" or "false consciousness." Correspondingly, positions on social issues—of citizens, leaders, and parties—cannot be derived from their positions on fiscal issues. Note that we do *not* define "social issues" as expensive welfare state programs, although some persons do. Rather, we focus more on issues like tolerance for new women's roles or multiculturalism, and other items measured in many citizen surveys on social tolerance. To say that social and fiscal issues should be analytically distinguished does not imply that they are do not overlap empirically. Social issues can have fiscal implications—such as providing extra funding for minority students. But social issues can also be pursued with no fiscal implications, such as Jimmy Carter's appointing more minority lawyers as federal judges. By contrast, the class politics model implies the opposite: (1) fiscal issues dominate social issues; (2) social issue positions derive from fiscal issue positions; (3) specifically the left is liberal on social and fiscal issues, and the right is conservative. The NPC reflects a more general socio-economic differentiation and professionalization. We test these competing interpretations below, via correlations between fiscal and social issues. As class politics is replaced by the NPC, correlations between fiscal and social liberalism decline.

3. Social issues have risen in salience relative to fiscal/economic issues. This change is driven by affluence: As wealth increases, people grow more concerned with lifestyle and other amenity issues—in addition to classic economic concerns. We document this change with several citizen survey items. Recognition of these changes spurred some neo-Marxists to rethink socialist theory (e.g., Harrington 1989; Bowles and Gintis 1987).

4. Market individualism and social individualism grow. Neither individualism implies a return to tradition; indeed the NPC is most clearly opposed to the statist European right. Both individualisms foster skepticism toward traditional left policies, such as nationalization of industry and welfare state growth. But the NPC joins "market liberalism" (in the past narrowly identified with parties of the right), with "social progressiveness" (previously identified with parties of the left.) This new *combination of policy preferences* leads NPCs to support new programs, and follow new rules of the game.

5. *Questioning the welfare state.* Some NPC citizens, and leaders, conclude that "governing" in the sense of state-central planning is unrealistic for many services—economic and social. Although not seeking to reduce services, NPCs question specifics of service delivery and seek to improve efficiency. They are skeptical of large central bureaucracies. They are willing to decentralize administration or contract with other governments or private firms—if these work better. "Work" includes citizen responsiveness as well as meeting professional staff criteria. In difficult economic times—like the 1970s stagflation—NPCs can become fiscally conservative, as specified in propositions below. But they are clearly distinct from the traditional right (e.g., Reagan, Thatcher) that focuses on simply cutting government. Many observers feel that national governments have lost much of their legitimacy; nation-states are too large, distant from citizens, and unresponsive. Federalism and regionalism claim new converts, especially in Western Europe. "Small is beautiful," and "think globally but act locally" are new mantras; many see local governments as serving citizens better than nation-states. This leads to efforts to develop smaller, more responsive governments, and new intergovernmental agreements—which happened in the United States and many other countries in the 1980s and 1990s. The European Union has undermined nation-states and reinvigorated regions and localities; conflicts in the former USSR and Yugoslavia have broken up the largest unit into confederations. In the United States and Britain, nonprofits and public authorities have taken a far more visible role, even shaping government policies in their own image, such as in health, education, and social service provision. In Eastern Europe, one of the first, dramatic reforms after the fall of communism in 1989 was reviving thousands of local governments—small towns that had been abolished in the past few decades. Many U.S. cities are criticizing their existing service delivery modes and experimenting with such alternative patterns of service delivery as contracting out services, using new technology, and the like. Neighborhood governments, block clubs, and other small-area associations are emerging the world over, simultaneous with declines in turnout and interest in national elections. This new decentralization and volatility may be more citizen responsive, but it causes problems for provision of large public goods, like national defense or coherent national policies.[2] The new character of leadership and decision-making is thus open to criticism by many intellectuals and displaced political leaders—these were loud and sometimes successful in displacing initial NPC leaders in Eastern Europe and Italy in the 1990s (see Chapter 3).

6. *The rise of issue politics and broader citizen participation; the decline of hierarchical political organizations.* The NPC counters traditional bureaucracies, parties, and their leaders. "New Social Movements" and "issue-politics" are essential additions to the political process. These movements encourage govern-

ments to respond more directly to interested constituents. By contrast, traditional hierarchical parties, government agencies, and unions are seen as antiquated. Activist and intelligent citizens, who refuse treatment as docile "subjects" or "clients", articulate new demands. They thus organize around new issues of welfare state service provision, like day care or recycling paper. The media grow more visible and important, as new issues and developments rapidly emerge and frequently change, making NPC leadership often volatile and turbulent. New groups seek to participate in general policy formation (rivaling parties and programs); and may press to participate in service delivery (rivaling government agencies, clientelist leaders, and unions). NPC's are thus seen as "rocking the boat"; they mean to. Conflicts with traditional particularistic leaders whose political support depends on clientelistic patronage are particularly acute, such as in Southern Italy or Chicago.

7. *These NPC views are more pervasive among younger, more educated and affluent individuals, and societies.* The NPC has emerged with basic changes in the economy and the family, and is both encouraged and diffused by less social and economic hierarchy, broader value consensus, and spread of the mass media. Further factors driving toward the NPC are analyzed in propositions below, summarized in Figure 2.9.

Past Steps Toward a New Interpretation

Our interpretation builds on and extends prior formulations that revise class-based politics.

Class Politics

The core idea from the class politics tradition is that people may be ranked from high to low—often as upper, middle, or lower class. This class cleavage in turn explains political cleavages—in particular campaign statements of political candidates, party programs, and citizen voting patterns. A major political issue is redistribution—how actively government redistributes wealth from the more to less affluent.

The basic idea is ancient and was stated forcefully by Karl Marx: Social classes differ by their relations to the means of production. Class divisions define political cleavages when members of social classes become self-consciously *proletarians* or *bourgeois*. Marx held that as class consciousness rises, social categories move from being classes *an sich* (turned inward or literally *in themselves*) to classes *fuer sich* (acting *for themselves*). We broadly follow Marx in defining class as rooted in occupational/labor market differences.

Class politics includes these core elements:

1. Political cleavages derive from occupational cleavages, especially between white- and blue-collar workers; blue-collar workers and the economically disad-

vantaged oppose parties they identify as supporting persons higher in occupation and income.

2. Labor unions and socialist political parties express the society's class cleavages and appeal to blue-collar workers. Membership in such groups similarly follows occupational cleavages.

3. Political issues and campaign statements tend to be oriented toward work and production (salaries, working conditions, health insurance, etc.).

4. Social issues (like abortion, ecology, women's roles) are less salient than economic issues, or are addressed by linking them to economic issues (e.g., by stressing economic implications of social issues and using terms like exploitation).

5. Parties and voters can be classified from left to right.

Most work on political behavior in the mid-twentieth century started from some version of this class politics approach. In *Political Man*, which synthesized a wide range of work and served for decades as the leading textbook for political sociology, Lipset (1981, 460–461) used "an apolitical Marxist analysis.... Political systems ... must be analyzed in terms of their social class structure." Verba and Nie's (1972) influential work similarly offered a "standard model" of participation that was essentially class politics. Logistic analyses showing party differences in voting of distinct occupational subgroups by Heath et al. (1991), and Hout et al. (1995) suggest "trendless fluctuation", i.e. continuing class politics over recent decades. Many other statements overlap, but we cite just these to illustrate the mainstream social science concern with class politics. Leading textbooks on social stratification present similar views (e.g., Coleman and Rainwater 1978; Vanneman and Weber 1987).

Note a subtle conceptual stretch in how social scientists have defined class. Dahrendorf's influential work (1959, 157–206) exacerbated this stretch; he argued that cleavages between white- and blue-collar workers often were superseded by more complicated occupational cleavages. He differed from Marx in noting that social groups had increased in number and political importance. Dahrendorf was among the first to stretch the concept of class by redefining it as "conflict groups generated by the differential distribution of authority in imperatively coordinated associations" (204). Giddens (1980, 108–12) similarly emphasized workplace subdifferences but retained the term *class*, as did Wright (1985, 64–104), who even specified a twelve-category "typology of class location in capitalist society," including "1. bourgeoisie," "2. small employers," "4. expert managers," "5. expert supervisors," down to "12. proletarians." Wright explicitly included not just ownership but skill level and managerial responsibility.

Many writers similarly interpret race as a *temporary* or *false* version of class, asserting that time or more active organizing efforts should join racial minorities into a broader coalition of the disadvantaged. Ethnicity in general and race in particular have been treated as peculiarly American aberrations that should weaken over time. Gans (1962) made this argument forcefully, especially for white ethnic groups. Wilson (1978) and Patterson (1977) elaborated it for racial minorities.

Ethnic or racial politics involve using ethnic or racial cleavages in organized group and party activity; this is analogous to class politics as defined here. Ethnic politics has long sparked controversy, first simply in its documentation and second among political theorists. Ethnicity was so marked about 1900 in Chicago that a University of Chicago political theorist considered the European class-politics tradition inadequate and launched *group theory* as an alternative (see Bentley 1908; and his follower Truman 1951). Dahl (1961) interpreted past ethnic politics as declining in New Haven because of Mayor Richard Lee's reform style.

The success of African-American local leaders in the 1989 elections led many to ask if *deracialization* was occurring. According to Perry (1991, 182), "Deracialization essentially refers to the campaign style of several of the victorious African-American candidates who chose to downplay racial themes in their campaigns to attract white voter support." Electoral results in New Haven or Atlanta suggest deracialization or *transethnic politics* to some scholars (Kilson 1989; Summers and Klinker 1991; Pierannunzi and Hutcheson 1991). A sophisticated African-American activist from Chicago strongly disagreed: "Race is such an overriding factor in American life that to support its elimination or diffusion as a factor in elections through deracialization is folly" (Starks 1991, 217).

The New Class

In the early 1970s, Irving Kristol, Aaron Wildavsky, Seymour Martin Lipset, Alvin Gouldner, and others asked, sometimes skeptically, if a "new class" was emerging (see Bruce-Briggs 1979). Their new class was college educated, young, substantially more "liberal" than most voters, their examples predominantly American. Why "class"? Because it involved a distinct relation to the means of production: The new class depended on government, sometimes directly for jobs as government staff (especially social workers, teachers, or other service providers), or indirectly as public interest lawyers, advocacy journalists, community organizers, and others who sought to make government more activist and responsive to the disadvantaged.

Weaknesses of this approach are that it depends too narrowly on a self-interested concern with jobs and specific views of government. We concur with the New Class emphasis on social issues. But we disagree with the government job formulation: The new views are broadly shared among younger persons, not just those who depend on government. In contrast to the New Class hypothesis, we find generally increased criticism of government, at least of its hierarchical/bureaucratic services. We show below how such changes are driven by a

diverse set of factors. The New Class formulation is particularly weak in gloss-
ing over economic and fiscal issues, as considered below.

More recent work on the New Class has distinguished cultural from technical workers, specified support for more precise policy issues, and assessed European patterns (e.g., Brint 1984, 1994; Brint, Cunningham, and Lee 1997; Berger
1987; Kreisi 1989; Weakliem 1991).

Related Formulations

Several studies differ from New Class writers in focusing less on government
and more on education and shifting criteria for jobs, for example, Parsons and
Platt (1973), Boudon (1974), and Jencks et al. (1979). Other related themes: a
general decline in social stratification (especially particularistic) (Grusky and
Hauser 1984); "dealignment" of traditional "class cleavages" from party programs and candidates in much political behavior work (Franklin 1985; Franklin
et al. 1992); the continued expansion of social tolerance in studies of civil liber-
ties (Smith 1985; Weil 1985); "consumerism" as a reaction to big firms (Coleman
1974); the pervasiveness of "new social movements" (Bowles and Gintis 1987);
and government strategies to improve services (Clark and Ferguson 1983, ch.
10). These multiple strands of research converge at several points, especially in
questioning traditional class politics. The ferment demands systematization.

Political culture is defined as patterned rules of the game involving political
processes. In this respect, we depart from past works that invoke *culture* as an
explanation without probing its sources (e.g., the tradition stressing basic values, following Parsons, 1937) and we are closer to recent urban work that seeks
to identify consistent leadership patterns, under such labels as "regimes" (Stone
1989), "mental maps of mayors" (Wollman 1992), or simply "leadership" (Judd
and Parkinson 1990). Still, our concern is less with such general labels than
with formulating specific prepositions about how governments make decisions.
More specifics on the political cultural approach used here are in Appendix 1.

Emergence of the New Political Culture:
Evidence of Its Growing Importance

This section presents brief evidence to document the emergence of the New
Political Culture. Far more is in subsequent chapters. We show here that the
seven definitional elements above increasingly describe Western political systems. We draw on surveys of citizens and leaders in the United States and Europe over the past several decades, which show progressive emergence of the
NPC, especially among younger persons. Causes driving these changes are introduced in the next section.

The Shift to NPC in Underlying Values: Intergenerational Value Changes

Intergenerational value change was initially explored by Inglehart (1971), who hypothesized that basic value priorities of Western publics had been shifting from a Materialist toward a Postmaterialist emphasis—from giving top priority to physical sustenance and safety, toward belonging, self-expression and the quality of life. From this work two key hypotheses emerge:

1. *The Scarcity Hypothesis. An individual's priorities reflect the socioeconomic environment: One places the greatest subjective value on those things in relatively short supply.*

2. *The Socialization Hypothesis. Value priorities do not adjust immediately to the socioeconomic environment; a substantial time lag is involved since basic values largely reflect the conditions of one's pre-adult years.*

The scarcity hypothesis is similar to the principle of diminishing marginal utility in economic theory. The recent economic history of advanced industrial societies has significant implications in the light of this hypothesis, for these societies are a remarkable exception to the prevailing historical pattern: The bulk of their population does *not* live with hunger and economic insecurity. This has led to a gradual shift: Needs for belonging, esteem, and intellectual and aesthetic satisfaction became more prominent. There is no one-to-one relationship between economic level and the prevalence of Postmaterialist values, for these values reflect one's *subjective* sense of security, not one's economic level per se. But generally, prolonged prosperity encourages Postmaterialist values; economic decline has the opposite effect. These two propositions are essentially social psychological; we link them to more specific economic and social structural factors in Section IV.[3]

These two hypotheses were initially tested in a cross-national survey conducted in 1970 with representative national samples of citizens in Great Britain, France, West Germany, Italy, the Netherlands, and Belgium. Respondents indicated which goals they considered most important from a series designed to tap economic and physical security, on the one hand; or belonging, self-expression and the nonmaterial quality of life, on the other hand (Inglehart, 1971: 26ff.). Those whose top two priorities were the former were classified as pure Materialists; those whose top priorities were the latter were classified as pure Postmaterialists. Those choosing a combination of goals were classified as mixed. (Appendix 2 lists the Postmaterialist scale items.)

As predicted, younger persons raised in more prosperous families emphasize Postmaterialist items. Figure 2.1 depicts this pattern in the pooled sample of six West European publics. Despite crossnational differences, the basic pattern is similar: Among older groups, Materialists outnumber Postmaterialists enormously; as we move toward younger groups, the proportion of Materialists declines and Postmaterialists increases. Updates by ourselves and others show broadly consistent results through the 1990s (e.g., Inglehart 1997).

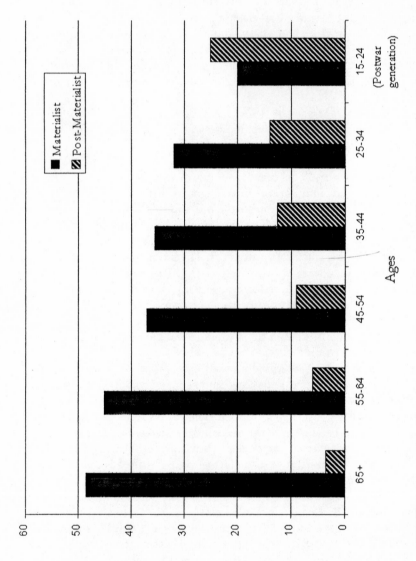

FIGURE 2.1 Value Type by Age Group, Among the Publics of Britain, France, West Germany, Italy, Belgium, and The Netherlands in 1970

Might these Figure 2.1 differences simply reflect life-cycle effects: Might the aging process bring ever-increasing emphasis on economic and physical security? Figure 2.2 traces the balance between Materialists and Postmaterialists within birth cohorts from 1970 to 1988 with pooled data from six nations—more than 190,000 interviews. Each cohort's position at a given time is calculated by subtracting the percentage of Materialists in that cohort from the percentage of Postmaterialists. Thus, at the zero point on the vertical axis, the two groups are equally numerous (which is about where the cohort born in 1946–1955 was located in 1970).

There is no sign of the overall downward movement that would appear if age differences reflected life-cycle effects. Each cohort retains its relative position with striking consistency throughout the eighteen-year period. Short-term fluctuations are significant: Each cohort swings downward briefly in 1977 and again in 1980–1981. These are period effects linked with economic recessions, as indexed by inflation. Yet by 1986, inflation had fallen to near the 1970 level. With period effects thus held constant, there is no indication of gradual conversion to Materialism that a life-cycle interpretation would predict. Young persons have a reputation for "idealism" that recedes with age; but these findings suggest that the core definitions of idealism have substantially shifted over time.

That we find a much narrower gap between the 1966–1973 cohort and its predecessors—narrower than the gap between the two other postwar cohorts and their predecessors—further indicates that these value differences reflect historical change rather than a permanent life-cycle tendency for the young to be less Materialist than the old. The narrowing of this gap after the 1970s reflects effects of the relatively uncertain economic conditions on the youngest cohort in these years. This may represent a slowing of the earlier trend, from more consistently prosperous years.

Citizen Assessments of Government Growth: Postmaterialism and New Fiscal Populists

Some observers of the young since the 1980s suggest that they have grown more conservative. Our results refute this for the items in the Postmaterialism Index. So do several dozen other social liberalism items repeatedly administered from the 1950s to 1990s (see the extensive review in Smith 1985). The main areas showing a conservative tilt are government spending, tax questions, and crime (Rempel and Clark 1997). The shift toward fiscal conservatism was at the core of Clark and Ferguson's (1983) New Fiscal Populists. The class politics lenses led the general public and social scientists to ignore or misinterpret these developments. That is, the last decades have seen moves (1) toward social liberalism (captured in the Postmaterialist index and other items), *and* (2) toward fiscal conservatism. These two ostensibly impossible or at least mutually contradictory trends (in terms of the traditional class political model) demand in-

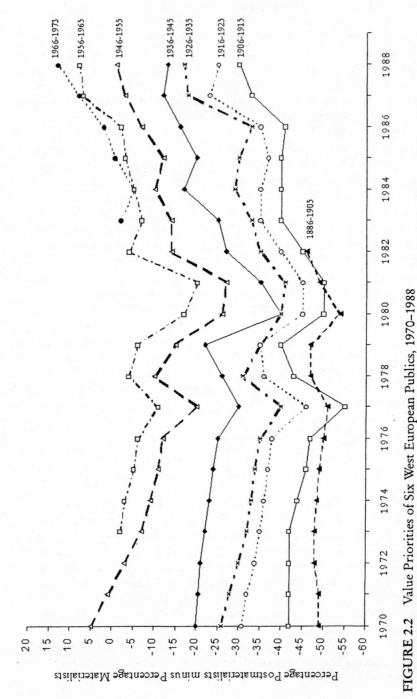

FIGURE 2.2 Value Priorities of Six West European Publics, 1970–1988

Source: Based on data from representative national surveys of publics of France, Great Britain, West Germany, Italy, Belgium, and The Netherlands, interviewed in European Community surveys of 1970, 1973, and Euro-Barometer surveys 6 through 29.

terpretation. This is a critical issue that the New Political Culture analysis can illuminate. We pursue it in several ways.

A first is to ask how citizens reporting Postmaterialist responses answer other social and fiscal policy items. Most Postmaterialists take a progressive stand on social issues—and have moved sufficiently far from the traditional left position on economic issues that—under current circumstances—they often support fiscal conservatives.

One should be cautious, however, in characterizing Postmaterialists as economically or fiscally conservative. On social welfare issues, they tend to be slightly more liberal than the electorate as a whole, depending on question wording. But they no longer endorse the traditional leftist position that the expansion of government is progress. On the contrary, they are suspicious of big government, insofar as it encroaches on individual autonomy. A key characteristic of Postmaterialists is concern for self-expression.

In short, their basic values make the growing Postmaterialist segment of society a potential constituency for New Fiscal Populism. Let us demonstrate this point. First, are Postmaterialists liberal on key social issues? A massive body of survey data, from twelve Western nations, suggests yes, on most social issues.

Table 2.1 presents some of these findings for ten European nations. They demonstrate that Postmaterialists are markedly more liberal than Materialists (or those with Mixed values) on social questions ranging from women's equality to terrorism, protection of the environment, Third World countries, and use of nuclear power. By and large, Postmaterialists are almost twice as likely as Materialists to take the "liberal" position.

Figure 2.3 similarly shows that Postmaterialists are markedly less likely than Materialists to support censorship of books, to have xenophobic attitudes toward immigrant workers, or a nationalistic outlook; and they are markedly *more* permissive on abortion.

How Pervasive Is Class Politics Versus the New Political Culture Among U.S. and French Mayors and Citizens?

To push one step further, consider *interrelations* between fiscal and social liberalism. A class politics model implies a clear positive relation: fiscal liberals are also social liberals. The NPC analysis suggests the opposite: no clear relationship. We test these competing hypotheses in several ways, with data for both leaders and citizens. Political leaders, abundant evidence suggests, have more ideological coherence and awareness than average citizens (e.g., Converse 1975). As leading carriers of political culture, they should show similar but stronger patterns than among citizens. We tested these hypotheses with data for mayors, using mayors' surveys from the Fiscal Austerity and Urban Innovation (FAUI) Project. Consistent with the citizen analysis just presented, we also expected differences by age cohort: *Younger mayors should evidence less class politics.*

TABLE 2.1 Postmaterialist Liberalism on Social Issues (percentage who "strongly agree" with following positions)

"Women should have the same chances as men to gain political offices."
Materialist	38
Mixed	52
Postmaterialist	70

"More severe penalties should be introduced for acts of terrorism."
Materialist	80
Mixed	69
Postmaterialist	38

"Stronger measures should be taken to protect the environment."
Materialist	59
Mixed	61
Postmaterialist	74

"Economic aid to Third World countries should be increased."
Materialist	17
Mixed	19
Postmaterialist	32

"Nuclear energy should be developed to meet future energy needs."
Materialist	25
Mixed	22
Postmaterialist	10

Source: Combined 10-nation data from Euro-Barometer survey #19 (April, 1983). Results weighted according to population of each country. Unweighted N = 9,789.

We analyzed mayoral data from the United States and France, expecting *France to illustrate more class politics, and the United States less*—for several reasons specified in propositions below. Our hypotheses were clear, but the results supported them in far more striking manner than we anticipated. We first computed simple correlations (Pearson r's) between (1) an index of fiscal liberalism, and (2) an index of social liberalism, for U.S. and French mayors.[4] Results are in Figure 2.4. Older French mayors (over age 50) show the traditional class-politics association between fiscal and social liberalism. But for mayors aged 40 to 50, the relationship drops to zero, while for those under 40, it flips to negative. These New Mayors were a much noted phenomenon when they won many *mairies* in the early 1980s; their fiscal conservatism was striking, but it was combined with many "youthful" themes: citizen participation and other nontraditional issues that seemed "peculiar" to most political commentators (Balme et al. 1986–

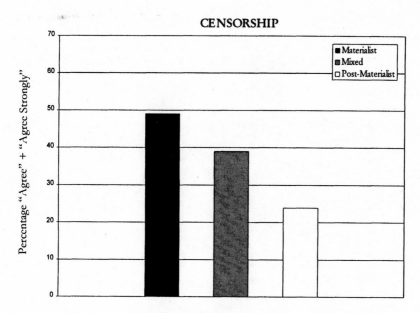

"There are some books that should be censored."

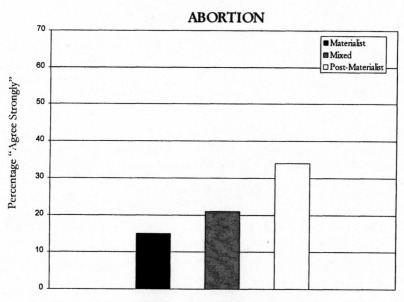

"Liberalization of abortion is a good thing."

FIGURE 2.3   Social Attitudes by Value Type
Source: Combined data from Euro-Barometer survey 21 (April, 1984), N = 9,745.

XENOPHOBIA

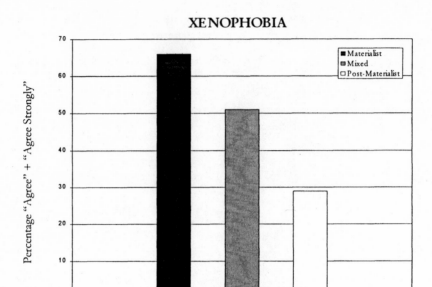

"There are too many immigrant workers in this country."

NATIONALISM

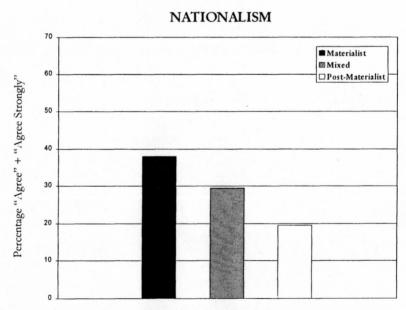

"One should be ready to sacrifice oneself for one's country."

FIGURE 2.3 *(continued)*

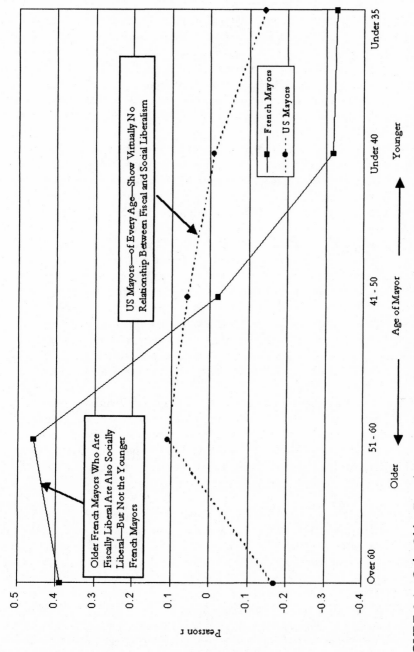

FIGURE 2.4 Only Older French Mayors Report Traditional Ideology: Correlations Between Fiscal and Social Liberalism for US and French Mayors, by Age

1987). But initial commentators did not recognize the degree of social liberalism these results imply: The young who were more fiscally conservative were also *more* socially liberal than other young mayors. There is a weak but insignificant trend in this direction among U.S. mayors; for U.S. mayors of every age, fiscal and social liberalism are virtually unrelated. French mayors of every age report more ideologically structured views than American mayors. But the senior French mayors, who grew up in a time of more scarcity and class conflict, report more traditional class politics policy preferences. These traditional class cleavages drop to zero among the middle-age French mayors and are turned on their heads by the young mayors.

Does the class politics pattern we observe for older French mayors derive from "French ideology" versus "American non-ideology"? No. Results from a decade-earlier survey of U.S. mayors were much closer to these findings for the French mayors. Conclusion: The New Political Culture is distinctly New. It was just emerging in our 1976 U.S. survey, found then only among the first term populist Democratic mayors (see Figure 2.5).

Note that these r's are quite distinct from *differences in levels* of fiscal or social liberalism. The only such difference across age categories, for U.S. and French mayors, was that the French mayors under 50 were slightly more fiscally conservative. Newer leaders often claim greater citizen responsiveness, consistent with *City Money* (Clark and Ferguson 1983) (results not shown).

Citizens are almost identical to U.S. mayors: They show practically no relationship between fiscal and social liberalism. This is clear in several social and fiscal liberalism items for citizens in twelve European countries and the United States. Further, even when we separated by age, relations remained nil for all age cohorts. See Table 2.2.[5]

Consider next the causal structure of social and fiscal liberalism, again with U.S. and French mayors. We estimated multiple regressions to explain fiscal and social liberalism, with social background characteristics as the main predictors. We find patterns analogous to those for the r's. That is, the French mayors show much more predictable patterns than American mayors. Adjusted R^2s for the French equations are high = .25 to.44; for American mayors these are less than one-sixth as strong: .03 to .08! American mayors are all over the ideological lot: Their positions are explained weakly by the same measures that worked well for France. In particular U.S. political parties are *unrelated* to either fiscal or social liberalism (Table 2.4). This marks a shift from just a decade earlier—in our 1976 U.S. survey the New Deal cleavages were still clear: mayor's party had the expected associations with fiscal liberalism, as did other social characteristics. Results were also far stronger, as expected, for the older than the newer mayors (the party beta was .44 for second term or more, but just .28 for first-term mayors; full regressions not shown). We have thus identified an historical turning point: After the late 1960s, the ideological and party cleavages of the New Deal began to decline in the United States, and through the 1970s mayors

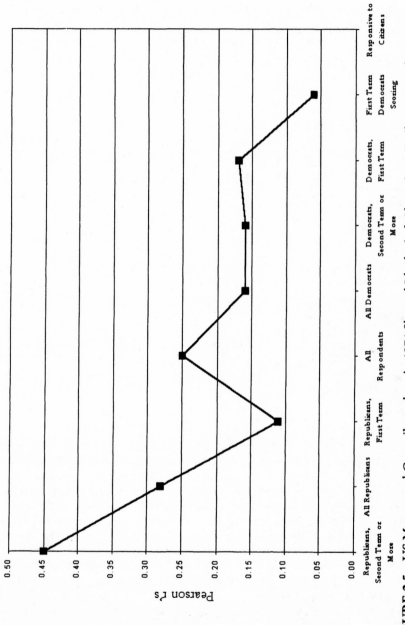

FIGURE 2.5 US Mayors and Councilmembers in 1976 Showed Ideological Clusterings Similar to French Mayors in 1983

Note: Traditional ideology is measured here by a high r between social and fiscal liberalism.

TABLE 2.2 Citizens in the US and Europe Show Low Ideological Clustering

For European Citizens

			V148 *Less Govt in Economy*
Age 60-80	V57	Less Different Sex Roles	0.008
	V150	Protect the Environment	-0.0126
Age 45-59	V57	Less Different Sex Roles	0.0648
	V150	Protect the Environment	-0.0287
Age 33-44	V57	Less Different Sex Roles	0.0126
	V150	Protect the Environment	-0.0462
Age 15-29	V57	Less Different Sex Roles	-0.0346
	V150	Protect the Environment	-0.0198

For US Citizens

	Federal Taxes Are Too High	*Federal Taxes Should Be Cut by 1/3*	*Support Proposition 13 (tax cut)*
Civil liberties/crime	0.009	0.078	-0.094
Race-gove should play an active role	0.053	0.058	-0.106
School integration	0.022	0.005	-0.071
Women's rights-govt should play an active role	-0.034	0.023	-0.04
Abortion	-0.03	-0.022	-0.065
ERA	0.01	-0.021	0.012

Note: Correlations between fiscal and social liberalism items are low or insignificant. Data are for 2000 US citizens, surveyed in the 1978 National Election Study, University of Michigan. Statistics are Pearson r's, with values exceeding about .05 significant at the .01 level. (Our computations.) Cf. also Clark and Ferguson (1983), p. 372.

Source: EuroBarometer 19, April 1983. Survey of 9790 citizens in France, Belgium, Netherlands, Germany, Italy, Luxembourg, Denmark, Ireland, Great Britain, Northern Ireland, Greece. V57 = Q. 136: "Do you agree or disagree with women who claim that there should be fewer differences between the respective roles of men and women in society? 1. Agree 2. Disagree." V150 = Q. 236: " <Do you agree or disagree> that stronger measures should be taken to protect the environment against pollution. 1. Agree strongly 2. Agree 3. Disagree 4. Disagree Strongly." V148 = Q. 234: " <Do you agree or disagree that > government should play a smaller role in the management of the economy? 1. Agree strongly 2. Agree 3. Disagree 4. Disagree Strongly."

TABLE 2.3   Multiple Regression of Sources of French Mayors' Fiscal and Social Conservatism

	Fiscal Liberalism		Social Conservatism	
	Multiple R	0.570	Multiple R	0.708
	R Square	0.325	R Square	0.501
	Adjusted R Square	0.254	Adjusted R Square	0.441
Independent Variables	B		B	
M08 Mayor's Party (1=Communist, 5=Right)	-0.118 ***		-0.063 ***	
D22 Mayor's Education (High = most ed)	-0.146 **		0.045 ***	
D23 Mayor's Relig (1=None, 4=Practice Regly)	0.064 ns		-0.086 ns	
D16R Mayor's Age (Year Born 1=old, 6=young)	-0.024 ns		0.031 ns	
D17 Mayor's Sex (1=male, 2=female)	0.409 **		0.141 ns	
CITRSPS Mayor-Citizen Respvsns Index	0.062 **		0.015 ns	
D18 Mayor's Occupation	-0.034 ns		0.019 ns	
M17 Percent Foreign-Immigrants	0.014 ns		-0.007 ns	
L07 Income/Tax Base of City 1982	0.000 ns		0.000 ns	
(Constant)	3.687		0.477	

Note: This shows the b (unstandardized regression coefficient) for each independent variable. The significance of each b is shown by ns=not significant; *=sig, $<.10$; **=sig, $<.05$; ***=sig $<.01$.

Source: French Fiscal Austerity and Urban Innovation Project.

TABLE 2.4 Multiple Regression of Sources of US Mayors' Fiscal Liberalism and Social Conservatism

	Fiscal Liberalism		Social Conservatism	
	Multiple R	0.260	Multiple R	0.342
	R Square	0.068	R Square	0.117
	Adjusted R Square	0.037	Adjusted R Square	0.088
Independent Variables	B		B	
LPARTY Myr's Pty(1=Repb,1.5=Indp,2=Demo)	-0.085	ns	0.058	ns
EDMAY Education of Mayor (18 pt scale)	0.001	ns	-0.017	**
LCATHMY Mayor Catholic (1=yes, 0=no)	0.077	ns	0.087	*
TERMMY2 Number of Terms Served as Mayor	-0.029	ns	-0.018	ns
SEXMY2 Mayors Sex (1=male, 2=female)	0.096	ns	-0.153	***
CITRSPS Mayor-Citizen Respvsns Index	-0.056	**	-0.006	ns
LNONWHMY Non-white Mayor (v145z)	0.181	ns	-0.143	ns
LBLK30 Percent Population Black, 1980	0.401	ns	-0.199	ns
LFORNSTK Percent Foreign Stock	0.103	**	-0.030	ns
LV904R Per Capita Income 1979 (v904)	-0.069	ns	-0.161	**

Note: This shows the b (unstandardized regression coefficient) for each independent variable. The significance of each b is shown by ns=not significant; *=sig, <.10; **=sig, <.05; ***=sig <.01.
Source: US Fiscal Austerity and Urban Innovation Project.

with new ideologies increasingly came to power. In surveys from the 1980s and 1990s, American mayors look ideologically "unstructured"; we stress that this is a recent development.

Analogous regressions (using Euro-Barometer and World Values Survey data) for citizens in Europe and the United States show the same pattern as the correlations: They show much less clustering than for the French mayors (results not shown).

Note that all these findings are consistent with three of our seven key points about the New Political Culture. They support: #1, fiscal and social liberalism must be explicitly distinguished; #3, the classic left-right dimension has declined; and #6, these NPC views are more pervasive among younger persons and societies. We pursue these points further in Chapter 4.

The historical "dealignment" that these findings document has not been properly interpreted to date. Nor has, more specifically, the rise of market individualism, especially among leftist political leaders. We have shown with our French team collaborators that these survey results did not emerge easily: Many younger French mayors broke dramatically with classic ideological positions of their parties. Such as the Communist Mayor of Le Mans who was kidnapped by his staff for "collaborating" with citizens to reduce taxes and staffing (e.g., Balme et al. 1986/1987). Nevers (1989) stressed the dramatic changes by the French Socialist Party, which after 1968 moved away from party hierarchy toward citizen participatory meetings, and, under President Mitterand, embraced elements of fiscal conservatism and decentralized certain national welfare state programs to local government. We consider similar dramatic changes elsewhere in Chapters 3 and 4.

Less Class Voting

Ironically, as policies of the classic welfare state *succeed*, problems that engendered them recede and class conflict withers as a political issue. Although working-class voters still disproportionately support left parties, and middle class voters support right parties, over the past four decades social class voting has substantially declined in many societies. Still for some researchers, these remain controversial points, and the magnitude of change depends very much on the metric used to measure it. A first simple measure of these changes is the Alford Index, which shows a clear decline of class voting (in Figure 2.6). If 75 percent of the working class voted for the left, and only 25 percent of the middle class did so, the corresponding Alford class voting index would be 50 (the difference between the two figures). This was the approximate position of the Swedish electorate in 1948, but it fell to 31 by 1985. Norway, Sweden, and Denmark have traditionally had the highest class voting, but it fell steeply over three decades. In the United States, Great Britain, France, and West Germany, in the late 1940s and early 1950s, working-class voters were more apt to support the

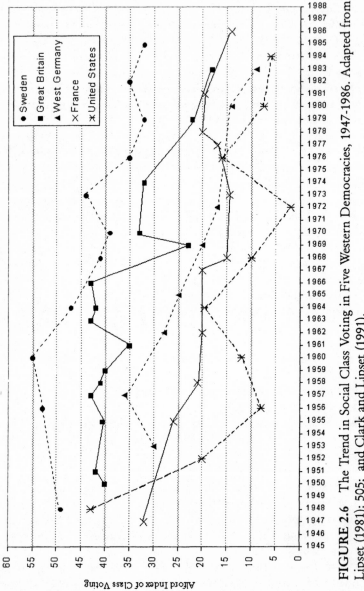

FIGURE 2.6 The Trend in Social Class Voting in Five Western Democracies, 1947-1986. Adapted from Lipset (1981): 505; and Clark and Lipset (1991).

left than middle-class voters by margins ranging from 30 to 45 percentage points. This had shrunk to 8 to 18 points in the mid-1980s. Tradition maintains class politics, but it erodes as middle class (often Postmaterialist) voters shift their support to left parties, and working class voters shift to right parties in defense of traditional social values or to new parties (nationalists in many European countries; Inglehart, 1977; Lipset, 1981), as elaborated in Chapter 4.

A lively exchange was sparked over these issues after Clark and Lipset (1991) published "Are Social Classes Dying?" The main counter-argument came from Heath et al. (1991), Hout et al. (1995), and Goldthorpe (1994), who held that class politics measured by voting shows no decline but trendless fluctuations over the past twenty to thirty years. The exchange has continued in several dozen papers, considered in Chapter 4. For now we simply mention that Heath, Hout, and Goldthorpe all use single-country data for the United States or the United Kingdom and a very simple model. But two major studies of more than a dozen countries that use slightly more complex models find different results: more variations, cross-nationally and over time; and both suggest a decline in class voting: Franklin et al. (1992) and Nieuberta (1995).

Less Clientelism

The 1980s and 1990s have also seen increasing criticism of clientelist politics, attacked as "corruption," "patronage," and "machine politics" from Japan to the United States. Often led by the media and opposition politicians, critics have had dramatic impacts: in deposing the entire political leadership in Italy, in undermining traditional "rules of the game" from Taiwan to the Clinton White House, to Mayor Daley's Chicago. Advocates of the New Political Culture oppose traditional clientelism, with considerable success, as several cases show in Chapter 4.

The decline of class politics and clientelism, and rise of the NPC, are increasingly strong, clear, and dramatic. What are the dynamics of this transformation; how and why did it ever occur? Note that the breakup in class politics and clientelism paralleled the rise of new political issues. Indeed, we propose that

3. *The broad shift toward market/individualism in economic policy by many political parties would have been impossible without the concomitant introduction of social issues to complement traditional fiscal/economic issues.*

This is a strong argument, the components of which of which consider next.

Causes of the New Political Culture

Where and why does the NPC emerge? A quick summary of our analysis is in three figures. First are the main elements of Class Politics, in Figure 2.7. Second is the New Political Culture, in Figure 2.8. The major factors driving political systems away from Class Politics toward the New Political Culture are

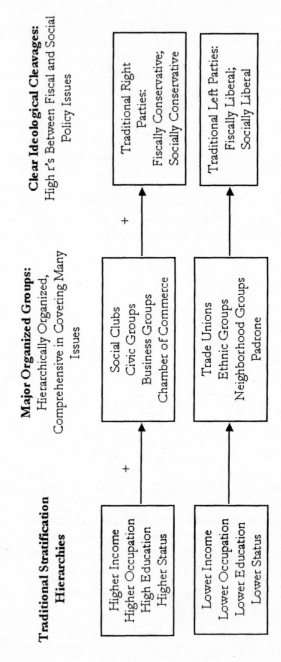

Salient Political Issues:

Primarily Materialistic, Work/Production Oriented

Redistribution of Income by the State

Power over the Workplace and Income Generation

Social Issues Subordinated to Fiscal Issues

Left Parties "Progressive" on Social Issues

Clear Ideological Cleavages:

High r's Between Fiscal and Social
Policy Issues

Major Organized Groups:

Hierarchically Organized,
Comprehensive in Covering Many
Issues

**Traditional Stratification
Hierarchies**

Higher Income	+	Social Clubs	+	Traditional Right
Higher Occupation		Civic Groups		Parties:
High Education		Business Groups		Fiscally Conservative;
Higher Status		Chamber of Commerce		Socially Conservative

Lower Income		Trade Unions		Traditional Left Parties:
Lower Occupation		Ethnic Groups		Fiscally Liberal;
Lower Education		Neighborhood Groups		Socially Liberal
Lower Status		Padrone		

FIGURE 2.7   Class Politics: Major Components

Organized Groups:
Fewer Class Based Organizations
More Specific Issue Oriented
Non-Hierarchical
Media Oriented
Weaker Parties and Clientelism

Salient Political Issues:
Fewer Economic/Workplace Issues Than in Class Politics
More Social and Cultural Concerns
Consumption/Lifestyle Issues
Personal Satisfaction
Social Tolerance
More Attractive Physical Environment

Cleavages:
1. "Reform": i.e., Pro-NPC Politics Against Traditional Class Politics, and Patronage/Clientelism
2. Among NPC Persons: over Regions, Neighborhoods, Relative Emphasis on Different Consumption Styles

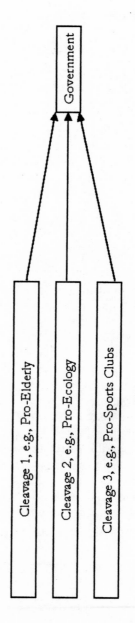

Cleavage 1, e.g., Pro-Elderly

Cleavage 2, e.g., Pro-Ecology

Cleavage 3, e.g., Pro-Sports Clubs

Government

FIGURE 2.8 The New Political Culture: Main Components

in Figure 2.9. The rest of the chapter discusses each of the causal factors as blocks of interrelated propositions, usually moving from left to right in Figure 2.9.

Three General Principles Guide Subsequent Propositions

What drives the shift toward the New Political Culture? Our specific propositions fall under the three general ideas, concerning *hierarchy, empowerment,* and *structural conditions.*

Hierarchy Propositions

By virtue of their standard operating procedures, *hierarchies (social, economic, or political) generate reactions against hierarchy.* This is the Leveling Principle. Thus large factories generate large unions, which seek to level the factory hierarchy. We explore several corollaries and implications of the Leveling Principle below and apply them to political parties, government, the economy, the family, and religion. The Principle is austerely simple:

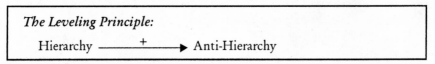

The Leveling Principle:

Hierarchy ——————+—————→ Anti-Hierarchy

The antihierarchy movement may be championed by a "vanguard party," either in a literal Leninist sense or more as a social movement (for unionization of workers, women's rights, new religious cults) highly organized or not. Such antihierarchy movements often spark conflict by identifying an opposing "class" (bourgeois, male chauvinists, heathens), which in the polar case generates conflicting dichotomies of good and bad, just and unjust—at least in the rhetoric.

But if this Leveling Principle captures the flavor of hundreds of conflicts of the late nineteenth through mid-twentieth century, the post-1968 years saw hierarchies weaken enough to generate distinct dynamics. That is, as hierarchy declines, people grow less willing to invest energy in a movement (e.g., labor union, socialist party) just to level the hierarchy; instead they are more likely to participate in new forms of activity:

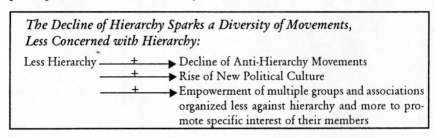

The Decline of Hierarchy Sparks a Diversity of Movements, Less Concerned with Hierarchy:

Less Hierarchy ————+————→ Decline of Anti-Hierarchy Movements
——————+——————→ Rise of New Political Culture
——————+——————→ Empowerment of multiple groups and associations organized less against hierarchy and more to promote specific interest of their members

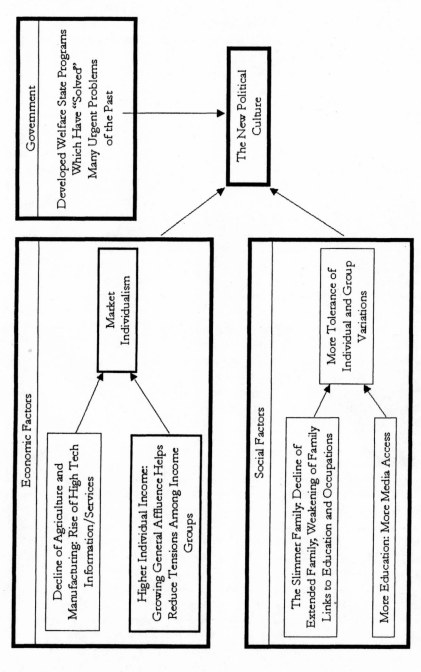

FIGURE 2.9   Factors Driving Toward the New Political Culture

We leave as exogenous to our theory the explanations of where and why hierarchy should rise or decline, since the dynamics of economic hierarchy are quite distinct from religious or family hierarchies. Some propositions below suggest factors associated with declines in several hierarchies, like more education, but we leave it for others to model seriously specific dynamics of change in each hierarchy. Our focus is on the sociopolitical *consequences* of hierarchy.

Empowerment Propositions

Pace Hegel and Marx, politics is not all thesis and antithesis. Part of mobilizing (e.g., for an ecology movement) is developing the skills and concerns among citizens that help them to form and participate in organized groups. An illiterate, feudal peasantry does not immediately spark political activity. In Poland in 1990, in the first postcommunist local elections, some townspersons were eager to vote but more than once asked "when is Warsaw sending us the list of candidates"? In most of the world, for decades political parties have generally chosen their candidates with minimal input from average citizens; lists of party candidates are normally presented to voters as a fait accompli. (See the Hoffmann-Martinot chapter.) The United States and Taiwan are among the few countries in the world to hold "primary" elections, permitting average citizens to vote on party candidates. If party hierarchy was accepted as normal in the past, today many citizens feel that no party is responsive to their concerns. As citizens acquire more personal resources in the form of social capital (education, communication skills, personal experience participating in voluntary associations, richer networks of social contacts), they are more likely to join issue-specific organizations (for neighborhood cleanups, crime watch, women's issues, or whatever), than to rely on political parties and elected leaders. They are then more likely to question party leaders and other hierarchies. Our logic here is simple:

The Empowerment Proposition:

Individuals Acquire   More Participation

Organizational and   +   In Civic and Political

Communication Skills   ⟶   Groups

The factors driving empowerment are more education, media access, income, occupations that generate more interpersonal skills, travel, and exposure to civic organizations—elaborated below.

At the close of the twentieth century, we find considerable variation in how adequately social and political dynamics are captured by the Leveling Principle or the Empowerment Principle. Unions and socialist parties remain strong in Scandinavia; the United Kingdom still has clear class politics (making the Tony Blair election of 1997 a dramatic shift from the recent past); many less developed countries still have rigid hierarchies. Yet even within these same countries, new variations are emerging. To stay with the Scandinavian countries, one finds more women elected to their national parliaments than elsewhere in the world, considerable greening of the left parties, tempering of traditional class conflict themes by unions, and serious dismantling of the welfare state, which for decades most of the world identified as distinctly Scandinavian. Why should such differences emerge and grow? A first core answer is that as hierarchies decline, other factors grow in explanatory importance. Why do these processes obtain in some locations but not others? Certain general structural conditions serve as contextual factors that shift operation of these processes.

Structural Conditions Affect General Transformation Rules Shifting Specific Rules of the Game

Empowerment skills are largely individual; structural conditions are also important, like the degree of conflict or political consensus among the citizenry or tolerance of political opposition (which totalitarian systems prohibit). These structural characteristics include quasi-necessary conditions for aspects of the New Political Culture to emerge, and factors that spread it faster. Other structural characteristics include partisan elections, proportional representation, and similar legal structures that favor parties and weaken new social movements.

Some general processes are so powerful that they transform rules of the game in many countries and cities. Industrialization in the past transformed entire societies away from more local, often agricultural-based ties. The time of industrialization varied by country, since nations were more autonomous in the past. This has changed. The most powerful similar force at the end of the twentieth century is globalization: No nation or city can today escape at least some elements of global processes that transform many rules of the game for national and local policies. In the 1980s and 1990s the world grew smaller. Tariffs fell, international trade and investment grew rapidly, migration of people rose in some locales—but quite unevenly. Simultaneously, most national governments gave local officials more autonomy, decentralizing many components of national welfare states. The net effect was for international markets to favor those cities—with investment, trade, and tourists—that seemed attractive. Cities with high tax burdens, bad ecology, and poor reputations suffered corresponding losses. Leaders who feared becoming "losers" increasingly sought to make their policies internationally competitive. New was the pressure to compare specific performance to others world wide (such as in tax rates, travel times, and many quality of life measures increasingly published in popular magazines and used by consulting firms advising corporations about location decisions). This prepared the biggest change of the century for left leaders, who felt increased pressure to abandon state-centralism and cut taxes and services, especially when they were at higher levels than elsewhere. Pressures toward ever lower taxes and fiscal conservatism grew clear, but so did others—"corruption" charges increased in these years, as global standards were applied even in locations like China, when the U.S. Congress frequently threatened its "most-favored-nation" status for tariffs due to "human rights violations." Italian firms complained in the 1990s that local political bribes essential to do business had grown so high that they were priced out of international markets. This was seen as a significant factor behind the collapse of the Italian political system in 1993 (see Chapter 3). Globalization reinforces the importance of markets and bigger markets. In brief, several elements of the NPC are driven further by globalization, never alone, but combined with other national and local factors identified in propositions below. Global considerations that we have listed tilt the balance against clientelism, in particular, and favor the NPC.

We derive more than twenty specific propositions below from these three general ideas. Stressing derivations from the three adds theoretical elegance. Still, it is simpler to communicate new developments using more standard institutional and topic areas. We thus consider in the following sections: government and political parties, the economy, the rise of social issues with the slimmer family and new social movements, and the decline of clientelism and its socioreligious roots.

Important Caveats: Several propositions in this chapter refer to long-term trends (growth of income and education) that are clear over fifty to one hundred years. However, some trends slowed with economic stagnation in the 1970s, and some reversed in the 1980s. Income per capita was generally constant in most of Western Europe and North America from about 1970 to the mid-1990s. But education kept growing in many countries. Although these propositions posit simple linear relations, the theory in no way denies that empirical patterns cycle or reverse. The slowing of economic or educational growth does not refute the propositions but, rather, illustrates the need to analyze not just their change in linear manner but to relate changes to specific attitudes and other behaviors specified in the propositions. The propositions are ceteris paribus probabilistic statements, which means that there can be important exceptions to them, since myriad other factors also operate. The combined effects of these caveats decrease the observed coefficients in the statistics.

Well-educated persons can be snobs or engage in subtle and sophisticated forms of racial discrimination and develop verbal defenses for all sorts of behavior. Less-educated persons often just express their feelings more directly. The media and opinion leaders develop and diffuse numerous negative stereotypes, for example, of immigrants, the underclass, and racial minorities. Efforts by the media to make a story *dramatic* or by organized group leaders to *heighten public consciousness* can boomerang in creating exaggerated stereotypes, prompting overly negative *labeling*. The net effect may be that some young (even highly educated) persons whose main contact with urban problems is national media develop exaggerated and stereotyped fears of crime and minority populations.

There are always disparities among survey responses, political programs, and *revealed preferences* on such issues as social tolerance. One can detect more subtle discrimination with more subtle methods. But these issues are so widely known to social scientists and, especially for racial tolerance, have been carefully documented through comparisons such as multitrait, multimethod matrices (see for examples Weil 1985) that they are not pursued here.

Hierarchies and Their Opponents: Political Parties and Governance Processes Which Incorporate or Exclude the New Political Culture

New movements often organize to counter an "unresponsive hierarchy":

4. *The more hierarchical the social institutions, the more likely powerful opposition groups are to emerge, challenging the hierarchies and pressing for egalitarian reforms.*

This is *The Leveling Principle: Down with Hierarchies* (cf. Clark 1985–1986) used in several subsequent propositions. Reducing traditional hierarchies—of nobility and the estates, the church, the military, land and property ownership—have long been classic European leftist programs. In countries or cities with rigid hierarchies, we thus expect more persistent class politics and less NPC. If the hierarchy is centralized and monolithic (like a large monopoly corporation), the opposing movement or union tends to develop and retain the same character. Strong left parties, close to unions, were the natural response to rigid social and economic hierarchies of many European societies for much of the twentieth century. This changes when, for reasons exogenous to our theory, the hierarchies flatten or differentiate.[6] As these hierarchies themselves diminish in reality or in salience, their political importance for parties opposing them should too. Hence American society with its more egalitarian traditions and past (absence of standing military, state church, aristocracy, etc.) generates more moderate proposals for social redistribution of income and status than do more hierarchical societies. To Americanize Hegel: no antithesis for want of a thesis. Strong opposition groups and parties weaken as hierarchy declines. Thus, in countries, regions, or cities with more equal distributions of income, property, and the like, one should find less conflict—and smoother emergence of the NPC.

Consider some key structural characteristics shifting operation of the Leveling Principle. These might be seen as "assumptions," but we consider them system characteristics that may be stronger or weaker. The first is the degree of legitimacy of the hierarchy in the minds of those affected by it. The more illegitimate the hierarchy, the more powerful are its leveling effects. Legitimacy often seems weaker for those lower in a hierarchy. The second structural characteristic is the degree to which political opposition is tolerated. The Leveling Principle operates most powerfully in a democratic context. Under an absolutist monarchy or dictatorship, it is harder for Leveling to succeed. There must be room for opposition to emerge. The dramatic importance of this idea is illustrated in the rapid demise of Eastern European Communist leaders in 1989 after Gorbachev indicated that citizens could have more voice in selecting leaders. We next add a few more general ideas, then apply them to specific institutional areas.

There also must be enough persons to support an issue for it to take on significance; Quintuplets of Iceland have less clout than Women. Numbers count:

5. *Demographic growth of a sector increases its legitimacy and power. The more persons in a political system who support a policy, the more likely it is to succeed.*

Social categories whose members generally share preferences on a public policy are termed *sectors*. A demographically expanding sector encourages policies consistent with that sector's preferences. Analysts often use social background characteristics (like age cohorts) to identify sectors and possible corresponding changes in political culture. Demographic expansion of a sector can come from two sources: (1) migration and (2) differences in natality/mortality across sectors. Daniel Elazar (e.g., in Elazar and Zikmund 1975) has creatively developed the first approach, showing how distinct migration streams from Europe to the United States, and across the United States, helped implant distinct political cultures along the way.

The second demographic process is that a sector (e.g., Catholics) has higher birth rates and/or lower death rates than others: then its sector size expands. Several of our propositions, like those concerning more young and highly educated persons, build on this basic Demographic Principle. Combining the Demographic and Hierarchy principles permits tracing political cultural reactions back to past and distant hierarchies that live on in the politics of their carriers. Immigrants from Russia, Eastern Europe and the Middle East have helped spread terrorism and radical themes to Western Europe and the United States for generations. The closest American analogue to these hierarchies and the European feudal system was slavery in the South. Though slavery was abolished in 1865, most blacks were still unable to register to vote until after the civil rights victories of the 1960s. But when they finally registered, political impacts followed— for blacks and others. Black politics after the 1960s shares many anti-hierarchical elements with European egalitarians: From Martin Luther King to Harold Washington, a central issue was mobilizing the poor and disadvantaged, through voter registration, mass demonstrations, and marches. Blacks thus added a radical tone to American politics, which was blended in the late 1960s with the northern union organizer tradition by campus activists (cf. McAdam 1988) and subsequently spread by radical students, feminists, environmentalists, gays, and even the elderly using such labels as the "Grey Panthers." Television and activists' meetings helped export this American blend around the world.

These movements are drastically changing the rules in many countries. Consider just American political institutions, from the U.S. Congress to cities and voluntary associations. Chicago is a particularly dramatic case. For half a century it was dominated by an unusually hierarchical Democratic Party. Black

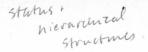

mobilization changed Chicago's political culture only in the 1980s. Clark has conducted an oral history of Chicago in these years with William Grimshaw. Our interviews with activists reveal the hatred of former Mayor Daley and his Democratic machine. Tactical ploys to "unveil" its hierarchical, oppressive quality were consciously used again and again to mobilize black supporters. As an organizing tactic Martin Luther King typically chose openly racist and potentially violent places to organize, like Birmingham, Alabama, where Police Chief Bull Connor instructed his men to use electric cattle prods against demonstrators. But as many African Americans moved to northern cities, the civil rights movement sought to follow them.

Dorothy Tillman and another King coworker, Jesse Jackson, thus helped mobilize black support against Mayors Daley and Byrne and eventually persuaded U.S. Congressman Harold Washington to run for mayor of Chicago. How did they mobilize? In the same way and with many of the same people as under Martin Luther King: Find a hierarchical opponent. Demonstrate against it using sit-ins and marches (nonviolent but media-visible). Try to force the hierarchy to use violence to stop your demonstration. Third parties (including television viewers) will then rally to you as supporters.

M.L. King and his followers chose to organize in Chicago in 1969 in part because of the national image of Daley from 1968, when, during the Democratic presidential convention, Daley (still hierarchical) had actively used police to break up street demonstrations. He and the national Democratic Party (and Vietnam-scarred President Lyndon Johnson) came under much political fire; in the national media they became the major domestic resistance to peace and a more radical political program (Tillman 1986: 155–158). Daley moved away from hierarchy in the 1970s, as did most European and some Asian governments and organizations—which illustrates the *converse* of the Hierarchy Principle:

4A. *As hierarchy declines, it is harder to mobilize against it.*

In the 1950s and 1960s, Conrad Adenauer in Germany and General DeGaulle in France, were iron-fisted symbols of hierarchy, against which egalitarians could effectively organize opponents. The May 1968 demonstrations in France were the most dramatically successful, helping topple De Gaulle. France, Germany, and many countries in Western Europe and the rest of the world have grown far more egalitarian since then, especially in styles of political leaders. The Chinese Tinanmen Square events and Eastern Europe shakeups in 1989 illustrate the pervasiveness of these cultural pressures. This *decline in hierarchy* is a particularly powerful source of decline in traditional class politics.

4B. *Decline in hierarchy has in turn brought a decline in traditional left and right allegiances of citizens to political parties.*

This idea is pursued in Chapters 3 and 4. Recall that we do not seek to explain where and why hierarchies decline since this demands integration with theories of private firms, families, and other social institutions; we thus leave the tasks to other theorists and focus on *consequences* of change. One aspect does deserve mention: Strong hierarchy often generates strong egalitarian groups, who in turn often make strong demands to level economic or religious hierarchies by using the State—the classic case is socialist/communist groups. But even Marx suggested that this was undesirable, and after the "dictatorship of the proletariat" (a.k.a. strong temporary hierarchy) the state should "wither away." How is the NPC different? The answer turns on changes in preferences of citizens. More income and education should encourage citizens to grow more fiscally and socially individualistic, which over time undermines support for strong egalitarian policies—such as those followed by People's Republics for many decades. When Russians and Poles grew so affluent and educated that they were ready to risk their jobs to fight for democracy, they also wanted the State to provide less strong central policies of equal treatment and grow more sensitive to differences in citizen preferences (i.e., individualism rose). In Western countries, "strong egalitarian" policies are far more powerful in the rhetoric of social movement leaders than in actual government policies, although clearly policies shift back and forth on issues like affirmative action for minorities. But to explain many of these dynamics demands analysis of intellectuals versus intellectuals, parties, and organized groups as much as or more than of the impacts of major hierarchical social institutions, which our propositions seek to capture.

The social consequence of more "individualism" is a decline in value consensus. But it may be modest (I like pizza, you like steak) or profound (all heathens must die!). Consider the more profound differences first, since they raise obvious problems for NPC governance. These deeper "basic values" have concerned theorists since Weber and Durkheim. Opposing the Leveling Principle is:

6. *The Consensus-Market Principle: The greater the value consensus among citizens, and the more that public policies reflect these values, the less citizens turn out to vote, support organized groups, parties, and a (hierarchical) bureaucratic state pressing for change.*

Major differences among population subgroups is a classic rationale for a strong state: to preserve order. This was Hobbes's Leviathan argument. But the polar opposite of the strong state is not inevitably his state of nature; markets of various sorts are also possible. Markets may depend in turn on a few government-supported institutions—enforcement of contracts, rules of law, and so on, as Spencer, Durkheim and others stressed—but not a massive state hierarchy.

The Consensus-Market Principle adds more power in combination with the Hierarchy Principle. A corollary follows: *The legitimacy of hierarchy is maintained if many citizens feel that pressing problems would persist or grow worse if the hierarchy disappeared.* This "need" for hierarchy is illustrated by the former Yugoslavia, a classic case of multiple regions, religions, and language groups that would, and have, fought bitterly. The central state hierarchy persisted due to lack of consensus; when it weakened, the lack of consensus erupted. Variations are found around the world in the emergence of new ethnic, regional, and linguistic "sub-nationalisms." Yet the converse of this situation also follows: As fundamental socioeconomic and value differences decline—as in most European countries in recent decades—so should hierarchical states, parties, and related institutions. Less fundamental social and value conflicts imply less urgent support for a strong state to "right wrongs." This is consistent with Marx's observation that the state, as an instrument of repression, would disappear under socialism or at least communism. This is the essence of the Consensus-Market Principle.

But if decline in social hierarchy and greater value consensus may have weakened support for Leveling among *citizens*, these preferences do not immediately reach political leaders and policy, since specific programs usually come from political parties.

7. *The more ideologically coherent and structurally hierarchical are the political parties, the less likely the emergence of the New Political Culture.*

This is the first application of the Leveling Principle to a specific institution: the political party. The NPC breaks with the past by challenging the traditional left-right classification of social and fiscal issues; it thus is rejected by party regulars who hold to this tradition and by incumbents whose positions are threatened. By contrast, in political systems with structurally weak and ideologically bland parties, the NPC is more likely to penetrate party programs and be adopted by candidates for office.

Several surveys show similar NPC patterns for U.S. and European *citizens*, but NPC *leaders* seem fewer in Europe. Parties appear as a critical distinguishing factor: The United States has weaker parties, more easily penetrated by new issues. In most of the world, new parties must often be formed to launch new issues. Why is the United States different?

Primary elections held by most American parties make candidates far more responsive to voters. Candidates must be elected by all voting members of the party to win endorsement as party candidates for the general election. This primary election system is absent in Europe and Asia, strengthening party leaders.

Non-partisanship, that is, elections prohibiting candidates from using any party labels, further weakens party control. About half of U.S. cities (and many Canadian and Australian localities) use nonpartisan elections, even though parties sometimes informally support candidates. Only a few elections in Europe are held this way (e.g., for special districts), although nonpartisanship is being explored in several countries.

Parties are strengthened further when *split-ticket voting* is impossible, such as in Italy, where voters can only choose all candidates for a single party. By contrast, in many partisan election systems, like the United States or Norway, voters can split their ticket by choosing individual candidates from two or more parties. This helps explain the Italian Communist Party's success with the new social movements: A young feminist-ecologist in Italy would have to vote for the Red Party, and all its candidates, whereas in Norway she could vote for one Green and one feminist candidate in two different parties.

Proportional representation (PR) according to parties in a legislature further increases party control. By contrast, candidates elected by a simple majority of voters in a geographic constituency or ward are less beholden to a party. The United States and Britain generally use such *constituency elections*, and Continental Western European countries use mainly PR (Rokkan 1970: chs. 4 and 5).

Party strength thus varies cross-nationally and across localities, encouraging comparisons to assess Proposition #7, which we pursue in Chapter 4. Again, Chicago is the classic outlier in the United States, where party strength until recently made it closer to Europe than to Texas or California.

Note an important consequence for those parties that *do* embrace NPC themes: *They tend to lose working-class voters.* Rhetoric of gay rights, flag-burners' rights, and animal rights drives out blue-collar voters. Tony Blair alienated coal miners by weakening traditional Labour appeals (see end of Chapter 3). The extreme U.S. example was the 1972 Democratic presidential candidacy of George McGovern, which drove major union leaders to endorse the Republican candidate Richard Nixon. Indeed, if NPC leaders take over a party, and impose the new policy on local officials and citizens who resist (like McGovern and still more Blair since the Labour Party is stronger than the Democratic Party) this can weaken or even reverse Proposition #7—which deals more with the past where NPCs were in a minority resisted by traditional leaders. In the United States and Britain, angry workers have only the big right parties to vote for (which fuels little organized groups like militias, the Ku Klux Klan, etc.), but in Continental Europe, with PR, New Right parties flowered in the 1990s after many socialist and communist parties embraced NPC issues. These New Right parties (neofascist, etc.—see Boxes in Chapter 4) are thus in part reactions *against* the success of NPCs in their political systems. The rise of NPC and then New Right parties changed the character of national politics in most West European countries in the 1980s and 1990s. Over many years, the extreme racist and xenophobic leaders should decline in popularity if their supporters grow more affluent and educated; but in the shorter term they enjoy *more* success in the socially fragile, media-sensitive, and volatile political systems of NPC-like societies. Some people understandably find class politics and clientelism, with their relatively stable and centrist parties, more attractive.

8. *New social movements organize locally and nationally in extra-party organizations more often when established party and elected leaders are perceived as unresponsive to movement concerns.*

This is the Social Movement Mobilization Proposition. For instance, the Chicago Democratic Party under Mayor Richard J. Daley in the 1960s and 1970s, and the French Communist Party into the 1980s were widely perceived as "closed." To wit: A University of Chicago law student named Abner Mikva went to the local Democratic Party regulars and asked if he could volunteer to work with them. Question: "Who sent ya?" Answer: "Nobody." Reply: "We don't want nobody nobody sent." Mikva became an important "independent Democrat," fighting the "Machine" for years thereafter. By contrast, Democratic Party organizations in most other U.S. cities have been more easily penetrated and changed; such openness and adaptability is a major reason for the historical continuity and success of the two major American parties through most of the twentieth century (cf. Lipset 1981), compared to the more organizationally and ideologically closed European parties. By refusing to adapt, they have more often been supplanted by others when their environments changed.

8A. *Multiparty systems discourage new social movements by permitting many parties to address more specific issues. New social movements are stronger and more pervasive in systems with few parties.*

The extreme example was Poland in 1991, where some 200 parties emerged, including those for Beer Drinkers and Safe Sex.

Even if American and British parties seek to respond to citizen-voters, the few parties inevitably frustrate many citizens on specific issues. This party stability encourages new social movements more in the United States (and Canada, Australia, and Britain, which share many legal party arrangements), just as it drives faster change by smaller parties in Continental Europe (and those countries around the world with similar legal arrangements like PR).

The Italian Communist Party (PCI) illustrates these dynamics. Comparison with the French Communist Party (PCF) shows that "other factors," especially leadership, remain important to explain party adaptability. In the 1970s and 1980s, the French PCF remained true to its Leninist-Stalinist past, while the Italian PCI (with the Spanish Communist Party) defined a new Eurocommunism. The Italian Party did not resist the new social movements, like the French PCF, but swallowed them. The PCI thus created major "caucuses" within the Party in the 1970s—of feminists, gays, ecologists, and others. Movement sentiment for these caucuses brought many younger voters to the PCI (Ercole and Martinotti 1989); simultaneously votes for the French PCF declined precipitously (see Chapters 3 and 4 for more on Italian Communists). Young French voters supported a variety of new social movements, and turned out for elections far less than older persons. Why was France different?

8B. *More centralized national governments, and higher population concentrations in larger cities, generate parties that are stronger, more centralized, less ideologically adaptable, and less citizen-responsive. Party centralization correspondingly encourages protests and various forms of extra-party movements, including new social movements.*

France was more centralized than most West European countries, at least in elite administrative and cultural institutions, and remained so through the 1990s (but cf. Thoenig 1986). The greater ideological stress on decentralization than exists elsewhere flows from the more hierarchical past. General De Gaulle incarnated the hierarchical tradition in his speeches and personality in the 1960s,

thereby reinforcing anti-hierarchical views among younger French persons. Decentralization was further encouraged by Socialist Party dominance of many
local governments—from the 1940s through the 1970s—in part since the Socialists seldom held power nationally. Decentralization thus became a major plank
of the Socialist program. Within the Socialist Party a new tendency emerged in
the late 1960s stressing *autogestion* (self-management)—in discussion groups like
the Club Jean Moulin, in the student movements of May 1968, and in subsequent decentralization reforms by the Mitterand government (Nevers 1989;
Bernier 1989). The ideological leader of *autogestion*, Michel Rocard, became
prime minister in the late 1980s. France illustrates well several components of
Propositions 8, 8A, and 8B, our Social Movement Mobilization Propositions:
French hierarchy leads social protest to focus more on "decentralization" and
democracy than in countries like Switzerland or the United States where hierarchy is comparatively weak and less an issue. Yet France shares the Western
democratic tradition, and was surpassed in its state hierarchy by Eastern Europe
and China after World War II. The East European and Chinese events of 1989
recalled the Paris of May 1968, in that they were such strong reactions against
state hierarchy and pro-democracy that they left little room for other issues. As
hierarchy declines, generally, we see more attention to other NPC themes. Thus
only in the late 1980s did ecology become politically important in France, a
decade after it did in Germany and Italy, despite numerous nuclear reactors on
French soil.

Economic Organization Changes: Sources of a New Market Individualism

We first consider changes in economic organization then trace their effects
and parallel developments through the framework in Figure 2.9. Three fundamental shifts in economic organization illustrate declining hierarchy: (1) the
decline of agriculture and family firms in the early twentieth century; (2) the
rise then decline of large manufacturing firms over the twentieth century; and
(3) the rise of small, high-tech service firms in the late twentieth century. Each
dominated but still did not quite displace the last; all three coexist in parallel
situses.[7] What changes over time is the size of each situs, that is, the proportion
of the labor force working in these different organizational conditions. Changes
in the three are roughly similar in the United States, Europe, and Japan, with
the United States leading slightly in the rise of services.[8]

Situs size changes helped redefine business culture, as well as political culture, over the last century. How? One cause is increasing specialization and
unique combinations of tastes that individuals can refine and express more fully
as their incomes rise. People in stark poverty first need food, clothing, and
shelter. With more income, they indulge progressively more elaborate and varied tastes. But as such complexity increases, it grows harder to plan centrally;

decentralized, demand-sensitive decision-making becomes necessary.[9] Hierarchy weakens. We thus formulate an economic corollary of our Scarcity Hypothesis above:

9. *Markets, ceteris paribus, grow in relevance as income rises.*

Private goods come increasingly from more differentiated and submarket-oriented small firms, especially in such service-intensive fields as "thoughtware," finance, and office activities. By contrast, huge firms are in relative decline, especially for traditional manufacturing products like steel and automobiles. Some two-thirds of all new jobs are in firms with twenty or fewer employees in the United States and many European countries (Birch 1979); the proportion is still higher in Japan if one includes both autonomous companies and those affiliated with larger firms. These small firms emerge not by chance but because they out compete larger firms. Why? Technology and management style are critical.[10]

10. *The more advanced the technology and knowledge base, the harder it is to plan in advance and control activities administratively, both within a large firm, and still more by central government planners.*

Technological changes illustrate how new economic patterns are no longer an issue of capitalism vs. socialism or public- versus private-sector control but frustrate administrative control efforts by anyone. As research and development generate increasingly critical inputs for new products and technologies, it is harder for distant administrators of that firm to direct or define in advance, and still harder for outside regulators or political officials seeking to plan centrally (as in a Soviet five-year plan, to use an extreme case). Certain plastics firms have as much as one-third of staff developing new products, and the entire product line changes in less than five years. Computers, biological engineering, and robotics illustrate the dozens of areas only vaguely amenable to forecast a few years ahead, and hence to central control. One can define a goal, such as cheaper energy, or a drug to cure cancer or AIDS, and allocate staff and budget administratively; but just which line of work will best yield results, and when, is essentially unplannable. This turbulence and unpredictability in the economy parallels the political turbulence of the NPC. The new economic turbulence, especially in locations like the former Soviet countries, have brought massive unemployment and considerable disorder in many towns and industries, especially traditional steel- and coal-based heavy industries that the Soviets often located in one-firm factory towns. Western Europe and the United States have suffered similar if less extreme dislocations, again most visibly in heavy industries concentrated in small towns with little economic diversification. When top managers leave town, the mass of blue-collar workers experience much despair, and few have the skills to become the small entrepreneurs who spark growth in larger cities.

11. *Smaller firms are less subject to state regulation and controls and thus are more nimble.*

The new job creation rate in the United States is almost twice that of Europe, even though income levels and technologies are roughly similar. This seems due in part to greater regulations on firms and thus more paperwork for each change—and correspondingly higher costs to start a new firm. More benefits are guaranteed by European welfare states (unemployment, sick leave, etc.) to each worker in the (large and officially regulated) firms. Smaller firms often escape such regulations, either because they are legally excluded or they (sometimes illegally) do not report their activities. In closely regulated economies like Italy or Eastern Europe, these non-reporters are thus labeled the "underground economy." Smaller firms often employ more part-time and non-union workers, which helps explain the decline by about half in the percent of the labor force unionized from the 1940s through 1980s in much of Europe and the United States (cf. Rempel and Clark 1997).

A major sociopolitical implication of these economic changes is *decline in traditional authority and hierarchy*. Current technologies require fewer unskilled workers performing routine tasks, or a large middle-management bureaucracy to coordinate them, than did traditional manufacturing, as in steel, automobiles, and so on. High-tech means increasing automation of routine tasks. It also demands more professionally autonomous decisions. More egalitarian, collegial decision-making is thus increasingly labeled a hallmark of modern society, by analysts from Habermas and Parsons to consultants in business schools who teach the importance of a new "corporate culture"—illustrated by *In Search of Excellence* (Peters and Waterman 1982), the number-one non-fiction best-seller in the United States for some time and widely read by business leaders in the United States and Europe. Employees are encouraged to be more involved in collegial definition of tasks, take more responsibility, and be more rewarded for individual contributions—rather than collective union negotiations for a "class" of workers or by civil-service or seniority rules. Many older, larger firms have sought to adopt aspects of this corporate culture to compete with dynamic smaller firms (strong evidence on this point is in Chapter 4). Bill Gates thus became the Marilyn Monroe of corporate America in the 1990s. This trend is not just imposed by top management but often driven by employee preferences: Several U.S. personnel studies indicate that employees report less job dissatisfaction with wages or benefits than with collegiality of work conditions and similar factors (Farnham 1989).

These internal organizational changes are reinforced by the general economic environment. Big and little firms have experienced major consolidations—enhanced by growth of multinationals, the 1970s oil boom and subsequent bust, leveraged buyouts, rise of the Eurodollar and Euro markets, and worldwide trade expansion. All these factors combine to undermine the (sometimes) genteel hierarchy of the familistic and quasi-monopolistic tradition of business still powerful in Europe in the 1950s and, later, in Asia. It paralleled a more general culture of hierarchy and deference in the family, church, and elsewhere.

When these strong forces for change do alter business practices, this leads naturally to questioning traditional bureaucratic-hierarchical arrangements in other domains—like welfare state agencies. This in turn fuels demands for more marketlike individualism, which grew far more politically emphatic in the 1980s. Some was just cyclical faddism; but many elements we list are more profound and enduring.

A fundamental consequence of these changes is a shift in the fault lines of economic conflict, as these flow into the political system: The class-based economic right and left over the past century were commonly owners and managers of large manufacturing firms *versus* manual workers, often in labor unions. As this characterizes less and less the economic condition of the labor force, support declines for this traditional political cleavage. The old cleavage can correspondingly be replaced by new issues more easily than if there had been no such changes in the economy—as Proposition 3 states.

Although much research on these points comes from the United States, Western Europe, and Japan, pressures for analogous changes are underway elsewhere: from the Glasnost of the former USSR to the velvet revolutions of Eastern Europe and Italy to more decentralized state planning in China to displacement of traditional family/clientelistic oligarchs like the Shah of Iran or Marcos in the Philippines to decentralizing presidential and traditional party dominance in Mexico. Global international pressures and media coverage make national isolation increasingly difficult, although our propositions still propose specific reasons why all places are not identical. The turbulence and conflicts of fundamentalism that followed the Shah in Iran, and grew into a major force in much of the Middle East, and the fragility of democracy in the former Soviet areas, remind us that the end of one hierarchy does not imply smooth consensus. Indeed, multiple conflicts—and correspondingly greater political uncertainty— are part and parcel of weakened hierarchy and cause many to lament the loss of security and stability of the ancien regimes. Every regime, alas, has its flaws.

Rising Income:
More Affluence and Less Social Tension

Besides these workplace relations and attitudes, a growing economy increases income to individuals. More income in turn brings important political cultural consequences, although many are indirect. Consider:

12. *The higher the level of income and the more continuous the rate of economic growth, the less powerful are political parties, and the less salient are radical programs like fundamental economic redistribution.*

The turmoil of the Great Depression in the 1930s and World War II encouraged leftist parties. People tend not to rock the boat when things go well, but crisis generates demands for political change. Simple stagflation (after years of prosperity) leads to dissatisfaction with incumbents. Stagflation in the 1970s encouraged electing conservative parties—in many countries, like Britain, Germany and the United States. The Mitterand socialists were an apparent exception: Elected in 1980, they initially pursued classic socialist policies of nationalizing industries and expanding social welfare programs. But citizen dissatisfaction mounted, New Mayors were elected in 1983 (who, as we show in Figure 2.4, were often fiscally conservative but socially liberal). By the mid-1980s the French socialists essentially redefined socialism, embracing such unorthodox socialist issues as efficiency and fiscal conservatism. The French socialists thus chose to adapt their program to changes in the society, and stayed in power, unlike the French communists, who refused ideological deviationism until well into the 1990s (Becquart-Leclercq et al. 1987; Clark et al. 1987; Balme et al. 1987). Yet ferment on the left in Spain and Italy led the communist parties in those countries to large changes in the 1970s. Debates correspondingly emerged about the appropriate ideological position of leftist parties internationally, partially captured in the next proposition.

13. *The higher the level of income and the more steady the economic growth of a society, and the more stable and affluent is each individual, the more fiscally conservative they are.*

Higher income for individuals, and societies, permits more choice. As income rises, it is more technologically difficult to define priorities in advance and harder to plan through established (especially national) programs—for both central governments and large private firms. If the private-sector solution is for small, nimble firms to displace the large, then for national governments an analogous policy is to decentralize the welfare state and other programs to smaller units and local branches—to encourage tailoring programs to local preferences. One next logical step, for some, is privatization, permitting individuals to choose, like consumers in a classic market for consumer goods. As people grow more affluent, they are not satisfied with standardized medical care, education, or theater—they want tailor-made items and are willing to pay for them. The normal corollary is less political support from the affluent for at least some and sometimes all government services (or at least taxes). Similarly, as income rises for all, the number of economically secure persons grows, and they are likely to criticize as bureaucratic and unresponsive those social programs that may have seemed quite adequate just a decade or two earlier. When it grows clear that this dissatisfaction comes not just from a small affluent elite but increasing numbers of voters/taxpayers, old policies start to be rethought. "Innovation" becomes fashionable for government. The strength of this proposition should increase with the progressiveness of the tax system, the degree of redistribution (from rich to poor) of government services, and the separableness of the goods supplied.[11] Yet even with a tax system taking the same proportion of income from citizens at all income levels, zero redistribution in services, and pure public goods, the higher absolute contribution paid by the more prosperous leads them to fiscal conservatism. Similarly, the further above the average an individual voter, or group of voters, the more fiscally conservative they should be (Clark and Ferguson 1983: 177; Hoffman and Clark 1979) since the marginal increase in taxes paid to services received rises continually with income.

These last comments point to the interdependence between the private and public sectors to explain citizen reactions toward continued government growth. We next consider government characteristics more explicitly.

Government Growth:
Welfare State Dynamics

14. The more extensive and complete the adoption of welfare state-type programs, the less the pressure for continued growth of these programs and of government in general.

Success is the main problem of the welfare state. Many goals of leftist parties have been achieved, and proudly applauded by Social Democrats from Scandinavia to U.S. Democrats. The ideological issue this poses is: What next? The question has both a technical or managerial logic (what programs can build on each other) and an electoral logic (what will citizens support). Over the last few decades both ideological and party commitment to leftist goals by European and U.S. voters has substantially weakened. This is clear in several measures, such as the decline of class voting, that is, the degree to which income, occupation, and similar social status indicators explain party voting, as Figures 2.4, 2.5, and 2.6 suggest. Further related analyses are in Chapter 4.

Public ownership of industry, once viewed by the left as a solution for many social evils, is supported today by only a minority of West European publics, including Materialist, Mixed, and Postmaterialist subgroups (Eurobarometer 19, results not shown). National differences here are revealing: Support for classic leftist policies—redistribution of income, state government control and planning of the economy—is strongest in the least developed European countries like Greece and Ireland. Conversely, these policies enjoy least support precisely where the policies have moved farthest—as in Denmark and West Germany (Inglehart 1990). If carried still farther, one may even reach the point where (as was sometimes the case in Russia and Eastern Europe) state control is viewed as a policy of the right.

15. If government grows more rapidly than the private-sector economy, support for reduction in government programs is more likely.

This was clear in the 1970s, when economies stagnated but government spending and taxes continued growing. The consequence was an increased *"tax bite"*— the share of one's income paid to support government. Result: less net income for individuals. Such loss of income was characteristic of ten European countries, Canada, the United States and Japan from 1976 to 1985 (except Finland) (cf. Mouritzen and Houlberg 1988: 38 for 1978 to 1986, and Wolman and Goldsmith 1987 for 1976–1982). These were critical years for the rise of fiscal conservatism.

Let us stress that most New Political Culture supporters are uncomfortable with the fiscal conservatism rhetoric of the traditional right. The NPC seeks more efficiency. Lower taxes are preferred if money is visibly wasted, but most important, better spending, more responsible management of limited funds—particularly in times of slow or negative economic growth when all feel economically squeezed.

Evidence: Among the most dramatic, and researched turnarounds of this sort were the United States state referenda, from California's Proposition 13 (in 1978) to Massachusetts's Prop. 2½ (in 1980), which cut property taxes nearly in half. Surveys of who supported cuts in government spending often showed that, analyzing some seventy factors, citizens who considered their governments "corrupt, inefficient, and overstaffed" were particularly prone to support the referenda (cf. Ladd and Wilson 1985; Reid 1987). Similarly, the 1989 defeat of the Liberal Democratic Party in Japan's Senate was interpreted as largely due to increasing dissatisfaction by Japanese citizens with overstaffing and inefficiency (Kobayashi and Iwagami 1989 analyze these changes with surveys over more than a decade).

Consider next how these economic and government dynamics combine with social issues to generate support for the New Political Culture.

New Social Issues Often Extend
Individual Rights to New Domains

More individual freedom, combined with equal treatment, is a "deep structure" underlying many specific social issues. The clearest instances are those demanding extension of rights of the general (or "majority") citizenry to a minority or new group—feminism thus seeks equal rights and treatment for women in the workplace and other social institutions, including the family. Ethnic minorities, immigrants, and racial subgroups seek to end discrimination, that is, not to apply criteria that treat *Gastarbeiter* differently from native workers. The young, elderly, homosexuals, handicapped, and animals—or their advocates—can similarly demand "equal" treatment. Former U.S. President Jimmy Carter championed this principle internationally while in office in his world concern with "human rights" that has continued to spread globally and increase in power. Is the ecology movement an exception? It demands active government intervention to prevent despoiling nature. One might present this as "nature rights"—extending to trees and air the rights of people. Not too great an extension beyond human and animal rights, perhaps, but different in means required. Since trees cannot speak out, ecologists must speak for them, urging political leaders to defend nature against noxious gasses, liquefied chemicals, and physical destruction—or at least protect the persons who would be harmed by these changes in nature. Civil rights are increasingly extended to new groups (like children and animal rights) and to new policy areas (like do citizens have the right to burn the flag?)[12]

Related concerns go back decades, but they grew more politicized in the 1960s. "Demands" become "needs" when governments recognize the claimants' legitimacy. Needs may then be incorporated managerially in specific programs and aid formulas of public agencies. Feminists don't just ask men to be more egalitarian; they want the state to punish men who are not. Parents similarly grow liable to state intervention if they mistreat their own children. Similar policy dynamics basically hold for many social issues. As governments have intervened further in many social processes, demands have sometimes shifted from "equality of opportunity" to "equality of achievement." The first stems from the Lockean rights concept that persons should be permitted to exercise their rights freely. Equality of achievement is more activist and depends on state intervention: Its success may be monitored by quotas (e.g., percent of women hired for a job) or similar means.[13]

What is new is using state regulations and programs to enforce individual rights and equal treatment in progressively more policy areas. If these are the government policy outcomes, let us move back to their sources.

From Market Individualism to Social Individualism: The Rise of Social Issues

16. *Younger, more highly educated persons support more socially liberal issues. Although they support the output of many welfare state programs, they also prefer increased efficiency in service delivery and the corresponding lower costs and taxes. These changes in fiscal/administrative preferences are largest (a) among more afflu-ent persons, and (b) in affluent societies with extensive welfare state programs, and (c) among younger persons.*

If market individualism is increasing, so is social individualism in many policy issues. What factors contributed to this rise in social issues? The lower paths of Figure 2.9 summarize our propositions. Driving both market and social indi-vidualism is "more free choice." We provided descriptive evidence of the spread of social individualism in several survey items above. Why does individualism spread?

Higher incomes permit more economic choices and pursuing a wider range of tastes, including social issues. These in turn pose new demands on govern-ment, like more egalitarian school teaching. Why are public issues increasingly social? In part via a simple extension of the Scarcity Hypothesis: As basic eco-nomic concerns are met, new concerns arise. These increasingly involve con-sumption more than production—women's roles, day care, the elderly, nuclear waste disposal, clean air, culture, sports, leisure. Less salient are work-related issues like "the right to strike," social security or unemployment insurance.

The hottest national issues in the United States in 1989 were abortion, who may burn the American flag, and drugs—strikingly noneconomic policies. In 1989 in China, the USSR, and Eastern Europe the major issue was not more guns nor more butter but more democracy. This was the year that communists chose to end communism in much of the world.

Situs-type reasoning also applies to political issues: Many old issues and cleavages are still in place, but they dominate the political agenda far less than earlier. Economic needs do not disappear; they are complemented by others, which join but do not displace economic concerns.

Consider more specific factors:

17. *The higher the education of an individual, or average level of a social unit (country, city), the greater the support for classic issues of civil rights, civil liberty, and tolerance.*

Education increases tolerance. Support thus grows with education for classic survey items like would you permit a communist to speak to your school or permit his/her book to be in the school library or accept a person of different social background as a marriage partner. Tolerance on such issues has consistently increased since surveys of them began in the 1940s to the present in the United States and Europe (cf. Smith 1985; Weil 1985; Ward and Greeley 1989; Davis 1989; Brint, Cunningham, and Li 1997).

Effects of education tend to be more pronounced in a less hierarchical society, that is, one whose educational system tends to inculcate egalitarian norms; for example, education has a less strong impact on tolerance in some European countries, especially Germany and Ireland, than it does in the United States (Weil 1985; Butts 1997).

Education also has more impact when it exposes students to contrasting interpretations of what they knew from their parents. Travel and more "cosmopolitan" social contacts, like education, have similar effects. Combined with travel and the worldly sophistication influence of television, it undermines the traditional intolerance of the parochial. When you understand the enemy, simplistic stereotypes of "foreign devils" grow less compelling.

A few foreign migrants to a country may bring cosmopolitanism of the exotic and heighten social tolerance. But mass immigrations, as in most West European countries in the 1980s, dampened this trend. Migrant workers met visible antagonism during economic recessions in Germany and elsewhere. In France, migration of many Arabs and black Africans in the 1970s and 1980s heightened their social and political salience. Simultaneous with a general rise in tolerance, especially by youth and the highly educated, was a resurgence of anti-immigrant themes and political success of the French far right around Le Pen after 1986 (Hoffmann-Martinot 1989). One would expect more anti-immigrant politics in regions and cities with the most immigration. This seems the case in Britain, Germany, and even Scandinavia judging from the success of parties and candidates on anti-immigrant themes in the 1980s, sometimes joined with antitax measures. The immigrant issue even drove French communist mayors and the national PCF to lead in promoting anti-immigrant legislation.[14]

Nevertheless, if ceteris were paribus, increased education should reduce support for anti-immigrant and other socially "unprogressive" programs.

Most of our propositions identify income and education as exerting separate effects. However, education and income are moderately intercorrelated at the individual level, more so with city-level data. And some political/social effects may be driven by both. Two related candidates are "altruism" and support for "public goods," which several studies suggest rise with income as well as education (Wilson and Banfield 1971; Becker 1982; Inglehart 1990). These remain controversial points, in part since the precise conceptualization and measurement of the phenomena remain vague. We leave them as hypotheses to be explored.

The Dynamics of Cultural Change: Social Issues

Lying behind changes in many specific social issues are (1) a slimmer family, and (2) new social movements, including related religious and ideological groupings.

A Slimmer Family

Major trends here parallel those we identified in the polity and economy. Hierarchical decline is a central dynamic.

18. The family and intimate personal relations have increasingly become characterized by more egalitarian relations, more flexible roles, and more tolerance for a wider range of behavior.

The traditional family has slimmed.[15] Fewer young people marry; they marry later; they have fewer children; far more women work instead of just living at home; divorce rates have risen; parents and grandparents less often live with children (e.g., Cherlin 1981; Forse 1986; Hernandez 1986; our chapter 4).

Paralleling these socio-demographic changes are changes in attitudes and roles concerning the family. Indeed, attitudes toward the family have changed more than almost any other social or political item in the past twenty to thirty years, especially items like should women work outside the home? Announcing changes since the 1960s are such popular labels as "new rules," "liberation," "yuppies," the "Me generation," "greening," "consciousness-raising," and many more. Although these developments started earlier in the United States (cf. Reich 1970; Yankelovich 1981), their impacts may be even more profound in more hierarchical and traditional societies of Europe and Asia (Mendras 1997). Conflicts in many hierarchical societies often flow from more politically dramatic differences between age cohorts than in the (historically) more consensual egalitarian societies like the United States, Canada, and Australia. For instance, an item posed to a national sample of young French persons asked if they felt closer to an older French person or a young Arab; a majority reported the young Arab (Balme et al. 1986–87; SOFRES 1985)—at a time when Arabs had become widely criticized in France! The politics of fundamentalist Christians and Muslims often stresses women's roles as central to their agendas, illustrated by heated conflicts in the 1990s in France and Turkey over when and where Muslim women should or should not wear traditional dress or cover their faces.

Besides internal family dynamics, the slimmer family determines less the education and jobs of individual family members. The great transformation of society from *Gemeinschaft* to *Gesellschaft* over the last century was driven by spinning out key functions from the family to other institutions. Since 1945, increased economic well-being and government support programs have expanded choices to individuals and cumulatively transferred more functions than ever out of the family, such as public health, daycare, and student loans. Individuals thus value less "particularistic" family relations as they have grown decreasingly important for other essential activities.

Families are decreasingly responsible for raising children and placing them in jobs. Schools have assumed more responsibility for intellectual training—as well as emotional and general cultural training. Children rely less on their parents to support their education expenses—scholarships and public support have brought more access, especially to higher education. But while all these trends evolved over a century or more, their magnitude in the 1970s and 1980s is new. The proportion of age cohorts pursuing postsecondary education has vastly increased in most of Western Europe. Scholarships covering basic living costs as well as tuition for higher education have risen dramatically—even to being universally available to all high school graduates in the Netherlands, for example. Higher education has literally become "mass" education since the 1960s in Western Europe and the United States.

Fewer children work in family firms (farms, shops, etc.). Social mobility studies show decreasing effects of parents' education and income in explaining childrens' occupational success; simultaneously effects of education have increased.[16] The proportions of wives and mothers working in jobs outside the home have increased dramatically, in the United States and in many European countries. With children and wives less at home and less dependent on the family for key activities, as children grow older they perceive a less family-dependent world and pursue more individual concerns at a younger age and more fully. This is also true of parents, especially mothers, whose jobs remove them increasingly from traditional roles. Similarly, older persons rely less on their children for continued economic support and more often live physically separated from their children than a few decades back. Governments help.

How do these family changes link with changes discussed above? The slimmer family, first, facilitates greater individuation and differentiated pursuit of tastes. Tolerance for more diverse lifestyles should similarly grow. Second, it helps legitimate extending rights to new types of persons and activities. Still, new groups did not arise smoothly. Although changes in economic organization, more affluence, and family roles encouraged the New Political Culture, social movements still played an independent role.

The Rise of New Social Movements

New social movements fill the gap between individuals/families and political leaders. The most obvious movements date from the late 1960s, pressing for civil rights, first for blacks in the United States and soon thereafter for feminist issues, ecology, the elderly, and so on. Support for these rose as traditional parties and leaders did not respond as fast or fully as activists hoped. Active citizen participation remains exceptional: Leaders are always, by definition, an elite. Still average citizens support such movements in myriad ways, noted in survey items like "trying to convince friends" of a cause, volunteering time, contributing money, and so on. Such items from the World Values Survey show the younger, socially liberal respondents nearly twice as active as average.

A repeated U.S. citizen survey shows a near doubling from the late 1960s to the late 1980s in the number of citizens participating in group activities, letter writing, visiting political leaders, contributing money, and volunteering time for social and political groups (Brady, Nie, and Verba in draft). Another two-time replication over the same period concerning government agency responsiveness (Schumaker, Cigler, and Faye 1989) shows similar results: Direct contacts doubled for many organized groups, especially neighborhood groups. This doubling almost directly matches the drop in voting turnout for elections over the same period. Many citizens, these results suggest, find choices among political candidates too distant from their concerns even to vote; established parties and leaders are seen as "irrelevant." Local groups and specific issues bring out more autonomous support. Grass roots ecology movements in France and Poland saw substantially increased support, often by teenagers and persons in their twenties, in the late 1980s.[17]

One explanation for such movements is social psychological: As the family declines in holistic, emotive, and role-defining functions other groups rise in importance. Several social psychological theories suggest such functional substitution among institutions (e.g., Parsons and Platt 1973). Extending this perspective culturally, Wildavsky and Webber (1986) argue that four quasiuniversal political cultures have persisted for centuries. But the 1970s saw growth in their fourth culture: the "egalitarian" or "communal," which provides cultural self-definition for its members by attacking outsiders, thus defining themselves as distinct and creating more internal egalitarian unity. In periods of activism, group leaders seek to "raise consciousness" of both outsiders, like political leaders, and insiders who are potential but inactive group members. For example, leaders of feminist and gay groups would suggest how to handle hard social situations for individual women and gays, substituting for the family. Informal "discussion circles" thus sprang up as thousands of individuals sought to address new concerns. Our point is even echoed by two economists of neo-Marxist background (Bowles and Gintis 1987, esp. pp. 152ff.) who argue that a narrowly instrumental interpretation of social movements should be expanded to include participants' benefits from movement participation, especially a sense of satisfaction and working out specifics of new role definitions. Emotive terms have correspondingly spread from familial and religious contexts to many others, like "forming a community," changing the "discourse," "social bonding," and so on. These surfaced in post-1968 student rallies and have diffused further since.

Functionally analogous, often, are quasireligious movements. New sects, cults, transcendental meditation, scientology, and others have grown even more numerous in some European countries than the United States (see the extensive studies by Wuthnow and Bainbridge, e.g., 1989). And some of these religious movements have dramatically increased in political impacts, from Muslim fundamentalism in the Middle East to electronic preachers (TV evangelists) and direct-mail campaigns for political candidates in the United States. Fundamentalist Christians and Muslims became major political forces in many countries by the 1990s.

How can we reconcile such "intolerant commitment" of social movements with the increased tolerance we observe? Similarly, how to reconcile the demands for increased government regulation of even intimate social relations with the broader support for social tolerance we see in surveys? Our interpretation: by distinguishing leaders from followers. Leaders of all political movements tend to be more extreme than their followers; moreover, the leaders of new activities are likely to oversell their cause in hopes to mobilize—especially in heated negotiations with political leaders or in media appeals; and they often succeed when political leaders take them as spokespersons for new social issues. But followers, as indicated by the results we reviewed for the general citizenry, are growing increasingly tolerant even while supporting new social movements. These leader-follower differences are documented in Rempel (1997). That citizens may support several groups, not just one, should also lead them toward more tolerance, as Simmel, Coleman (1957), and others argued. This leader-follower distinction is often missed by political leaders who deal primarily with group leaders.

Although social movements are centuries old, they shift from smaller, more isolated, and informal groupings to larger, formal, and unified political movements when political leaders do or do not respond. The rise of ecology movements into parties in many European countries illustrates this clearly: The open, decentralized Swiss parties endorsed green issues rapidly; the centralized French parties were slow to do so. The success of new social movements (NSMs) in institutionalizing new cultural norms and values over the past two decades is counterbalanced by a decline in legitimacy of traditional hierarchies, ranging from factories and unions to the traditional family to churches, schools, and governments. (Lipset and Schneider 1983 provides baseline data updated in numerous scattered surveys.) Strategically, some new groups sought to present issues in ways that "establishment" groups could or would not respond to. To explain the emergence and success of such new social movements thus depends both on social psychological dynamics, coming from (a) the declining family and new social identities, and (b) the (perceived) unresponsiveness of established institutions. When both seem responsive, new social movements should decline—which widely happened in the 1990s, as past NSM issues had become official policies of many governments.

Clientelism, Religion, and Media: Facilitating or Retarding Factors

Four remaining factors encourage or retard operation of the propositions already discussed. Political clientelism and religious practices that stress personal relations retard the NPC, whereas professional administration and media use encourage the NPC. These four are fundamental factors differentiating Northern Europe from Southern Europe. They combine on a dimension of political culture that varies from abstract, impersonal "issue politics" to specific, personal contacts and "clientelism."

19. *The New Political Culture is more likely to emerge in political contexts stressing issues rather than clientelism.*

The political culture of clientelism and ethnic politics conflicts with several NPC components. It is harder to break with organized group loyalties and bureaucratic work rules if the personal relations they embody are highly legitimate and at the core of political exchange and reward. These personal loyalties make the network of personal relations more legitimate vehicles for policymaking than in a more individualistic (even atomistic) society. Why and how are such dense political/social contexts important? Consider first traditional religious patterns and then more recent developments that shift their effects.

20. *Nonstate religions, such as Protestantism in Catholic countries and nonconformist Protestants in Protestant countries, tend to emphasize individualism, which leads to more abstract issue politics, whereas state religions and Catholicism stress more personalistic ties, encouraging clientelistic politics.*

Protestantism emphasizes salvation through the individual's good works, and thus a direct (super-) personal relationship to God. By contrast, for Roman Catholics the Church is a critical social intermediary, providing confession for one's sins and granting absolution. These traditional theological differences may recede over time but still persist in cultural outlooks that they helped shape. The abstract and moralistic conceptions of politics continue in much of Northern Europe and New England in the United States (Elazar 1975), whereas per-

sonal loyalty is more valued in Catholic settings (cf. evidence of persistent international differences in Ward and Greeley 1989 and Mendras 1997). Clark (1975)
joins these general religious differences to specific components that affect political culture. They form a distinct "Irish ethic" of sociability, trust, localism,
practicing Catholicism, and social conservatism, which in turn legitimates political patronage. Catholicism thus supports more intense personal contacts,
countering the abstract and impersonal issue politics of Protestants. In many
U.S. cities Irish Catholics emerged as leaders in building political organizations
on such personal ties. Their persistence, as in Chicago until the 1980s, discouraged abstract issue politics and an NPC style. Chicago's revolution came in
1983 with the election of Chicago's first black mayor, Harold Washington. He
and most of Chicago's blacks are Protestants who find the clientelism of machine politics "immoral and dishonest"—in contrast to Chicago's more
clientelistic (and Catholic) Hispanics. The black-Hispanic differences underline
the importance of religious factors distinguishing two similar low-income groups.
Further factors preserving/discouraging clientelism are in Clark (1997a).

The emphasis on abstract ideology encourages candidates to stress issues over
personal favors. Analysts following Samuelson (1969) term these public goods
versus private or separable goods. But public goods are harder to use to build
coalitions and can create intense debate. Causality is hard to ascribe, but an
"elective affinity" is clear between issue politics, public goods, and consensus as
a social and political style. The British and New England ideals of civility and
gentlemanly behavior, the New England (and Scandinavian) emphasis on una-
nimity and participation by all citizens as a moral duty—these contrast markedly with politics in Roman Catholic countries where interests are explicitly
discussed, politics is more openly conflictual, and is widely considered "dirty"
if not immoral. Politics is correspondingly not something to encourage "good
citizens," women, or children to engage in; it is delegated instead to professional
politicians (Clark and Ferguson 1983: 120–134; 242–243; Elazar 1987: 142ff.;
Durant, Lyons and Fitzgerald 1989; Clark and Jeanrenaud 1989). Such politicians deal in separable goods, "cut deals," and are expected to be openly
conflictual. Their politics is more a zero-sum game, and coalitions are minimal
winning coalitions to minimize the spread of booty. By contrast, the NPC leans
more toward public goods like strict environmental controls. This also permits
taking power away from "politicians" and delegating more autonomy to administrative staff via the professional city manager and similar "reform" government mechanisms (such as nonpartisanship and other factors we listed above
that weaken parties). The Scandinavian Ombudsman can survive politically
only where elected officials are willing to give up claim to an obvious source of
clientelistic rewards. The "Ombudsman" of Naples and Dublin and Chicago is
the *padrone*. Major "consolidation reforms" of local governments also succeeded
largely in Scandinavia and Britain, and failed in most Catholic countries of
Southern Europe in the 1970s (Goldsmith and Page 1987). This abolishing of

the smallest units to consolidate into metropolitan government was weakly resisted by local officials and their citizens in the Northern European Protestant countries, but in the South was seen as an attempt to break off valued personal ties and was thus defeated. The legal structure reinforces similar patterns: Italian *assessori* are elected council members who head administrative agencies (like water, etc.)—the opposite of the American/Canadian/Australian "city manager" government, which in some cases by law prohibits individual council members from having any communication with administrative staff (to prevent personal favors). Political parties held together by close personal ties are more resistant to change than those lacking such ties. Yet the nonideological style of the traditional machine could still adapt to shifts in ideology (as represented by the NPC) if all else were equal (this happened in Chicago in the late 1990s under Mayor Richard M. Daley). Factors not "equal" are the importance of personal relations via patronage jobs or contracts of clientelistic politics, used to solidify ethnic, religious, and union groups. These can offer vigorous resistance to efficiency policies of the NPC.

Non-Western countries and religions include similar but sometimes contrasting dimensions. For example, the Japanese emphasis on thorough and extended discussion by key participants in a decision has a resemblance to the New England town meeting but lacks the individualist underpinning. Clientelistic relations are embedded in many traditional Japanese associations, which overlap with more formal organizations—like neighborhood groups and political parties with local and national government representation. So is the Japanese family a strong and persistent source of particularistic ties and a model of ritualized and intense personal relations that echo in many workplaces and political institutions—from tea ceremonies to bowing precisely fifteen, twenty-five, forty-five, or ninety degrees to persons of varying status. Clientelism is correspondingly pervasive in Japanese politics, as in much of Asia, even though "reform" attacks on clientelism became an increasingly central cleavage in several Asian countries in the 1990s.

Some traditional factors are weakening, such that Inglehart (1990) found the Protestant-Catholic differences in economic growth in the late nineteenth century had reversed by the mid-twentieth century. Similarly, clientelism has declined even in areas like southern Italy and Spain in recent decades. Two factors are salient in such transformations:

21. *The more professionalized and bureaucratized the national welfare state, the more issue politics are likely to prevail over personalistic or clientelistic politics.*

Observers of the political machine like R. K. Merton and E. C. Banfield saw its decline coming with the U.S. New Deal and corresponding impersonal criteria for allocating welfare and social services (cf. Clark 1975, 1993a). The proposition is analytically sound, but many other factors retard its implementation. For example, in a national context where clientelistic politics is powerful, national programs are more often created or administered in a manner to support existing clientelistic patterns. Thus Roosevelt's New Deal and many Great Society programs helped bolster clientelistic machines in cities like Pittsburgh, Newark, and Chicago. The same holds in much of Southern Europe, Japan, and many Third World countries. In such contexts, the welfare state simply provides more resources for established groups to allocate to their followers. Proposition 21 thus stresses not just more welfare spending but whether resources are allocated to encourage or discourage personalistic relations.[18]

22. *The more important are mass media, the less important are clientelistic patterns.*

The more widespread the ownership of radio and television—and the more they carry politically significant content—the more they undermine personal ties as information resources and exchange mechanisms of politics. It is hard to rouse party "militants" from a comfortable TV and beer; similarly, simple but very popular past recreation activities of direct personal relations (card games, bingo, dominos, gossip—staples of clientelistic political organizations) are undermined by new media pleasures. Observers in Spain and Italy particularly stress this media impact in contexts with strong clientelistic traditions (Bettin and Magnier 1991; Giurickovic 1996). As the media rise in political importance they permit direct contact between a political leader and individual citizens, which can undermine clientelistic personalism.

The media emerged as a powerful force in the 1980s and 1990s as television coverage of politics grew more continuous and often more critical. Simultaneously, as parties and traditional groups like unions weaken, the media fill the gap faster than many alternatives. Usually, television is not controlled by a single ideological group or political party (unlike many newspapers and magazines) and, even if controlled by the national government, in most democracies this constrains television to appeal to the general citizenry. Hence the media can help increase the impact of the general citizenry. Research on the media lags behind these changes, but the main relevant studies are reviewed in Rempel and Clark (1997). They show moderate media effects. The costs of political campaign advertising escalate when candidates use television and radio more actively. In the past many volunteers, union workers, and others who did not bill leaders for their time did not demand that candidates find cash to pay them "up front." The media do, as do the increasingly professionalized and very expensive marketing, polling, advertising, and political consulting firms that emerged as major political forces in the 1990s in the United States and Western Europe. The correspondingly great pressure on candidates to raise vast sums of money—often five or more times greater than just a decade earlier—in turn led many NPC leaders to engage in sometimes questionable fundraising. Bill Clinton in the 1996 U.S. presidential campaign, and many French New Mayors (Carignon, Noir), confronted such problems. The more powerful media also focus citizen discontent by exposing details of (even rumored) corruption among political leaders with a vigilance and righteousness that catches many leaders off-guard.

With parties weakened and wounded, the media demand ever more detail, invoking the rights of the general citizenry. Few dare oppose.

The Internet further decentralizes information potentially far more than the mass media, since individual users can choose the sites to visit, create their own political groups, and maintain active contacts across the globe. Groups like ecologists have been assisted in this way, but even German Skinheads coordinate themselves via email in the 1990s. Very small and extreme groups especially in isolated small towns can help each other substantially via the new technology. Internet use was still confined to relatively elite groups in the 1990s who already embraced many NPC tendencies, but over time the Internet and associated computer technologies may reach deeper and bring still more and unclear changes.

Proposition #22 is weakened if political leaders can tightly control the media. Censorship threats or direct state ownership of media created many intermediary cases in countries like (earlier) Spain, Yugoslavia, or most Peoples' Republics. If media grow so tightly controlled as to be scorned by most citizens, however, personal relations are in turn strengthened as sources of political information.

Thus the NPC should emerge more readily among Protestants, where clientelism is weak, in countries with professionalized administrations, and where citizens actively use the mass media.

Summary

We defined the New Political Culture with seven elements distinguishing it from class politics in the first section. The second section showed how our analysis builds on past related work. The third offered evidence from several surveys of citizens and political leaders to indicate that class politics is still strong in some areas (such as among older mayors in France) but substantially displaced by the New Political Culture in others (such as U.S. mayors in recent years, younger French mayors, and younger cohorts of citizens in most of Europe and the United States). The last part explains such patterns in a set of twenty-two propositions that specify where and why the New Political Culture emerges (outlined in Figure 2.9). These propositions have been illustrated and supported with evidence from varied sources in this chapter. The next chapters assess the same propositions in many different contexts.

Notes

1. We use political culture differently from some past analysts, as grows clear in what follows. The reader who prefers a more abstract formulation of our distinctive approach should consult the Appendix. This chapter was planned from outset as the introduction for this volume. It was revised from a paper first presented at the American Political Science Association, Atlanta, August 1989, and the session on the New Politi-

cal Culture, Research Committee 03, Community Research, World Congress, International Sociological Association, Madrid, July 9–14, 1990.

Most data used in this chapter, and others below, for citizens and political leaders are available for analysis by others through the Interuniversity Consortium for Political and Social Research, P.O. Box 1248, Ann Arbor, MI 48106. Or contact the authors (see Preface).

2. This illustrates a more general pattern: Centralization encourages public goods, while decentralization encourages private goods and responsiveness to individual citizens (Clark 1975: 285).

3. "Postmaterialist" here and below refers to the concept and specific index of Inglehart, although most statements apply to the New Political Culture more generally. These two propositions are from Inglehart; most institutional/structural propositions below are from Clark. But the chapter is a joint product.

A pervasive social science notion is that basic personality structure crystallizes before adulthood, with little change thereafter. This does not imply no change during adult years. In some individual cases, dramatic behavior shifts occur; human development never stops (Brim, 1966; Brim and Kagan, eds., 1980; Riley and Bond, 1983). Nevertheless, human development seems more rapid during pre-adult years than afterward, and most evidence suggests less basic personality change in one's later years (Glenn, 1974, 1980; Block, 1981; Costa and McCrae, 1980; Sears, 1981, 1983; Jennings and Niemi, 1981; Jennings and Markus, 1984).

4. The b's and betas showed the same pattern as the r's. Data were collected in 1983.

5. We reviewed past surveys for changes but found little data. Few items have used identical wording over time. And most survey items before the 1970s did not separate fiscal from social liberalism but combined them in one general index.

6. The sources of declining monolithic power are elaborated in propositions for national systems in Clark (1974) and for local systems in Clark (1968).

7. We adapt the concept of situs from Benoit-Smullyan (1944) and Bell (1973: 377) to refer to parallel but distinct sectors of social organization, each with its partly distinct rules of the game (or culture).

Increasing automation of agriculture, and still more of manufacturing, implies that these situses continue to provide substantial output (measured in physical or monetary units), even while declining in relative labor force size. But for social and cultural consequences, physical outputs are less important than the proportion of the labor force in each situs.

Whether the shift from agriculture to manufacturing brought less hierarchy varied by context. For individualistic yeoman farmers it did not; for caste-like peasants it often did (cf. Moore 1966 and related debates).

8. The U.S. service sector comprised 22 percent of the labor force in 1900, 44 percent in 1950, and 65 percent in 1980 (Liesner 1985). Chan-ung Park helped us compute percentages over the twentieth century from this and other sources for most European countries and Japan.

9. Socialist theorists reached similar conclusions. "Let us consider the role of competition in a model of socialism. The word has undesirable connotations to many a socialist, yet it is inconceivable to imagine choice without competition among suppliers of goods and services.... A theater competes for an audience with other theaters by trying to be better...." Nove (1989: 18); cf. also Harrington (1989).

10. Debate continues over the contributions to economic growth of large versus small firms. Critics of small firms emphasize that many small firms are spinoffs of larger ones; that they may exist as suppliers to a few larger firms (common in Japan); that they have much higher death rates than larger firms; and that small firms often depend on larger firms such as automotive firms near Detroit, or finance firms near Wall Street. Small firms may also be less attractive to employees: less unionization, fewer benefits such as health care and pensions, and fewer job guarantees, especially because small firms fail more. On the other side, smaller firms permit more individual employee input, can be more democratic, and although they more often fail, failures may, in fact, be buyouts by a larger firm that offers increased opportunities to former employees of the small firm. Such points were actively debated in 1994 when the Clinton administration sought to use tax benefits to encourage small firms. But hard evidence on the magnitude and specifics of these points remains scarce or partial. Nasar (1994) is an overview of work by small-firm analysts Frank Levy, John Haltiwanger, Scott Schuh, Steven Davis, and David Birch. (See also Harrison 1994). Our key point, however, is that small firms provide powerful, widely admired models of egalitarian, participatory organizations. Their nimble adaptiveness leads persons familiar with them to criticize large organizations, especially governments, that fall short in these respects. That the Clinton administration accepted these arguments and sought to act on them shows the persuasiveness of the small-firm model. Similarly, the magazine written for managers of the 500 largest U.S. firms, *Fortune*, regularly covers small firms and exhorts its readers to adopt the decentralized, egalitarian approach of the model small firm. Even if this model were empirically refuted, the fact that it has been a powerful point of reference that helped change big firms and governments is the central point here.

11. Separable here is the opposite of public goods in Samuelson's (1969) sense. Clark introduced the term separable to refer to a type of government service, thus differing from "private" goods which are uniquely consumed by individuals.

12. Even this might be derived from the logic of rights extension to a new group rather than a new "policy arena" if we consider that President George Bush sided with "flag rights" and against "burners' rights" when he proposed a constitutional amendment in 1989 to protect the American flag. For especially non-U.S. readers, we add a comment on our text by Donald Rosdil: "The issue was initially raised by social conservatives. They took a stand on the flag issue because it represented symbolically a deeper challenge to their cherished values of patriotism, acceptance of authority, self-sacrifice for the nation, etc., by a rising adversary political culture." The opposing side publicly burned more flags, and the issue heated up until it reached the president.

13. The dynamics of "progressive" and "conservative" social issues are contrasted in Rempel and Clark (1997).

14. This violation of the traditional social progressivism of the left was spurred by large numbers of immigrant workers moving into public housing in communist cities. Since immigrants cannot vote in France, they just weakened communist electoral strength (Schain 1988). The negative impact of immigrants on social liberalism is exacerbated by the fact that foreigners cannot vote in France. By contrast black Americans and many Hispanic immigrants to the US are quite politically active, as immigrants have often been since the 19th century. The French-US difference in citizen responsiveness seems due to French mayors characterizing citizens as well as organized groups as generally pressing for more spending, whereas US mayors explicitly distinguish citizens from or-

ganized groups, and see just groups as pro-spending (in our FAUI data). Public officials in many countries have grown increasingly concerned that whether voters or not, immigrants often have access to welfare state services, and thus raise burdens on taxpayers. Which services should be denied to legal, or illegal, immigrants has sparked many political debates in the last decade. These have been particulary troubling to left parties and citizens.

15. So many young persons live together in varied contexts that the label of "family" is often antiquated. We retain it for linguistic simplicity, albeit the intended referent is more broadly "persons living in various forms of intimate social arrangements, including regular and irregular cohabitation."

16. U.S. mobility studies from the late nineteenth century onward report few changes until the 1960s (Grusky 1986) but major changes since: Hout's (1988) replication of Featherman and Hauser (1978) showed that effect of origin status on destination status declined by 28 percent from 1962 to 1973 and by one-third from 1972 to 1985. Considering welfare state effects, Hauser and Grusky (1984; 1987) analyze sixteen and twenty-two countries, finding more mobility in countries with socialist and social democratic political leadership. See also Grusky (1994). However such findings sparked a counter-reaction by some mobility researchers, who suggest no real change, only "trendless fluctuation" in mobility (e.g. Shavit and Blossfeld 1993). This debate directly parallels, and involves some of the same protaganists, as the debate over class politics. See Chapter 4.

17. Previously these issues were more dominated by national organizations, often with a more established outlook (Swianiewicz and Kowalczyk 1989).

18. Clearly issue politics can mix with clientelism. For example, Walder (1986) shows how traditional Chinese administrative clientelism joined with the ideological concerns of Maoist Marxism after 1945 to provide a joint set of criteria for promotion of staff and resource allocation.

19. We sharpened many of these ideas in discussions of the Political Culture Group, which Clark created with Aaron Wildavsky, Daniel Elazar and Seymour Martin Lipset in 1984. The Group held small meetings every year or so in the 1980s and 1990s.

Appendix 1:
The New Political Cultural Perspective

Just as a New Political Culture is emerging, so does a new analytical framework help capture its dynamics.[19] Our framework has grown through comparisons among (mainly) European countries, Japan, and the United States and thus encompasses more structural sources of variation than more limited purviews. The importance of political culture grows more apparent as one compares across quite different political systems, since basic political assumptions then change. Indeed, the concept of political culture first emerged in cross-national work, especially by Max Weber and then Almond and Coleman (1960). At any one time, one can describe citizen preferences—like support for a more active welfare state or opposition to women working outside the home—as part of political culture. And if one compares across units—age cohorts, cities, nations—that differ on these key preferences, and these preferences in turn are distinctly important (after controlling other variables) in explaining a policy like raising taxes, then we can say that these preferences helped cause the tax increase. But if culture includes individual preferences, it is also more.

In contrast to some who suggest that political culture is a residual variable, to be introduced after everything else is considered, we stress that it includes the quintessential elements of a political system—those deep structures defining basic rules of the game—that if the analyst can identify help understand how and why the players play as they do. We thus build on Max Weber, Emile Durkheim, and Talcott Parsons. Understanding the rules does not permit predicting a single game's outcome; political participants are active players who operate within and around the rules. We are not biographers of individuals or governments; unlike historians, we seek not to explain the unique. Yet our approach is more concrete and empirically informed than that of economists who usually analyze economic actors seeking to maximize their utility without identifying specific elements comprising a utility function. We thus complement economists and related public choice analysts who leave empty, or exogenous, the content of preferences of citizens, groups, and leaders. In this middle position, we do not attempt to know or measure all preferences of citizens and leaders; only those necessary to analyze the core processes in our framework. This does not imply any less "rational" a conception of mankind; it simply attends to concerns that rational choice theorists usually ignore. Thompson, Ellis, and Wildavsky (1990) concur with us on this and many points.

Our framework uses several middle-level concepts, such as "fiscal conservatism" and "social liberalism," although they are no more than very partial summaries of total sets of preferences. Still they are foundations of most political cultures and policymaking. Fiscal conservatism has informed classic debates over government growth, a critical element of left-right party continua for the last century. "Social liberalism" we use in part to stay deliberately close to past work by other social and political analysts. Both of these are rooted in deeper values such as egalitarianism and individualism.

We deny that political culture implies a unique and distinct theory or methodology; we see it first as a perspective that interpenetrates what people do in their political lives. Second, for analysts, it similarly refers to patterned values and norms that can be measured with survey data, fieldwork, textual readings, content analysis, discourse analysis, and other methods. We find that some "postmodernists" have a useful core of relativistic views but disagree when they press so far as to deny the legitimacy of science, of systematic evidence, and claim that they obviate past work. Brint and Kelley (1993) offer a useful critique of such postmodernist developments from a perspective close to ours.

What is new in the New Political Culture? The NPC is an ideal type, like the bourgeoisie. Concrete individual citizens and leaders vary in the degree to which they match the type. We do not include every recent political development. Our concern is not to explain everything new, but those fundamental elements that we can interpret analytically, particularly the seven distinguishing characteristics in the first section.

Basic concepts include *political culture*, by which we refer to enduring rules of the game: those general *values* defining important ends (like equality) and more specific *norms* concerning how roles should be performed (such as more citizen participation). These values and norms are often articulated more forcefully by political leaders than by most citizens, such that it often is illuminating to examine leaders as "carriers," to use Max Weber's term, for alternative cultural models. Citizens may be less outspoken but over time reelect new types of leaders to office (like Green/ecology leaders in many countries) or vote out clientelists, thereby indicating a clash over legitimate rules of the game. Sets of norms cluster in *roles*, which are aggregated into *institutions*, like the state or a party. Personalities of individuals, and expressions in their behavior, as in street demonstrations or voting, are in part unique; we consider only those personality and behavior elements consistent enough to express underlying cultural outlooks.

Yet unlike some anthropologists, *we by no means posit culture as deterministic or unchanging. A major focus in this chapter is to clarify the dynamics of change in political culture, in specific propositions.* Change flows from dynamic tensions among socio-economic and political conditions. Critical specific changes are often introduced by candidates for political office, who frequently articulate new conceptions more fully than average citizens. But they only succceed when citizens endorse their views. The framework outlined here can be applied to processes in several specific national contexts concerning citizens, organized groups, parties, and political leaders (e.g., Clark 1994a; Clark and Rempel 1997; and the chapters below).

The Renaissance of Political Culture

Political rules of the game have shifted. The concept of political culture fills an analytical void by identifying specific rules of the political game and conditions under which they hold. The concept of political culture is enjoying a renaissance, in work by Webber and Wildavsky (1986), Thompson, Ellis, and Wildavsky (1990), Lipset (e.g., 1996), Elazar and Zikmund (1975), Knoke (1981), Brint (1994), Putnam (1993), Ferman (1996), and earlier work by the two of us. But culture has been analyzed in many ways. Our approach differs rather substantially from simplistic formulations that contrast "structure" and "culture" or "materialist" and "idealistic." *Indeed culture for us is often a key dependent rather than an independent variable.* Most propositions in this chapter show how and why the NPC emerges and changes past rules of the game. A range of sources—economic, political, religious, and institutional—generate change. We evolved our approach not from pure deduction, but through interpreting specific critical developments that other approaches could not. How?

Postmaterialism

Inglehart (1971) introduced "Postmaterialism" to capture changes in political culture away from materialist issues. The Postmaterialism concept has been refined and tested using increasingly rich data on citizen preferences from as many as 300,000 persons in forty-two countries (Inglehart 1990, 1997). A Postmaterialism scale has repeatedly captured value shifts. Postmaterialists are younger and more common in recent age cohorts than materialists, and differ on a range of other social and political items.

New Fiscal Populism

In the mid-1970s, many American governments began cutting spending. Why? Especially visible was Proposition 13, which in 1978 cut property taxes in California. Yet Clark and Ferguson (1983) showed that cuts did not come from the traditional right, Republicans, but mainly from a new sort of political leader, the New Fiscal Populist (NFP). NFPs were often Democrats but parted from the traditional left in being fiscally conservative on at least some issues, while continuing the traditional left position on most social issues. Their (1) fiscal conservatism was combined with a (2) social liberalism by (3) breaking with traditional organized groups, like labor unions, and appealing instead to (4) individual citizens in populist style, especially via the media (5) emphasizing productivity improvement and "public goods" policies. These views, citizen surveys suggest, are broadly shared; indeed new citizen preferences explain much of the success of NFP leaders. NFPs emerged earliest in U.S. cities, since their parties were weak. Changes came later at the U.S. national level and in Europe, where parties were stronger. Clark had grown sensitized to culture as meaning more than citizen preferences in earlier work which showed cities with numerous Irish Catholics spent more, due to their support for an "Irish ethic" which legitimated patronage and clientelism. Thus "rules of the game" were critical above and beyond Downsian individual preferences, as considerable evidence made clear (Clark 1975).

Steps Toward a New Political Culture

The broad similarity, but useful complementarities, of Inglehart's Postmaterialism and Clark's New Fiscal Populism led us to extend the two approaches in this chapter. The initial Postmaterialism formulation, unlike the New Class, did not center on government growth. It thus did not suffer like the New Class formulation when fiscal conservatism surfaced in the 1970s. It focused mainly on citizens and their policy preferences, and less on leaders and political systems. Its causal dynamics were more social psychological than institutional.

By contrast, the NFP analysis was more concerned with political leaders, and how they emerge (or are discouraged) by political system characteristics. NFPs resemble the New Class on social issues, but not fiscal issues.

The New Political Culture builds directly on Postmaterialist and New Fiscal Populist analyses, adding elements in the core definition, and new structural propositions that link social and political system characteristics to specific attitudes and political processes.

Appendix 2:
The Postmaterialism Index

The Postmaterialism items have been used extensively in citizen surveys, such as the Eurobarometer Series administered approximately every six months from 1973 to the present. These same items have been used in surveys in the United States from 1972 through 1988, and in many other countries, including the 1981 and 1990 World Values Surveys, which surveyed national samples of persons in twenty-two countries, many outside Europe. More than 250,000 responses are thus available on selected items that have been repeated, plus many related items with which they can be compared, along with standard socioeconomic data.

The initial scale in Inglehart (1971: 28ff) included four items:

"If you had to choose among the following things, which are the two that seem most desirable to you?

1. Maintaining order in the nation
2. Giving people more say in important political decisions
3. Fighting rising prices
4. Protecting freedom of speech"

Postmaterialists were defined as those who answered "more say" and "freedom of speech"; materialists answered the two others; other responses were coded as "mixed."

In 1973 the original four items were supplemented with eight more:

5. Maintaining a high rate of economic growth
6. Making sure that this country has strong defense forces
7. Seeing that the people have more say in how things get decided at work and in their communities
8. Trying to make our cities and countryside more beautiful
9. Progress toward a less impersonal, more humane society
10. The fight against crime
11. Progress toward a society where ideas are more important than money
12. Maintain a stable economy

Here the Postmaterialist items are 7, 8, 9, and 11. The rest measure materialist or physiological needs. Items have been asked in different combinations, ranked and reranked, and analyzed in many ways. See Inglehart (1985, 1990).

Part 2

Where Has the New Political Culture Emerged and Why?

3

Is There Really a New Political Culture?
Evidence from Major Historical Developments of Recent Decades

Terry Nichols Clark

This chapter reviews the emergence around the world of the New Political Culture (NPC) as outlined in Chapter 2. We consider some major political transformations in recent years to see how they link with the New Political Culture.

Emergence of the NPC? Some Dramatic Cases

When key ideas about the NPC were first presented (in Clark and Inglehart 1989 and in many subsequent settings), listeners were often skeptical that fundamental change was really under way. Even close friends and colleagues would politely disagree, countering with statements like "parties and classes are still central" or "these NPC developments are only temporary or transitional." As the NPC ideas circulated at various conferences and in preliminary publications, they gave rise to numerous debates. One concerns the decline of class politics, reviewed further in Chapter 4. Others concern the interpretation of events like the collapse of communism. As example after example continued to "deviate" from the established (class politics) view, more observers have begun to accept that basic changes are in fact emerging. Nevertheless, we still find, among sophisticated political observers, that perhaps a third remain skeptical of fundamental changes like the New Political Culture. Some of this is labeling, how to "name" new developments. And as Thomas Kuhn (1996), observed, few persons working with a theory (or political ideology, we might suggest, extending his theory) ever say "I was wrong" and change. Most change comes rather when "carriers" of old theories are replaced by younger persons.

For readers skeptical or open-minded about NPC-like developments, this chapter looks at some profound political transformations over the past decade or so. To complement the views of the author in interpreting these we draw heavily on the work of others who know the events closely from personal experience and who have reflected on which aspects do and do not fit with the New Political Culture (NPC) interpretations. This adds a bit of interpersonal objectivity. Dramatic evidence from these critical and well-known historical cases helps illustrate the sea change. Other brief cases are presented in boxes through this and the next chapter that consider parallel trends.

Our concern in this chapter is not to test propositions about where and why the NPC emerges (we do in Chapter 4) but to provide evidence of emergence of some key elements of the NPC—such as the rise of populist democracy, decline of traditional parties, rise of social issues and issue politics, weakening of clientelism, and mobilization of the young and women—sometimes even in countries that one might consider unlikely locales for emergence of NPC-type politics.

The Collapse of Communism

Perhaps the most profound political transformation of the late twentieth century was the self-destruction of Communist leadership in Eastern and Central Europe and the former Soviet Union. It was a powerful reaction against Communism as a totalitarian hierarchy controlling the economy, polity, and much of social life. Just how to interpret these developments will busy many persons for decades. Here we ask if *some* processes link to *parts* of the NPC. Consider income and the economy first. As the resources of average citizens (education, income, media exposure) increased from the 1950s through the 1970s, the state-centered economies of Communist countries adapted minimally to complexities of postindustrialism. Pressures mounted for change. From factory floors in Poland to the Kremlin's elite, people searched for something different. Efforts toward incremental change in Gorbachev's *perestroika* were rapidly swamped by a rush of quasi-revolutionary events. Free democratic elections were announced and then held in 1990 across Eastern and Central Europe.

How to document and interpret these rich events? The Fiscal Austerity and Urban Innovation (FAUI) Project held a conference in Warsaw in March 1990. Eastern Europeans there expressed a strong interest in participating in an international effort to assess the emerging new democracies and to compare specific practices with the West. They created the Local Democracy and Innovation Project, coordinated by Harald Baldersheim, including some twenty participants from Hungary, Poland, and the Czech and Slovak Republics. The East European teams met every few months in 1990–1991, completing case studies of the transition to democracy by selected local governments, analyzing voting and participation patterns, and conducting national surveys of mayors, council members, and administrators. We actively discussed interpretations of these events as new evidence came in (cf. Clark 1993; Pateri 1991). Some of the most dramatic reportage came from Polish mayors who were invited to prepare biographical accounts of the transformation. Consider one microhistory. The Revolution in Lubanie, a Polish town of 5,000, is described by the new mayor:

> I will never forget this hot summer day in 1990. The town hall was filled to the brim. Windows wide open, 11:00 A.M. They (the communists) have already seized the chairmanship with 10 votes against 6. They are confident they will share all other spoils between themselves. But perhaps they hurry too much. . . . A break before the vote for a mayor. . . . Lively discussions in groups. My wife asks me to give up my candidacy; there are 10 of them against our 6. Chairman proceeds with the session. A few councilors, who encouraged me to put up my candidacy, look at me asking—what is my decision? Oh yes, I will. As the candidates are named, I feel that hardly anyone believes my chances, not even my supporters. I confirm my candidacy with a detached voice. I was cool, everything I wanted was to present my program. . . . I didn't have notes and after my presentation there were some mean comments. I addressed them extensively and received a standing ovation. My opponent's speech did not go down very well. He read mostly from his notes . . . . The commission left to count votes, then returned. I have never heard such a silence, like in a church. I won 9 to 8. The burst of joy among the public. People tossed me up igh in the air. The "old guard" were leaving the hall, their heads low.

The mayor's comments document remarkable fragility and unpredictability, the importance of small groups of individuals and organizations, personal appeals, and sometimes luck that drastically contrast with the strong, clear hierarchy that had long been common in Poland. How well does the East European transformation to democracy fit the NPC? Consider the interpretation of Polish social scientist Wisla Surazska (1995), who organized the mayors' biographies project and summarized general patterns. She asks how these developments match some available literature:

> The first years of post-communist local government have already been the subject of extensive research. Among the most comprehensive studies, two approaches can be distinguished. The first one is pragmatic and descriptive; it covers the local government structures and functions as part of a more general subject of public administration reform in the "transition" countries. The work by Hesse, Derlien and Szablowski belong to this category. The second approach is represented by authors, such as T. Clark and H. Baldersheim et al, who adopted models and methodology from their previous research on local institutions and politics in Western democracies. This second category of research illustrates certain problems arising when the models and methods developed in one socio-political reality are being transferred into another and quite different one.

Clark has developed a list of strategies with which local government may respond to a situation of fiscal stress that has typically occurred in developed countries since the early eighties. Clark found that an innovative response to fiscal stress was more likely to occur when a new mayor and council were elected with a new mandate. He assumed that the introduction of elected local government in Eastern Europe created similar circumstances of a new mandate and extended his research to this new area. Following his previous work in democratic societies, Clark (1993) assumed that behind the most fundamental change, democratization, even "more profound than a shift of parties or from communism to capitalism" was the rejection of the traditional hierarchy. According to Clark's "leveling principle," hierarchies, especially those with little in the way of legitimacy, generate powerful opposition parties and movements aiming at egalitarian reforms. This happens in particular when "legal structures, media, and other institutions permit the articulation of social conflict" as in Eastern Europe during Gorbachev's *perestroika*.

Clark's model of political leadership changes is based on the key factors of modernization, such as economic and technological growth, the spread of mass education, mass media communication, economic and social diversification, etc. An increase on these variables should result in various scenarios of political transformation, depending on the strength of socio-political hierarchies. Thus, when the existing hierarchy is strong and rigid, then a Soviet type scenario (which Clark identifies with the corporatist one) is likely to prevail. If the strength of the hierarchy is medium, at least five scenarios are possible: unionist, clientelist, ethnic-regional, church leadership, and populist leadership. If the initial hierarchy is weak, then two scenarios are likely to follow the change of political leadership: the increase of importance of voluntary associations or the so called "new political culture" based on post-materialist values and resulting in an increasing civic involvement in local affairs.

Since Communist regimes were distinct as to the rigidity of their hierarchies, Clark's model would have predicted that political leadership change should result in adopting corporatist rules, or at least those that are typical for the medium hierarchy level (see above). But, as Clark admits himself, the unionist solution was not very likely to occur in post-Communist transition since Communist regimes had not allowed for independent unions. As it happened, the only country which entered the transition process with strong unions, that is Poland with its mass Solidarity trade union, provided little confirmation for Clark' s predictions. Although Citizens' Committees, which won the first local elections in Poland with 44.3 % of the vote, did originate from Solidarity, nevertheless, they were more of a local civic associations type than of a union. In fact, Citizen's Committees were often in conflict with Solidarity trade union, and when such a confrontation occurred, the union was most often on the losing side; it received only 2.5% of votes nationwide. It was clearly not Solidarity as a union that attracted Polish voters but a local civic organization, quite similar to those described by Clark in the scenario of the New Political Culture. But such a scenario was designated in his model only as a response to a high level of economic development and "low hierarchy" circumstances, whereas in Poland these crucial dimensions did not obtain at that time.

Note that this turbulence and movement style was distinctly characteristic of Poland and several other Central and East European countries immediately after the fall of Soviet Communism in 1989. But over the 1990s, the looser groupings and parties were consolidated and many disappeared, whereas those that remained successful moved more in the direction of Western social democratic parties. They developed stronger organizations, tighter national-local linkages, and often more coherent programs. This was the tendency that Clark (1993) suggested was most likely for Eastern and Central Europe, since so much hierarchy persisted. How then explain the NPC-like character of the immediate post-Soviet years, discussed by Surazska? It was in part the product of intellectuals like Havel and Klaus in the Czech Republic and other nontraditional party leaders who won the first elections.[1] This early elite included more highly educated persons who themselves were closer to NPC tendencies than most persons in their societies; they were visibly anticommunist, which in the early years almost sufficed to win. But they were political amateurs and were supplanted in the later 1990s by more professional and more organized parties and leaders.[2] How about ethnicity/nationalism as a source of the transformation? Surely nationalist sentiments have been powerful in Central Europe for hundreds of years. But much of their force, and success, was driven by resentment against the hierarchical domination of the Soviet Union, as well as against earlier foreign rules from the Czars and Habsburgs in past centuries to the German Nazis and Soviet Russians in the twentieth. Nationally autonomous politics of any sort barely ever developed. Thus movements of personal and political liberation were often fused with anti-hierarchical, anti-foreign ideology. In this general sense, the decline of Soviet-style hierarchies with Gorbachev's *perestroika* paralleled the decline of slavery in America or of the hierarchical states of Western Europe after 1968. The consequence of such decline has often been the emergence of new socio-political moments, as the NPC propositions consider.

We do not doubt that some aspects of these momentous changes do not fit the NPC discussions, but at least parts of them do. In particular the Leveling Principle seems broadly to fit changes in the economy, the central state, and foreign domination. It also seems broadly consistent with some other major political changes. Consider Italy.

The Italian Political Revolution

Another profound transformation of a political system: Italy in the early 1990s. Almost simultaneous with the East European developments, national party leaders, cabinet members, parliamentarians, and mayors of many cities were all removed amid scandals and legal battles over *Tangentopoli*—the monstrous new word for the all-consuming system of bribery and payoffs to political leaders for government favors and services. Hundreds of leaders were brought to trial, many jailed. This was followed by elections that brought a complete

new set of parties, leaders, and, some claimed, new rules of leadership. As in
Eastern Europe, our FAUI participants were active in surveying and interpreting these events. Enrico Ercole comments on the key developments as they
relate to the NPC propositions.[3]

> The Italian case seems to be an interesting test of the New Political Culture
> model. Italy in fact starting from the Fifties went through a dramatic economic
> development (miracolo economico, the Economic Miracle, with an average growth
> rate of 5.3% from 1950 to 1958 and 6.6% from 1958 to 1963, compared to respec-
> tively 3.0% and 4.2% in the US), which eventually led to important social and
> demographic change. As a consequence of this process we would expect diffusion
> of post-materialistic values in Inglehart's (1977) terms, and change in the political
> arena in the sense described by Clark (1983, 1994) as New Political Culture. The
> dramatic economic development is well known and can be described with the
> help of a few results about occupation and quality of life. Occupation in agricul-
> ture went down from 44.0% in 1946 to 11.7% in 1986, illiterate people from 12.9%
> to 3.1%, infant mortality from 64.6 to 10.3 per thousand new born babies, while
> consumption of electricity rose from 301 to 2,867 per capita Kwh, number of
> telephones from 13 to 272 per 1000 inhabitants and people who go on vacation
> every year from 13.2% to 42.8%. The Economic Miracle was territorially differ-
> entiated, with a spread of industrialization from heavily industrialized regions of
> the Industrial Triangle of the Northwest to the regions of Terza Italia (Third
> Italy) in the Northeast and Center (Bagnasco, 1977) while the more agricultural
> and traditional South (Mezzogiorno) was only partially involved in the process.
> We find 7.6% of the occupations in agriculture in the North, and 17.8% in the
> South: similarly illiterate people are 1.4% in the North and 6.3% in the South,
> while consumption of electricity is 3.557 in the North and 2.297 in the South and
> diffusion of telephones respectively 370 and 240. We find as well territorial divi-
> sion in other issues, such as post-materialistic values, which are diffused among
> 30% of the young people in the North but only among 20% in the South (Cavalli
> and De Lillo, 1988). Patterns are similar in the level of civicness and institutional
> performance (Putnam, 1993: 96–99).
> When we turn to the political system, we find a country which has experi-
> enced more than 50 governments in the last 50 years, but with the permanence in
> power of the same party—the Christian Democrats—as major component of gov-
> ernment coalitions, which seems to reflect the cynical comment by Prince Tancredi
> in the novel *The Leopard,* that "If we want things to stay as they are, things will
> have to change." The only important change was at the end of the Sixties when
> the Socialist Party was included in the government coalition along with Christian
> Democrats and the small center parties allied with the Christian Democrats. Yet
> the modernization which came with the economic boom was not without conse-
> quences, even if the political system remained highly stable.[4]
> An outcome of the modernization of the fifties and sixties was a flourishing of
> social protest movements in the late sixties and early seventies, ranging from pro-
> tests of unions, to students, women and civil rights (Tarrow, 1989). These move-
> ments eventually gave rise during the late sixties and seventies to new parties,
> such as the extreme left parties (expressions of student and women protests more

than the working class), the Radical pro–civil rights party (Partito radicale), and the Greens (Verdi). Later appeared in the northern regions the Leagues (Lega Nord), an anti-tax and anti-party-system party, and a catholic anti-Mafia party in Sicily (Rete). But they were not important in numerical terms, and they could have representatives in Parliament only because of the almost pure proportional electoral system then working in Italy, which allowed 2 to 6 MPs to have a share of only 1.5% to 2% of the votes. Protest movements also had an indirect effect on the party system in that the issues raised by them became part of the political programs of the traditional parties. The Communist Party for instance has been transformed from inside by the presence of members coming from the experience of students, women, civil rights, and ecologist movements. Evidence on these points comes from the survey of delegates to the 1979 Congress of the Communist Party where, when asked about their attitude towards non traditional (i.e., of non-working class) forms of protest, delegates with a movement background showed a higher score than the others (Ercole, Lange and Tarrow, 1985). We can read in these terms as well Party decisions concerning the selection of several prestigious independent candidates, the quota of women among electoral candidates and internal committees, and the prohibition of smoking in assemblies by the then Communist Party. The fragmentation of the electoral base reflected disillusionment with traditional parties following the *voice* pattern (Hirschmann, 1970), while *exit* is shown by the rise of abstention from 7% in the early seventies up to 13% in early nineties. But once again these are changes in details of the general picture and not in the core of it.

In local government we find changes in both political personnel and actions implemented. Melis and Martinotti (1988) showed that city councilors changed in age, sex and occupational composition, with a larger presence of young, women, and employees in the tertiary sector. Similarly, we find a new consciousness of their role among mayors: they have called for a higher degree of autonomy, for both fiscal and political issues.

Mayors, through the National Association of Communes, were active in asking for a modification of the fiscal reform of 1972, which led in the following years to strict dependence of the Communes on central finance, in that State grants amounted to up to 70% of their resources. These eventually decreased to 43% in 1994. They were at the same time involved in actions aimed to reduce costs and supply better services, such as privatization, creation of mixed public-private companies for urban services, internal reorganization, diffusion of computers. A similar call for autonomy was directed towards the party system, which is known in Italy to have a stronger influence on the local level than in other European countries (Tarrow, 1977); for instance, frequently the type of coalition which rules the central government was "exported" to city councils, and national committees of parties frequently imposed their decisions on local committees. Evidence of the call for autonomy comes from the support of mayors for a proposed law on the direct election of mayors, which would have made them stronger vis-a-vis local and national parties.

New actions typical of the post-materialistic values and of a New Political Culture were also implemented by local governments, such as the building of cycling paths, the closing to traffic of city centers, the installation of recycling

bells (large containers placed throughout a city). These actions are no doubt related to post-materialistic values and New Political Culture but, once again, they
were marginal to the overall scenario, as well as easy to implement—in that they
were low-cost and highly-visible, but do not involve conflict with a counterpart
(Ercole, 1989: 250–255). We can then conclude that in Italy up to the early eighties we find a situation which is blocked, and we find but few and marginal innovations in a general scenario which is still quite far from the New Political Culture model. It is characterized by the persistence of "old" rather than "new" political culture, with the two main parties coming from the Cold War division (the
largest West European Communist Party on the left and the Christian Democrats
on the center-right of the political arena); a highly ideological political debate; no
alternation in power between left and right; the construction of a large Welfare
State with heavy aspects of clientelism and bribery and a low level of efficiency
and efficacy in provision of public services; a strong presence of the State in the
economy, including the credit system (a then popular joke said that the State
economy was established in Italy by Christian Democrats rather than Communists).[5] At the local government level we find as well a highly centralized situation both in terms of finance and local dependence, from laws dating back to the
fascist or pre–World War I period.

    We have to wait until the Nineties to find more radical changes. Referenda to
change the electoral law promoted outside the parties were successful in 1991 and
1993, and as a consequence there has been a change from proportional to first-
past-the-post system for three quarters of the MPs. At the same time the *Clean
Hands* (Mani Pulite) anti-corruption campaign launched in 1992 by magistrates in
Milan showed the mechanism whereby the parties in government exploited,
through bribery and kickbacks, their positions and swept away an entire generation of politicians, many of them corrupt. At the party system level we see a
dramatic increase of votes for Lega Nord, which eventually became the second
party in the populous and rich region of Lombardy; the transformation in 1991
of the Communist Party into a new Party of the Democratic Left (Partito
democratico della sinistra) and a new "traditional" Communist Party
(Rifondazione comunista); the creation of the Forza Italia (Go, Italy) party by a
media tycoon which received 20% of the votes in national elections in 1994; the
transformation in 1994 of the neofascist party Movimento Sociale Italiano into
the new rightist party Alleanza Nazionale (National Alliance), which doubled
its vote from 1987 to 1994. But the striking fact is the destruction of past governing parties: Christian Democrats went from 34.3% in 1987 to 11.1% in 1994, and
then split into three small parties, while their allies in government coalitions—
socialists, social democrats, republicans and liberals—disappeared (Waters, 1994
and Donovan, 1994). Turning to local government, the new electoral law with a
dual ballot between mayoral candidates from the first ballot going forward to the
second run allowed persons to become mayors of the largest Italian cities with
almost no previous experience in politics (and—not unsurprisingly—more true in
the modern North than in the traditional South) such as professors, professionals,
managers, magistrates, employees in the tertiary sector. They have stronger power
in that their resignation brings along the resignation of the city council, and mayors choose the aldermen (not councilors, but department heads or assessori).

Among the actions often implemented by newly elected mayors is the hiring of a city manager on a time-contract basis to supervise the local bureaucracy, as well as using the media to communicate with the population, bypassing the traditional mediation of local parties. The National Association of Communes, whose secretary has been elected the mayor of a large city in the South with a previous career in management, has been very active on issues such as local finance and urban policy. It has to be noted that the mayor is stronger vis-a-vis local parties, while the national leader is still chosen by the MPs.

We may interpret these changes with an incremental model, as the explosion of a slowly-growing unbearable situation in terms of incapability of political actors, blockage of the political system, inefficiency of the public sector, lack of autonomy at the local level. Or, as we suggest, as the consequences of the release of an external constraint, that is, the presence of the Soviet block, which encouraged alternatives to the Christian Democratic regime. There was no longer any reason to give electoral support to inefficient governments with Christian Democrat-led coalitions. Other factors have contributed to the process, such as an economic scene dominated by family capitalism, the clientelistic culture, the division between a more industrialized north and a more traditional south, though we consider these less relevant. The process is more evident at the local level, where the new electoral law, different from the national one, has given more power to mayors vis-a-vis local and national parties. If our suggestion is correct, then we could conclude that the external constraint on Italian politics did not allow for the creation of a New Political Culture. There were only marginal aspects of it until release of the external constraint allowed for a full expression of the phenomenon. Of course we still need more evidence from future studies and we also are aware that other factors play an important role along with the release of external constraint in explaining the dramatic changes in Italian politics. And again the characteristics of Italian society may certainly give a specific flavor to the New Political Culture model compared to other countries.

The Left Moves Right:
Transformation of Socialist Parties the World Over

Even if most political systems have not seen as dramatic breaks with the past as Eastern Europe or Italy, one litmus test of profound change is the transformation of party programs. It is no surprise that parties of the right or center, which traditionally favored "free enterprise" or "less government," should continue such programs. Some have added more emphasis on new social issues, thus incorporating more NPC concerns. But the more critical test of NPC ideas concerns Left parties. Following the theory, they may (1) Remain with past traditions and lose the growing NPC electorate, or (2) adapt, by embracing more NPC issues. We find both. The British Labour Party for instance did not substantially change its strong working class/union orientation through the 1980s and early 1990s, and continued to lose elections as its old electorate declined in size. But in preparation for the 1997 elections, Tony Blair and Labour abandoned their union ties, embraced NPC issues, and won a huge majority in Parliament.

How much have Left parties followed path #1 or #2 in other countries? Many moved from #1 to #2 from the late 1970s through the 1990s. Socialist parties around the world then largely abandoned their support of central state planning of the economy and embraced various market-linked ideas in their programs. Seymour Martin Lipset has charted this shift in a review of socialist policy statements from Europe, Asia, and Latin America. He summarizes:

> Beginning with the ideological changes by the German Social Democrats in their Bad Godesberg platform in 1959, but speeding up greatly in the last decade, most of the overseas parties of the Left have explicitly reversed their traditional advocacy of state ownership and domination of the economy and openly espouse the virtues of the market economy, of tax reduction, even of monetarism and deregulation (Lipset 1991: 184).

He goes on to detail specifics country by country. We present several cases in boxes in Chapter 4.

The NPC in Japan?

Wonho Jang completed a Ph.D. based on several years of work in Japan analyzing citizen surveys and Japanese FAUI data. He found many NPC elements, but not others. His causal analysis supports several propositions from chapter 2. He writes:

> The thesis examined whether the NPC is emerging in Japan, focusing on the dynamics of social structural and value changes in recent decades. Japan exhibits social and economic changes which encourage value changes. The society has become affluent, and the occupational structure has changed significantly in that the number of people employed in primary industries has decreased while those in high-tech industries has increased. The family structure has changed towards the slimmed pattern. Have values changed enough in Japan for development of the NPC? Based on several citizen surveys such as the World Value Survey and National Character Survey, significant value changes are found. Both individualism and post-materialism have increased significantly from 1950 to 1990.
>
> Based on analysis of Japanese citizen surveys, and using Franklin et al's (1992) method for international comparison of cleavage politics (a standard set of variables in a multiple regression model), the thesis shows that cleavage politics has been low and is declining. . . . Other key features of the NPC are also found. Support for conventional political organization such as the LDP and the SDP has declined significantly. Voting turnout rates have also declined significantly, exhibiting a decrease in support for conventional political participation. However, the last key feature of the NPC, an increase in new forms of political participation, has not been found in Japan.

Testing causal relations of NPC dynamics, age, income, education, professionals, and sex are included. Multiple regression analysis provides supporting results: Younger and more highly educated persons have more post-materialist values. Income has a positive effect on individualism.

Chapters 4 and 5 examine the relationship between the NPC and local politics in Japan. The hypotheses are: 1) younger and more-educated mayors demonstrate more NPC characteristics in policy preferences and 2) in cities with younger, more educated, and more affluent constituencies, mayors exhibit more NPC characteristics in their policy preferences. The first hypothesis is based on the scarcity and socialization principles and the second on the demographic principle which recognizes that demographic growth of a sector in the city increases its legitimacy and power. Variables tapping the NPC of the mayor's policy preferences are: 1) Anti-partyism, which indicates a negative relation to conventional political parties, 2) Populism which indicates how responsive mayors are to the public and how much mayors use media to appeal to the public, 3) SOCCONS, social liberalism, how much mayors support sex education and abortion, and 4) PRFSD, a selective spending index which indicates how much mayors are free from the left-right ideology in spending and individually selective in their spending preferences. Most have been used in testing the NPC in other countries (Clark et al., 1994). Results: 1) younger mayors are more populist, socially liberal, and more selective in spending; 2) more highly educated mayors are more antiparty oriented, and more selective in spending; 3) in cities with a higher proportion of youth, mayors are more antiparty oriented and socially liberal; 4) in cities with higher mean income, mayors are more selective in spending; 5) in cities with a higher proportion of professionals or tertiary workers, mayors are more antiparty oriented, populist, and selective in spending preferences.

A review of the literature on clientelism in Japanese politics suggests three characteristics of Japanese NPC mayors. First, these mayors oppose the clientelistic relationship between the LDP and the construction industry. They are less willing to have connections with the construction industry and therefore favor decreasing construction expenditures as a local fiscal policy. Second, they oppose the direction of the central bureaucracy and emphasize more opinions of citizens in local policy making. Third, the Japanese-specific NPC mayors are not entwined in the (more traditional) "Hoshu-Kakushin" ideology, which allows them to be "ainori (receiving endorsement from both the LDP and the SDP)" in local elections. Findings: Younger mayors show more support for decentralization in local policy making. In cities with higher proportions of professionals and tertiary workers, mayors support a decrease in clientelist expenditures, while in cities with a higher proportion of people employed in the construction industry, mayors do not support such cuts. In these pro-clientelist cities, mayors also do not support decentralization of local policy making. Finally, in these same cities, mayors tend to be less "ainori" in local elections (Jang 1996: chapter 7).

Case Studies: An NPC Mayor in Japan and
a Survey of Local Assemblymen

Mayor Tetsundo Iwakuni of Izumo City is an outspoken critic of traditional politics. A graduate of the elite Tokyo University law school, he pursued a first career in finance and was president of Merrill Lynch, Japan, until 1989, when he was elected mayor. He stood unsuccessfully for governor of the Tokyo Prefecture, but through his speeches and book, *Changing Our Way in Japan: The Second Message of the Mayor of Izumo*, he has been "making waves." Examples:

- he criticizes the "corruption politics" prevalent in Japan ever since the Lockheed Scandal in 1976
- his main solution to corruption: decentralization to the local level. Too many mayors are former bureaucrats of the national government, prohibiting true local autonomy
- administration should be service to citizens. He even extended city service delivery to weekends and holidays, and located some city staff inside large department stores to provide city services to citizens while shopping
- he paid for this extension of city services by cutting spending on road construction, a classic clientelist activity of many Japanese cities; it benefits organized pressure groups, particularly the construction industry, to the detriment of citizens and taxpayers
- Japan should be internationalized. He built the largest wooden dome in Japan since his Province is famous for wood products. But he imported all the wood from the U.S. since it was cheaper and symbolized his commitment to improving the trade imbalance with the US. He created joint agreements with several cities, especially in Korea and China, and sends his city manager to frequent visits
- women should be given more favorable treatment. When he took office, all 60 managers in Izumo City government were men; he hired 30 women managers.

(Wonho Jang kindly translated portions of Mayor Iwakuni's book.)

Mayor Iwakuni's effort to distance himself from the traditional parties is not unique. As early as 1980, a survey of 440 officials in 24 cities, wards, and towns found that 32 percent said they were independent of any party, which rose to more than 50 percent in small towns. Even though most are LDP party members, they do not want to publicize it. "There are ... reasons for such strange behavior. First ... candidates want unanimous recommendation from the regional associations.... Second is that an image of LDP assemblymen was damaged at the time because of the so-called Lockheed scandal. Local LDP members do not want to publicize their membership" (p. 13). Still, when he asked how often they met with party officials, the LDP members had about the same frequency of contacts as those in other parties: 49 percent said daily, about the same as for contact with residents (p. 23). (Moriwaki, 1984).

Activist Citizen-Consumers of Government in French Communist Cities

One might not look first to Communist-governed cities for NPC patterns, but if one finds traces of them *even* there, this suggests broader support for these patterns than some class-politics advocates suggest. Jacques Marsaud, city manager in the longtime Communist suburb of Paris, Saint-Denis, reports changes in his city and other left-governed cities in France that have remarkable similarities to general NPC trends:

Signs of evolution.
- An ever increasing importance accorded to the quality of services delivered to citizens, an increased attention to take into account its aspirations, notably those concerned with the daily environment.
- The development of "democratic practices" of local officials who try to multiply new sources of information, of consultation and participation of citizens (. . . neighborhood meetings, working groups with citizen representatives)
- A search for partnerships as broad and diverse as possible with other public agencies, with associations, with the private sector, with citizens to act more effectively.

Turning to causes of these changes, he lists:

- Social change and the evolution of needs, such as more participation by women and more concern for life-style issues, (citing Jean-Claude Vida, sociologist, director of local studies in the Saint-Denis City Hall)
- Decentralization
- The crisis of politics
Previously, the political allegiance of elected officials, the program of their party, the ideology to which they were attached preconditioned an important part of their local policies. The emergence of a new politics, of listening, of dialogue, of expertise, of reflection, of analysis of local situations today tends to replace the organizational referents and ideologies in crisis (Marsaud 1995: pp. 229ff.).

U.S. President Bill Clinton Advocates NPC Policies

President Clinton was first elected in November 1992, after campaigning actively against the federal government as distant, unresponsive, and hierarchical. He had been governor of Arkansas and vowed to bring lessons from other governments to Washington to make it better. Without seeking to evaluate what was implemented, one can see powerful NPC rhetoric in the policy statements. And these are what helped elect Clinton and Vice President Al Gore. Clinton's dramatic break with the New Deal Democrats of the past and illustration of many NPC issues has been commented on in detail by many. See for instance the box from his advisor/pollster Stanley Greenberg in the next chapter. Here follows a policy statement that illustrates the thinking of Clinton and Gore on these issues:

From Red Tape to Results:
Creating a Government That Works Better & Costs Less:
The Report of the National Performance Review

Vice President Al Gore
September 7, 1993

> "Our goal is to make the entire federal government both less expensive and more efficient, and to change the culture of our national bureaucracy away from complacency and entitlement toward initiative and empowerment. We intend to redesign, to reinvent, to reinvigorate the entire national government."
>
> —*President Bill Clinton Remarks Announcing the*
> *National Performance Review March 3, 1993*

Introduction

The National Performance Review is about change—historic change—in the way the government works. It's time we had a new customer service contract with the American people, a new guarantee of effective, efficient, and responsive government that puts our customers first and demonstrates to the American people that their tax dollars will be treated with respect for the hard work that earned them. The National Performance Review is about moving from red tape to results to create a government that works better and costs less.

This is a summary of the first product of our efforts. In it, we make hundreds of recommendations saving $108 billion over five years.

The Problem/The Solution

The National Performance Review looked to see how successful organizations—businesses, city and state governments, and organizations of the federal government—had made savings and efficiencies. The successful organizations had several things in common. They:

- Cut red tape—shift from a system based on accountability for following rules, to one where employees are accountable for achieving results.
- Put the customer first—listen to them, restructure basic operations to meet their needs, and use market dynamics such as competition and customer choice to create incentives for success.
- Empower employees to get results—decentralize authority and empower those who work on the front lines to make more of their own decisions and solve more of their own problems.
- Cut back to basics—abandon the obsolete, eliminate duplication, and end special interest privileges.

These characteristics constitute the four key principles around which we have based our report (National Performance Review 1993).

Many similar points were made in a U.S. national assessment of state and local government, led not by national, but by state and local officials. It concluded recommending:

- Stronger Executive Leadership
- Lean, Responsive Government
- Flatten the bureaucracy by reducing the number of management layers between the top and bottom agencies and thinning the ranks of the managers who remain.
- Deregulate government by reforming the civil service, including reduced use of veterans (1) preference and seniority; (2) streamlining the procurement process; and (3) making the budgeting process more flexible.
- A High-Performance Work Force
- Greater Citizen Involvement
- Reducing Fiscal Uncertainty
  (National Commission on the State and Local Public Service: 1993: 9–13).

Who is Left?

An important component of left party transformation to new issues is that old issues, and constituents, are left behind. One of the sharpest transformations was of British Labour to the New Labour Party. It won dramatically in 1997. At what cost? The negatives are clear, but their documentation and critique, if nothing more, provide clear testimony of the New Labour Party's incorporation of many NPC themes and abandonment of the old.

The anger of working class persons in Britain and the United States is not expressed in votes for New Right parties, in contrast to the Continent (for reasons outlined in Chapter 2 after Proposition #7). But individual citizen anger summarized below is similar to that articulated by New Right leaders on the Continent, examples of which appear in boxes in the next chapter.

The Hard Times of a Coal Town, Ignored in Booming Britain's Vote

GRIMETHORPE, England, April 16—The turnoff for this South Yorkshire mining town with the Dickensian name comes up shortly after an election billboard on the main road saying, "Britain is booming."

The ruling Conservatives put the sign up and it was about as far as they felt comfortable venturing toward this forlorn place. The residents of Grimethorpe are solid working class, resentful of the Tories for having shut down their coal pits and long loyal to the party with the name that sounded familiar to them, Labor.

Now, though, Labor has refashioned itself as "New Labor" and it is conducting a campaign for the May 1 national election aimed at wooing the beneficiaries of the boom with promises of low taxes and limited government spending. The targets are the voters of prospering Middle England. None of them live here.

This is the Britain that got left behind by the boom and is now being left out of the campaign. The new Laborites are just as scarce in places like Grimethorpe these days as the old Conservatives.

"The Labor Party isn't on the side of the working people anymore," said Ken Capstick, 55, a former miner and union official. He recalled that Tony Blair, the reformist leader of New Labor, paid a visit in December to celebrate the victory of the local member of Parliament in a by election and was gone in 15 minutes. "His footwork was so fast I thought he was Lionel Blair," Mr. Capstick said, referring to a popular British music hall dancer.

The boom has come at the cost of aggravating two divisions in British society, one between the rich and the poor, the other between the south and the north. And Grimethorpe, northern and poor, is at the bottom end of both equations, neglected and invisible in the current national debate.

People here will most likely vote Labor, if they bother to vote at all. Found in the ghettos of reinvigorated urban centers or in downtrodden rural villages close by affluent towns all over Britain, these are places that suffer from a shortage of jobs and an abundance of drugs and crime.

As you head toward Grimethorpe, you leave behind the Britain accurately portrayed by the boastful placard, a country whose restored civic centers, suburban shopping malls and leafy bedroom communities attest to the robustness of its recovering economy under the Tories.

Success is even in the air. Sheffield, the regional capital that was long a soot-blackened steel town, now claims the cleanest atmosphere of any industrial city in Europe.

Enter Grimethhorpe, however, and the roadside offers a different set of signals. There are red-brick row houses with their windows and doors boarded up and clutches of middle-aged men idling on the main street and in the parking lot of the Red Rum pub. The vast hillside sloping off to one side is covered with weeded-over crushed concrete and rusted cables.

An outspoken report from the Council of Churches for Britain and Ireland called "Unemployment and the Future of Work" chastised the political parties last week for ignoring what it called the growing problems of poverty, unemployment and social exclusion.

"When so many are living in poverty and unemployment, it is wrong to give priority to the claims of those who are already well off," the document said. "None of the political parties has put forward a program which offers much real hope of improvement to those in greatest need."

Though the report was supported by all church denominations and compiled by high-profile clerics and well-known economists, it did not attract lasting attention after its publication on April 8 because it prescribed a remedy of increased taxes, worker organization and government spending that no political party in post–Margaret Thatcher Britain will go near.

Prime Minister John Major and his Conservatives are campaigning on their success in reviving the country's economy, and Mr. Blair's Labor Party is saying it will preserve the gains and continue the progress by not raising personal income taxes for five years and not exceeding current Tory spending limits for two years.

"I keep hoping that the Labor Party is trying to grab the votes of the two-thirds and get them to pay attention to the other third," said Mike West, head of the church Industrial Mission office in Sheffield. "It's my only cause for optimism."

The Grimethorpe Colliery was shut down in 1993, one of the last networks of underground tunneling to be capped with concrete in a government pit-closing program.... The workers were the hard men of British industry, reviled by many for their union militancy and romanticized by others for their endurance in the face of the danger their hellish working conditions posed to their health and their lives and for the fervid family spirit of the embattled pit communities like this one. (Hoge 1997: 1, A6.)

Conclusion

The major transformations covered in this chapter, as characterized by their close interpreters, are consistent with core elements of the New Political Culture. They are not presented to test specific propositions but to indicate that major changes in political systems across the world include important elements of the NPC—reactions against hierarchy, rise of new parties and issues, weakening of clientelism, emergence of fragile new leaders. Cases below provide further evidence of transformations in recent years; those in boxes in the next chapter provide further illuminating cases that complement, illustrate, and enrich the analytical argument and FAUI results.

The next chapter turns to specific sources of these transformations toward the New Political Culture.

Notes

1. Here is a forceful 1992 statement by Vaclav Klaus, then Prime Minister of the Czech Republic, albeit to a foreign audience: *I am convinced that Adam Smith supplies us with a vision of where to go that needs no correction... All of that is of utmost importance in our part of the world just now because you will still be able to find that there are dreams of a paternalistic state .... Adam Smith knew that the market and its evolution is a spontaneous process that can't be planned, organized, or constructed. We are in our part of the world, under permanent pressure to create markets first and to "use" them after that. Everybody (especially our opponents) wants to see perfect reform blueprints based on a detailed sequencing of individual reform measures first. They do not want to participate actively in the often difficult and traumatic transformation process. They used to think in terms of "building socialism" and now they want to "build" markets. They want, therefore, to introduce the invisible hand of the market by means of a visible and omnipotent hand of a government bureaucrat. The Adam Smith message is, however, clear: "We have to liberalize deregulate, privatize at the very early stage of the reform process, even if we are confronted now and will be confronted with rather weak and, therefore, not fully efficient markets."* Klaus (1996).

2. Jerzy Bartkowski adds a caveat concerning Civic Committees. Just how autonomous they were from Solidarity is unclear, since in the first democratic election there was great pressure from the Solidarity leaders and public opinion to preserve a single list of candidates against the Communists.

3. During the spring of 1997, while I (TNC) was at the Department of Political Science and Sociology, University of Florence, I discussed these same issues with several experts there, asking for their interpretations. Most reported the same key points as Enrico Ercole, including his emphasis on the end of the Cold War, which many non-Italians do not appreciate. Italy borders on Yugoslavia, and the Italian Communists were a major domestic political force for nearly half a century. Many Italians voted Christian Democratic largely to oppose the Communists from 1945 until the Cold War ended. Only then could domestic pressures for change express themselves actively, and they burst forth with decades of bottled-up energy and resentment toward the traditional parties and leaders, which practically disappeared. Enrico Ercole prepared his comments for this volume.

4. For a general description of economic, social and political characteristics of Italy since 1945 see Ginsborg (1990) and Sassoon (1986). A thorough description of the Italian institutional system is in Hine (1993).

5. 2) Because of political instability and incapacity of government, which makes it a republic without a government (Allum, 1973), an imperfect two-party system *(Galli and Prandi, 1970)*.

4

Assessing the New Political Culture by Comparing Cities Around the World

Terry Nichols Clark

with considerable assistance for more than a decade from
Jerzy Bartkowski, Zhiyue Bo, Lincoln Quillian, Doug Huffer,
Ziad Munson, Eric Fong, Yun-Ji Qian, Mark Gromala,
Michael Rempel, and Dennis Merritt *

This chapter examines evidence for the New Political Culture (NPC) ideas in Chapter 2, primarily with urban data for countries participating in the Fiscal Austerity and Urban Innovation (FAUI) Project.[1] Our Chapter 2 propositions, combined with data for more than 7,000 cities, help us locate social and political differences with a theoretical framework that captures and explains many of them. For instance, why do welfare states grow or decline, who votes for left parties, where is environmentalism successful, why are women included or excluded from politics? Many narrow theories, considering

* The FAUI teams supplying wave after wave of data from around the world deserve first thanks for making this chapter possible. In Chicago we pooled national data by checking comparability and converting items to standardized international variables. My wonderfully diligent and creative coauthors worked more than a decade on these and all manner of related tasks which often seemed to have no meaning or no end, as new data sometimes arrived weekly. They helped with hundreds of memos and preliminary analyses. Many draft papers summarized earlier work (e.g., Quillian, 1990; Clark and Quillian, 1992; Clark, Bartkowski, Quillian, and Huffer, 1994; Miranda, Boyne, and Clark, 1994), but the current chapter took shape only in the last year as final data and analyses came together My coauthors deserve much of the credit and did much of the hard background work. I deserve the blame, as I had much of the fun, especially near the very end, conducting final statistical analyses and writing.

a single topic or country, propose answers to such questions that fail when considered elsewhere. What conditions or assumptions are critical to make underlying processes operate? Many theories implicitly assume a context of class politics. This chapter thus contributes to the sociology of knowledge as well as to political analysis by showing how different cultures redefine legitimate rules of the game—for several social science theories as well as political leaders and citizens. Some critical and illuminating cases are presented in boxes throughout the chapter. Note that while the NPC propositions taken together provide a theory of major change, each proposition can be tested separately; we do this below, and find that some hold powerfully, while others do not. Results by individual proposition are summarized in the Conclusion.

The propositions consider three patterns of politics: the NPC, class politics, and clientelism. For centuries, clientelism was the form of governance of traditional elites, often in agriculture-based societies; it continues in much of the world. Class politics arose with industry in the nineteenth century, and mobilized strong parties that persist in the late twentieth century. Advocates of clientelism and class politics fight to survive. But in many cities and countries, a new set of rules is growing. Yet the new rules often remain blurred due to interpenetration by clientelism and class politics. In most of the world, citizens have changed their preferences about life and politics faster than party leaders or most political analysts. The NPC issues include more direct and active citizen democracy, environmentalism, abortion, and similar lifestyle concerns. By contrast, material issues like pay, workplace conditions, and housing for the disadvantaged are more central to class politics. Strong parties often continue some allegiance to class politics, and in most countries party leaders choose candidates for elections. The U.S. pattern of holding primary elections, where citizens vote on candidates for the party, is but one sharp illustration of the generally weak U.S. party system. Thus, where and how NPC patterns may triumph politically depends in a key way on parties, as we find in striking detail in the rest of this chapter.

One set of propositions suggests that the NPC emerges more fully and forcefully in cities with less hierarchy (Proposition #4) and where citizens have more resources, such as more education (#16), higher income (#12), and more professional and high-technology service occupations (#10).

A second process persists in other cities and neighborhoods: class politics, built especially on working class unions and socialist parties. It remains most powerful in cities and societies with hierarchical cleavages and socioeconomic differences (Proposition #4) and where citizens have fewer resources, as measured by more blue-collar workers (Proposition #5) who encourage organized groups, mayors, and council members to articulate more redistributive policies (#4). Even if socio-economic changes in cities erode this older working-class base, strong parties may continue these programs and politics after citizens have changed their preferences. How much parties buffer political leaders is thus a critical intervening variable.

The NPC and class politics are often political antagonists. What encourages one discourages the other. They are confused and intermingled in national politics, most regions, and larger cities, since the larger electorates are more heterogeneous in their preferences and support larger and more powerful political parties. But new patterns emerge more distinctly by comparing localities, which differ more; this illustrates how urban research can clarify major national and international changes as well as central debates in social science.

Technical details are in the appendix; results in the text are presented simply, often with just plus and minus signs to make them clear for non-statistical readers.

Measuring the New Political Culture

Like much of social and political life, the NPC is complex. We thus use not a single, simple definition, but seven key points. Although this captures the phenomenon more adequately, the multidimensional definition makes testing it complex. We examine several key elements below, stressing those measured best with the data available. Recall the key elements defining the NPC:

1. *The classic left-right dimension has been transformed.* People still speak of left and right, but definitions are changing. Left increasingly means social issues, less often traditional class politics issues.

2. *Social and fiscal/economic issues are explicitly distinguished.* Positions on social issues—of citizens, leaders, and parties—cannot be derived from their positions on fiscal issues. One can identify the distinctiveness of these two types of issues via correlations between them. As class politics is replaced by the NPC, correlations between fiscal and social liberalism decline. *Social* and *fiscal* or *economic* issues are core political concerns of contemporary societies. *Fiscal liberalism* is support for increasing governmental spending; *social liberalism* or *progressiveness* implies social tolerance—for example, of homosexuals and others who deviate. Citizens' support for these concerns is measured by leading surveys such as the General Social Survey of the National Opinion Research Center and World Values Surveys. On such issues as gender roles, tolerance of communists and homosexuals, and racial discrimination, most respondents and researchers consistently classify questions in *liberal* versus *conservative* directions. Items used below were adapted from these citizen surveys.

3. *Social issues have risen in salience relative to fiscal/economic issues,* and

4. *Market individualism and social individualism grow.* The NPC joins "market liberalism" (in the past narrowly identified with parties of the right), with "social progressiveness" (often identified with parties of the left). This new *combination of policy preferences* leads NPCs to support new programs and follow new rules of the game.

5. *Questioning the welfare state.* Some NPC citizens and leaders conclude that "governing" in the sense of state-central planning is unrealistic for many services. Although not seeking to reduce most services, NPCs question specifics of service delivery and seek to improve efficiency

6. *The rise of issue politics and broader citizen participation; the decline of hierarchical political organizations.* The NPC counters traditional bureaucracies, parties, and their leaders. "New Social Movements" and "issue-politics" are essential

additions to the political process. By contrast, traditional hierarchical parties, government agencies, and unions are seen as antiquated.

7. These NPC views are more pervasive among younger, more educated, and affluent individuals and societies. This last point identifies causes of the NPC, as do the Chapter 2 propositions.

To assess defining elements and their causal associations, this chapter draws largely on the FAUI Project. Key variables and relations hypothesized in the NPC theory are in Figure 4.1. This is our "operational model" of variables used to test the theory with the FAUI data. Most tests were completed with multiple regression analysis to assess the impact of each individual variable in the model.

We begin by introducing some key items that measure the NPC and then shift to factors associated with or driving the NPC. National averages varied moderately on social and fiscal preferences, but, on many items, variations were substantial within each country, as registered in the standard deviations. The Appendix reports national means, standard deviations, and full text of questionnaire items.

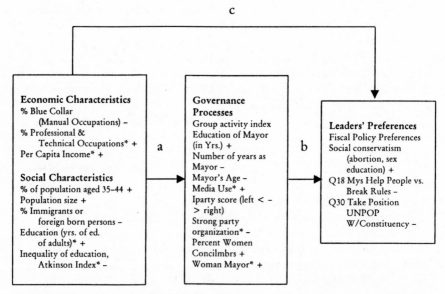

FIGURE 4.1   Global Model with Hypotheses Concerning Emergence of the New Political Culture

Note: A plus sign after a variable indicates that a higher value measures or should encourage the NPC. Three variables have no signs as their effects are more complex, as discussed. Asterisk indicates that it is included in alternative models due to intercorrelations among variables.

Source: Variables from the Fiscal Austerity and Urban Innovation (FAUI) Project. Data are incomplete for some countries. The FAUI study is discussed further in the Appendix.

Measuring NPC Tendencies

Social Liberalism: Abortion and Sex Education

The salience of social issues is central to the NPC. Social issues were measured by two items posed to the mayor and council in many countries: abortion and sex education. Both were summed in an index of social conservatism (SOCCONS). Other items were asked in individual countries but not consistently across countries. Abortion is a live social issue in many societies, even though it, like many political issues, is defined quite differently by different political subcultures. Mayors and council members are lower on the NPC if they give more socially conservative responses (high on SOCCONS). The full items and index formulas are in the Appendix. Acronyms like SOCCONS are reported in the text and tables to help the reader find explanations in the Appendix.

Fiscal Policy Preferences of Mayor and Council

The classic left-right continuum, from the nineteenth century to Anthony Downs (1957), is big versus small government. To tap this continuum, the FAUI survey asked the mayor and council members if they wanted to spend more, the same, or less in up to thirteen policy areas (PRFAVG). We completed some analyses using just preferences for redistributive spending, targeted primarily to the disadvantaged (including social welfare, public health and hospitals, and low-income housing [REDISTX]). Redistribution is a concern of the classic left.

How use spending items to test for the NPC? One way is via correlations with SOCCONS. In standard class politics, the r should be high; as one moves toward the NPC, it should decline. The problem in testing this operationally is that a correlation cannot be computed for an individual mayor but must be computed across subsets of mayors—which limits its use in more complex models. We explore alternatives to correlations below.

NPC Governance Processes

Several governance process changes are associated with the NPC, including the decline of hierarchical parties, the rise of single-issues, increased salience of the media, and direct appeals to citizens. Governance measures thus come mainly from these survey items:

- How important political parties are in slating candidates, election campaigns, and policymaking are combined in a Strong Party Organization Index, SPOIX. Unlike most variables, parties show strong and consistent national differences; we thus analyze parties by separate countries.
- How active are several local organized groups, GRPACT. But note that this includes all kinds of organized groups like businesses and unions, so it is not a clear measure of NPC.

- How important the media are in elections and general news coverage, MEDIA.
Social characteristics of the mayor and council convey at least a symbolic statement that many persons assume related to more concrete governance processes. Like the woman in Brooklyn who, when asked by a pollster if she took ethnic background into consideration in her voting decision replied: "ethnic, smethnik; I only care if he is Jewish!" The implicit assumption is that politicians like me understand my preferences, even if I don't know details of their program. We thus include:

- Education of mayor, in years of formal education, MAYED.
- Mayor's age, IV144.
- Mayor's religion (Catholic or not, CATHMY, or in Catholic countries, how often the mayor participated in religious ceremonies).
- Mayor's gender, FEMMAY.
- Percent women council members, PCTWOMC2 and FEMCOU2.

Two attitudinal items tap governance processes:

- Populism: "About how often would you estimate that you took a position *against* the dominant opinion of your constituents," IV142.
- "Break rules" an item that taps the salience of respecting rules: "If a leader helps people, it doesn't matter that some of the rules are broken"—agree or disagree, IV130.

Socioeconomic characteristics of localities:

- Percent blue collar is a classic measure of social class and political cleavage, IPCTBLUE.
- Professional and technical workers as percent of the labor force taps a postindustrial economic dimension, IOCPROF.
- Income per capita, measured at the city and national level, INCOME1, INCOME2.
- Percent population age 35–44 representing persons reasonably young but politically more active than persons in their twenties; persons 35–44 in the 1980s and

---

Background: Montreal politics was traditionally clientelistic and dominated by strong political parties. It was a major upset when a new mayor took office in 1994:

Le Monde Headline: An Ecologist Mayor Elected in Montreal

In an election that undid all predictions, Montreal citizens elected Sunday December 6 a new mayor, neophyte in politics and horticulturist by profession.

The victory—surprising Pierre Bourque and his new party Vision Montreal (center right) with about 47% of the votes, testifies to the depth of discontent of the inhabitants of the second largest city in Canada (after Toronto).

M. Bourque promised to rebuild the beauty of Montreal, which he judged "dirty", to freeze property taxes, and reduce the size of the city administration. He is also committed to attacking the poverty which troubles 30 percent of the population. This "green" candidate, unknown a few months ago, took the media up short: none supported his candidacy or predicted his victory. Tramier (1994).

BOX 4.1 New Mayors, the World Over

Note: Quotations in Boxes are set in italics; non-italicized text is by Terry Clark.

1990s were also growing up in the activist 1970s, which should increase their NPC tendencies, IPOP3544.

- Percent immigrants or foreign-born persons, FORNSTK.
- Mean number of years of education completed by city residents, IMEANEDU.
- Inequality of education among city residents, Atkinson Index, a simple hierarchy measure, IATKEDU5.

More information on the variables is in the Appendix.

Testing NPC Hypotheses

The hypotheses flow directly from the propositions in Chapter 2. Key hypotheses that we can test with these FAUI data are summarized in Figure 4.1, where a + or – sign after each variable indicates its hypothesized relationship to NPC processes. For example, percent Blue Collar (manual occupation) has a – indicating the hypothesis that blue collar residents decrease NPC processes.

Explaining NPC Governance Processes

Table 4.1 reports a first test of the NPC propositions that shows the impact of economic and social characteristics on governance processes. These match path a in Figure 4.1. Our economic propositions (#9–#13 in chapter 2) identify markets (versus nonmarkets), high-tech occupations, small firms, and higher income as factors encouraging less hierarchy in the workplace, more choice for individuals, and more related NPC characteristics. The hierarchy and politics propositions suggest that hierarchy encourages strong and militant political parties and protest groups, which discourage the NPC (propositions #4-7, 16, 17). To test these ideas, we computed multiple regressions to explain each variable listed across the top of Table 4.1 and used those down the left side as independent (explanatory) variables. The first row thus shows that localities with higher percentages of blue-collar residents had more group activities, more elected officials from left parties, and stronger party organizations. Similarly, they had fewer women council members and mayors, more older mayors, less educated

---

Voters jolted the Japanese political establishment today by choosing television personalities not affiliated with any party to lead the nation's two most important cities.

The outcome of the local elections was a stunning rejection of traditional politics and traditional politicians.

The most closely watched race, for Governor of Tokyo, was won by a former songwriter and author, Yukio Aoshima, 62, who spent only about $800 as a candidate and did not bother to campaign....

In Osaka, ... the governorship went to Knock Yokoyama, a onetime comedian who campaigned on a bicycle. The name that Mr. Yokoyama uses comes from his days with a comedy group whose members portrayed themselves as boxers.... Mr. Yokoyama, 63, easily defeated the expected winner, a former national Vice Minister who was backed by all of the major political parties. "Osaka voters were saying no to the existing political parties," Mr. Yokoyama declared tonight after his victory (Kristof. 1995).

BOX 4.2   TV Stars Defeat Politicians in Tokyo and Osaka Governor Races

TABLE 4.1   Impacts of Economic and Social Characteristics on Governance—Results

Independent Variables	Percent of Relations That Supports NPC Propositions	Group Activity Index	Iparty Score (left to right) where + = right	Strong Party Organization	Percent Women Council-members	Woman Mayor	Mayor's Age	Mayor's Years of Education	Media Importance
Economic Characteristics									
% Blue collar (manual occupations) –	100%	+	–	+	–	–	+	–	–
% Professional & technical occupations* +	100%	0	+	–	+	+	0	+	0
Local income + National	50%	–	0	+	+	0	0	0	+
income +	60%	0	0	–	–	+	–	–	0
Social Characteristics									
% of population aged 35–44 +	33%	+	0	+	0	0	+	0	0
Education (yrs. of ed. of adults)* +	71%	–	+	–	–	–	0	+	+
Population size +	100%	+	0	+	0	0	0	+	0
% Immigrants or foreign-born persons –	75%	+	0	+	0	0	0	+	–
Inequality of education, Atkinson Index* –	75%	+	+	–	–	–	+	–	+
Average for all variables	74%								

Note: The table shows the impacts of economic and social characteristics (down the side) on the governance process (across the top). Results are for FAUI cities pooled for all countries with data available. Estimates from eight OLS multiple regressions, one for each governance characteristic. Dummy variables were included to test for individual country effects, with weak results. The first column summaries are based on whether results match the chapter 2 propositions as summarized in Figure 4.1. The hypothesized + or – signs are repeated here for each independent variable, where + means the impact of the variable should be positive on NPC characteristics. To compute the first column percentages, positive or negative findings are used, zeros are omitted.

  * = included in alternative models due to intercorrelations among variables.

Source: FAUI cities pooled for all countries with data available; wball4, wbdum2, sball6t.

The average company will become smaller, employing fewer people

The traditional hierarchical organization will give way to a variety of organizational forms, the network of specialists foremost among these.

Technicians, ranging from computer repairmen to radiation therapists, will replace manufacturing operatives as the worker elite

The vertical division of labor will be replaced by a horizontal division

The paradigm of doing business will shift from making a product to providing a service

Work itself will be redefined: constant learning, more high-order thinking, less nine-to-five

Look at the numbers: IBM now (in 1993) employs 302,000 people, down from 406,000 in 1985; Digital Equipment, 98,000, down from 126,000 in 1989. But then these old-line computer companies compete against the likes of Apple, with 15,100 employees, Microsoft, with 13,800, and Novell, with 3,500, each of whose market capitalization—the total value of its outstanding stock—exceeds Digital's. . . . Research by professors Erik Brynjolfsson and Thomas W. Malone of MIT's Sloan School of Business indicates that while the number of employees per company increased until the 1970s, it has been decreasing since then, particularly in manufacturing.

Why should more economic activity be devolving upon smaller companies? . . . Brynjolfsson found that even as the typical company in his study eliminated 20% of its employees over ten years, it tripled its investment in information technology. . . . "Routine work is organized well in large hierarchical companies. Innovation and knowledge-work type activities . . . thrive best under the incentives of small firms." Just ask any of the legion of millionaires at Microsoft. (Kiechel: 1993, pp. 39-40.)

BOX 4.3 How We Will Work in the Year 2000: Six Trends That Will Reshape the Workplace

mayors, and weaker media. All eight of these results are suggested by the propositions. The first column ("Percent of Relations that Support NPC Propositions") shows the percent of results supporting the NPC propositions. The first row shows 100 percent, since eight of the eight results support the propositions. Subsequent results are less neat.

Cities with high proportions of professional and technical occupations show the expected results: Such cities have fewer left parties, weaker parties, more women mayors and council members, and more highly educated mayors.

We measured income at the city level and nationally (detailed in the Appendix), but results supported the propositions less well: Higher local income was associated with more women council members and media, as expected, but also with fewer group activities, and stronger parties, which were not expected. The group activity measure is conceptually ambivalent since it includes all kinds of organized groups. Too few countries asked about "new social movements" to analyze separately (they were added in more recent surveys). Thus the finding that there are fewer groups in richer cities reflects in part simply less active unions, business groups, and other traditional group activities, that is, less class politics–type mobilization. Similarly, higher-income localities in some countries like the U.S. often are affluent suburbs with fewer poor persons and thus less *local* class politics—again, what we would expect.[2] This point is explored in Boxes 4.20-4.23 on Inequality. The strong party organization result is bound up with country-specific party differences, elaborated below.

National income is associated with weaker parties, as expected, and more women mayors and younger mayors. But, contrary to our hypotheses, the more affluent countries have *fewer* women council members and *less* educated mayors. These two unexpected results seem due to intervention by political party leaders in several countries. That is, in the poorer East European countries, the Communist Party actively recruited women as council members (but not less educated persons); conversely, in the high-income Scandinavian countries, socialist parties often put forth relatively less educated council members and mayors.[3]

Considering the other causal variables, we see that localities with more persons aged 35–44 have more group activities and stronger parties, but this age cohort has no impact on the left-right party index, women elected officials, and media importance. We sought to measure not youth (e.g, persons under 25) so much as younger adults, more politically active than those younger. We experimented with other age cohorts but chose this one also to match the survey work by Inglehart and others (Clark and Rempel 1997). This age cohort also includes persons who were young in the activist 1970s to permit testing our Propositions #1 and #2 about youth socialization in Chapter 2. This cohort should thus reflect the 1960s and 1970s social movements and political activism. We do find these patterns for group activity and strong parties. But there is no consistent impact across other NPC governance measures, especially for women leaders. We experimented with several measures of age composition of local residents, but the main problem that emerged is that age is seldom distinct: It is often associated with a variety of other important socioeconomic characteristics, not all of which are fully incorporated in these models, in part since the residential location patterns differ across countries. For instance, in many countries, persons in this age group live disproportionally in suburbs, which are in turn associated with several other characteristics. But this is a general problem affecting all ecological measures. In testing general propositions, one should expect "probabilistic" patterns, which often but not always fit the propositions; clearly the propositions are not "deterministic."

Education is a central variable in our theory and indeed has relatively strong and consistent impacts on all the NPC governance measures. Localities with more highly educated residents have fewer organized group activities. Note that this city-level pattern is the *opposite* from that commonly reported for *individuals* (e.g., by Verba and Nie 1972, whose "standard model" is that the affluent and more educated participate more in politics). Our results differ since we consider cities rather than individuals, that is, locations with higher proportions of more educated persons, the extreme versions of which are college towns like Boulder, Colorado, or Cambridge, England. These locations usually have less poverty, fewer blue-collar workers, and less of the classic leftist base for political organization. The organized groups tend to be "new social movements" that are poorly represented in our "group activity index," which includes more of the traditional groups: business, labor, and the like. (See Appendix.) The activism of the highly educated, we hypothesized, undermines the traditional groups, just as it undermines strong hierarchical parties; these results appear in Table 4.1. However, we do not find the hypothesized higher proportions of women council members and mayors in these locations, although we do find the expected positive result for the media.

We theorized that younger and more highly educated citizens support NPC patterns. We did not offer hypotheses about the age or education specifically for elected officials in Chapter 2, but it is reasonable to expect that they are like citizens, in that younger and more highly educated leaders should broadly represent NPC patterns. We find younger mayors more common in cities with more blue-collar workers (not expected), with numerous citizens age 35–44 (as expected), and where there is more inequality (not expected). These weak relations might be seen as consistent with a Downsean hypothesis (Downs 1957) that mayors seek first of all to represent citizen preferences, such that the mayor's own characteristics (like age) should not matter; indeed we find no relations (zeros in Table 4.1) for five of the nine independent variables considered for mayors' age.

More highly educated mayors are more common in cities with fewer blue-collar workers, more professionals, more citizens age 35–44, in larger cities, with more immigrants, and less inequality. All relations fit the NPC theory except for immigrants.

Structural characteristics include population size: Larger cities have more active organized groups and stronger parties, as we would expect given tendencies of organizers to work in larger locations, since they can generate more votes in national elections. Similarly, traditional face-to-face relations are weaker and citizen value consensus is lower than in smaller towns. The theories of Toennies, Durkheim, and others about ecological concentration suggest that larger cities should have more diverse populations, denser and variegated social interaction, and more cosmopolitan, socially tolerant citizens—that is, more NPC. We did not formulate propositions about city size per se but did about "value consensus" (Proposition #6), which is moderately related with city size, so it suggests the hypothesized relations for groups and party strength; we had no hypotheses about the other dependent variables.[4]

Similarly, locations with more immigrants have more active groups and stronger parties, reflecting past political traditions of these locations, including strong worker-

---

A major international study of voting (of national samples of citizens in sixteen countries) by Franklin et al. (1992) reports conclusions that link to our findings about the decline of class varying by country (and party programs and leadership):

A development process that links changes in social structure to the evolution of party systems clarifies much of what has happened in recent elections around the world. In those countries where cleavage politics [like blue-collar versus white-collar voting] *continues to dominate, changes in the electoral fortunes of left parties are modest and linked to changes in social structure. In those countries where cleavage politics no longer dominate, party choice depends on other factors. In some countries (Australia, New Zealand, and France) left parties have benefited from their new freedom to appeal to voters beyond their traditional client groups; in other countries (Britain and Canada) they have suffered from a hemorrhage of votes, as right-wing parties have succeeded in appealing beyond the bounds of their traditional electorates.* (Franklin 1992: 403). This dramatically ended in Britain, of course, with Tony Blair and New Labour in 1997.

BOX 4.4   Class Voting Has Declined Where Parties Have Changed Their Programs

Robert Putnam's (1993) striking work on Italy supports many NPC propositions. Southern Italy, with more hierarchy and political clientelism, contrasts with the northern region. The book documents these differences in the stark and precise details of alienated voters and desultory civic participation. Local officials quickly reply to mail requests in some northern towns, whereas in southern towns some never replied to repeated requests in phone and in person. The intriguing twist is Putnam's interpretation locating these geographic differences in a historical and cultural context that dovetails with our propositions. He identifies the sources of these differences in centuries past. Some city states in the Renaissance developed considerable local democracy and participation (albeit with an elitist flavor), like Florence and Venice, which sparked local voluntary associations that in turn generated a "social capital" among residents in the form of trust and cooperative activities. These continue to present. But in the south, by contrast, foreign powers were heavy-handed administrators of local residents, leaving no space for legitimate democratic processes. Hence, the Mafia and personal contacts instead helped individuals navigate around the bureaucratic blockades. The culture of the north includes more market and social individualism, more entrepreneurship, issue politics, and group activities. People in the south lack the trust to work together as individuals, so problems fall back on government and bureaucrats, who administer passive citizens. The national government and clientelistic party system, which leaned toward and was staffed heavily by persons from the south, was brought down by newly formed organized groups, the Leagues in the north, as discussed in the last chapter. These regional contrasts support our Chapter 2 propositions about the Consensus-Market Principle, Hierarchy, issues, and clientelism. They document how rules of the game interpenetrate specific institutional performance patterns in ways that directly parallel our analyses in this volume, as Putnam acknowledges (1993: xv, 83ff.).

BOX 4.5   The New Political Culture in Renaissance Italy?

based parties (like New York City and larger European cities). Countries vary in urban concentration of immigrants. Norway is the extreme case, with Oslo having the great majority of immigrants in the country; immigrants are more dispersed in Britain and many other countries. Further, locations with more inequality in their residents' educational attainment (i.e., more hierarchy), have as hypothesized stronger groups and fewer women elected officials, but inequality does not show the hypothesized patterns for parties and media: Parties are weaker and more often on the right and media are stronger. We explored four such measures of inequality (for income, education, occupation, and national origin) for U.S. cities in more detail (Clark 1994a), as more complete data were available for U.S. cities. Results indicate more urban autonomy in the United States in that local leaders respond more to local inequalities via the local political system, detailed below.[5]

Explaining Leader's Preferences

We next consider four leaders' preference measures: two fiscal items, citizen responsiveness, and social conservatism. We analyze how well these are explained by the economic, social, and governance characteristics from the last section. The analysis tests the Figure 4.1 hypotheses shown in paths b and c. Results are in Table 4.2.

TABLE 4.2 Impacts of All Variables on Leaders' Preferences—Results

Independent Variables	Fiscal: All Areas	Fiscal: Redistributive Items	Nonresponsiveness to Citizens	Social Conservatism
	Policy Preferences: Dependent Variables			
Economic Characteristics				
% Blue collar (manual occupations)	+	0	–	+
% Professional & technical occupations	–	–	+	0
Local income	0	+	0	0
National income	+	+	–	+
Social Characteristics				
% of population aged 35–44	0	+	0	–
Population size	0	0	0	–
% Immigrants or foreign born persons	0	0	0	0
Education (yrs. of ed. of adults)	–	–	–	0
Inequality of education, Atkinson Index	–	–	0	+
Governance Characteristics				
Group activity index	0	–	+	0
Education of mayor (in years)	0	0	+	–
Number of years as mayor	0	0	0	–
Mayor's age	0	0	p	+
Media use	–	–	–	–
Iparty score (left < – > right)	–	–	0	+
Strong party organization	0	+	0	+and–
% women councilmembers	0	0	0	+
Woman mayor	0	0	0	+
Catholic mayor = 1; non-Catholic mayor=0	+	–	+	+
Percent of relations that support the NPC propositions	n.a.	n.a.	67%	77%

Note: This table shows the impact of all (independent) variables down the side on the four preference items across the top. These estimate paths b and c of Figure 4.1 but omit path a. Four main OLS multiple regressions were computed. Some variables were added and deleted in alternative specifications due to intercorrelations among the independent variables, especially mean education of citizens.

Source: FAUI cities pooled for all countries with data available; wball3, 4.xls.

Is active participation critical for democracy? The common answer is yes, from Tocqueville's contrast of New England and France to Verba and Nie's (1972) studies of who participates to Putnam's (1993) work on Italian regions. Hence recent declines in participation in many countries have led most interpreters to sound an alarm (Putnam 1995; Lipset 1995). For instance the Dutch launched investigations of the problem when turnout fell (Denters and Geurts 1992).

Participation in politics is central to our New Political Culture, but we differ from many observers on some key points:

1. *Declines* in voter turnout, party membership, and activities of traditional parties—in certain specific contexts—we interpret as *positive evidence of the NPC.* Why and in what contexts? When voters change faster than parties. Because the traditional parties for decades have been slow to adapt to new citizen concerns; some adapt a bit, but virtually none as rapidly or completely as specialized organizations, since parties must join many issues together for broad appeal (Poland in the early 1990s was an exception with over 200 parties). This means addressing multiple issues, unlike a single-issue group—focused on abortion or recycling, and so on. And seriously active citizens want informed professionalism on such issues, not platitudes of generalist party leaders.

2. *Putnam is concerned that membership and activity are declining in some voluntary groups,* especially in the United States. But membership is rising in other groups, especially broad membership groups that lack the face-to-face proximity and social support of traditional neighborhood and close personal contacts. This means that he, mistakenly perhaps, discounts the rise of ecology groups, although they have substantially grown.

3. *The most dramatic innovation in participation in decades is the Internet:* It permits enormously powerful information and professional expertise to reach everyone with a modem. University of Chicago students immediately react against Putnam's interpretation of decline since he deliberately excludes Internet/World Wide Web browsing and related computerized activities. We lack serious detailed research, but student papers have documented enormous psychic involvement of many computer groups on topics ranging from Zionism to lesbianism to ecology. Political activists increasingly rely on email and Internet links for coordination of their activities (even Neo-Nazi skinheads in Germany) (Cowell 1997). Such groups can achieve almost instant globalism, dramatically overcoming ecological barriers to organization. Virtual communities can be more intellectually meaningful than ecological communities, which may preserve a personal touch. As the world grows more intellectual, ideas may count more in such matters. I offer here an extension of Durkheim's *Division of Labor* argument regarding solidarity, in contrast to those who held that solidarity could only persist in ecological communities.

BOX 4.6   Where Is the Civic Culture? Heterogeneity, the Working Class, and Affluent Towns: Ecological Concentration Reverses the Verba/Nie "Standard" Political Participation Model

The two fiscal policy items concern spending on (1) all items and (2) redistributive items. Cities with more blue-collar workers have leaders who support more total spending, but not on redistribution. Conversely, those with more professional and technical workers favor less spending in general and on redistribution—all findings as expected. Contrary to a simple self-interest hypothesis, however, we find that more affluent cities, and cities in more affluent countries support *more* redistributive spending. This seems to reflect two things: (1) Ecological separation of poor persons makes poor persons and their leaders less willing to support more local spending, even for

4. *Local organized groups are less important in more affluent communities.* This directly contradicts the Verba/Nie "standard" pattern, which holds that persons higher in income, education, and occupation participate more actively. Why the contradiction? Because an important spur to much participation is discontent or social conflict: parents dissatisfied with schools, increases in crime and gang activity, irresponsible political leaders—all these fuel dissent and provide a rationale for organization. But note: The opposite holds if you live in Utopia, or the closet earthly version, a homogenous town with many persons like you, especially upper-status suburbs or rural towns, small in population. Then you have no reason to organize because you have what you want already! This hypothetical extreme illustrates the more general point: Localities with dramatic social heterogeneity should have *more* participation, *despite* the lower socioeconomic status of many residents. American central cities like Chicago and New York have moved further in this direction in the last few decades, becoming home to more affluent young urban professionals as well as more poverty-stricken persons while losing the broad middle class to smaller suburbs. I have documented this phenomenon for some time (e.g. in Clark 1981: 50ff.)I but know of almost no studies that have recognized the fundamental point that social homogeneity reverses the "normal" participation pattern. Vincent Hoffmann-Martinot (1992) did complete one paper growing out of similar concerns, where he estimated "normal" participation for French cities and then examined deviant cases above and below the predicted levels. There were often local crises that sparked participation, such as a succession crisis after the death of a traditional mayor or floods and other natural disasters. This is perhaps the most detailed study to date of the contextual causes of local political participation.

5. *Combine now the above points and ask what they imply for the NPC in regard to participation and political involvement.* Most likely: less traditional politics, lower turnout for "normal" (especially class politics-oriented) candidates, more involvement with electronic communities, less neighborliness in locality-based organizations. But these patterns shift with the type of locality: People should organize more locally if problems rise that local activity can address. If social cleavages divide the population, these can be salient directly, or indirectly in issues like schools, drugs, and crime. But even in more homogeneous towns and neighborhoods with more affluent residents, there are issues like recycling garbage, bicycle paths, crime watches, and schools. Activities linked to children, consumption, and aesthetics (parks, lighting, pollution) are far stronger already among the more affluent, educated, and especially women who participate, actively, on these kinds of issues. Dramatic differences are documented across U.S. FAUI cities in the causes of participation patterns for (1) black-oriented organized groups (sparked by Atkinson inequality) versus (2) ecology groups (sparked by higher education, income, and occupation) in Clark (1996.).

BOX 4.6   *(continued)*

social programs—exacerbated especially in counties like the United States by a concern that high taxes may drive out the nonpoor. This fits with the Atkinson inequality result: More inequality is associated with support for *less*, not more spending in all areas and for redistribution. (2) Many affluent, younger persons do support redistributive programs (a result from citizen surveys e.g., in Rempel and Clark 1997), especially in college towns and affluent suburbs where there are few poor persons, tax implications are small, and an ideology of altruism toward the disadvantaged can be stronger.

The most powerful result for both fiscal items is that left parties favor higher spending, but not in every country. Parties are country-specific and demand separate

One line of NPC propositions stresses that traditional parties alienate the young, the educated, and professionals, who often join new social movements or occasionally reshape older parties (like the PCI in Italy or several Swiss parties). What about the working class, the unemployed, and the disadvantaged? They have often grown alienated from the left, which they earlier supported, as leftist parties turned from Red to Green or a combination of Red and Green. In the United States and Britain, elections by single constituencies and with "first past the post" rules discourage new parties, but in Continental Europe, with proportional representation, new parties emerge continuously; many since the 1970s have moved away from centralist issues. Soon thereafter, most European countries elected New Right and nationalist leaders in larger numbers than since the 1930s, stressing such issues as "right to life, anti-women's liberation, traditional moral values, military defense, law and order, anti-minority rights, and xenophobia." (Ysmal 1990: 2) Often replacing the declines of socialists and communists, the new right parties have won some 10–20 percent of the votes in many European countries. Analyzing the values of right party supporters, Ysmal finds that of eight factors, antidemocratic values and anti-immigrant views are among the most important in explaining party support (in national surveys of citizens in France, Germany, and Italy).

The open racist and nationalist rhetoric is striking. Listen to perhaps the most important New Right leader in Europe, France's Jean-Marie Le Pen, responding to the question: *Do you believe that some persons are superior and some races inferior?*

Answer: *Yes there are some persons and minds that are superior ... egalitarianism is a myth and a stupidity (une sottise). Similarly, between the races there exist undeniable differences....*

I cannot say that the Bantous have the same ethnological aptitude as Californians, because that is simply contrary to reality. Citizens are equal in law, but people are not. ... I am French, I prefer the French. I feel myself linked to the world through ties that are hierarchical (cited in Schweisguth, 1988: 12).

This discourse of a leading European politician contrasts with the United States, where almost no national candidate has spoken this way since George Wallace in 1968. When Pat Buchanan started to run for president in 1996 on nationalist and anti-immigrant issues, he sparked a huge negative reaction by leaders of both political parities and the media and soon withdrew—yet his rhetoric was far milder than European New Right leaders. This suggests a more dominant social liberalism in the United States. While American citizens may talk privately like Le Pen, political candidates cannot.

BOX 4.7   The Rise of Right/Nationalist Parties in Europe

analysis, to which we turn shortly. Similarly, some Table 4.2 results appear insignificant but take on meaning when we consider indirect effects and country differences. For now just note that cities with more blue-collar residents have mayors who favor more spending in general, but not on redistribution. This shows that the move away from support for the disadvantaged by left parties is found not just in the U.S. Democratic Party but is a more general international pattern that holds here in our pooled data. By contrast, persons age 35–44 do not favor more spending in general but *do* support more redistributive spending—perhaps showing their 1960s legacy, in contrast to blue-collar workers, who seem to have grown more fiscally conservative. However, cities with more educated citizens are more fiscally conservative. Catholic mayors favor more spending in general, but less on redistribution. Cities with more powerful parties have leaders favoring more redistributive spending, whereas those with more powerful media have more fiscally conservative leaders. These two last results hint at the key role of parties, pursued shortly.

In his drastic redirection of the French Socialist Party in the early 1980s, Francois Mitterand showed other socialists around the world how their parties could incorporate markets and participatory democracy. In the 1970s, Mitterand led a socialist party whose official objective was "rupture with capitalism." The lead statement at the 1979 party congress was strong and clear: "Our objective is not to modernize or temper capitalism, but to replace it with socialism. . . . The so-called economic laws that the right presents as eternal are in fact only the operating principles of the capitalist system." (Quote in Schweisguth, 1988: 2.)

Yet by 1988 Mitterand proposed no nationalizations, not even the companies which he, in a government with the Communists, had nationalized in 1981, and which the right had privatized when they returned to power in 1986. The slogan on campaign stickers was no longer "class conflict" but France United, "La France unie."

The intervening years had seen many battles as socialists fought within their party. The victors, such as Michel Rocard and Edouard Balladur, were increasingly those who favored direct democracy, citizen participation, decentralization of more functions of the national state to local government, less central planning, and more reliance on free markets and individual initiative. Schweisguth interprets this as a new combination of the market right with the cultural left in terms nearly identical to our New Fiscal Populism (Schweisguth, 1988 and n.d.)

BOX 4.8   Francois Mitterand: Pied Piper of a Global Socialist Transformation

The citizen responsiveness item asked the mayor and council members "about how often would you estimate that you took a position *against* the dominant opinion of your constituents." NPC leaders should be more responsive to citizens, as we suggested in defining the NPC (in characteristic #6). Do cities with NPC socioeconomic and governance characteristics have leaders who say they are more citizen-responsive? Moderately (see Table 4.2). Two characteristics did not show that pattern: cities with more blue-collar workers had *more* citizen-responsive leaders, while those with more professionals reported *less* citizen responsiveness. Education works as hypothesized: Leaders are more responsive in cities with more educated citizens. And as expected, Catholic leaders are less citizen responsive. Group activities, however, depress citizen responsiveness—indicating conflict between "greedy factional interest groups" and citizen-responsive leaders[6] And as hypothesized, cities with more powerful media also have more citizen responsiveness—each encourages the other.

Results for these first three preference items in Table 4.2 are theoretically fair; most are in expected directions, but some are not. By contrast, results are much stronger for the most theoretically appropriate measures of NPC preferences: abortion and sex education, combined in the index of social conservatism. Note that below its column is a high 77 percent of relations that support the NPC propositions, whereas only 67 percent do for nonresponsiveness. No such percentages appear for fiscal items since the fiscal propositions that posit contextual characteristics (like combinations of high taxes and low local wealth) are not included in this table.

Considering social conservatism, cities with more blue-collar workers had more socially conservative leaders; larger cities, and those with a larger 35–44 age cohort, were less socially conservative—all as expected. Unexpectedly, cities with higher educational inequality were more socially conservative. Educa-

＜

Deep changes in French society have made many traditions obsolete. A team of social scientists led by Henri Mendras has documented dramatic change in newsletters and books (e.g. Mendras 1980, 1997; Dirn 1992). For instance:

Union Decline
  In elections for the workers' committees of 1989, votes for non-union members (26.4 percent) for the first time dethroned the CGT (25.1 percent),. Some observers interpret this as an act of defiance toward the traditional unions. The CGT is the national union dominated for decades by the strong Left parties.

Small Firms
  The union result is tightly linked to the rise of small firms, since CGT votes have barely changed in firms with 1000+ employees—which still elect less than 2 percent of non-union members. But small firms (under about 50) elect 45 percent non-union members, and employees in small firms grew at over twice the rate of large firms from 1966 to 1987 (3.7 versus 1.7 percent). (Source: Dirn, 1992).

Organized Groups
  Ever since Napoleon suppressed voluntary associations, and Tocqueville declared him victorious, France has been contrasted with America on this civic dimension. But times have changed. In the 1970s, 25,000 associations were created annually. This rose to about 50,000 in the 1980s. A 1991 survey of 11,000 associations showed that they were mainly in sanitation and social services (33 percent), culture (15 percent), education (14 percent), leisure and tourism (11 percent), and sports (9 percent). While the class-oriented unions are in decline, the new associations seem distinctively oriented toward consumption and post-industrial concerns, plus aid to the disadvantaged. (Source: Dirn, 1992)

Ecology Groups
  From 1977 to 1992, new voluntary associations of all sorts grew over 20 percent each year in France. But those concerned with "defense of the environment" grew 132 percent. Source: Forse (1993).

BOX 4.9 Is France Still Napoleonic, or Leninist? Unions Decline, Small Firms Grow, and Voluntary Organizations Spread

tion of citizens was unrelated to social conservatism.[7]

As expected, more highly educated mayors and women mayors and council members were more socially liberal, older mayors more conservative. The media were more powerful in more socially liberal cities. And cities with left parties were more socially liberal, although as we show below, this varies strikingly by country.

Do Political Parties Constrain Emergence of the NPC?

Vincent Hoffmann-Martinot's chapter (Chapter 5) reviews studies of parties in many countries, which suggest that strong, hierarchical parties, like the traditional French and Italian parties, alienate citizens, decrease turnout, and drive younger persons to new social movements. This is a general but not universal trend as Hans Geser emphasizes in his chapter (see Chapter 7). He shows that Swiss parties incorporated young activists quite successfully. In many other countries, by contrast, young persons concerned with ecology and other new issues joined new groups or remained alienated. In brief, parties vary considerably across countries and cities in ways that seriously affect the political system. Indeed parties are the most important single participants, in many locations, in refocusing actions and policies of other participants, like organized groups and elected officials. The United States is an international exception, having weak parties but more active organized groups and citizens in some locations.

One's awareness of just where a political system is located, and why, only emerges via numerous comparisons with others. We held conferences with experts from many countries for years, heard many cases cited, but could not tell precisely how large differences were until directly comparable results became available. Without systematic data one just cannot say precisely how distinctive or universal any city or country is. We explore some intriguing ways to capture differences in party arrangements with the comparative FAUI data. Most of these international analyses we undertake for the first time in urban research. Results clarify several continuing international debates over class politics, new social movements, and roles of political parties. How?

Consider first at a simple table of national averages of Strong Party Organization (Figure 4.2). France, Italy, and most West European countries had strong, organized parties (black bars); by contrast, the United States, Canada, and Australia are world outliers with their weak parties. In these three former British colonies, the Victorian reform tradition is alive and strong in institutions like nonpartisan elections and the professional city manager; in Britain itself, parties grew more dominant after World War II, especially the Labour Party and associated unions, until the 1980s, when Margaret Thatcher and her Conservatives imposed their policies on local governments with a vengeance (Chandler and Clark 1995). Simultaneously, after 1989 ingenious Eastern Europeans celebrated the flowering of democracy by creating parties for, among others, Beer Drinkers and Safe Sex. This efflorescence was soon overshadowed by the return to national leadership of former communist parties in Poland and Hungary, but the communists were far weaker than in the Soviet days; they lacked a majority in their national parliaments and many cities, so governance was through complex coalitions of many new parties and groups (cf. Clark 1993; Swianiewicz and Clark 1996). Our case study of the Italian party system in Chapter 3 similarly illustrates the dramatic collapse of hierarchical parties. In brief, some countries have strong hierarchical parties, but fighting party hierarchy is globally popular.

The United States and Taiwan are the only two countries with primary elections where citizens vote on candidates for parties to run in general elections. Worldwide, the common pattern is that party leaders choose candidates for public office. This brings ideological coherence and control by national parties and more generally constrains local autonomy and innovation, whatever the legal structures of government. The common defense of strong parties is that they occur in multiparty systems, which give voters more choices. National diversity among parties is surely greater in Continental Europe than in Britain and former British Commonwealth countries (United States, Australia, and Canada). Proportional representation in varying forms and multiparty governance have long been staples of Continental European government. But despite diversity across parties this still means that each (normally national) party generally

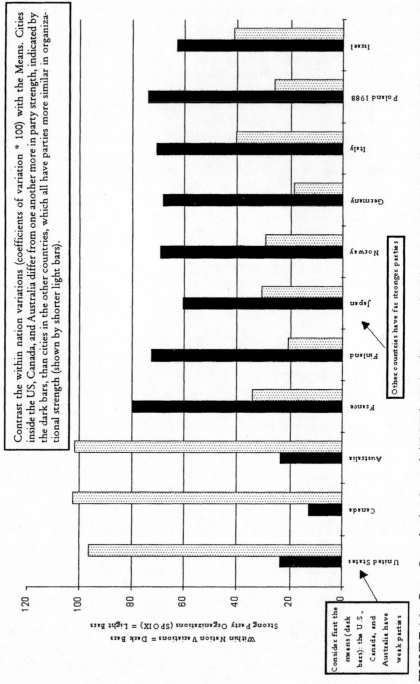

Contrast the within nation variations (coefficients of variation * 100) with the Means. Cities inside the US, Canada, and Australia differ from one another more in party strength, indicated by the dark bars, than cities in the other countries, which all have parties more similar in organizational strength (shown by shorter light bars).

Other countries have far stronger parties

Consider first the means (dark bars): the U.S., Canada, and Australia have weak parties

Within Nation Variations = Dark Bars
Strong Party Organizations (SPOIX) = Light Bars

FIGURE 4.2   Party Organization Strength (SPOIX): National Means and Within Nation Variations Show Two Different Patterns

dominates in choosing candidates and policies across the national territory inside its own party. Hence the emergence of new rules, like our New Political Culture, should be retarded by strong parties. This was our Proposition #7 in Chapter 2, which we now explore.

What is party strength, and how to capture it? One dimension is organizational. This is central in the tradition of urban politics led by Edward Banfield (1961: 235ff), who pointed out that Chicago had strong party organization while New York City had weak parties. This, in turn, Banfield suggested, led to an inability of New York mayors to implement clear policies, since they became victims of day-to-day pressures from special-interest groups. He interpreted the 1975 New York fiscal crisis in this way. James Q. Wilson (1973/74) elaborated this further, conceptualizing parties as organizations that must offer incentives to their members and which vary in how they structure incentives to generate organizational coherence. Ester Fuchs (1992) extended their ideas by examining longer historical fluctuations and showing that New York, long lacking a strong party, had seen several fiscal crises. In each, business leaders were (temporarily) empowered as strong leaders (like the party in Chicago) and thereby imposed solutions that weak political leaders could not. Rowan Miranda (1994) was the first to test these ideas with a national sample of U.S. cities. Analyzing FAUI data, he found that the basic Strong Party Organization (SPO) thesis held strong: Cities with SPOs had fewer fiscal problems and lower spending levels, controlling other characteristics. Vincent Hoffmann-Martinot in this volume analyzes this same SPO Index for several countries, finding, for instance, that left parties had higher SPO scores. We used the same SPO index in Table 4.1 and found that cities with more blue-collar and less-educated residents had stronger SPOs, in many countries, as predicted. But taking the next step, from SPO to policy views of local officials (in Table 4.2), we did not find the pattern reported from Banfield through Miranda. On the contrary: Mayors in cities with higher SPO scores preferred *higher* redistributive spending.[8] How interpret these new results?

The SPO literature highlights the value of crossnational comparison: It makes explicit both the strengths and limits of a theory developed in one country. Country-specific analysts might wave a red flag emblazoned Not Generalizable and call for a halt to modeling here—concluding that unique historical circumstances made the United States different (cf. Przeworski and Teune 1970; Ragin 1987; Brint 1994:30ff contrasts recent work using case studies versus analytical variable approaches). This is surely true, but can we really say no more? Are there not characteristics of parties that make some more and others less likely to follow the SPO theory? Yes, and they are not country-specific but can be stated in general terms to permit testing in many national contexts. Two general characteristics of European political systems are critical here: local autonomy in (a) fiscal/administrative responsibilities and (b) in party organization and ideology. The administrative aspect is well known: European cities are less fiscally and administratively autonomous from their national governments than U.S. cities, thus permitting local European officials to engage in more "radical" programs or at least to articulate more "high spending" preferences but not to have to impose taxes to pay for them—albeit changes in the last two decades are generally toward more autonomy (with Britain being the exception). The second point has been less discussed and, to our knowledge, never systematically operationalized crossnationally. That is, parties vary in their national coherence, and the degree to which they permit local branches or candidates to choose programs that deviate from the national program. Party strength thus has two dimensions: organizational and ideological. How might we capture this second ideological dimension of party strength? Indeed, American commentators on parties have been less sensitive to ideology and programs than many Europeans, understandable given the greater salience of ideology in Europe (yet here again, we see convergence as NPC tendencies operate in Europe).

The U.S./European differences affected the dominant theories of coalitions. The American theorists Riker and Ordeshook (1973) review coalition theory, stressing Riker's Minimum Winning Coalition idea, which assumes that political resources are private goods from which noncoalition members are excluded. Parties may be the key actors but are not critical to the theory, as befits the American system. By contrast, Dutchman DeSwaan (1973), studying European governments, stressed Minimal Range Theory, which is based purely on ideology, to explain why parties join or do not join coalitions: Leaders seek to minimize the ideological range of views in their coalition. Parties only join if they are comfortable with the programs of their coalition partners. Riker and Ordeshook denied the value of Minimal Range Theory, perhaps showing an American bias. We hold rather that both elements should inform an adequate theory of parties: organization and ideology, and we use both below.

Stating the matter in terms of comparative party and policy differences, we posit that *the more local autonomy in a political system, especially in its political parties, the more that the attitudes and specific policy preferences of local officials should covary with local circumstances (wealth and other characteristics of local inhabitants) and the more the distinct preferences of local leaders can then explain local policy commitments (such as higher spending).*

We turn to evidence for this idea after considering class politics.

One of president Francois Mitterand's major policies was decentralization of the national state to local government. Paradoxically, the program was launched simultaneously with President Ronald Reagan's New Federalism. But whereas Reagan was hamstrung by a Democratic Congress, arguing that the policy came from the right, Mitterand's strong Socialist majority implemented *la decentralisation*. Effects are still being assessed, but decentralization seemed to heighten local initiatives, entrepreneurship, and civic activity—even with less money. One survey of 400 French public and private sector leaders reported:

	Agree	Disagree	No Opinion
Decentralization has brought local government and private business together	75	18	7
Decentralization has created better coordination of state and local activities	90	4	6

Source: Bernier, 1992, p. 50.

BOX 4.10   Decentralization: French and U.S. Contrasts

Class Politics and the New Political Culture: Conceptual Controversies and Mixed Evidence

Parties are pivotal in ways past analysts have often ignored. Consider recent work on class politics. The main findings change dramatically when parties are more closely examined. I presented some key NPC propositions in a paper with Seymour Martin Lipset, "Are Social Classes Dying?" (Clark and Lipset 1991), which helped spark a vigorous exchange about class politics.[9] For instance, Michael Hout et al. (1995), and John Goldthorpe (1994, 1996) countered that class was not dying at all. For evidence, they focused on about seven occupational categories to explain party voting, with only a few control variables. They and several others have generally studied one or two countries over the last twenty years or so, using sample surveys of individual citizens (see Lee and Turner 1996 for a summary). They report results, which they label "trendless fluctuation." That is, they suggest class has not declined in its impact on party voting, esp. in Britain and the United States, where much work has been done. Four major weaknesses of these studies are: (1) assuming that parties are constant over time in ideology and class-related issues, especially fiscal (rather than social) issues, since none are measured (2) ignoring specific occupational shifts, like the rise of professionals and decline in the proportion of manual workers, which transform the meaning of occupational class (3) biasing results by omitting critical variables other than occupation (their measure of class), and (4) imposing a simplistic conceptualization, such as asking "is class significant over time" rather than testing alternative models, such as how important are specific components of "class politics" versus "postindustrial politics." Postindustrial politics is the main candidate which Inglehart, Lipset, I, and others have proposed as an alternative to class politics. Most actual political systems have elements of both. To clarify the dynamics of class politics and the NPC, we must identify, measure, and compare their specific components in different political systems. How? The six definitional elements of the NPC state a clear and specific set of alternative hypotheses to class politics; indeed they were formulated largely to contrast with class politics. We offer evidence that substantially qualifies the class-is-trendless view in the next sections.

What specific evidence should we consider to assess class politics versus NPC tendencies? I focus on two simple questions, conceptually central to the class politics exchange:

1. Are parties changing? In particular, do they show more attention to social issues and less to fiscal issues than in the past? The class-is-trendless view suggests (and methodologically assumes) no change; the NPC view suggests change.

2. How much are parties ideologically structured around fiscal versus social issues? The class-is-trendless view suggest that fiscal issues dominate social issues and these are clearly linked to parties; the NPC posits greater salience for social issues and weaker links to parties.

Answers? In analyzing party programs, we find strong evidence supporting the NPC interpretation, specifically as stated in the first three of our NPC defining characteristics—#1 transformation of the left-right continuum, #2 distinguishing social from fiscal issues, and #3 the rise of social issues. But NPC tendencies are not universal; they are often stronger in contexts specified by our Chapter 2 propositions.

Are Political Parties Moving Toward the NPC in Their Programs? Often But Not Always

Parties are labeled "black boxes" by some class theorists. We must open the party "box" to see if parties remain constant over time and thus may legitimately be ignored as the class-is-trendless analysts do. Or, if *party agendas* shift toward NPC issues, even a constant relationship over time between occupation and party voting then clearly does *not* indicate "trendless fluctuation." Most class-is-trendless analysts like Hout et al. (1995) and Goldthorpe (1996) use methods that assume implicitly that parties do not shift in meaning in the periods they study. They simply analyze the relationships between citizens' occupations and their party preferences. Have parties changed their programs? Virtually no studies have been conducted in this tradition on social class and politics that have sought to determine if parties are indeed constant in their programs. Let us look.

The (potentially) critical role of parties in this exchange led me to acquire data on party programs from the Party Manifesto Project (of Ian Budge, Richard Hofferbert, and Hans-Peter Klingeman). The Manifesto Project coded platforms of 250 parties in twenty-eight countries for most national elections from 1945 to 1988. Each idea or "quasisentence" in a platform was assigned to a theme. The percentage of total space devoted to each theme was then calculated. These data permit us to monitor the shifting salience of themes across a rich set of countries and parties. For each party I tabulated five themes that differentiate class politics from the NPC. The hypothesized changes are in Table 4.3.

These hypotheses from Table 4.3 were tested first using all 250 parties, and second country by country. Two time periods were used: 1945–1972 and 1972–1988 since we expected NPC themes to rise after the early 1970s, as many new social movements then emerged. The first period was compared to the second to see if themes changed. This simple method for testing the hypotheses is consistent with the form of the data, since we have only data on the party programs, not on organization, membership or other characteristics. Results: Four of the five hypotheses were supported for the 250 parties. That is, the 250 parties showed increased attention over time to the two NPC themes (environmental protection and government and administrative efficiency) and less attention to two of three class politics themes. The exception was traditional morality, which did not decline. To assess specifics, we calculated t-tests for all parties in all countries combined; then we analyzed five major countries separately. Results for each of the five countries (in the right half of Table 4.4) are weaker than those for all twenty-eight countries combined (left half of table). This is partly a function of the low number of cases, such that while one country may appear "trendless," combining cases can generate a trend. One can observe the detailed patterns in Figures 4.3 and 4.4, which show results for the largest left parties in the United States and Germany. The U.S. parties changed least of all five countries toward NPC themes—only by mentioning Labor less (Table 4.4). The United States also differs from three of the four other countries on Traditional Morality; it rose for the United States in total (Table 4.4); it was stressed more often by Republicans in the Reagan and Bush years (but not by the Democratic Party) (Figure 4.3). Nevertheless, Traditional Morality did decline in Germany, France, and Italy (right half of Table 4.4), suggesting movement toward the NPC by parties in these countries. However, on Labor, the four European countries did not show the decreased emphasis found in all twenty-eight countries. More details on the Manifesto data and analyses are in the Appendix. Note that themes favored are marked plus (like Welfare State +), while those opposed are marked minus.

This simple evidence is such compelling support for the rise of the NPC that it is best left in this direct manner. One might probe (Goeff Evans did, orally), asking if such party thematic differences matter to citizens, in terms of their own preferences or their perceptions of where parties stand. Answer? Yes: Considerable evidence, such as in Heath et al. (1985, 1991), documents the salience of these very themes among citizens as well as the impact of such themes on citizens' attachments to parties. We return to class politics issues after examining another aspect of party impact.

Are Parties Structured by Fiscal or Social Issues? How Tightly Are They "Structured" for Elected Officials?

Let us now shift from national party programs to examine how ideologically structured parties are for individual mayors and council members. We consider how tightly

TABLE 4.3 Hypotheses Contrasting Class Politics and the New Political Culture to Test with Party Program Data

Theme	Hypotheses: Relative Emphasis on Each Theme by	
	Class Politics	New Political Culture
Environmental Protection	Less	More
Government and Administrative Efficiency	Less	More
Traditional Morality: Positive	More	Less
Labor Groups: Positive	More	Less
Welfare State Expansion	More	Less

Note: For instance, the first line shows that we hypothesize that Environmental Protection issues would be stressed more by parties that lean more toward the New Political Culture than toward Class Politics.

TABLE 4.4 Results from Content Analysis of Party Programs

		1. Results for 250 Parties in 28 Countries		2. Results for Five Individual Countries				
				Significance of Change				
		Average Space on Theme	Signifi-cance of Change	USA	Germany	France	Italy	Great Britain
Environmental Protection								
After	1973	3.69						
Before	1973	0.92	0.00	0.96	0.01	0.00	0.04	0.05
Gov-Admin Efficiency								
After	1973	2.70	0.00	0.69	0.07	0.68	0.08	0.15
Before	1973	1.90			down			
Traditional Morality								
After	1973	2.54						
Before	1973	2.31	0.59	0.15	0.10	0.13	0.07	0.99
				weakly up				
Labor +								
After	1973	2.16						
Before	1973	2.76	0.01	0.00	0.82	0.49	0.42	0.57
Welfare +								
After	1973	5.64						
Before	1973	6.40	0.02	0.72	0.09	0.08	0.44	0.33

Note: The mean percent of space devoted to each theme was compared in the two periods, and a T-test computed to indicate significance of the change. Results for all 250 parties in 28 countries showed significant shifts toward the NPC on four of the five themes. Details: The first row shows that 3.69 was the average percent of total space devoted to Environmental Protection themes by 250 parties after 1973. The second row shows that before 1973 just under 1 percent was devoted to Environmental Protection. This change from .92 to 3.69 after 1973 was significant at the .00 level. The probability that the change for Traditional Morality was significant was just .59—which is insignificant. The individual country scores are for the significance of the change. Example: The first row shows that there was not a significant change in space on Environmental Protection in the US (since .96 is way below the .10 level of significance), but the change was significant in the four other countries. The direction of all changes matched the hypotheses in Table 1 except for Govt-Adm Efficiency in Germany, which parties mentioned less after 1973, and Traditional Morality in the US, although this last change was only at the .15 significance level.

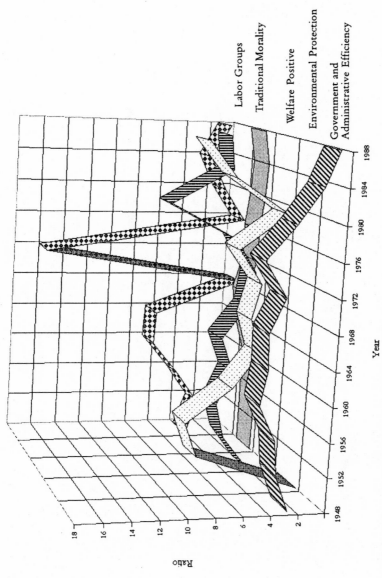

FIGURE 4.3 Changes of Themes in US Democratic Party Programs.

Note: The vertical axis shows the percent of total space devoted to each of the five themes in the chart. The categories are explained in the Appendix. Items like welfare were coded as positive and negative; only positive is shown.

Source: Party Manifestos Project.

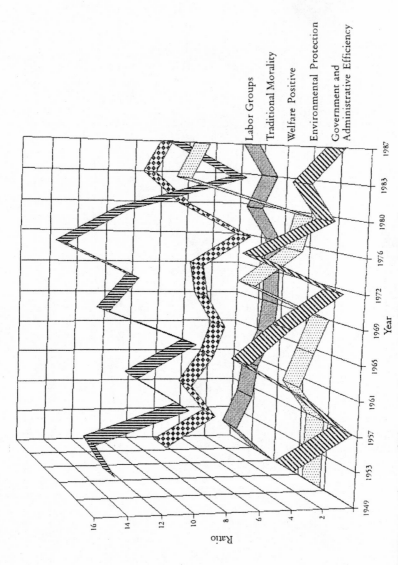

FIGURE 4.4 Changes of Themes in German Social Democratic Party Programs.

Note: The vertical axis shows the percent of total space devoted to each of the five themes in the chart. The categories are explained in the Appendix. Items like welfare were coded as positive and negative; only positive is shown.

Source: Party Manifestos Project.

Noting the emergence of new social and cultural issues among citizens and new organized groups, Paddock (1980) analyzed eleven U.S. Democratic party programs in eleven states to see if they had incorporated these new issues. They did *not* basically change from 1956 to 1980. Paddock analyzed eight issues, such as capitalism, redistribution, labor, and the like. Conclusion: *The New Deal model of conflict persisted within Democratic platforms throughout the period... The eleven Democratic organizations in this analysis showed little inclination toward embracing a social and cultural agenda.*

Reviewing national political debates, E.J. Dionne (1991: 11-12), *Washington Post* journalist, reaches conclusions close to ours by stressing that (national) party leaders remained ideologically trapped and thus ignored new citizen priorities:

Most of the problems of our political life can be traced to the failure of the dominant ideologies of American politics, liberalism and conservatism. The central argument of this book is that liberalism and conservatism are framing political issues as a series of false choices. Wracked by contradiction and responsive mainly to the needs of their various constituencies, liberalism and conservatism prevent the nation from settling the questions that most trouble it... On issue after issue, there is consensus on where the country should move or at least on what we should be arguing about; liberalism and conservatism make it impossible for that consensus to express itself...

The cause of this false polarization is the cultural civil war that broke out in the 1960s. Just as the Civil war dominated American political life for decades after it ended, so is the cultural civil war of the 1960s, with all its tensions and contradictions, shaping our politics today. We are still trapped in the 1960s....

It is easy to understand why conservatives would like the cultural civil war to continue. It was the Kulturkampf of the 1960s that made them so powerful in our political life. Conservatives were able to destroy the dominant New Deal coalition by using cultural and social issues— race, the family, "permissiveness," crime—to split New Deal constituencies. The cultural issues, especially race, allowed the conservatives who took control of the Republican Party to win over what had been the most loyally Democratic group in the nation, white Southerners, and to peel off millions of votes among industrial workers and other whites of modest incomes.

BOX 4.11 The American Democratic Party Changes Slowly

parties are linked to preferences on issues and how fiscal and social issues differ. Much past work has treated each country's parties as nation-specific. We sought to examine how much this was true. This requires a method of comparing parties, which means transcending their names to locate them on a more general scale. The most common among activists and analysts is a left-right classification generated by asking citizens or leaders, "How would you classify yourself on a left-right scale?" with answers like "Very Right, Right, Center, Left, Very Left." We similarly classified parties of each mayor and council member in every FAUI city and country on a general left-right scale (IPARTY) from 0 to 100. The left-right scores for each party came from citizen and expert surveys for each country (see Appendix for details). This IPARTY method is the first we have seen that permits such systematic comparison of parties internationally; we encourage others to pursue it or develop better methods in future work.

The IPARTY setup permits us to pose two central theoretical questions: First, *how tightly linked to the party's left-right classification are the policy preferences of an individual mayor?* We define an ideologically tight party system as one where a mayor (or citizen) who supports a right party also holds "right" preferences on fiscal and social policy items. As one moves toward the NPC, we expect such ideological tightness to weaken.

> "*Before reaching the presidency, Bill Clinton held to a strong conviction that the established party divisions had divorced politics from the lives of ordinary citizens. The people, he asserted, 'do not care about the rhetoric of left and right,' what he called 'stale orthodoxies.' The real people, he said, 'are crying desperately for someone who believes the purpose of government is to solve their problems and make progress'"*
>
> "*The Clinton solution represents a personal revolt against the lines and categories that blocked the formulation of a broad bottom-up vision. Such an approach challenges the organizing idea of the party of Lyndon Johnson. The plight of the poor and the unfinished business of civil rights are no longer the first principles of Democratic politics. Instead, Bill Clinton is seeking to reassociate his party with the American dream*" (Greenberg, 1995: pp. 276, 278).

BOX 4.12   Clinton Moves Away from the New Deal: an Assessment by One of His Main Pollster-Advisers

Thus party-policy tightness, as we measure it, indexes a non-NPC pattern. Second, *how important are fiscal compared to social issues in driving left-right party location?* Many class politics analysts posit one dimension, largely fiscal, as driving party location. The NPC instead stresses that new social and other issues increasingly drive elected officials, who may break with others inside their own parties if they disagree on these issues.

We measure both aspects of party dynamics and consider the competing hypotheses by analyzing how well the left-right *Iparty* score for each mayor is explained by his/ her answers to two *ideology* scales: *fiscal liberalism* (preferring more or less spending) and *social liberalism* (abortion plus sex education, the same items used in Table 4.2.) Results are illuminating. When we pool 1,033 mayors who answered these items in all countries, we find that the "party-ideology tightness" score is just 9 percent, which says that 91 percent of the variation in party affiliation of these mayors is *unrelated* to their fiscal or social views.[10] This suggests far more NPC-like looseness across all these countries than a classic, tight, left-right characterization. Addressing our second question, about social versus fiscal issues, both are important, but the fiscal index is about twice as important as the social index in explaining party affiliation when responses are pooled for all countries. Our Party Tightness Method can be repeated for any subgroup of mayors. Given the importance of national parties for such issues, we consider mainly scores by country. Results: In some countries, the party-ideology tightness index is minimal—scores are 1 percent or less for the United States, Canada, Belgium, and the Czech Republic, for example (Table 4.5). But in other countries, tightness jumps: to 31 percent for Britain and a high of 80 percent for Italy—huge differences in party ideological consistency! One could interpret this to say that parties are roughly thirty-one times more important in structuring mayors' policies in Britain than in the United States, Canada, or Poland.[11] In counties like the United States, with ideologically weaker parties, issue positions are practically specific to each mayor rather than defined by his or her party.

Next look at how much parties are structured by fiscal versus social issues. Again countries vary considerably. Britain leads in the dominance of fiscal issues (with the fiscal beta of .55 and social beta of .05). This probably changed substantially in 1997

The Italian Communist Party (PCI) transformed itself more dramatically and earlier than most other communist parties, showing the way for others around the world. The PCI's transformations illustrate the power of extraparty social pressures on even this officially Leninist organization, long linked to the Russian, East European, and French Communist parties, which held to the Leninist-Stalinist line much longer. The change came in two stages, according to PCI observers: first was to move toward clientelism, second toward new social movements:

    Embracing clientelism: *In [the 1970s in] the 'red zone'—the areas of central Italy where it has consistently received large percentages of the vote—the PCI has become an institutionalized distributor of patronage. Entrenched party functionaries have become functionally indistinguishable from the leaders of other Italian political parties.* Brunell (1986: 369).

    New social movements, and protest tactics: The PCI moved from a Leninist vanguard party to a patronage party to a movement party more concerned with homosexuals, feminism, and the antinuclear movement than with Eurocommunism. *Generational renewal and inclusion of former movement activists [i.e. young people who participated in demonstrations or New Social Movements during the late 1960s and early 1970s] within the party's grassroots cadre has affected its attitudinal structure at its base.* (Lange et al, 1990: 19). *In 1979, 61% of delegates to the provincial party congress had joined the PCI after 1969; 40.5% had once belonged to the Young Communist Federation, which was an Italian version of the Young Pioneers...The phase of mass mobilization introduced a very large new generation of activists into the party's ranks—about 20% of the delegates had participated in various social movements in the late 1960s or early 1970s. (p.22)*

    65.1% of delegates with movement exposure had a university degree

    19.1% of those from PCI families

    16.3% of those who had belonged to the Young Communist Federation

    However, the three post-1969 generations together positively and significantly affect the probability that unconventional behavior [conscientious objection, occupying a building, and blocking traffic] will be tolerated. (p.36) Probably because ... *all three [forms of protest] became frequent instruments of either mass or individual dissent [during the late 1960s or early 1970s in Italy].* These three forms had not been part of the PCI's platform. (pp. 35-37)

    The PCI was pressed by "social" pressures as well as strategic reaction to the Christian Democrats, who in the late 1960s and early 1970s were concerned about the rise of secular ethics. To counter it, the Christian Democrats took a strong position on abortion and nearly outlawed divorce. And as these policies were presented in a way that was perceived as dogmatic by a dominant hierarchical party, the unintended consequence was to drive the young and educated toward street protest, new social movements, and then the PCI. (Thanks to Mark Gromala for his research on the PCI and to Guido Martinotti for insightful discussion.)

BOX 4.13   The Greening of the Italian Communist Party

after Tony Blair and New Labour abandoned their traditional high-spending policies and won a substantial majority. In Italy, Christian Democratic mayors were *not* at all nationally consistent on fiscal policy; instead social issues dominated in structuring party alignments. On a national referendum in the 1960s, the Christian Democratic Party took a strong antiabortion position, while left parties opposed it, and won. Mayors, we see here, strictly followed the same party lines two decades later. Such rigidities contributed to transformation of the whole Italian party system in the 1990s.

    The main results of Table 4.5 are thus (1) low party-ideology tightness in most countries (with Italy the big exception), and (2) considerable diversity across countries in the dominance of social issues versus fiscal issues. We do not find that social issues are insignificant or spurious as a strong class politics approach might suggest, although Britain was the closest to this end of the spectrum. In most countries, economic and fiscal issues do *not* dominate party differences. Rather we find that *both social and fiscal issues are independently important* in their links with political parties. We computed a ratio of fiscal/social issues, but the very low scores of many components make some ratios loose meaning. In brief, this diversity clearly covers considerable variation in the degree to which party ideology dominates local officials. Some parties and national systems are dominated by national parties, like the British. But on the Continent, we find considerable diversity, with minimal structure in the new East European parties but great hierarchy in Italy. Of course, recall that these Italian data are from the last years of the ancien regime, which collapsed soon thereafter, as shown in Chapter 3. The hierarchical control by Rome, clear in the Table 4.5 results, contributed to the demise of Italy's traditional party system.

Where is Class Politics?

As Durkheim reminded us, science begins with comparison. Who cares if the occupation/voting relation is constant in one country over a few decades—as the class-is-trendless proponents report? For analytical meaning, a pattern must be demonstrated that transcends description of one or two countries. Comparing individual citizens suffices for many social psychological hypotheses, such as the age of party identification and socialization into new issues. But to understand social and political systems, a theory must also include structural characteristics. Obvious candidates are class and party, but how and why are they interrelated? Cracking this nut can let us see more closely where and why class politics persists or declines. Answers are largely absent from recent research, especially work on class politics like Hout, Brooks, and Manza (1995) and Goldthorpe (1994, 1996), since the researchers did not compare differences; they simply reported a "trendless fluctuation" that they conceived as constant. One way to cut into this more deeply is to look at historical change in parties, as we pursued above in the party manifesto analysis. A second approach is to compare political systems differing in their amounts of class politics and try to explain the differences. Comparing multiple social units, not just individual citizens, is key for most structural theories. Unlike most past work on changing class/party linkages, Nieuwbeerta and De Graaf (1995) include crossnational findings about class politics for citizens in several countries. Some related work does too: Przeworski and Sprague (1988), Inglehart (1990), and Franklin et al. (1992). All report substantial differences across time and countries. They reinforce Durkheim's admonition, which as restated by Przeworski and Teune (1970) urged researchers to test ideas with cross-system data so that country names disappear—because they are analytically transcended. For instance, the statement that class voting declines in the United States, but not Denmark, should be replaced by an effort to specify what analytical characteristics differentiate the United States from Denmark, like the strength of the unions and coherence of parties. Then

TABLE 4.5 Party Ideology Tightness Varies by Country: Fiscal vs. Social Components

Country	Party Tightness (Adjusted R Square)	Impact on Party of Fiscal Policy Preferences all areas	Impact on Party of Social Conservatism Index	Fiscal vs Social Impact (Ratio)	Number of cases
All Countries	**0.09**	**-0.28 *****	**0.05 ***	**5.6**	**905**
UNITED STATES	0.01	-0.12 **	0.01 ns	9.10	272
CANADA	-0.03	-0.16 ns	-0.27 ns	0.61	19
FRANCE	0.18	-0.42 ***	-0.16 ns	2.63	80
FINLAND	0.01	-0.12 ns			175
JAPAN	0.01	-0.19 *	0.05 ns	3.86	89
NORWAY	0.07	-0.27 ***			368
AUSTRALIA	0.33	-0.49 **	0.28 *	1.75	33
BELGIUM	-0.01	-0.19 ns			24
ARGENTINA	-0.04	-0.01 ns			24
CZECH REPUBLIC	0.00	0.02 ns	-0.12 ns	0.14	115
HUNGARY	-0.01		0.03 ns		75
SLOVAKIA	0.04	0.06 ns	0.28 **	0.21	51
GERMANY	0.07	-0.27 ***			137
ITALY	0.80	-0.03 ns	0.89 ***	0.04	50
BRITAIN	0.31	-0.55 ***	0.05 ns	10.90	200
POLAND, 1991	0.00	-0.08 ns			102
ISRAEL	-0.01	0.11 ns			49

Italy has by far the tightest party system

Italy's tightness comes mainly from social, not fiscal, policy issues

Note: We measure party tightness by the adjusted R2 of the regression of the left-right party measure of the mayor (IPARTY as dependent variable) on fiscal policy preferences (PRFAVG) and social conservatism (SOCCONS6). The Impact measures (second and third columns) are beta statistics from the regression computed by country. The Fiscal vs. Social Ratio is simply the ratio of the fiscal impact to the social impact (column two/column three), left blank for countries where one item was missing. Ns=not significant; * =sig. <.10; ** =sig <.05; *** =sig <.01

the two-country difference can be reformulated: In political systems where unions and parties are more coherent, class voting is encouraged.[12]

What can move class politics studies in this direction? First by comparing more countries, as in Nieuwbeerta and De Graaf (1995), although they study citizens atomistically within each country since they have only national citizen survey data. Second by comparing relations across other units, like cities or regions, as well as nations. This can increase the N enough to begin to generalize. Heath, Yang, and Goldstein (Undated) and Weakliem and Heath (Undated) are two nice papers that explore regional and local variations in class/party effects within Britain by Oxford researchers from the logistic tradition of Goldthorpe. Both papers pursue provocative system-type propositions. They find some interesting results on local differences: "Individuals from the same social class had very different propensities to vote Conservative in different constituencies ... constituencies seemed to vary in their level of class polarization (p. 14)." This dovetails with our Chapter 2 propositions and cross-city comparisons, such as those on inequality differences by city. Analogously, Brooks and Manza (1997) refine the simpler model used in their papers with Hout (Hout, Brooks,

---

Many prominent NPCs in America are Democrats, but some are Republicans. Consider William Floyd Weld, former governor of Massachusetts: 49 years old, born on a farm one mile square on Long Island from one of the Northeast's most established families. He ran on the theme "Tough on Taxes, Tough on Crime" in 1990. He spent his first year undoing what his predecessor, Governor Michael Dukakis, had spent his career establishing in the state government in the one of the most Democratic states in the Union The *Wall Street Journal* ranked him first among governors for fiscal policy; he cut total payroll by 12 percent in his first six months. He received surprisingly high marks from Democratic guru David Osborne, author of *Reinventing Government*. On "right to life," he says that the loss of a viable life is "a price I would pay to have government stay out of the thicket. I leave it up to the women." He named gays to his subcabinet and to judgeships.

He studied at Middlesex School, Harvard College, Harvard Law School, and Oxford and was the only candidate running who strongly supported gay rights and abortion rights. Weld's education agenda was similar to that in *Reinventing Government*, although somewhat more minimalist, following his libertarian tradition: He stood for a minimum state expenditure of $5,000 per child in a "competitive" system in which the money would follow students as they shopped for schools. With an upturn in the economy he would like to see more spent on open space acquisition (an exception to his libertarian position since he felt it was an area where government must be more assertive). He supported more money for prevention education (AIDS, teen pregnancy) to stop problems before they start.

When elected, he faced a $2.6 billion deficit in the first eighteen months. He repealed a 5 percent professional services tax ($160 million), shut down eight of thirty-four underused state hospitals, privatized many areas of departments, reducing the state work force by 8,000 (11 percent) by consolidation, attrition, and privatization, and shrank the highway department by 40 percent. Estimates are that privatization saved Massachusetts $273 million in 1992 and 1993 alone. He claimed partial credit for 110,000 new jobs created in Massachusetts in his first two years. Unemployment fell from: 9.5 to 8.5 to 6.9 in 1991, 1992, and 1993 (Lydon, 1992; Novack, 1993).

BOX 4.14   A Republican NPC: Governor of Massachusetts

and Manza 1993, 1994, 1995) by comparing citizens in different occupations—finding that professionals have grown increasingly NPC while managers have not. The striking increases of professionals and declines in production workers in most of the world are clear in Box 4.15. Many class theorists have not yet incorporated such changes.

Our FAUI data permit testing propositions about theoretically important structural characteristics. One powerful finding is that class impacts on party vary enormously by country and by city within countries. We find three distinct patterns linking class and party, summarized in Figure 4.5. These patterns open the door to structural explanations. The FAUI surveys included comparable items to mayors on political processes, analyzed here for seven countries with relatively complete data. One question asked if the mayor would prefer more, the same, or less spending in some thirteen areas—the PRFAVG item used above. To explain such fiscal liberalism, we analyzed characteristics of mayors and their cities in each country. Class politics is modeled in two key steps, shown in Figure 4.5. Step 1 (path a) shows the impact of percent blue-collar residents on party of the mayor and council members (more blue-collar workers should increase left council members); Step 2 (path b) shows the impact of party and blue-collar residents on the mayor's fiscal liberalism. The strength of class politics is shown by the regression coefficients (betas) for these key variables (details in Appendix Table 4A.3). Additional variables are included as controls. We find three main patterns:

- *strong class politics* in Finland and France (a and b significant)
- *weak class politics* in Canada, Japan, Norway, and Australia, where blue collar has little impact, but party sometimes affects mayor's ideology (insignificant a's and c's, mixed b's)
- the United States, where *race is powerful but class and party insignificant.*

Although policy preferences in France, Finland, and Norway are driven by parties and percent blue-collar residents, party is insignificant in the United States.[13] Consistent with our propositions about race and hierarchy in Chapter 2 and Clark (1994a, 1996), the most powerful factor explaining American mayors' policy positions is the percent of nonwhite residents: Mayors in cities with more nonwhite residents favor more government spending. Race is the American version of a class-based party, that is, race crystallizes mayors' policy preferences in America the way that class and party do in countries with stronger classes and parties. Race is the most visible and simplest indicator of hierarchy in American society. But take methodological note: We would have found no structure for the United States if we had only used party, as in Hout et al. (1995) for instance; this underlines the importance of including policy preferences along with party.[14]

What Kind of Hierarchy? Social or Political?

What is it about political systems that make some illustrate strong class politics, like France and Finland, and others far less? This is a central focus of the Chapter 2 propositions. But systematically testing them to interpret differences in party ideology and class salience, as identified in this chapter, is complex. Hierarchy is a powerful concept

here. More hierarchical institutions should generate antihierarchical politics. But as
hierarchy declines, so should antihierarchical politics. This comes from our Leveling
Principle (proposition #4) in Chapter 2. Its power here is in locating the context where
class politics should be strong and why it may decline: as hierarchy declines. It may be

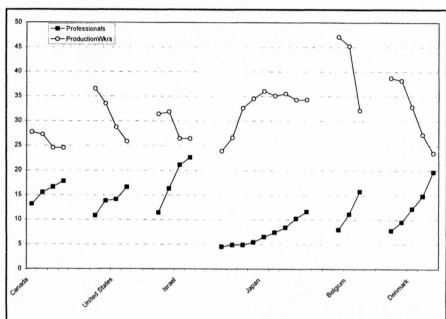

	Canada		United States		Israel		Japan		Belgium		Denmark	
	Profes-sionals	Production Wkrs	Profes-sionals	Production Wkrs	Profes-sionals	Production Wkrs	Profes-sionals	Production Wkrs	Profes-sionals	Production Wkrs	Profes-sionals	Production Wkrs
1951	7.1	38.4										
1960			10.8	36.5			4.5	23.9			7.8	38.7
1961	9.7	35.8			11.4	31.4			8	47.1		
1965							4.9	26.6			9.5	38.2
1970			13.8	33.5			6.5	36	11.1	45.2	12.2	32.8
1971	13.1	27.7										
1972					16.3	31.8						
1975							7.4	35.1				
1980			14.1	28.7			8.4	35.5				
1981	15.5	27.2			21.1	26.4			15.7	32.1	14.8	27.2
1983												
1985							10.2	34.3			19.7	23.5
1986	16.6	24.5										
1993	17.8	24.5	16.6	25.8	22.6	26.4	11.6	34.3				

Note: These charts on national workforce changes were compiled from data of the
International Labor Organization, which seeks to standardize national reports into internationally comparable categories. However, three sets of categories were used for the 1950-
1990s, which reduces comparability over time and across some countries (especially those in
Central Europe). The consistency of patterns that emerges practically everywhere, despite
obvious data inconsistencies, is striking testimony to the strength of the general trends.
    Source: ILO (1990, 1991, 1994, 1996).

BOX 4.15   Production Workers Fall and Professionals Rise as a Percentage of the
Total Work Force in Most Countries [Chart 1 of 3]

that France and Finland are more hierarchical societies, which in turn generates more class voting. This is consistent with many elements of their history and culture: the 1789 Revolution, battles by right parties against workers, bloody uprisings over the nineteenth and early twentieth century (and 1968!) that remain vivid even in recent

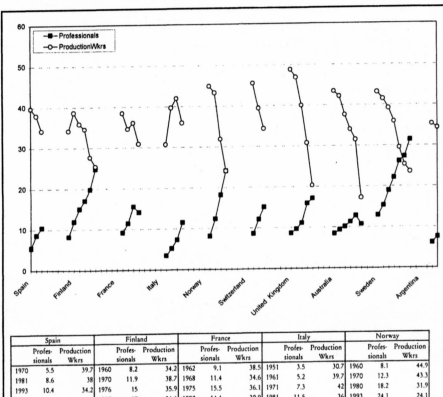

Spain			Finland			France			Italy			Norway		
	Profes-sionals	Production Wkrs		Profes-sionals	Production Wkrs		Profes-sionals	Production Wkrs		Profes-sionals	Production Wkrs		Profes-sionals	Production Wkrs
1970	5.5	39.7	1960	8.2	34.2	1962	9.1	38.5	1951	3.5	30.7	1960	8.1	44.9
1981	8.6	38	1970	11.9	38.7	1968	11.4	34.6	1961	5.2	39.7	1970	12.3	43.3
1993	10.4	34.2	1976	15	35.9	1975	15.5	36.1	1971	7.3	42	1980	18.2	31.9
			1980	17	34.6	1982	14.1	30.9	1981	11.5	36	1993	24.1	24.1
			1985	19.8	27.7									
			1993	24.8	25.4									

Switzerland			United Kingdom			Australia			Sweden			Argentina		
	Profes-sionals	Production Wkrs		Profes-sionals	Production Wkrs		Profes-sionals	Production Wkrs		Profes-sionals	Production Wkrs		Profes-sionals	Production Wkrs
1960	8.6	45.5	1961	8.6	48.8	1961	8.4	43.4	1960	12.9	43.2	1960	6.1	35.3
1970	12.1	39.4	1966	9.6	46.9	1966	9.3	42.2	1965	15.3	41.5	1970	7.5	34.3
1980	15.1	34.4	1971	11.1	40	1971	10.1	37.6	1970	18.9	39.2			
			1981	15.9	30.8	1976	11.3	34	1975	22.1	35.9			
			1993	17.1	20.3	1981	12.8	31.5	1980	26.1	29.5			
						1991	10.7	17.2	1985	27.3	25.3			
									1993	31.4	23.6			

Note: See base of Chart 1 for explanation.

BOX 4.15 Production Workers Fall and Professionals Rise as a Percentage of the Total Work Force in Most Countries [Chart 2 of 3]

popular history. Finland had great internal social conflicts, and many bloody incidents
that are still vivid. Still, quantifying the salience of these concerns for individual voters
and parties is complex. How can we measure hierarchy? Virtually every social and
political institution has some hierarchy, and people who vary in their social contacts
with each should thus be differentially affected by each. Such a broad formulation is
appropriate for social stratification in general, but we focus here on politics and class.
We can thus ask: Which institutions most affect the political process, especially class
politics versus the NPC and postindustrial politics? We consider briefly related litera-
tures, then empirical results.

Perspectives stressing economic and social bases of politics, from Karl Marx to
Seymour Martin Lipset's *Political Man* (1981), suggest using variables like occupation
and income of citizens. Following these ideas, we invested considerable effort acquir-

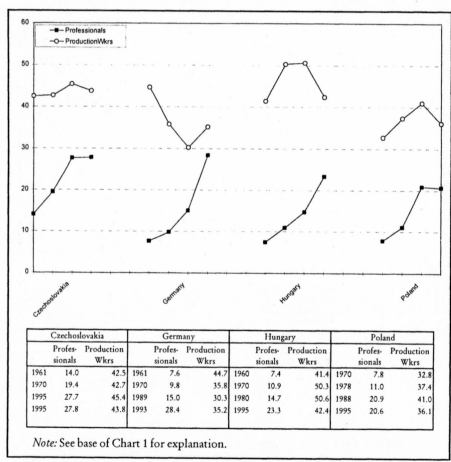

Czechoslovakia			Germany			Hungary			Poland		
	Profes- sionals	Production Wkrs		Profes- sionals	Production Wkrs		Profes- sionals	Production Wkrs		Profes- sionals	Production Wkrs
1961	14.0	42.5	1961	7.6	44.7	1960	7.4	41.4	1970	7.8	32.8
1970	19.4	42.7	1970	9.8	35.8	1970	10.9	50.3	1978	11.0	37.4
1995	27.7	45.4	1989	15.0	30.3	1980	14.7	50.6	1988	20.9	41.0
1995	27.8	43.8	1993	28.4	35.2	1995	23.3	42.4	1995	20.6	36.1

Note: See base of Chart 1 for explanation.

BOX 4.15   Production Workers Fall and Professionals Rise as a Percentage of the
Total Work Force in Most Countries [Chart 3 of 3]

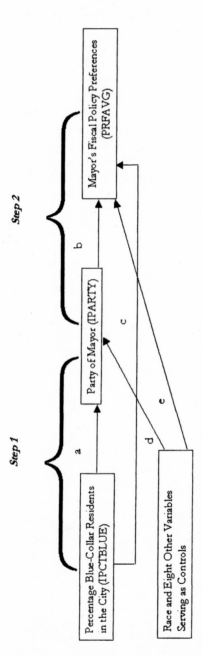

FIGURE 4.5   Why do Mayors Support Higher Spending? International Contrasts

Note: Class politics is measured by the strength of paths a, b, and c above, using data for mayors and their cities in seven countries. Three patterns emerge:

A. Strong class politics in France and Finland

Blue-collar residents elect left party mayors (strong path a), and left party mayors prefer more spending (strong path b).

Blue-collar mainly operates via paths a and b, but may have some direct effect on spending preference (path c).

B. Weak class but some party politics in Norway, Canda, Japan, and Australia

Insignificant a's and c's, mixed b's.

C. Race acts like class in the United States

Insignificant a, b, and c, but strong d and e paths from percentage nonwhite residents to party and policy preferences.

This figure summarizes multiple regressions to explain support by mayors for increased spending on an index of up to 13 municipal spending areas, PRFAVG. The same basic model was used in each country: Dependent variable: PRFAVG = Average spending preference of mayor on 13 FAUI items. Independent variables: LIPOPT = Log of city population; IMEANEDU = Mean level of education for the city's population; IPCINCT = Mean level of income for the city's population; IPCTSEC = Percent of the population in manufacturing; IPOP3544 = Percent of the population 35 to 44 years old; IPCTBLUE = Percent of the population who are blue-collar workers; IPARTY = Mayor's party position on 0–100 scale of left-right party ideology (low=left); IV144 = Age of mayor; CATHMY = Dummy variable for Catholic mayors (1=Catholic, 0=not); MAYED = Years of education for the mayor; MAYYRS = Years as mayor; FEMMAY = Dummy variable for female mayors (1=female, 0=male); FORNSTK = Percent of the population who are foreigners and/or immigrants.

Source: Fiscal Austerity and Urban Innovation Project surveys in each country. Data available for about 100 mayors in most countries.

ing data on inequality among citizens in many countries. We then computed measures of inequality using Atkinson's inequality indices. Data on inequality items varied considerably by country; for the United States we could create four: for education, income, occupation, and national origin of citizens. These provide clear measures that contrast small, socially homogenous towns (and low scores) with others like Chicago (and high inequality scores). These hierarchy/inequality measures performed powerfully for U.S. cities, as detailed in Clark (1994a, 1996). We found that even the deepest cleavage in American politics, race, could be localized and "explained away" by hierarchy. Let us clarify. Race explains much of the "left-right" ideological differences across American cities—a standard finding also in citizen voting behavior (e.g., in the Michigan tradition of Converse 1975 and Inglehart 1990). But this voting tradition builds largely on social psychological models and omits most of the social context surrounding political behavior. Stein Rokkan (e.g., 1967) did consider such contexts, and following his "minority" tradition we introduced our four hierarchy measures for each city to see if they might clarify the dynamics of race. Results were dramatic: Adding the four inequality indexes completely eliminated the importance of race in explaining group activities and related political processes (Clark 1996).

This result for U.S. cities provided a compelling test, and support, for the Leveling Principle. It encouraged us to pursue the same analysis in other countries. But it failed miserably outside the United States! That is, inequality among citizens in a city did *not* explain mayor's ideology and policy outside the United States. This contrast between the United States and other countries is clear in Table 4.6, where Atkinson inequality has strong effects in U.S. cities but is insignificant in all other countries. Why? The beginning of an answer is in the same Table 4.6, which shows that in contrast to the Atkinson result party effects are weak in the United States but strong in many other countries in explaining the mayor's ideology on a key issue: the degree of support for spending on social redistribution (public housing, public health, public welfare).[15] The

---

COLEMAN YOUNG, MAYOR OF DETROIT:

We are far from being the masters of our own destiny. We sure in hell don't control General Motors or Chrysler, Ford, or any of the major corporations that furnish jobs. We don't control insurance companies that charge us three times as much as they charge whites for automobile or home insurance. We don't control the businesses that have moved out of Detroit across Eight Mile Road and elsewhere in order to get away from blacks. Anybody who tells you something [different] is someone you ought to take a look at because that's a racist. Reminds of something that Martin Luther King said, "how do you expect us to pull ourselves up by a bootstrap when we don't have boots?". The mothaf..s stole our boots.

Source: *Washington Post*, March 31, 1989, section A, page 3.

HAROLD WASHINGTON, MAYOR OF CHICAGO:

Reagan and his mafia consider the cities a 'special interest group'. They believe we Democrats have 'bought' our constituents with social programs. They're determined to undermine us among the poor, minorities, students, working people, by cutting off funds to these folks. That's what the big spending cuts is all about. It sure as hell isn't about budget balancing. And it isn't that self-help bullshit. It's politics, period...

Source: Alton Miller, *Harold Washington*. Chicago: Bonus Books, 1989, p. 208.

BOX 4.16   How Have Leading Black Mayors Articulated Class and Race Issues?

TABLE 4.6   U.S. Cities Are Unique in Local Political Permeability

Part I: Dependent Variable:
Mayor's Redistributive Spending Preferences

	Effect of Atkinson Inequality of Education	Effect of Party
UNITED STATES	2.28 **	-1.11 ns
CANADA	1.52 ns	-0.22 ns
FRANCE	-2.14 **	-2.03 **
FINLAND	-0.10 ns	-9.10 ***
JAPAN	0.83 ns	-1.49 ns
NORWAY	-0.05 ns	-5.89 ***
AUSTRALIA	0.03 ns	-2.48 ***
ARGENTINA		0.05 ns
CZECH REPUBLIC		0.43 ns
SLOVAKIA		0.02 ns
GERMANY		-4.06 ***
ITALY		-2.08 **
BRITAIN		-3.05 ***
POLAND, 1988	0.89 ns	-1.23 ns
POLAND, 1991	-0.11 ns	-0.65 ns
ISRAEL		-0.13 ns

> *Only in the US does Inequality increase Mayors' spending preferences*

> *Parties drive policy in most countries, but not the US, Canada, or Eastern Europe*

Part II: Dependent Variable: Activity Level of All Local Groups

	Effect of Atkinso Inequality	Effect of Party
UNITED STATES	2.27 **	1.11 ns
CANADA	0.20 ns	-0.96 ns
FRANCE	0.05 ns	0.33 ns
FINLAND	0.90 ns	-1.06 ns
JAPAN	-1.12 ns	-1.64 ns
AUSTRALIA	-0.19 ns	0.30 ns
BELGIUM		-1.39 ns
GERMANY		-1.26 ns
ITALY		-1.96 *
BRITAIN		-0.49 ns
ISRAEL		-0.56 ns

> *The same inequality effect holds for organized groups as for mayor's spending preferences*

> *But parties are generally unrelated to local group activity levels, except in Italy where cities with Left parties also have more group activities*

Note: This table shows how different US cities are from those in most other countries in the permeability of the US political system to local social hierarchy. American cities with more inequality have mayors who favor more redistributive spending (Part I), and more active organized groups of all sorts seeking to affect the local political system (Part II). By contrast, parties have no consistent impact on these two items in the US. In most other countries, strong parties shape mayor's spending policies, and buffer mayors from the effects of social inequalities. This impermeability of the political system may in turn discourage groups from organizing locally. France shows the opposite pattern from the US, which seems explained by the importance of Communist and Socialist Parties in relatively low-income-homogeneous, working- class suburbs, the converse of the American affluent suburb.

The table highlights two contrasting causes of mayors' preferences for redistributive spending: 1. the Atkinson inequality index for education and 2. the Iparty score for each city. T-statistics are reported from a multiple regression which includes 12 independent variables, although just two are shown. The 12 include: Atkinson inequality, Iparty, media impact, mayor's age, mayor's years of education, female mayor dummy, proportion of population age 35-44, mean years of education of population. The first dependent variable is mayors' redistributive spending preferences (REDISTX); the second is the level of activities of all organized groups in the FAUI survey (business, unions, ethnic, neighborhood, etc., GRPACT). The same pattern holds when Atkinson Inequality of Income is used instead of Inequality of Education, but since the income data area available for fewer countries, education is shown here See Table 4.7 for income.

Right is high on the Iparty index, so negative coefficinets show that right party mayors prefer less spending. The t-statistic shows the magnitude of impact; its statistical significance is indicated by *** = sig. < .01 level, ** = sig. < .05, * = sig < .1, ns = not significant at .1 level.

Source: International FAUI Surveys; c\npc79.sps.

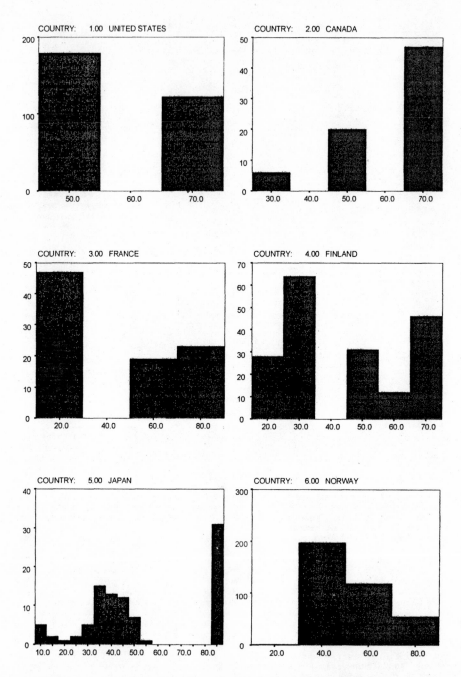

FIGURE 4.6   Countries Differ Considerably in the Range and Diversity of Parties Across the Left-Right Continuum

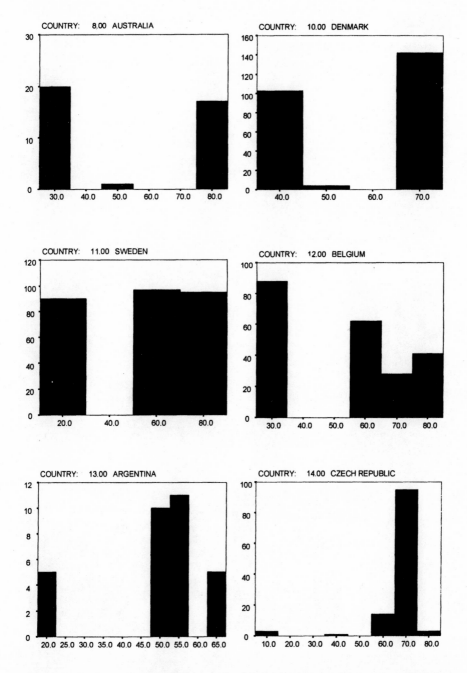

FIGURE 4.6 Countries Differ Considerably in the Range and Diversity of Parties Across the Left-Right Continuum

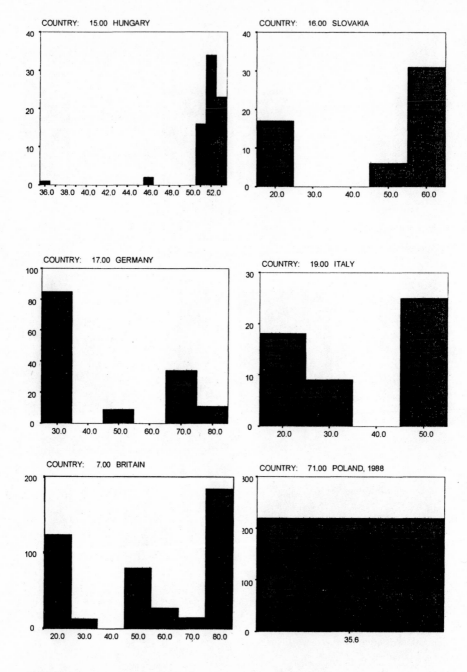

FIGURE 4.6 Countries Differ Considerably in the Range and Diversity of Parties Across the Left-Right Continuum

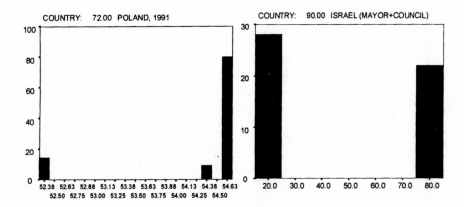

FIGURE 4.6   Countries Differ Considerably in the Range and Diversity of Parties Across the Left-Right Continuum

Note: The X values across the bottom are the IPARTY Left-Right scores that experts assigned each party. Right is high. The Y values up the side show the number of mayors in each party. Our SPSS graphics algorithm uses a different scale for each country, so note that while the two U.S. parties appear at the extremes, the Left-Right scores shown below them are closer to each other than for France and most other countries. The program did not calculate a histogram for parties with too few cases, so just two parties appear for Israel, although mayors are members of other parties.

Source: International FAUI Surveys.

Supreme Court Cases by Major Policy Area, 1933-1987						
Policy Area	*1933-37*	*1938-42*	*1943-47*	*1948-52*	*1953-57*	*1958-62*
Due process	5.20%	7.1	10.0	14.4	17.1	20.9
Equality	1.40%	1.0	2.7	4.9	5.1	5.2
Ordinary Economic	16.10%	8.0	5.9	5.9	5.3	4.0
Total N	792	764	659	507	490	593
Policy Area	*1963-67*	*1968-72*	*1973-77*	*1978-82*	*1983-87*	*Total (N)*
Due process	25.0	31.0	27.8	26.8	29.6	1,497
Equality	12.4	12.0	12.5	12.8	16.6	617
Ordinary Economic	3.6	2.8	2.6	2.8	2.9	416
Total N	659	717	836	793	749	7,559

Note: The percentages are computed vertically. For instance the top number on the left shows that   Due Process was 5.2 percent of all cases in 1933-37. These include cases that received one page or more in the *United State Reports.* Other categories such as foreign affairs are not shown here.

Source: Adapted from Pacelle (1991: 56-57).

BOX 4.17   The US Supreme Court Shifted in Cases Processed from "Ordinary Economic" to "Rights" Over the Last 50 Years

party systems look different indeed if one inspects the ideological range and distributions of parties inside each country. For a simple descriptive overview of these powerful differences, peruse the many different patterns in Figure 4.6. The X values across the bottom are the IPARTY Left-Right scores that experts assigned each party, Y values up the side show the number of mayors in each party. Contrast the United States, with two large parties both near the center (note that their scores are 50 and 70) with France and Finland, which have a wider range (from below 20 to over 80) and many parties scattered along the wide continuum.

Why is the United States different? It has more inequality than other countries, although higher levels of education and income (Table 4.7). These differences are in part due to greater ecological separation into legally distinct local governments in the United States than other countries, but U.S. inequality is similarly highest when calcu-

TABLE 4.7 The US Has the Most Inequality in Income and Education Among its Citizens, but Nearly the Highest Average Levels

	Atkinson Inequality of Education	Average Number of Yrs. of Education of Citizens	Atkinson Inequality of Income	Average Per Capita Income in US Dollars
UNITED STATES	32.24	12.12	79.01	$17,480
CANADA	32.36	12.40	79.88	14,120
FRANCE	15.32	9.78		10,720
FINLAND	25.77	10.30		12,160
JAPAN	25.18	11.34		12,840
NORWAY	20.50	9.77		15,400
AUSTRALIA	28.01	11.08	60.77	11,920
DENMARK	20.74	9.67	55.74	12,600
SWEDEN	16.72	10.47		13,160
BELGIUM				9,230
POLAND, 1988	5.51	9.45		
POLAND, 1991	5.62	9.49		

Note: The US and Poland stand at opposite extremes: the US is high in income and education, but also has the greatest inequalities. Poland is at the low end, although its educational attainment is very close to France and Norway. Most dramatic is Poland's equality of educational attainment (and lowest Atkinson score) of any country. The Atkinson Inequality Index is discussed further in the Appendix. These are national averages for cities in each country. Income data are lacking for several countries since the Atkinson indices require data for multiple income or educational levels, and most countries only disclose just average income by city, or no income data at all.

Source: FAUI international data files.

lated using national measures (Atkinson 1995, and see Boxes 4.20–4.23). Why should American cities be more sensitive to social inequality than cities in Europe or Japan? We sought, again, an answer generalizable across political systems.

A first hypothesis was that new leaders emerged more in the United States, like New Fiscal Populists (NFPs) who are socially liberal but fiscally conservative—identified in Clark and Ferguson (1983). Key to NFP emergence in the United States was their

---

Sam Eldersveld (1995) found a important deviant case: He enlightens us about America by showing how Ann Arbor is "un-American." It sharpens our thinking about political parties and democratic theory. The grand American tradition—the Federalist Papers/ Tocqueville/Almond/Verba/Putnam—stresses civic associations, not parties. American parties are often portrayed as a European peasant residue—for instance, the Merton/ Banfield/Wilson tradition stressed how parties helped the poor advance through patronage jobs and favors.

Eldersveld paints another picture. Unlike past work on local parties (usually studied in places like Chicago, Detroit or Gary), in Ann Arbor the parties are not the preserve of lower-status persons joined through patronage and favors. Instead the image is a squeaky-clean, highly activist, partisan government, where, yes, there is civic activism, but parties are the central participants. The city manager and staff are clearly subordinate to the parties. Unusual.

Parties are critical: We find careful documentation on how they help structure public issues, mobilize voters, link with civic and interest groups, and discipline elected officials. They recruit activists into politics in a manner more like the New England town meeting ideal of the League of Women Voters than the Chicago machine. When Abner Mikva was a law student at Chicago, he volunteered his services to the local party organization. They asked, "Who sent ya?" Answer: "Nobody." Reply: "We don't want nobody nobody sent." Such closed particularism (heightened by Irish Catholicism) is transformed in Ann Arbor into a more open and universalistic pattern. Politics is driven far more by policies and issues than the "non-ideological" parties of Chicago and Detroit ("What types of differences divide people here?" "Political views" answered 79% of Ann Arbor leaders compared to 19% in 25 other cities, p.178).

In the 1950s, business leaders and the Republican Party led in the council, but then the Democrats organized, and there has since been an actively competitive two-party system—which dramatically differentiates Ann Arbor from most U.S. cities. Eldserveld shows how the parties imitated each other in efforts to expand their voting base, although the most dramatic shift was in the 1970s when the Human Rights Party mobilized students and former students to turn out in vast numbers and brought young activists to power. Ann Arbor's council members have been young (in the 1970s 75% were under 40), often women (32% in the 1980s), and highly educated (75% had graduate degrees in the 1970s, 51% in the 1980s).

Does all this partisan activity make a difference? The turnout rates are not much above the U.S. average, but trust is. This is important for current debates by Putnam, Lipset, and others on the decline of confidence in all political institutions (e.g. in the *Journal of Democracy* 1995). For not only do Ann Arbor residents report "trust in local government to do what is right just about always or most of the time" (71% in Ann Arbor, 55% nationally)—More: they report "trust in the government in Washington to what is right just about always or most of the time" (50% in Ann Arbor, 29% nationally). Some differences from the national average are due simply to demographic composition (of Ann Arbor having a disproportionately highly educated, professional population), but some is probably also a spillover from the positive specifics of Ann Arbor partisan democracy.

BOX 4.18   Yes, America Has a Few Strong Parties

Our Atkinson Inequality indices for cities around the world show that U.S. cities have the most inequality of any country in our survey (Table 4.7). When the same indices are computed for citizens using national data, results are essentially identical (Atkinson 1995; Yi 1997). A decade or two ago many (U.S. and European) observers would interpret this as indicating America's "late" historical development of a welfare state. But with globalization and new recognition of market pressures, some ask if such inequality may point the way for other countries too. If so, then why? Saskia Sassen offers a bold statement from her detailed study of New York, London, and Tokyo. She chose the three as "global cities" and sought to identify recent changes in their economies and residential patterns linked to global economic developments. She assembled considerable original data on growth and decline in income and occupational shifts, by separate subindustries and neighborhoods and holds that they fit a common trend that spells more inequality.

I will examine to what extent the new structure of economic activity has brought about changes in the organization of work, reflected in a shift in the job supply and polarization in the income distribution and occupational distribution of workers. Major growth industries show a greater incidence of jobs at the high-and-low paying ends of the scale than do the older industries now in decline. Almost half the jobs in the producer services are lower-income jobs, and half are two highest earnings classes. In contrast, a large share of manufacturing workers were in the middle-earnings jobs during the postwar period of high growth in these industries in the United states and United Kingdom.

The expansion of low-wage jobs as a function of growth trends implies a reorganization of the capital-labor relation. To see this it is important to distinguish the characteristics of jobs from their sectoral location, since highly dynamic, technologically advanced growth sectors may well contain low-wage dead-end jobs. Furthermore, the distinction between sectoral characteristics and sectoral growth patterns is crucial: Backward sectors, such as downgraded manufacturing or low-wage service occupations, can be part of major growth trends in a highly developed economy. It is often assumed that backward sectors express decline trends. Similarly, there is a tendency to assume that advanced sectors, such as finance, have mostly good, white-collar jobs. In fact, they contain a good number of low-paying jobs, from cleaner to stock clerk.

These, then, are the major themes and implications of my study. (Sassen 1991: 9-10).

BOX 4.19   Inequality: The United States Leads the World, but London and Tokyo Are Close . . . Why?

reaction against traditional hierarchies, especially of political parties and interest groups like business and unions. NPC leaders saw these as mere "factions" in James Madison's sense of a selfish special interest pressing governments toward narrow benefits and wasteful programs. Citizens, by contrast, were the focus of NFPs, in their new rhetoric and processes of governance—such as stressing the media, surveys, and public meetings—hence we termed them "populists." President Bill Clinton, especially in his campaigns, illustrated this well. He abandoned most of the traditional welfare-state commitment of the Democratic Party, stressing instead the market and socially-liberal issues like racial tolerance, abortion and gay rights, even imposing these policies inside that most hierarchical of institutions, the military (See Box 4.12 on Greenberg). Social issues rose in salience in the U.S. in citizen surveys, leaders' speeches, and court decisions (e.g., Box 4.17). Yet as we reviewed salient new leaders in the 1980s and survey evidence from citizens (cf. Rempel and Clark 1997), outside the United States we found that many leaders and citizens endorsed socially liberal issues and participatory procedures but not always fiscal conservatism. Consequently, we broke up the NFP components. In formulating the NPC as a variant of the American NFP we thus stressed less

Whether inequality is increasing and just how much and where remains controversial. Inequality is linked for some to the decline of union power that began in the early 1970s and to growing economic instability, mass unemployment, and related "post-Fordist" restructuring processes (Aglietta 1987). Central to economic restructuring is the growing prevalence of small firms (Brown 1990; Hardiman 1990). Small firms grew salient in the early 1970s (Birch 1979), just as unions began to decline. Small firms are more apt to hire part-time or temporary workers, given small firms' sensitivity to short-term economic fluctuations (Baron 1984; Beck, Horan, and Tolbert 1978). In the United States, harder bargaining with unions and reduced wages and benefits grew more common in the 1980s as large-firm employers made explicit arguments that they had to respond to competition by smaller firms domestically and to global competition internationally. Workers in automobile, steel, and other industries often accepted "givebacks," inconceivable a decade or so earlier. In the 1990s these same issues sparked major strikes in Western Europe. Some researchers stress other aspects of small firms in the postindustrial transition: lower wages and less satisfactory jobs. Harrison and Bluestone (1988) and Harrison (1994) suggest that postindustrial *service* growth (e.g., in small firms) has been more in menial, unsatisfying jobs than in high-technology industries, as Bell (1973) maintains. However, on this point, research by Esping-Andersen (1994) indicates that the specific postindustrial sectors that grew the most varies greatly by country. In general, from analyzing changes in jobs and income in the United States, Germany, and Sweden from the 1960s to 1980, Esping-Andersen reports that postindustrial service growth more often produces a job *upgrading* and *declining* job polarization. This suggests that any deleterious effects on workers remain more subtle than some maintain. The nature of postindustrial *service* labor represents a decided upgrading from the past. His findings thus conflict with those of Sassen, leading one to wonder if Sassen focused too much on a certain real tendency in New York City, but which may not be generalizable. Still, labor in advanced industrial societies remains more temporary or part-time and more in small firms than in the past; such conditions pose new barriers to the ability of service *and* traditional manufacturing workers to promote economic and political interests concerning employment stability, health care and other job benefits, and social welfare protections for the unemployed. To conclude: The evidence and, still more, the interpretations stand in conflict. One way to contextualize the various findings is to assess their meanings for politics and for average citizens. The next boxes do this.

BOX 4.20   Inequality—Conflicting Evidence

fiscal policy preferences and more social liberalism and new processes of decisionmaking. We next consider this conceptual reformulation..

Do National Parties Always Constrain Mayors?

How refocus the hierarchy analysis to interpret both U.S. and non-U.S. patterns? Building on the findings above, that parties are more salient in most other countries, we next asked how might new leaders act if much of their battle to innovate was *inside* their own parties? That is, extending the NFP concept, we pursued the idea of the new entrepreneurial leader but sought to capture how he/she might specifically adapt to an environment of strong, constraining national parties—typical of most of the world. For instance, new mayors in France surfaced in the 1980s that we studied with our French FAUI team (Balme et al. 1987). Similar mayors were identified in other coun-

Equality is a powerful value in politics across the globe. How to reconcile it with observed inequality, especially in U.S. cities, which have the greatest inequalities of any major country? Americans stress individual "rights" in a quasilegal sense that persons in other countries often misinterpret. The meaning comes from the eighteenth-century tradition of John Locke and the American Founding Fathers who stressed that a critical right is *equality of opportunity*, guaranteed in the U.S. Constitution. But it has been in conflict with *equality of achievement*, which especially since the 1960s has been stressed by disadvantaged groups in the United States and elsewhere. American cities have more obvious poverty than most anywhere in Europe or Japan, compounded by racial conflict.

In 1996, chief executive officers of major American corporations earned about 200 times more than factory workers; in the 1970s they earned only 30 times more (National Public Radio broadcast, April 10, 1997). Yet of the ten most highly paid Americans in 1996, four were African-Americans: Michael Jackson, the singer; Michael Jordan and Magic Johnson, basketball players; and Oprah Winfrey, TV talk show hostess. All four illustrate self-proclaimed NPC patterns in that they came from modest backgrounds, worked hard as individuals, and achieved fame and fortune in "the entertainment industry." Their success depends on social liberalism of whites and reflects the enormous time and money that many Americans spend on leisure/entertainment activities rather than traditional production.

Seymour Martin Lipset (1996: 74–76) has contrasted tensions in America between achievement and equality: *The American commitment to equality of opportunity implies that achievement should reflect ability, justifies higher differentials in reward and rejects taxing the successful to upgrade the less advantaged. Europeans reared in postfeudal societies which assumed hereditary disadvantage and noblesse oblige find the idea that those with higher incomes should pay larger proportions of taxes much more acceptable than do Americans...economic inequality as measured by the ratio of income of the richest 20 percent of households to the poorest 20 percent is greater in America (11 times) than in all the other developed OECD countries, with Japan, at the other extreme with a ratio of 4. Other more egalitarian countries are Sweden Belgium, and Holland, with ratios of 4.5 to 5.5. Britain, Canada, France, and Italy fall in between, at 6 and 7. A 1995 New York Times review of research in this area reiterated that wealth is more concentrated in the United States than in other industrial democracies. Measuring concentration of wealth on a rising scale of zero to one, the U.S at 0.34, outranks Italy (0.31). Canada (0.29), Germany (0.25), France (0.25), and Finland (0.21). The top-earning 20 percent of Americans control 80 percent of the national wealth, while the lowest-earning 20 percent earn only 5 percent of all income. It cites the findings of economics professor Edward N. Wolff that "We are the most unequal industrialized country in terms of wealth."*

BOX 4.21   Interpreting Inequality: Major Sociocultural Differences

tries, like Denmark (Mouritzen 1992: 1–3). One salient aspect of the French new mayors was their challenging the national parties with new initiatives. The French "cumul" laws permit mayors to serve simultaneously in the national government, such that Jacques Chirac was simultaneously mayor of Paris and prime minister; many French mayors have long held seats in the National Assembly and are active in both national and local party organizations. The fear of being expelled from a party is serious for local officials in most countries. How then can they innovate? One view is that change only occurs at the top in centralized systems like the French (as Crozier 1967 argued), but we were skeptical as we saw many French local officials struggling to change their policies and their parties' programs. Some of the most dramatic changes

	Strongly Agree/ Agree the Government Should Provide a Job for Everyone		Agree Strongly/ Agree the Government Should Provide a Decent Standard of Living for the Unemployed		Agree Strongly/ Agree the Government Should Provide Everyone with a Guaranteed Basic Income	
	High Income	Low Income	High Income	Low Income	High Income	Low Income
United States	32	61	23	52	12	33
Great Britain	44	73	57	74	47	71
West German	77	84	61	72	45	66
Netherlands	60	82	57	68	39	58
Italy	70	93	55	76	53	80

Note: These are from national surveys of citizens.

Source: Adapted from Karlyn H. Keene and Everett C. Ladd, "America: A Unique Outlook?" *The American Enterprise*, 1 (March-April 1990), p. 118.

One must stress that despite exceptions like Michael Jordan, African-Americans have enjoyed much less success than other Americans, such that the proportion of nonwhite residents in a city was the prime force driving their leaders to advocate greater redistribution (Clark 1996).

BOX 4.22   How Much Should Governments Attack Inequality? Attitudes on Responsibility In Different Areas (Percent)

worldwide started in France, which stands as the archetypal centralized state. Thus, it is important to examine for how the NPC emerged there. It illuminates change dynamics in centralized systems.

Francois Mitterand took power nationally in 1980 in a coalition with the Communists. They nationalized banks and many industries, pursuing a strong socialist program. (See quotes in Box 4.8.) Fiscal problems followed rapidly, as did negative reactions in the polls. Many entrepreneurial leaders then presented themselves as mayoral candidates in center and right parties (and a few in the Socialist Party). They sought to differentiate themselves from traditional party leaders by their youthful enthusiasm, use of citizen meetings, and an often vague but politically effective call for new programs and policies. A dozen or more *Nouvels Maires* like Alain Carignon, mayor of Grenoble, were thus elected, and over the 1980s they increasingly rivaled the traditional leadership of the national parties. They selectively embraced elements of the NPC, responding to changes in French society that moved in this direction. These new mayors were studied by our French FAUI participants in detailed case studies of locations like Caen and Nimes. A nationally salient example was Mayor Bousquet of Nimes, president of the Cacherel designer company who defeated a long-time Com-

Proposition: Strong parties, we hypothesize, buffer their political systems from social cleavages, like inequality of education or income.

We illustrate the general point by contrasting two political systems:

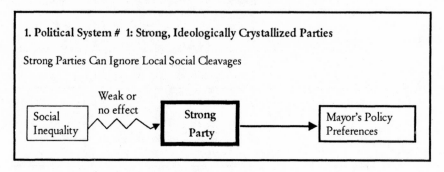

1. Political System # 1: Strong, Ideologically Crystallized Parties

Strong Parties Can Ignore Local Social Cleavages

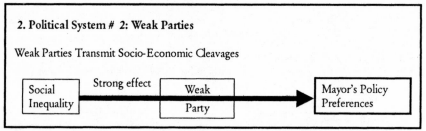

2. Political System # 2: Weak Parties

Weak Parties Transmit Socio-Economic Cleavages

FIGURE 4.7   Is the US Really Unique? How Parties Shift Effects of Socio-Economic Characteristics

Note: This more general proposition should interpret the US "uniqueness" in Table 4.6 by identifying party strength as a more general explanation

munist to become mayor (Becquart-Leclercq et al. 1987). He was fiscally conservative, anti-union, and privatized refuse collection—precipitating union violence. But he was explicitly liberal on the most controversial social issue in France, immigration, actively supporting Muslim immigrants to Nimes—a taboo policy for most mayors and parties. Several French New Mayors later had legal problems, such as accepting contributions from improper sources, which may have reflected their ambitious and aggressive entrepreneurship, lack of party funds for campaigns, and efforts by more traditional leaders to destroy them.

These mayors engaged others in their parties over central ideological issues. Indeed the party itself became the critical battleground for many mayors. As proposition #7 states: *The more ideologically coherent and structurally hierarchical are the political parties, the less likely the emergence of the New Political Culture.* A graphical version of this idea is in Figure 4.7, which illustrates Proposition #7 with two extreme examples of strong and weak parties.

Past empirical work on local parties, by Banfield and others, was largely American and focused little on programs and more on party organizations and material incentives. Initial work with the FAUI data by Miranda (1994) and Hoffmann-Martinot (this volume) similarly measured party strength with organizational items. However, we also posed several policy preference items in the FAUI surveys of mayors and council members. How analyze them to capture some dynamics of the French entrepreneurial mayors battling national parties? Our idea was as follows. To capture how much mayors deviated from their national parties, we started with the FAUI survey of policy preferences of all mayors in each country. We used the two basic policy preference items analyzed above, fiscal liberalism (PRFAV) and social conservatism (SOCCONS), and for each created a national average for each party. We then compared each individual mayor's policy positions to those of other mayors in his party by computing a "policy distance" measure: subtracting the individual mayor's position from the national mean of all mayors in his party. This is conceptually analogous to a "loss function" in the public choice tradition from Anthony Downs (1957) and others, except that we deal with mayors, not citizens, by party. The basic idea can be restated in a simple equation:

$$\text{(1) Mayor's Policy Distance} = \left| \begin{array}{ccc} \text{Mayor's Policy Position} & - & \text{National Average} \\ \text{(for each mayor)} & & \text{(for all mayors in} \\ & & \text{that party)} \end{array} \right|$$

This gives us a Policy Distance Score (DPRFAV) for each mayor in each country, computed as an "absolute value" ignoring plus or minus signs, since our concern was the magnitude of the deviation, not its direction.

Next we add the idea of party organizational strength, following the notion that the stronger the party, the harder it is for the mayor to pursue and implement "deviant" ideas. Conversely, the weaker the party is organizationally, the easier it should be for the mayor to pursue and implement new ideas and policies.

Methodologically, we incorporate these considerations by weighting the policy distance measure (from equation 1) by the reciprocal of the strong party organization index (SPOIX):

$$\text{(2) Strong Policy Distance (SPD)} = \text{Mayors' Policy Distance} * 5/\text{SPOIX}$$

The five was added simply because the mean score for policy distance from equation (1) was five times less than that of SPOIX. The SPOIX and SPD indexes are contrasted by country in Table 4.8.

Two country groups are clear: first, the United States, Canada, and Australia, with weak parties, more independent mayors, and correspondingly high SPD scores; second are the West European countries, with generally dominant parties. Still, each country holds important variations, indicated in the standard deviations. How does SPD work?

Buffering by parties, we hypothesize, *is strongest for mayors ideologically closest to their national parties and when these parties are organizationally strong.* (This extends the logic of

TABLE 4.8   Strong Party Organization and Strong Policy Distance, National Means

	Strong Party Organization index	*Strong Policy Distance Index*5*
	SPOIX	SPD*5
UNITED STATES	23.66	27.08
CANADA	12.89	· 36.79
AUSTRALIA	23.58	30.43
FRANCE	79.92	7.02
FINLAND	72.61	3.05
JAPAN	60.73	2.73
ISRAEL	62.85	12.57
GERMANY	68.34	2.60
ITALY	70.76	6.77
ISRAEL	62.93	7.94

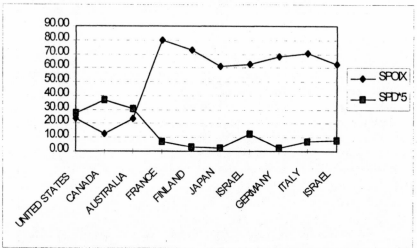

Note: These are national means of the Strong Party Organization Index (SPOIX) and Strong Policy Distance Index (SPD*5). SPD is a combination of ideological distance and party organizational strength for each mayor, following equation (2) in the text. A high SPD score shows that a mayor is distant from his national party on fiscal and social policy issues, and that his party is organizationally weak. Two sets of countries emerge clearly on both indexes: US, Canada, and Australia, with weak parties and mayors with higher ideological distance, and the other countries (Western Europe, Japan, and Israel) with strong parties and mayors who deviate less in ideology from national party programs. SPD is multiplied by five in the chart to make the scores more comparable to those of SPOIX.

Source: FAUI International Data files.

Leveling hierarchy and citizen/consumer responsiveness are major trends for both U.S. governments and business. Heroes in business magazines like *Fortune* and *Business Week* are executives like Bill Gates of Microsoft, whose highly egalitarian management style has shaken traditional corporate boardrooms. General Motors and even IBM have been eclipsed by Microsoft and the small Silicon Valley firms that challenge established hierarchies. The big firms have worked hard to change. Similar themes are discussed in Europe, but research on effects is limited. One study from the Harvard Business School on changes from 1977–1992 in the Fortune 100 (largest U.S. corporations) found:

    * *In terms of size, most firms became leaner and flatter. They downsized, delayered, and restructured, usually with the stated purpose of becoming less hierarchical and more network-like. Yet layoffs were not always effective. They had a positive effect on performance only if they went beyond being just reductions in headcount and were instead occasions for radical restructuring.*

    * *There was a clear trend towards active as opposed to passive corporate governance. Management performance was more actively monitored and CEO turnover was common. Forced CEO turnover had, on average, positive consequences for firm performance, suggesting the value of a more active corporate governance regime.*

    * *There was a concerted effort to change the firm's culture. Over 90% of the firms adopted formal total quality management practices as a way to change their firm's culture and become more open, participative, and responsive to customers needs. But not all these initiatives paid-off. The best results came to those who moved early and stayed committed to their change initiative* (Nohria 1996: 1-2).

These results come from analyzing value added to the firm from 1977 to 1997 using seven variables in regressions, which shows that several factors, including Total Quality Management, have independent positive impacts.

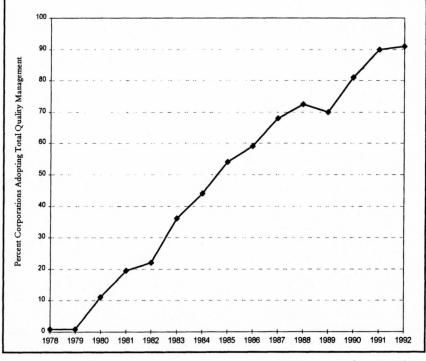

BOX 4.23   Corporate Culture Shift

proposition #7 from Chapter 2.) Mayors in such locales should be less sensitive to specifically local cleavages and concerns and respond more to party-endorsed national policies. We test for such party buffering effects by estimating regressions like those in the models used above to estimate Table 4.1 but compute them separately using the split-halves technique. That is, we divided all mayors in each country into two halves on the Strong Policy Distance measure: the low half closest to their national party ideologically and with strong parties, the second half most distant and with weak parties. This permits us to test the impact of different factors on local policy. The buffering hypothesis can be tested by comparing the coefficients for two sets of mayors: entrepreneurial mayors should respond more to local cleavages, since they have sought the freedom to deviate from the national parties and probably depend more on local input for their policies; the other half of the mayors, closer to their national parties, which give them more ideas and organizational support, therefore "need" local support less and should thus respond less to local cleavages and concerns. This idea is presented graphically in Figure 4.7.

A hot, continuing issue is how to implement the social concerns of the New Political Culture. When discrimination is visible, the solution is simple: treat everyone equally. But for persistent social inequalities, such as gender, class, and race, what to do is much harder. Especially when helping disadvantaged groups directly conflicts with universalism, or "market principles" of treating all equally. Here ideology enters in complex ways; leaders clearly vary in their tradeoffs among equality versus achievement in general, but even on the left the more specific, harder choices concern policies which may favor more equality of opportunity *versus* equality of achievement. Although Bill Clinton and the U.S. Democrats embraced individualism in some areas, "affirmative action" remained highly controversial through the 1990s. Here is a revealing case that illustrates the powerful commitment of the Democratic Party on these matters.

The Democrats' Quota System

In dealing with affirmative action, President Clinton has apparently seized on the slogan "reflect, don't retreat" while he awaits the findings of a bipartisan commission. But before he embarks on yet another timid assertion of presidential leadership, President Clinton would be wise to reflect on the presidential nominating rules of his own party. There the full extent of the Democratic party's institutional commitment to race and gender preferences underscores the likely failure of any affirmative action commission that the president might appoint.

Delegate selection rules for the 1996 Democratic National Convention provide that the national and state Democratic parties must "adopt and implement affirmative action programs with specific goals and timetables" for five minority groups: African-Americans, Hispanics, Native Americans, Asian/Pacific Americans and women. While the rules profess to prohibit quotas, each state delegation, and the convention as a whole, must be divided equally between male and female participants. Moreover, at-large seats are "reserved" for members of the above named minority groups to meet the representation "goals" typically established by a demographic study of the Democratic electorate in each state.

While these rules started as a commendable effort to ensure minority participation, in practice they are enforced with the rigidity of quotas. Indeed, during the 1992 Clinton campaign, I found myself in the uncomfortable position of assisting Mr. Clinton's delegate selection team, like all of its Democratic counterparts, in counting the number of women, African-Americans, Asians, Hispanics and other party-sanctioned minority groups.

BOX 4.24   Social Quotas and Equality: What to Do?

What did we find? Our key socioeconomic hierarchy measures are the Atkinson inequality indexes of education and income. Recall that inequality was insignificant in impact on mayors' spending preferences in each country except in the United States (in Table 4.6). This is what led us to try to explain why the United States was distinct. Here is the answer. When we divided cities into halves on Mayors' Policy Distance (SPD) the results were consistent with this emerging interpretation. That is, we found that Atkinson inequality among citizens had more impact on mayors' policy preferences in cities with *high* SPD scores—those cities where mayors are more distant from their national party and parties are organizationally weaker—just as we expect (Table 4.A4). By contrast, for the other half of the cities—those with mayors *low* on SPD and thus *closer* to their national parties—Atkinson inequality among citizens has less impact on the mayor's policy preferences. This pattern holds in four of the six countries for which we had data (Table 4.A4 in the Appendix). When we computed the same analysis with just SPOIX, results were far weaker; that is, the combination of party strength plus

---

Consider a typical example: A state is allotted 100 convention delegates. Seventy-five of these delegates must be elected at the district or caucus level. The remaining 25 "at large" delegates are held in reserve pending a final examination of the gender, ethnic and racial characteristics of the 75 delegates elected at the district level. Although any Democrat is eligible to run for these delegates positions, the rules mandate that the district delegates be evenly divided between men and women. Consequently, in a district with 10 delegates, if the voters elect eight male and two female delegates, the party rules dictate that three male delegates be replaced with three female delegates.

The state party must then tally the ethnic, gender and racial characteristics of all the district delegates. If the tally shows that the makeup does not match the state's representation "goals," then the state's "at-large" delegates are "cherry-picked" from among those individuals possessing the group attributes necessary to bring the entire delegation into compliance with affirmative action criteria.

Ostensibly, the purpose of these rules is to encourage those groups who have historically been under represented in the party. But rather than provide for equal opportunities, the Democratic Party's rules—as my own experience revealed—dictate equal outcomes based on race and sex. In short, convention delegates are increasingly selected on the basis of their status as members of defined groups, rather than as individuals with unique ideological principles, commitments and beliefs.

And there is no limit to those who qualify for "minority" status. The New York Democratic party's 1992 affirmative action plan, for example, guaranteed niches for, among others, African-Americans, Latinos, Asian/Pacific Americans, Native Americans, women, people with a high school education or less, the physically handicapped, and lesbians and gays.

These quotas can't simply be dismissed as the work of a voluntary organization. The Democratic Party, like the Republican, receives millions of dollars in Taxpayer funds. Were there any delegates with the courage—and standing—to challenge the system, the federal courts might well find the Democratic Party's use of federal dollars to promote racial and gender set-asides to be in violation of both Title VI and VII of the civil rights law. Even more important, however, the Democratic Party's nominating rules embody the ideological commitment of the party and presumably its leader, Bill Clinton, to race and gender set-asides. Until President Clinton revamps these rules, not much credence can be given to his promise for an honest review of this country's affirmative action policies.

Mr. Friedman was the deputy general counsel to the 1992 Clinton campaign. He is an attorney in Washington (Friedman 1995).

BOX 4.24 *(continued)*

Background: When Vincent Hoffmann-Martinot was at Harvard, we had lunch in Cambridge with a militant New England ecologist (my cousin Chalmers Hardenberg), and Jean-Yves Nevers, visiting from France. Chalmers talked of ecological terrorism, like traveling to Norway to sink whaling boats in their own harbors in the thick of night. Who did this and why? Where and why is ecology successful? The two Frenchmen kept probing about fund raising, staff-organization, and similar secular questions. Chalmers interrupted: "You are asking the wrong questions. To understand the deep ecology movement, you need to understand New Age religion." This floored the Frenchmen: "Qu'est-ce que c'est le New Age?" We talked about it for weeks, pursuing it with Lincoln Quillian, who grew up in Irvine, California (in Orange County, see chapter 8), and had attended a summer school called Pegasus which exposed him to New Age activists. He offers some remarkable insights, including why Irvine citizens joined their militant ecologist Mayor Larry Agran, in organizing chains of people holding hands to stop all traffic at rush hour on the Orange County expressways. They wanted fewer people. Donald Rosdil, an expert on radical-left-progressive American cities, maintained that Agran was one of the most successful militant-ecologist mayors in America. He organized an international association of (not too many) cities to pursue more powerful ecological agendas. Who would join him in demonstrations, and why? Voici le New Age:

Rather like "Christianity" or "liberal", the term "New Age" describes not so much a uniform and coherent set of beliefs as a diverse and overlapping group of ideas and practices that extend from the border of popular psychology to beliefs in the supernatural. What is usually described as "New Age" includes adherents of acupuncture, herbal medicine, reincarnation, meditation, massage, auras and colors, hypnosis, yoga, astrology, palmistry, clairvoyance, numerology, astral projection, and organic foods (to name but a few). These beliefs sometimes conflict and are not the province of any single organized group or groups; nevertheless, these practices tend to appear side-by-side in new age magazines, and disciples of one branch of new age are often familiar with others.

Despite such diversity of belief, I would argue that there are certain themes common to most forms of new age belief. Most notably New Age beliefs share a holistic perspective on the self and the world. New agers (my term) tend to believe that there is a sort of ultimate oneness between the self and the cosmos: many of the exercises practiced by different branches of new age are attempts to give the individual a sense of better connectedness with the universe, and so to empower the individual by providing a better understanding or ability to tap into some sort of ultimate force of nature. Yoga, for example, is an exercise that helps the new age discipline begin to sense the connections, and the ultimate oneness (in new age terms), between the mind (or spirit) and the body. Acupuncture leads towards a similar goal. Herbal medicine and traditional remedies stress the connectedness between nature and the body; beliefs in reincarnation manifest the belief that there are spiritual continuities between generations; the belief in psychics demonstrates the connection between the mind and physical reality. It is little wonder that with such holistic perspectives new agers should be supporters of strong environmental protection - they would describe those who willfully pollute as lacking a consciousness of their own connectedness to nature. To pollute is one example of having lost sight of the whole of existence, focusing instead on only the parts. As the *Daily Aspectarian*, Chicago's new age magazine, says of "workaholics": "They must learn to relax their attachment to the details and start embracing the unity of existence, or suffer health complications. Often times, there are periods of retreat and time away from community involvement to redefine one's service to something higher than money, a job and one's business." That something higher involves knowing the linkages between self and universe. Such knowing is achieved through introspection; it is usually a turning inward, such as that manifest in yoga or meditation, that is the correct path to this ultimate knowledge. For all of its emphasis on connectedness and the whole of existence, new age manifests a distinctly individualistic orientation.

If there seems to be a connection with sixties drug culture, of course there is. But the "drug" element in most sects of new age is absent, as it is recognized that drugs may be ultimately harmful. Further, there is little of

BOX 4.25   Ecology and the New Age Militants: Some Brief Ethnography and a Conceptual Postscript

the confrontationalism and angry renunciation that accompanied the drug counterculture: new age practitioners by and large lead normal, often "yuppie", lives. New age believers congregate at occasional conferences, seminars, classes, retreats, and organic food stores. Together they support an industry that profits by selling crystals (used as focal points for meditation - a pickup from American Indians), herbs and incense; bringing Hindu holy men to the states to lead classes in meditation, self-understanding and yoga; and publishing New Age books and magazines (including Shirley McClaine's book on remembering her past lives - a bestseller).

Despite all their unconventional beliefs, new age adherents are not necessarily anti-technology. There is an acceptance of work and material needs; conventional medicine is accepted by most new age practitioners but it is thought to deal only with one facet of bodily health. Herbal and New Age medicine, on the other hand, is through to treat the whole person. Similarly there is little enmity between believers of different new age ideas. New agers generally accept that others may need to follow their own paths to interpersonal and interpsychic understanding. Indeed, there is a strong de-emphasis of competition and confrontation in new age. New age games are designed precisely to be non-competitive, and often to increase trust among participants. For example, games where groups of people form a long sort of snake-like line and close their eyes, and have to keep them closed while their group leader leads them around obstacles; or games where people learn to relax and fall down, trusting that their partner in the game will catch them. Some of these games border on mass hypnosis. One of the most popular games at Pegasus was "energy ball", which involves forming a circle with of twenty to thirty people with one person at the center. Everyone closes their eyes and a group leader gradually encourages everyone to visualize a giant ball of energy made up of positive emotions or energy. They visualize the ball moving toward and ultimately engulfing the person in the center. The idea is that the person in the middle is spiritually rejuvenated by the positive energy transmitted by the others.

Unsurprisingly, New Age has borrowed from religions of the far east and the practices of American Indians. But probably the most pervasive influence is from South Asia: Buddhism, Hinduism and Jainism have left lasting marks on new age beliefs - Yoga, meditation, and the ultimate place and oneness of all are adopted from Hinduism. This influence is left, however, only selectively, since elements of these religions not consistent with the holistic-oneness orientation of new age are dropped. The ascetic ethic of the holy men of north India, for example, is adopted by new age groups in only limited ways, and the emphasis on ritual purity/impurity central to caste is nowhere in new age. There is a sort of individualistic twist that most Hindu beliefs lack in the concern with the specialness of the individual self (each having its unique aura) that is echoed in the fact that discovering this ultimate reality is usually a process of turning inward and unlocking one's hidden potential - a process of personal growth.

I am not sure when one would say that new age started, but it achieved large proportions only in the 1980s. Some pockets of new age belief assert that a sweeping change in world consciousness is imminent: that a new consciousness that recognizes the interconnectedness of all is sweeping the globe (or at least the United States). However exaggerated some of these claims may be, the growth in new age belief through the 80s has been undeniable. No doubt they have had at least some political impact. For what New Age and Larry Agran have broadly in common are their holistic concerns - evident in Agran's focus on national and world issues (his "Center for Innovative Diplomacy") and the environment (ozone protection legislation, and Agran's volunteers giving away small plants door-to-door as a reminder to preserve Irvine's environment). Although they lack Agran's pragmatic political orientation, I would guess the New Age community in Irvine supports Agran overwhelmingly.

Lincoln Quillian

This New Age outlook overlaps with pantheistic or naturalistic philosophy of the early leader of the American Sierra Club, John Muir, and more recently the deep ecology of Dave Foreman, co-founder of Earth First! The grizzly bear, the wolf and the spruce tree had as much right to exist for them as human beings. That natural order itself is sacrosanct. "Until we learn to respect these others as our equals, we will be strangers and barbarians on Earth." (Foreman 1991: 192; cf. Fox 1981).

BOX 4.25 *(continued)*

ideology add considerable power to the analysis. We thus commend this sort of approach to others.

How should IPARTY behave in the split halves analysis? Recall that IPARTY is our international left-right party score, and following traditional class politics, we expect left parties to support more redistribution. They do in some countries, as we saw in the three types of class politics presented above (in Figure 4.5). With our SPD analysis, we can push those results one step further and transcend the country names. The hypothesis is clear: Cities with stronger parties, and where mayors are less ideologically deviant, should show more class politics. We measure class politics here by the impact of IPARTY on the mayor's redistributive policy preferences. When we split by halves, this is exactly what we find: more impact of IPARTY on spending for those mayors closer to their national party. The generalizing power of the SPD analysis is clear: In seven out of seven countries this effect holds—at least in direction (there is no clear measure of statistical significance for this situation.)

Percent blue collar, like Atkinson inequality, is a local social cleavage. But with an important difference: Karl Marx baptized it the Proletariat, and many national parties use working-class symbols and are linked to trade unions. That is, the national party ideology of class politics, especially of left parties in many countries, stresses responsiveness to the working class. The more "independent" half of the mayors on our SPD measure, although we did not ask them about the working class, showed their independence from traditional class politics by responding *less* to local blue-collar workers. The other half of the mayors, more loyal to national parties, responded *more* to blue-collar workers. This resembles the NFP pattern of *City Money* mayors, like Pittsburgh's Peter Flaherty or New Labour's Tony Blair, who started from left parties but over time grew independent of unions and traditional class politics programs—appealing instead to the more general citizenry (Clark and Ferguson 1983). This pattern holds in four out of five countries in Table 4.A4, with Japan being the exception. This makes sense since Japan has almost no blue collar/class politics tradition for strong parties to uphold (cf. Wonho Jang Ph.D. and in Chapter 3; Hoffmann-Martinot, this volume).

In summary, we do find clear party buffering effects. And we have transcended the national differences by introducing the more general party buffering analysis. Splitting each country's mayors into halves, we find empirical support (in Table 4.A4 in the Appendix) for the theoretical pattern illustrated in Figure 4.7. That is, parties interact with other local variables to shift impacts of nonparty factors. Most national studies have been insensitive to theses large party effects on other participants in decisionmaking.

The Slimmer Family: Education, Women's Roles and Careers, Feminist Moments

Many slimmer family ideas from Chapter 2 can be pursued more sensitively with data for individuals rather than entire cities. Paul Butts (1997) does this in Clark and Rempel (1997). He analyzes details of women's roles and attitudes, including abor-

Country	Divorces per 1,000 existing marriages	
	1960	1983
Belgium	2.0	6.8
Denmark	5.9	12.7
Federal Republic of Germany	3.6	8.1
France	2.9	7.7
Italy	-	0.9
Luxembourg	2.0	6.4
Netherlands	2.2	9.4
United Kingdom	2.2	12.2

Source: *Eurostat Demographic Statistics* (Statistical Office of the European Communities, Luxembourg, 1985).

BOX 4.26   Divorce Rates in Selected EEC Countries, 1960/1983

tion, divorce, family values (such as single parents raising children, a woman choosing to have a child without a steady partner), general sexual morality (several items on sexual freedom, having an affair while married, etc.), homosexuality, and prostitution. Butts finds that men and women are more tolerant of women's new roles if they have more education, are younger, and are less religious. Still, he finds important contextual effects: Education is *less* important in more religious, Catholic countries like Poland and Ireland. Catholic religion thus has a conservative effect, but so does Protestant religiosity, especially in predominantly Protestant countries. His results come from some 14,000 individuals (about 1,000 in each of fourteen countries in the World Values Survey, conducted with general encouragement from Ronald Inglehart). Butts tests for factors considered in related literature: age, education, occupation, income, union membership, religiosity, marital status, size of town, gender (male and female responses were analyzed separately), and so on, using multiple regression analysis. Although Butts lacks data over time, his results for age and education generally sup-

Mayor Larry Agran of Irvine, and the box above on the New Age movement, lead to the more general question: Who supports antigrowth movements (a strong ecology indicator) in U.S. cities? We found them more common in cities with residents who were more educated, affluent, and worked in professional and technical occupations and if they were in New England or on the Pacific Coast—areas with attractive physical environs, thus offering more amenities and enhancing consumption politics. The ecology movement, and such findings, pose deep problems to standard theories of urban development of Paul Peterson, Harvey Moloch, John Logan, and Clarence Stone—which posit that cities want continuous growth since it should benefit their residents' land values, that is, classic secular, materialist interpretations. We propose the NPC theory as a stronger explanation in Clark and Goetz (1994).

BOX 4.27   The Anti-Growth Machine

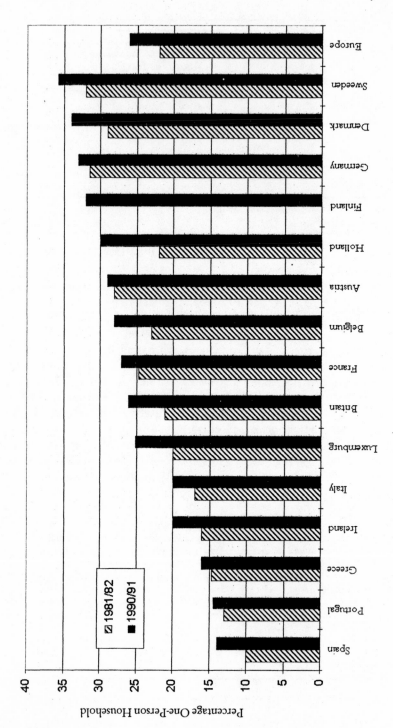

FIGURE 4.8   Percent of One-Person Households Rose in the 1980s
Source: Adapted from Mendras (1997: 161).

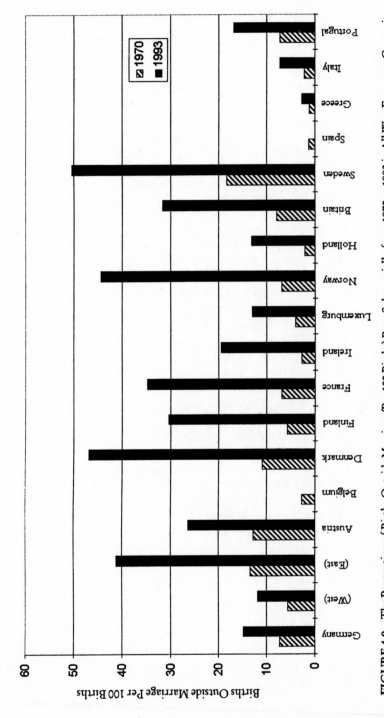

FIGURE 4.9 The Proportion of Births Outside Marriage (Per 100 Births) Rose Substantially from 1970 to 1993 in All West European Countries
Source: Mendras (1997: 168).

port the Chapter 2 propositions about the slimming family and support for new social movement issues. Broadly similar results are in Stoetzel (1983) and Mendras (1997).

Other studies have documented many of the processes we discuss about the slimmer family. For instance, the percentage of women who entered the labor force rose in most countries in Western Europe and the US: from 62 to 79 percent in Sweden and from 50 to 69 percent in the United States between the early 1970s and early 1990s. Consequently: "The two-earner couple has become more common than the one-earner couple in most modern countries" (Smeedling, Danziger, and Rainwater 1995: 3). Similarly, divorce rates rose between 200 percent and 600 percent in Western Europe from 1960 to 1983 (Box 4.26). In Sweden and the United States, almost half of all marriages end in divorce (Johnson 1987: 78). The percentage of one-person households and proportion of births outside marriage rose substantially from the 1970s to 1990s in every West European country for which we have data (Figures 4.8 and 4.9).

Do these processes shift if we examine their components in local decision making? Yes indeed. As many U.S. and West European observers might expect, we find that cities with more educated residents have more women council members and mayors—in most countries. Not so in Eastern Europe (especially Poland) or France. Why not? Two factors are important here, that suggestively illuminate more general rules about these governments, their parties, their (lack of) new social moments, and corresponding resistance to the NPC. Citizens have gradually increased their support for social tolerance as education has risen (as Butts and others show), but education effects were smaller in Poland and Ireland, where the Catholic Church is powerful in affecting what is taught. The opposite is true in France, where public schools have been militantly secular and often anticlerical since the 1880s (cf. Clark 1973). The Church and party hierarchies and the strong central state have been so dominant that local voluntary groups have traditionally been discouraged (Napoleon suppressed them as potentially dangerous, and public meetings were barred for much of the nineteenth century). But in recent years, voluntary associations have been growing rapidly in France, especially concerning ecology (see Box 4.25). Still, women's groups have been weak in France and in other countries with strong Catholic traditions like Italy, Ireland, and Poland. But the traditionally strong *parties* in these countries, often on the left, have embraced many social issues, especially abortion. Second, in Eastern Europe the Communist leadership, just before its 1989 demise, made a concerted effort to appear progressive without sacrificing its key policy tenets (on economic issues). How? It presented numerous women as party candidates for council and mayor.[16] Combine this with no primary elections and (especially in France) strong left parties in towns with less-educated citizens, and the result is that many women are elected *despite* citizen preferences. We lack direct evidence on citizen preferences by locality to clinch this point, but the consistency of the relationship between education of the population and women elected officials in most other countries and similar results from surveys of individuals (like Butts 1997) supports this explanation. Britain, with its strong parties but more activist women, still shows only a weak and insignificant positive relation between the average level of education for citizens in a city and percent women elected officials (in Table 4.9).

TABLE 4.9   Cities with More Educated Residents Have More Women Leaders, But Not in Poland or ... Why Not?

Pearson Correlations (r's) of Mean Educational Level of the Adult Population with:

	Percent Women Council-members	Female mayor (1=female, 0=male)
	PCTWOMC2	FEMMAY
	r	r
UNITED STATES	0.22 **	0.11 **
CANADA	0.45 **	0.14 *
FRANCE	.	-0.03
FINLAND	0.58 **	0.16 **
JAPAN	0.26 **	.
NORWAY	0.20 **	0.13 **
AUSTRALIA	0.28 **	.
DENMARK	0.34 **	.
SWEDEN	0.42 **	.
BRITAIN[b]	0.08	.
POLAND, 1988	.	-0.06
POLAND, 1991	.	0.04
ISRAEL	.	.

*** Correlation is significant at the 0.01 level (1-tailed).
** Correlation is significant at the 0.05 level (1-tailed).
* Correlation is significant at the 0.10 level (1-tailed).
[a]Cannot be computed because at least one of the variables is constant.
[b]British result is r of femcou2 and percent college educated, only signficant at .254 level.

Note: The straightforward finding is that education generally increases women elected officials; most r's are positive. The interesting question is why some are not: Poland and Britain.
Source: FAUI International Surveys.

The Royal Society for the Protection of Birds (RSPB) has more members than the Labour, Conservative and Liberal Democratic parties combined. The society's total membership has increased thirteenfold since 1971, to 860,000, while all three parties have lost membership over the same period. The Economist (1994: p. 49).

BOX 4.28   Britain Is for the Birds

The interesting general story here is therefore how the party system and local rules of the game encourage or suppress new social movements in ways that generate these striking differences among the political systems. Indeed, these intriguing structural effects directly contradict the associations for individuals in citizen surveys. This supports Proposition #8 from Chapter 2: social movements tend not to emerge where parties are stronger and more ideologically closed.

A related analysis considers the mayor's support for abortion, one of our key items in the social conservatism index SOCCONS. We analyzed abortion support by country, since parties are critical in shifting dynamics in ways ignored by most persons in a single country. The America/Northern European individualistic scenario (which broadly holds in these countries) is that more educated citizens and leaders and organized women should promote this quintessential women's issue. But in other countries this fails altogether: Educated populations are unrelated to the mayor's abortion support.

Here the general pattern illuminates the national "idiosyncrasies" of those countries that seem to "deviate." Yet they deviate "meaningfully"—as explained, again, by our more general principles.

Globalization

Globalization affects many other processes that we have documented, but to date it remains beyond the reach of social scientists to capture many specifics. A few bits of evidence still emerge from our analyses. Comparing U.S. cities in their fiscal policies from the 1960s through 1990s, we find a decline in impact of local characteristics explaining local policies. Local unions, mayor's policy preferences, even local income and education decline in significance (Clark 1996: 63-65). International pressures have long been clear in smaller countries, at least for their export sectors. New is the degree of penetration into central government, welfare policies, and larger countries. It is extremely difficult to disentangle specific globalization components from other forces, but consider a few strong examples from locations that long resisted such pressure. The French elected the Socialists to power in 1997, but an explicit central theme in the campaign was how much welfare-service and job-creation policies must be cut due to global pressures. The British elected Tony Blair the same year, and a central issue was how much to participate in the European Union, since it was a major international force preserving worker benefits. At international socialist party meetings in the 1980s and 1990s, former German Chancellor Willy Brandt was a major force pressing for international regulation of workers' conditions, since many socialists feared that left to national decisions the welfare state would be lost. But in the 1997 international socialist meetings, representatives of this view were increasingly ignored, and within the Germany Social Democratic Party how much to preserve this international concern was hotly debated (Personal discussions with SPD leaders, Chicago, November 1996; International Herald Tribune 1997.). Even more globally isolated for many years was China; it thus is a strong test case. But in the 1990s, it drastically increased its efforts to attract foreign investment and succeeded in expanding exports even to supplant Japan as the major source of the U.S. trade imbalance. Inside China this was accomplished by certain provinces concentrating on global exports. We did a small analysis of this extreme case, which indeed showed that those provinces that attracted the most foreign investment grew the most economically and had the fewest state-operated firms; they were more often in coastal areas, some of which had special lower taxes like Guangdong (Clark and Yi 1996). Each of these cases illustrates global pressures moving policies toward parts of the NPC.

The Media and Clientelism

The media are increasingly important for politics, particularly for the NPC. This chapter considered the causes and correlates of media importance above (e.g. in Table 4.1) and suggested that the media can empower citizens by providing them with more information and new ways of thinking about authority and politics. Television has spread simultaneously with new social movements and active proponents of change, like the Polish Solidarity movement, Boris Yeltsin, and Italian magistrates attacking corruption. The media strengthens their hand while weakening *padrone* who used to keep most information. In Chicago, my students in years past seeking to do research (like Esther Fuchs 1992) had to be invited to bars by Democratic Party leaders just to learn basic facts, such as what laws were on the floor of the Chicago City Council. Pending bills were not recorded, numbered, or made available to the public or the press. This changed only when Mayor Harold Washington adopted a Freedom of Information Act in the 1980s, a minor revolution, especially for the media, who thereafter dug much deeper. We do not pursue *consequences* of media impact in this chapter, however, since we did in Rempel and Clark (1997), but report just one dramatic case, which joins clientelism and the Leveling Principle through the media (Box 4.29).

Measuring media impact on politics and hierarchy is decidedly difficult. Here is a striking case that speaks forcefully to conceptual issues of the NPC.

Not only has television influenced and unified the way the Italians speak today, it has also exercised an immeasurable cultural impact. It has even helped change the country's laws: The courtroom episodes of the American television serials that Italians buy and rebroadcast continuously have aquatinted provincial audiences with the oratorical and procedural duels between prosecutor and defense counsel that mark criminal trials in the United States. To Italians, this adversary system based on common law has been a fascinating novelty; their country's penal procedures are derived from Roman law, giving the prosecution preponderance. When the Italian Parliament in 1988 passed legislation introducing features of the Anglo-American system of criminal justice, including a broader possibility for cross-examination in court, lawmakers and lawyers spoke about the new "Perry Mason trial". Italians, finding themselves defendants or witnesses in a court of law for the first time in their lives, addressed the presiding judge as "Vostro Onore," the video translation of "Your Honor." The is not the way to speak to an Italian magistrate who expects to be called "Mr. President" or "Your Excellency". Often the smiling or annoyed judge would tell the defendant: "You are not Perry Mason, and we are not on TV here!" (Hoffman 1990: 6, quote located by Lorna Ferguson)

BOX 4.29 American Media Confront Roman Hierarchies

Clientelism, like the media, is a subtle and sensitive phenomenon to ask about in surveys. Many FAUI teams were deeply interested but felt unable to include clientelism-related items that might offend respondents or lower response rates. We did include two items in many countries: "If a leader helps people, it doesn't matter that some of the rules are broken"—agree or disagree; and, "How important is the ethnic, national, and religious background of candidates in slating and campaigns for your city council?" But if these items tap aspects of clientelism, they index other things too. For instance, an NPC candidate can endorse "breaking rules" set by hierarchical bureaucrats. And parties (like the U.S. Democratic Party in Box 4.18) may officially apply ethnic quotas as a socially progressive policy. We thus pursue clientelism not with the survey items but in ethnographic work. For instance, we showed how clientelism was supported or fought in different U.S. cities, depending on the city's more general rules of the game: Republican and New Fiscal Populist cities (like San Diego and Pittsburgh) defined clientelism very stringently and officially attacked minor acts, whereas Ethnic/clientelist and Democratic cities (like Gary, Boston, and Chicago in years past) tolerated many openly clientelist practices (Clark 1994c). For instance the word "clout" in Chicago refers to statements of politicians boasting how much clientelist power they have to get things done. Another term marks the threat posed by, and resentment toward the NPC: the label "Yuppie" (an abbreviation for *Y*oung *U*rban *P*rofessionals that spread widely). It was coined by a Chicago journalist to refer to people no solid Chicago beer drinker would want in his bar. It showed how much Chicago's dominant culture and politics were unlike that of "young urban professionals," whose numbers and political impact dramatically rose in the 1980s and 1990s, threatening Chicago's clientelist politics. In places like Palo Alto or San Diego, where "young professionals" were long socially and politically dominant, one does not find such visible cultural conflict. These examples extend earlier work that showed how Irish-Americans, building on their sociability and trust, were unusually successful as clientelist political leaders (Clark 1975). Similarly, French and some American universities followed clientelist practices (Clark 1973, 1997). These cited works explicitly consider propositions similar to those in Chapter 2 about clientelism, but their ethnographic evidence does not permit quantitative testing.

Conclusion

Of the twenty-two propositions from Chapter 2, this chapter could not test five, and six were indirectly or weakly tested. Eleven were quite directly tested (summarized in Table 4.10).

We find contrasting results in terms of our three types of propositions: those concerning hierarchy, resources, and transformation rules. The clearest support was for *hierarchy propositions*, as measured by workers in the city's labor force: high percent blue collar decreased the NPC, and high percent professionals increased it—using several measures of NPC governance (women mayors, weak parties, etc.). However, the

TABLE 4.10   Summary of NPC Propositions and Results

	1-Scarcity	2-Pre-socialization	3-NewSocialIssues	4-DownWithHierarchies	5-Demographic	6-Consensus	7-CoherentParties	8-NSMsVs.Parties
			Tested Indirectly					Tested Indirectly
Economic Characteristics								
% Blue Collar (Manual Occupations) -	H			H	H	H	H	
% Professional & Technical Occupations* +	H			H	H	H	H	
Local Income+	M			M	M		L	
National Income+	M			M	M		H	
Social Characteristics								
% of population aged 35-44 +		M-L			M-L		H	
Education (yrs of ed. of adults)* +		M-H			M-H		M	
Population size +					H	H	H	
% Immigrants or foreign born persons -					H	H	H	
Inequality of education, Atkinson Index* -				M-H	M-H	M-H	H	
Governance Characteristics								
Catholic mayor=1 non-Catholic mayor=0 -								
Strong party organization index -				H				
Media +				M-H			X	

TABLE 4.10　Summary of NPC Propositions and Results *(continued)*

	9-MarketsRise	10-AdvTech	11-SmallFirms	12-HiIncome/WkPrys	13-HiInc/FiscCons	14-MoreWelfState	15-Gov	16-Young,ed,socib
	Not Tested	Not Tested	Tested Indirectly			Not Tested	Not Tested	
Economic Characteristics								
% Blue Collar (Manual Occupations) -								
% Professional & Technical Occupations* +			H	L	L			H
Local Income+				M	L			L
National Income+								
Social Characteristics								
% of population aged 35-44 +								
Education (yrs of ed. of adults)* +								
Population size +								
% Immigrants or foreign born persons -								
Inequality of education, Atkinson Index* -								
Governance Characteristics								
Catholic mayor=1 non-Catholic mayor=0 -				X				H
Strong party organization index -								
Media +								

TABLE 4.10   Summary of NPC Propositions and Results *(continued)*

	17-HiEd/ MoreTToler.	18-Slimmer Fam (Non-FAUI Data Support)	19-IssuesVs Clientelism (Bardy Tested)	20-Protest/ NPC	21-Prof WdfState (Not Tested)	22-MediaVs Clientelism (Indiredy Tested via Media/NPC Relations)
Economic Characteristics						
% Blue Collar (Manual Occupations) -						
% Professional & Techncial Occupations* +						H
Local Income+						L
National Income+						
Social Characteristics						
% of population aged 35-44 +						
Education (yrs of ed of adults)* +	L					L
Population size +						H
% Immigrants or foreign born persons -	H					H
Inequality of education, Atkinson Index* -						
Governance Characteristics						
Catholic mayor=1 non-Catholic mayor=0 -				H		
Strong party organization index -						
Media +						X

Note: Most propositions were tested in Tables 4.1 and 4.2. Results are summarized as H=Highly supported, M=Medium support, L=Low support, X=the variable used to measure the proposition, Blank=not tested. Many propositions using individual characteristics like age, education, and income were supported with citizen data in Clark and Rempel (1997), but this table summarizes only city-level results from this chapter. Source: International FAUI Surveys.

Propositions are listed across the top, measures down the side.

A plus sign after a characteristic indicates that a higher value should encourage the NPC.

Atkinson inequality measures of income and education had clear impacts on leaders only in the United States.

Resource propositions were only moderately supported: Cities with more affluent and highly educated residents more often had powerful local media (as hypothesized) but did not consistently have more women elected leaders or weaker parties (as also hypothesized). By contrast we found strong support for these resource propositions in large-scale surveys of citizens in many countries, where more affluent and educated persons, younger in age, generally supported NPC views like abortion, new women's roles, more citizen participation, and the like (Clark and Rempel 1997). The disparity between the citizen and city-level results seems due to (1) ecological difficulties of disentangling associated variables in city-level data, but also (2) contextual effects, such as people shifting their policy preferences depending on who their neighbors are. For instance, if few poor reside in a city, the mayor may represent the actual views of most (affluent) city residents in supporting more generous redistributive programs.

This example of a contextual effect is close to our third type of propositions: *transformation rules* that explain how structural patterns shift effects in different sociopolitical systems. The most dramatic results concerned parties and how they shifted impacts of other variables, like inequality of the population in terms of income or education. Inequality initially seemed to have no impact on leaders' policy preferences, except in the United States (with its weak parties). But we sought to explain these apparent "country" effects with the critical underlying variables. To do so, we measured Strong Policy Distance by combining (1) the distance of the mayor's personal ideology from that of his/her national party, with (2) party organizational strength. Using this new measure to split the mayors into two halves (high and low within each country), interesting results emerged even in countries with strong parties. Specifically, individual mayors who were ideologically distant from their national parties and had weaker local parties acted more like NPC mayors—by responding more to citizens and inequality and less to party organization or blue-collar workers. More generally, strong parties had many other effects, such as left parties nominating more women council members and mayors even in cities with more blue-collar workers (especially in Eastern Europe). Most observers and analysts, particularly of U.S. cities, have downplayed parties, but in most countries of the world they are the most critical type of participant in urban decision making. The diversity of parties, however, and their interrelations with many other social and economic characteristics makes disentangling effects a challenge. Only by using the massive and precise data on these matters that the Fiscal Austerity and Urban Innovation Project assembled over more than a decade could we identify and clarify such patterns. The data are now available to others

Even negative or zero relations take on heightened interest in crossnational context, where we can ask *why* relations fall to zero in some countries but not others. The general logic of the Chapter 2 propositions is thus often compelling. But as they are largely ceteris paribus statements of separate processes, they are usefully complemented by the contextual effects that this chapter has detailed, especially those concerning party systems.

Notes

[1] Our main units are termed "municipalities" or "communes" in many countries. They are relatively autonomous general local governments. We use these terms as well as "cities" and "towns" interchangeably, following common usage.

[2] The same persons can act differently in regional or national politics, a common U.S. phenomenon, where in taxpayer referenda, government employees of one level often voted against taxes for the other levels.

[3] Indeed cities with stronger parties had less educated mayors (Pearson r = -.08, sig. at.002 level, for all countries pooled, but this is largely due to cross-national differences, suggesting that national party policies drive the pattern. In the 1997 British Parliamentary election, almost a quarter of the new MPs were women. "The new Labour Party will be the most socially diverse parliamentary force ever assembled, with women making up almost a quarter of its MPs, more blacks and Asians elected than ever before and a youthful contingent unprecedented this century. All-women shortlists in target seats have ensured that the 101 Labour women have been elected to Parliament out of 419 MPs...more than double the number in the last Parliament." Henderson (1997:2).

[4] Geser's (unpublished) comprehensive synthesis of past work on local parties stresses that population size drives several related processes.

[5] We did not have propositions about the sources of Catholic mayors or years as mayor, so omit these from Table 4.1, but include them in the next step of the path model, leading to policy preferences, where we did have hypotheses about them.

[6] Cities with more active groups have mayors who say they are less responsive to citizens (Pearson r = .15, sig. < .000); effects are strongest in the U.S., Canada, Japan, and Australia, and insignificant in France and Finland, again indicating that parties mediate this pattern.

[7] We were surprised as this zero relation, so we examined it by country and found that simple correlations were near zero in most countries. We respecified a regression of social

TABLE 4.F1   Correlations of Mean Number of Years of Educaton of Adult Population With Other Variables Shift Across Countries

	Local Income	Pct. Blue Collar
UNITED STATES	0.66	-0.85
CANADA	0.67	
FRANCE	-0.31	-0.68
FINLAND	0.49	-0.29
JAPAN	0.84	-0.80
NORWAY	0.53	-0.85
AUSTRALIA	0.81	-0.61
DENMARK	0.67	-0.75
SWEDEN	0.75	

Note: These are Pearson r's. Local income is sometimes a more general wealth measure, and in France is a tax base measure, "fiscal potential," computed by the national government from a complex formula. This may make it behave differently from other countries, but no more precise income measure is available for French cities.

conservatism with just mean education and the two income variables to see if we could separate effects of these three independent variables, but again found insignificant results for education—although it was nearly significant in the US. This weak result seems most likely due to ecological association of income and education and their relations with other variables, especially percent blue collar and Atkinson inequality; these effects are hard to distinguish with city-level data. France and Finland are remarkably different from most other countries; see Table 4.F1.

That is, higher income traditionally leads individuals to more right party support, and thus more conservative social views, while education leads to more socially liberal views. But with city-level data, such income and education effects tend to suppress each other. The most direct solution to such ecological association is to analyze data for individuals, as in Clark and Rempel (1997), and indeed results in that volume from several large citizen surveys (e.g. Butts 1997; Brooks and Manza 1997) consistently show that more highly educated persons are more socially liberal. See also the section on slimming of the family and Boxes 4.20-4.23 on this point.

[8] Similarly, in separate analyses by country, we find that the U.S. is the main country where SPOs are negatively related to spending, while other countries show weak or inconsistent relations. Martin Saiz is pursuing these points in Geser and Saiz (unpublished).

[9] Martin Lipset and I organized four conferences, generating many papers. Several books are out or in progress, such as Nieuwbeerta (1995); Lee and Turner (1996). Some 470 persons subscribed in the first four days to an email-Internet news group on Social Class that Michael Rempel and I started in 1997. Communicate with us at stdmire@icarus.uchicago.edu.

[10] Tightness is operationalized as the adjusted $R2$ of the regression of Iparty on the Fiscal and Social liberalism indexes; see note to Table 4.5.

[11] One should consider such numbers only approximations since the numbers of mayors and parties vary by country, as does their degree of variation within each country. See Achen (1975).

[12] Good examples of system propositions in nearby research include Budge and Keen (1990), which elaborates a very clear set of deductive propositions about where and why different sets of parties join coalitions and shift policies. Although stated as X causes Y-type propositions, they are tested with data for 20 nation states. Similarly Klingeman, Hofferbert, and Budge (1994) use several general models to analyze how specific party programs and coalition participation shift policy effects—although unfortunately neither of these studies addresses changing programs to consider post-industrial politics themes.

[13] Finnish citizens similarly show more class voting and fewer postmaterialist value cleavages than Norwegian citizens in Knutsen (1990).

[14] These results come from Ordinary Least Squares (OLS) regression and measure class with percent blue-collar workers in each city. OLS is appropriate as we measure party in a manner useful for cross-national research. As mentioned above, the basic idea is to assign each party an IPARTY (I for international) left-right score from 0 to 100, based on 1. expert rankings 2. citizen surveys and 3. coding party programs. The three ranking methods intercorrelate highly. Analogous methods can measure over-time changes in one country. We estimated the same model for individual parties as dependent variables in logistic regressions, since many class-is-trendless researchers strongly advocate this method. The key findings in Figure 4.5 were near identical using either OLS or logistic regression. Differences of this magnitude usually do not change with the method, but we are never sure until we try. My colleagues and I continue to explore variations with such models, using more occupational

categories, different ways of classifying parties, adding other variables, etc. Given the controversies in recent exchanges over class politics, we recognize that the results are controversial and thus offer the data to others to pursue as they like.

[15] Might a path model like Figure 4.5, modeling indirect effects of hierarchy through Iparty, as well as direct effects, show more impact of hierarchy on redistributive preferences? No. We tested the model and found insignificant effects for six countries, two with the wrong sign, and one where indirect effects held as expected: the U.S..

[16] I grew aware of this thanks to an unpublished paper by two young Polish social scientists, both named Swianiewicz, who documented the pattern with Polish FAUI data, ethnographic materials, and personal observation. Pawel Swianiewicz served as a city council member in Warsaw, and spent a too short 11 months in Chicago. Mrs. Swianiewicz added a sociological focus on women. Ewa Jurczynska and Janet Stametal brought more details in the Workshop in Urban Policy at the University of Chicago.

Appendix:
The Fiscal Austerity and Urban Innovation Project

The Fiscal Austerity and Urban Innovation (FAUI) Project grew over fifteen years into the most extensive study of local government in the world. In the United States it includes surveys of local officials in all municipalities over 25,000 population, about 1,000. In some thirty-eight other countries analogous studies are in progress. Although Project costs exceed $19 million, they have been divided among Project teams so that some have participated with quite modest investments. Our goal is to document and analyze adoption of innovations by local governments and thus to sharpen the information base of what works, where, and why. The Project is unusual if not unique in combining a large-scale, sophisticated research effort with decentralized data collection, interpretation, and policy analysis. The Project's potential to help cities provide better services at lower costs has heightened interest by public officials. The wide range of survey items makes the database unique for basic researchers on many related topics. Some data are available to interested researchers via the Interuniversity Consortium for Social and Political Research, Ann Arbor, Michigan and more from our Internet sites. Contact tnc@spc.uchicago.edu. The Project remains open to persons interested in participating in different ways, from attending conferences to analyzing the data or publishing in our *Newsletter*, annual volume *Research in Urban Policy* (JAI Press), and the Westview Urban Policy Challenges Series.

Background

The Fiscal Austerity and Urban Innovation Project emerged in the summer of 1982. Terry Clark, Richard Bingham, and Brett Hawkins had planned to survey how sixty-two U.S. cities adapted to austerity. We circulated a memo summarizing the survey and welcomed suggestions. The response was overwhelming: People across the United States and several other countries volunteered to survey leaders in their areas, covering their own costs. Participants were initially attracted by the opportunity to compare cities near them with others. As it seemed clear that we would cover most of the United States, others volunteered to survey remaining states. The result was a network of some twenty-six U.S. teams using a standard methodology to survey local public officials; the teams pooled their data and then made the information available to all. The Project spread internationally in the same manner, with more countries joining over several years.

Although the Project emerged quite spontaneously, it built on experiences joining many participants. In the 1970s and 1980s, a few large empirical studies had major impacts on urban policy analysis. Social scientists and policy analysts increasingly use such studies, but data collection costs are so high that each individual cannot find a grant to collect data he might desire. Research funds have progressively declined, yet urban research has increased in sophistication and scale. A collective effort thus offers clear payoffs. This situation, recognized in the late 1970s, was the focus of a conference in 1979 where twenty persons presented papers that reviewed the best urban policy research to date, outlined central hypotheses, and itemized critical indicators that might be collected in future work. Seven participants (Terry Clark, Ronald Burt, Lorna Ferguson, John Kasarda, David Knoke, Robert Lineberry, and Elinor Ostrom) then extended the ideas from the separate papers in "Urban Policy Analysis: A New Research Agenda." It was published with the separate papers as *Urban Policy Analysis, Urban Affairs Annual Reviews*, Vol. 21 (Sage Publications, 1981). Several persons and many topics from that effort found their way into the FAUI Project.

The Permanent Community Sample (PCS), a national sample of sixty-two U.S. cities monitored over twenty years, provided a database and research experience on which the Project built. Many questionnaire items and methodologies for studying urban processes were derived from the PCS. Several hundred articles and books used the PCS; the most comprehensive was Clark and Ferguson, *City Money* (1983). Basic research and public policy issues have both been addressed, such as how fiscally strained are cities and what solutions can they adopt? These and related issues have been pursued in the United States in conferences, workshops, and publications involving the Department of Housing and Urban Development, U.S. Conference of Mayors, International City Management Association, Municipal Finance Officers Association, and their state and local affiliates. Similar groups have participated internationally, such as the German Association of Cities and many individual local officials.

Project participants came to know each other through professional associations such as the American Political Science Association, International Sociological Association, and European Consortium for Political Research. Meetings in Denver and San Francisco in August 1982 facilitated launching the Project. The international component developed via the Committee on Community Research of the International Sociological Association, which organized a conference in Essen, Germany, in 1981. This Essen meeting and a Mexico City meeting in August 1982 helped extend the Project to Western Europe and other countries.

Since it began in 1982, the Project's conferences have been held regularly around the world, often with meetings of larger associations, especially the European Consortium for Political Research in the spring and American Political Science Association in the summer.

The Survey:
The Most Extensive Study to Date of Decisionmaking and Fiscal Policy in U.S. Cities

The mayor, chair of the city council finance committee, and chief administrative officer or city manager have been surveyed using identical questions in each city of the United States over 25,000—nearly 1,000 cities. Questionnaires were mailed; telephone followups and interviews were used to increase the response rate. Questions include fiscal management strategies the city has used from a list of thirty-three, such as contracting out, user fees, privatization, across the board cuts, reducing workforce through attrition, and deferred maintenance of capital stock. Other items concern revenue forecasting, integrated financial management systems, performance measures, management rights, and sophistication of economic development analyses. The first wave of U.S. data collection was completed in the winter and spring of 1983. Unlike most studies of local fiscal policy, the Project includes items about local leadership and decisionmaking patterns, like preferences of the mayor and council members for more, less, or the same spending in thirteen functional areas. Other FAUI items are policy preferences, activities, and impact on city government by twenty participants, including employees, business groups, local media, the elderly, city finance staff, and federal and state agencies. Several items came from past studies of local officials and citizens, thus permitting overtime comparisons of results. Project participants often share new data for the first year and then make them available to others.

Participants and Coordination

The Project Board, chaired by William Morris, former mayor of Waukegan, Illinois, includes civic leaders and public officials. Terry Clark is coordinator of the Project. Most decisions evolve from collegial discussion. Many participants have ten to twenty years of experience in working together as former students, collaborators in the past studies, and coauthors of many publications. Mark Baldasarre and Lynne Zucker developed the U.S. survey administration procedures. Robert Stein played a lead role in merging U.S. Project data from twenty-six teams with data from the U.S. Census and elsewhere. Paul Eberts coordinated surveys of counties and smaller municipal governments involving more than a dozen other persons in a closely related study. Participants include persons who helped devise the study, collect or analyze data, or participate in conferences and policy implementation activities. A first wave of data collection was completed in the United States and most European countries in the mid-1980s. A second wave began in 1996 in Korea, Japan, and the United States; in some countries third and forth waves have been completed. Other surveys to assess changes have been conducted in several countries and U.S. regions.

FAUI Project Participants in the United States

ARIZONA: Albert K. Karnig

CALIFORNIA: Mark Baldasarre, R. Browning, James Danzinger, Roger Kemp, John J. Kirlin, Anthony Pascal, Alan Saltzstein, David Tabb, Herman Turk, Lynne G. Zucker

COLORADO: Susan Clarke

WASHINGTON, D.C.: Jeff Grady, Richard Higgins, Charles H. Levine

FLORIDA: James Ammons, Lynn Appleton, Thomas Lynch, Susan MacManus

GEORGIA: Frank Thompson, Cal Clark, Roy Bahl

ILLINOIS: James L. Chan, Terry Nichols Clark, Burton Ditkowsky, Warren Jones, Lucinda Kasperson, William Morris, Tom Smith, Laura Vertz, Norman Walzer, Harry Kelley

INDIANA: David A. Caputo, David Knoke, Michael LaWell, Elinor Ostrom, Roger B. Parks, Ernest Rueter

KANSAS: Paul Schumaker

LOUISIANA: W. Bartley Hildreth, Robert Whelan

MAINE: Lincoln H. Clark, Khi V. Thai

MARYLAND: John Gist

MASSACHUSETTS: Dale Rogers Marshall, Peter H. Rossi, James Vanecko

MICHIGAN: William H. Frey, Bryan Jones, Harold Wollman

MINNESOTA: Jeffrey Broadbent, Joseph Galaskiewicz

NEW HAMPSHIRE: Sally Ward

NEW JERSEY: Jack Rabin, Joanna Regulska, Carl Van Horn

NEW YORK: Paul Eberts, Esther Fuchs, John Logan, Melvin Mister, Robert Shapiro, Joseph Zimmerman

NORTH CAROLINA: John Kasarda, Peter Marsden

OHIO: Steven Brooks, Jesse Marquette, Penny Marquette, William Pammer

OKLAHOMA: David R. Morgan

OREGON: Bryan Downes, Kenneth Wong

PENNSYLVANIA: Patrick Larkey, Henry Teune, William Van Vliet, Susan Welch

PUERTO RICO: Carlos Munoz

RHODE ISLAND: Thomas Anton, Michael Rich

TENNESSEE: Mike Fitzgerald, William Lyons
TEXAS: Charles Boswell, Richard Cole, Bryan Jones, Robert Stein, Del Tabel, Robert Lineberry
VIRGINIA: Robert DeVoursney, Pat Edwards, Timothy O'Rourke
WASHINGTON: Betty Jane Narver
WISCONSIN: Lynne-Louise Bernier, Richard Bingham, Brett Hawkins, Robert A. Magill
WYOMING: Oliver Walter

The international participants are among the leading urban analysts in their respective countries and, in several cases, direct major monitoring studies with multiyear budgets including collection of data directly comparable to those in the United States. Gerd-Michael Hellstern, University of Berlin, initially coordinated the European teams. Harald Baldersheim provided much help with Western Europe and led the Local Democracy and Innovation Project in Hungary, Poland, Slovakia, and the Czech Republic. Ed Prantilla coordinated the Project in six Asian countries. The survey items were adapted to different national circumstances while retaining the core items wherever possible to permit crossnational comparisons. The year of the survey is listed after the country if it was anlayzed in this volume.

International FAUI Teams

ARGENTINA: 1991 Martha Landa
AUSTRALIA: 1990 John Robbins
AUSTRIA: H. Bauer
BELGIUM: 1990 Dr. Stassen, Marcel Hotterbeex, Catherine Vigneron, Johan Ackaert
BULGARIA: N. Grigorov, O. Panov
CANADA: 1988 (Western Canada), 1990 (Ontario) Andrew S. Harvey, Caroline Andrews, Dan Chekkie, Jacques Leveilee, James Lightbody, Mary Lynch
CHINA: Min Zhou, Yun-Ji Qian, Zhiyue Bo
CZECH REPUBLIC: 1992-93 Michael Illner, Jiri Patocka
DENMARK: Carl-Johan Skovsgaard, Finn Bruun, Poul Erik Mouritzen, Kurt Houlberg Nielsen
FIJI: H. M. Gunasekera
FINLAND: 1985 Ari Ylonen, Risto Harisalo
FRANCE: 1985 Richard Balme, Jean-Yves Nevers, Jeanne Becquart-Leclercq, P. Kukawka, T. Schmitt, Vincent Hoffmann-Martinot
GERMANY: 1993 B. Hamm, D. H. Mading, Gerd-Michael Hellstern, Oscar Gabriel, Volker Kunz, Frank Brettschneider
GREAT BRITAIN: 1987 (administrators), 1994 (councillors and mayors) Michael Goldsmith, James Chandler, George Boyne, Bryan Jacobs, Keith Hoggart, Peter John
GREECE: Elias Katsoulis, Elisavet Demiri
HONG KONG: P. B. Harris
HUNGARY: 1992-93 G. Eger, Peteri Gabor
INDONESIA: Hatomi, Jonker Tamba
IRELAND: Carmel Coyle
ISRAEL: 1990 Daniel Elazar, Avraham Brichta
ITALY: 1987-88 Guido Martinotti, Enrico Ercole, Annick Magnier, Gianfranco Bettin
JAPAN: Hachiro Nakamura, Nobusato Kitaoji, Yoshiaki Kobayashi
KENYA: Daniel Bourmaud
NETHERLANDS: A. M. J. Kreukels, Tejo Spit, Bas Denters

NIGERIA: Dele Olowu, Ladipo Adamolekun
NORWAY: 1985 Harald Baldersheim, Helge O. Larsen, Jonny Holbek, Sissel Hovik, Kari Hesselberg, Nils Aarsaether, Solbjorg Sorensen, Synnove Jenssen, Lawrence Rose, Per Arnt Pettersen
PHILIPPINES: Ramon C. Bacani, Ed Prantilla
POLAND: 1988, 1991 Gregory Gorzelak, J. Regulski, Z. Dziembowski, Pawel Swianewicz, Andrzej Kowalczyk, Jerzy Bartowski, Leszek Porebski, Ewa Jurczynska, Wisla Surazska
PORTUGAL: J. P. Martins Barata, Maria Carla Mendes, Juan Mozzicafreddo, Carlos Silva
REPUBLIC OF KOREA: Choong Yong Ahn
SENEGAL: Abdul Aziz Dia
SLOVAK REPUBLIC: 1992-93 Gejza Blaas, Miroslav Hettes
SPAIN: Cesar E. Diaz, Teresa Rojo, Lourdes Nieto
SWEDEN: Hakon Magnusson, Lars Stromberg, Cecilia Bokenstrand, Jon Pierre, Ingemar Elander, P. O. Norell
SWITZERLAND: A. Rossi, Claude Jeanrenaud, Erwin Zimmermann, Hans Geser, Erwin Ruegg, Andreas Ladner
TAIWAN: Fang Wang
TURKEY: U. Ergudor, Ayse Gunes-Ayata
YUGOSLAVIA/SLOVENIA: Peter Jambrek

Participation in the Project is open and teams continue to join, especially outside the United States, as they learn of the Project and find ways to merge it with their own activities. Austerity links the less affluent countries of the world with others who can learn from them.

Research Foci

Project participants are free to analyze the data as they like, but past work indicates the range of concerns likely to be addressed. The seven-author statement "Urban Policy Analysis: A New Research Agenda" (cited above) outlined several dozen specific hypotheses. Many specific illustrations appear in Project publications such as the seven volumes of *Research in Urban Policy* (JAI Press) completed to date, T. N. Clark, ed., *Urban Innovation* (Sage 1994), Terry Clark, Gerd Michael Hellstern, and Guido Martinotti, eds., *Urban Innovations as Response to Urban Fiscal Strain* (Berlin: Verlag Europaeische Perspektiven, 1985), and several country-specific reports, including William J. Pammer, *Managing Fiscal Strain in Major American Cities* (New York: Greenwood Press, 1989). More than 200 papers have been presented at Project conferences or published separately, listed in the *Newsletter*. Some general themes follow.

Innovative Strategies Can Be Isolated and Documented

Showcase cities are valuable to demonstrate that new and creative policies can work. Local officials listen more seriously to other local officials showing them how something works than they do to academicians, consultants, or national government officials. Specific cases are essential to persuade. But since local officials seldom publicize their innovations, an outside data-collection effort can bring significant innovations to more general attention. Questions: What are the strategies that city governments have developed to confront fiscal austerity? How do strategies cluster with one another? Are some more likely to follow others as a function of fiscal austerity? Case studies of individual cities detail strategies identified in the survey.

Local Governments That Do and Do Not Innovate Be Identified: Political Feasibility Can Be Clarified

One can learn from both failure and success. Local officials often suggest that fiscal management strategies like contracting out, volunteers, and privatization are "politically infeasible," that they may work in Phoenix but not in Stockholm. Yet why not—specifically? Many factors are hypothesized and some studied, but much past work to date is unclear concerning how to make such programs more palatable. The Project is distinctive in probing adoption of innovations, tracing diffusion strategies, and sorting out effects of interrelated variables. A full range of political leadership and urban decisionmaking process variables has been collected, extending past work on community power and regimes internationally. The Project also probes interrelations of strategies with changes in revenues and spending.

National Urban Policy Issues, Regionalism, and Globalization

In several countries, reductions in national government funding for local programs compound fiscal austerity for cities. How are cities of different sorts weathering this development? Cities are undergoing some of the most dramatic changes in decades. When city officials come together in their own associations or testify on problems to the media and their national governments, they can pinpoint city-specific problems. But they have difficulty specifying how widely problems and solutions are shared across regions or countries. The Project contributes to these national urban policy discussions by monitoring local policies and assessing the distinctiveness of national patterns. The Project summarizes nationally fiscal strain indicators of the sort computed for smaller samples of cities. Types of retrenchment strategies are being assessed. Effects of national program changes are being investigated, such as stimulation-substitution issues. A lengthy report of key national trends in twelve countries has been published by Poul Erik Mourtizen and Kurt Nielsen, *Handbook of Urban Fiscal Data* (Odense, Denmark: University of Odense, 1988), and P. E. Mourtizen, ed., *Managing Cities in Austerity* (Sage 1992). Regional differences can be mapped by aggregating the local data to multiple regional levels, within and across countries. Global similarities, competitive pressures, and diffusion patterns are being assessed across the 7,000-plus localities for which we have assembled data around the world.

Conclusion

The Project is such a huge undertaking that initial participants doubted its feasibility. It was not planned in advance but evolved spontaneously as common concerns were recognized. It is a product of distinct austerity in research funding, illustrating concretely that policy analysts can innovate in how they work together. But most of all it is driven by the dramatic changes in cities around the world and a concern to understand them so that cities can better adapt to pressures they face.

Samples, National Data, and Checking

Most national teams mailed questionnaires to local officials in all municipalities in their country above a certain population size, like 25,000 in the United States. Smaller countries used lower population size limits to raise the N. The units studied were commonly termed communes, municipalities, cities or (in Britain) districts. These are the main local general governments in each country. We did not survey specialized authorities like transit districts. But we do include suburbs as well as central cities. As specific names vary by country, we do not seek to use consistent terms but refer interchangeably to our units as cities, localities, and municipalities. More detail on the samples in each country is in Mouritzen (1992) and Mouritzen and Nielsen (1988).

Data for population, economic, fiscal, and other nonsurvey data were assembled by national teams as well as in Chicago, where we pooled the national data and checked them for validity and consistency. We generally compared data that came in machine-readable form to hardcopy publications. Most teams also supplied several raw questionnaires that we verified against the final data files as a check on data entry and file merging. We found very, very few errors but did discover some inconsistencies in decimal placement, for per capita computations, and similar matters that we spent many months correcting and documenting. The care and effort of the hundreds of persons worldwide that went into this effort was remarkable and is deeply appreciated. The data now stand in archives, available via the Internet, so that others may readily access them. Several thousand files have been assembled—procedural memos, coding schemes, original language and English translations of questionnaires, national and pooled international data from surveys and nonsurvey sources. These data, which totaled just over 1,000 megabytes in 1997, are available inexpensively on CD Roms or one Iomega Jaz Cartridge, which permits using standard IBM-PC search and indexing programs. Most data files are in SPSS/PC or Windows format.

A few general points about the FAUI research. Separate national teams in the FAUI Project conducted surveys using a core of common items given to mayors and council members. Teams added other data—demographic, fiscal, and the like—for national samples of cities in each country. Beyond the common core was some variation, especially in nonsurvey data. New data arrived every few weeks for years; we updated continuously. By the late 1990s, we had some data for more than 7,000 localities in twenty countries. However, not all variables are available for all countries. We could have restricted analysis to variables available for all countries, but this "listwise" method for handling missing data eliminates many countries for which we have many variables. Some analyses were completed listwise, but we more often used the "pairwise method," analyzing all cases available for each "pairwise" combination of each individual variable with all other variables. Consequently the numbers of cases and countries included varies from table to table. This diversity is consistent with our analytical effort to test general propositions about political processes rather than precisely describe a "representative" sample of cities or countries. For most key variables we have tested relations for all cities pooled across all countries, as well as by each individual country. Space limits restrict what is here, but we include selections of the major analyses.

Comments on major variables:

SOCCONS = social conservatism, computed by summing abortion and sex education questions to mayor and councilmembers. Scores for Italy and France were based on the abortion item plus the international mean for sex education for all countries that did have sex education responses, since sex education was not asked in these two countries. To check that this adjustment would not affect results, we recomputed the IPARTY regression in

Table 4.5 using spending and just abortion. The coefficients were virtually unchanged: for example, betas for Italy: .890 for just abortion; .893 for abortion and imputed sex education; for France: -.138 for just abortion, -.158 for abortion and imputed sex education. Other statistics like b's were similar.

INCOME1, INCOME2. Income data came from each national census in national currencies. To analyze differences within each country, we created a standard (Z) score for each city that is its deviation from the country mean: Income1. The Income1 scores were also used in some pooled crossnational analyses to permit comparing cities that are rich in national terms. But to capture crossnational differences in income, we used Income2, which is the national average income per capita in 1986 (World Bank 1988). Both income measures are included in some analyses that then capture both types of income effects: relative national and absolute crossnational differences.

Atkinson Inequality Indexes. Social science has a long tradition of inequality indexes, including the Lorenz curve, Gini coefficient, Theil's entropy, and more. They help to operationalize the concept of hierarchy. Atkinson (1975) contributed by joining social welfare theory with statistical measurement to generate a flexible but powerful methodology for capturing the degree of hierarchy in an income distribution. Like other social welfare economists, he used income as a simple quantitative aspect of social welfare. We extended the approach to related social hierarchies, like occupation and education. Atkinson's index increases with inequality, but the exact increase depends on the coefficient alpha. The researcher can set the alpha in the defining equation:

$$I_r = 1 - [\Sigma \, (Y/\overline{Y})^{1-\alpha}(P_i)]^{1/(1-\alpha)}$$

where

I_r = Atkinson's Index of Inequality
Y_i = income of income class i (e.g., persons from \$5,000 to \$10,000 annual income)
$\overline{Y}$ = mean income for the social unit (the city)
P_i = proportion of income earned by income class i
α = the exponential coefficient that the analyst can vary to specify the rate at which inequality affects the overall Index

The index subtracts from one the ratio of a city where each individual is equal in income to the mean of the actual income distribution in that city. Thus I_r declines as the income distribution grows more equal. The magnitude of this decline in I_r is also affected by alpha. As alpha rises, more weight is attached to transfers at the lower end of the distribution; at infinity, only transfers at the bottom are taken into account. Thus one can vary the alpha coefficient to emphasize, or de-emphasize, the effect of a small improvement in income by the poorest income group. Although Atkinson and most interpreters discuss this as *the researcher's choice*, one can assign alpha values to match different political cultures—a leftist political culture is presumably more sensitive to the lowest income groups and should value a higher alpha more than would conservative political cultures. Accordingly, four alpha values were chosen in computing each of the Atkinson indexes from .5 to 0., -.5, and -1, a range of alpha values recommended by Atkinson and researchers who have refined the index (e.g., Bartels and Nijcamp 1976; Schwartz and Winship 1979).

For this study, sixteen Atkinson indexes were created for the United States, with four alpha scores each for income, occupation, education, and national origin. However, results for U.S. cities showed that indexes using each of the four alpha scores were quite similar (most r's over .9). Thus, despite the theoretical appeal of assigning different alpha coefficients to the Atkinson index, these results suggest that such (slight) variations in method for measuring inequality/hierarchy generate minimally different results. Consequently, only four indexes were retained, one each for income, occupation, education, and prestige of national origin. These four Atkinson indexes were in turn moderately interrelated but not enough to generate substantial multicollinearity; all were below .5 except occupation with income (r = .51). Further computational specifics, intercorrelations among the four indexes and related inequality analyses are in Clark (1994a). Data availability in other countries limited us to Atkinson indexes of inequality of education, income, and in a few countries, occupation.

Data and Analysis Procedures

Party Manifestos Data set CMPr3 (Author A. Volkens), Comparative Manifestos Project, Science Center Berlin, Research Unit Institutions and Social Change (Director H.-D. Klingeman) in cooperation with the Manifesto Research Group (Chairman I. Budge). These data come from coding the party "manifestos" or programs for national parties, often issued for nation elections. Programs were coded in a large international project for 250 parties in twenty-eight countries from 1945 to the present (the project continues). Each distinct idea was considered a "quasisentence" and classified into one of fifty-six categories. Many categories involved national or international issues (foreign policy, peace) or did not fall clearly into more traditional left-right or New Political Culture themes. We selected nine themes that differentiated traditional left-right versus the NPC reasonably clearly. But the number of mentions for four of these was so low that they were deleted: Marxist analysis, nationalization, free enterprise, antigrowth economy. Five were retained, defined as follows:

- Environmental Protection: Preservation of countryside, forests, etc.; general preservation of natural resources against selfish interests; proper use of national parks; soil banks, etc.; environmental improvement.
- Government and Administrative Efficiency: Need for efficiency and economy in government and administration; cutting down civil service; improving governmental procedures; general appeal to make the process of government and administration cheaper and more effective.
- Traditional Morality: Positive: Favorable mentions of traditional moral value; prohibition; censorship and suppression of immorality and unseemly behavior; maintenance and stability of family; religion.
- Labor Groups: Positive: Favorable references to labor groups, working class, unemployed; support for trade unions; good treatment of manual and other employees.
- Welfare +: Welfare State Expansion: Favorable mentions of need to introduce, maintain, or expand any social service or social security scheme; support for social services such as health service or social housing. Note: This category excludes education.

The units reported on the Y (vertical) axis of Figures 4.3 and 4.4 are the percent of quasisentences that the manifesto devoted to each theme. Given the form of these data the simple hypothesis that was tested was that NPC themes rose after 1973. Thus two subperiods were compared: 1945 to 1973 and 1974 to 1988 (the last year currently available). The mean percent of space devoted to each theme was compared in the two periods, and a T-test computed to indicate significance of the change. Results for all 250 parties in twenty-eight countries analyzed together showed significant shifts toward the NPC on four of the five themes; the exception was traditional morality, which showed no change.

Frequencies, Correlations, and Regression Models

To consider relations among key variables, simple descriptive statistics are reported in scatterplots, barcharts, and correlation matrices. These communicate key relationships at the same time that they show that no relations are deterministic; indeed some are quite modest. All key relations are next considered in regressions, to see how much bivariate relations may shift or decline when other variables are simultaneously considered for their impacts on the same dependent variable. We model each key block of variables (social, economic, governance) using a path-type sequence.

Recursive regression models were used to explain each block of variables, including most other causally prior variables. Variables were drawn from past work by ourselves and others such as Clark and Ferguson (1983), the Fiscal Austerity and Urban Innovation Project annual *Research in Urban Policy*, and Clarke (1989). Variables not identified above are briefly described here. Most regressions were estimated with pairwise deletion of missing cases, which retains the full number of cases available for each bivariate relationship. For instance, in the United States, with as many as 1,030 cases, this meant that for Census variables we often had relatively complete Ns, while variables from the FAUI and ICMA surveys had lower Ns since their response rates were 40–65 percent. Practically all important results we checked in several ways to see how robust they remained. We tried listwise deletion. We compared regression coefficients with simple correlations and looked for consistency. We compared results across varied regression specifications to see if key findings consistently held. For instance, we reestimated simpler regression models, deleting subsets of variables that were somewhat multicollinear and which had low Ns. We completed analyses using the methods of Heckman (1979), Olsen (1980), and others to check for sample selection bias due to Ns differing by variable and found minimal bias (details in Clark 1994a: 241-255).

Methods of Analysis: Pooling Cities, Country Effects, Etc.

Much past research by ourselves and others analyzes cities in a single nation. A near-unique aspect of the FAUI Project is to have not just census data but original survey data on decisionmaking and related processes for cities in many countries. Data come from many teams, who followed an international model closely but not always exactly. This means that some items are not available in some countries (mainly since some teams omitted or modified survey items). This poses problems if one wants to test, for example, for the impact of education on social liberalism of the mayor, controlling "other variables" like city population size and percent blue collar residents. Consider a not unusual situation: Five countries have full data, but ten more lack from one to three variables, and the missing variables differ for each country. If we estimate multiple regressions separately in each country, we observe some differences but are never sure how much of the differences are due to differences in available data or actual national differences. The solution to this problem turns on one's goal. If we were area specialists seeking to generate a "representative sample" precisely comparing three countries, we could report national means for variables from each country and test for significant differences across countries. However, our primary concern is not such description but to identify general processes that encourage or discourage the New Political Culture. Thus a second analytical approach is to pool (combine the data) for all cities from all countries and analyze interrelations among variables for those cities that have available data. We often use the pooled approach below, but conducted most analyses by country as well. Consider reasons for pooling: (1) One powerful argument is that differences on key variables like means are often small or insignificant across nations. But (2) there are large variations across cities *inside* almost every country, as shown by high standard deviations and similar statistics. (3) The numbers of cases are modest within some countries (under 100) but exceed 7,000 when all are combined. Higher Ns mean that statistical significance is more likely, other things equal. But (4) especially important: the higher N makes it more possible to disentangle closely associated variables. By contrast in one country with a low N, variables like percent blue collar and mean education are so highly interrelated that their effects are very hard to disentangle. (5) More complex models can be specified, including more independent variables, which may be too closely interrelated to include in analyses with lower Ns. (6) Some national effects are clearly "idiosyncratic" in the sense that they are not "general processes" likely to affect many other countries in broadly similar manner. For instance, Prime Minister Margaret Thatcher and her government politicized and changed governance patterns in British local authorities so extensively that it is hard to compare British localities to themselves a decade earlier. Yet many general processes still operate in British cities (such as percent blue-collar citizens declining, and parties shifting their programs) in ways that encourage including Britain in some manner. Although this is an extreme case, it is simultaneously true that every nation, and city, is unique. It does not inevitably follow that there are no common patterns. And since our main concern is to identify major common patterns, our general methodological solution is to pool the data for many countries. This reduces the salience of unique patterns.

What of "country effects"? Obviously cities differ across national boundaries in some respects. We sought to pose more general survey questions to avoid subtle details of administrative specifics, budget cycles or the like. For instance, the questions posed to council members and mayors concern more general governance and policy issues. One indicator of the success of the effort to pose general items is that national differences on many items are small. A second simple method is to examine Pearson correlations (r's) for several countries; in each country the r is computed for the same two variables (like percent women council members and average citizens' education in Table 4.10). Achen (1977) pointed out that national differences identified in this way are biased if nations differ in the total amount of variance; he recommended calculating slopes instead (such as b coefficients in OLS regressions). We occasionally report such r's because of their greater communicative simplicity, but have also pushed on to regressions. However to keep the text more accessible to readers, we have sought not to present regressions in the text, but to include a few here in the Appendix. A third method we have used in analyzing the pooled data, is to add "country dummies" (i.e., dummy variables equal to 0 if a city is not in that country, and 1 if the city is). Consdier for instance, a 10 variable multiple regression model to explain social conservatism with 10 independent variables like percent blue collar, etc., pooling data for five countries. We can assess "country effects" by adding four country dummy variables (for all countries except one). If all regression coefficients for all country dummy variables are zero, this suggests that the 10 variables in the model (not the country dummies) have reasonably explained differences among the countries. If, for instance, the countries differ in percent blue collar, and we include for each city in each country its percent blue collar as one of our 10 explanatory variables, then we are succeeding in doing just what we attempted: to show how national differences may be explained away if we analyze the proper variables, like percent blue collar. Still, if the country dummy variable coefficient remains significant and positive for one country, this tells us although the common pattern holds for cities in general, but in that one country social conservatism remains higher than in the reference country (the one whose dummy variable is omitted) even after considering the effects of the 10 variables. Some other studies report strong country effects on citizen attitude items (e.g., Brint, Cunningham, and Li 1997). In general, we found much weaker country effects. This is largely because local units vary substantially *within* as well as *across* countries. We thus captured much of the variation that Brint et al. found only at the country level since they used national samples of citizens and had no subnational data except for individual citizens. We have sought to probe further such situations where country effects persist. One way is to analyze separately cities by country for countries that differ. However, such efforts, as well the identification of "country effects," are confounded when variables are not consistently available across countries. Thus what may at first appear to be a "country effect" could, in this example, result if no data were available for percent blue collar persons in cities in that country. We have sought to incorporate country dummies in all pooled models and to pursue any significant results but often found that what seemed to be significant "country effects" as measured with these dummy variable were most common in countries with the most missing variables. This is fully to be expected and is the same way that modeling of all sorts proceeds, with or without any statistics. That is, for centuries travelers have sought to explain national differences and to posit more general interpretations quite like our blue collar example. But only as more countries become considered, and more variations are collected on key variables, can one assess the adequacy of the posited interpretation. Here for instance is average spending preferences by country, in Figure 4A1. A few national averages are higher—Israel and Slovakia—but the range and standard deviations of cities within each country is considerable. Tables 4A1and 4A2 reports country means and standard deviations for key variables in our analysis, showing this same general pattern.

Elaboration of Class Analysis, as Summarized in Figure 4.5

We use core survey items in Table 4A3 plus socioeconomic variables assembled by our FAUI Project participants in each country and by researchers in Chicago. Items in Table 4A3 not explained above include:

• FORNSTK = Immigrants or foreign born, the proportion of persons in a city born outside the country. Data are not fully comparable in each country, but we are at the mercy of each national census for such items.

• IPCTBLUE = Percent blue collar or manual laborers as proportion of labor force. For the United States, this includes the proportion of city residents whose occupations are listed as: private household services; protective service occupations; farming, forest, and fishing occupations; precision production, craft, and repair occupations; machine operators, assemblers, and inspectors; transportation and material moving occupations; and handlers, equipment cleaners, helpers, and laborers. Other countries use similar measures.

• IPARTY = We devised IPARTY to permit crossnational party comparisons, as in Table 4A3. This is an internationally comparable measure of left-right party ideology on a 0 to 100 scale, not distinguishing fiscal from social liberalism (low score is left). Scores came from one of two main sources. First was Castles and Mair (1984), who used 115 experts to rank political parties on a left-right 10-point scale in many countries. Second, for countries not in Castles and Mair we used a survey where citizens affiliated with each party placed themselves on a general left-right scale (Sani and Sartori 1983). For France party scores from Castles and Mair were adapted by our French FAUI participant Vincent Hoffmann-Martinot to incorporate recent developments. The third source we compared against was Klingeman, Hofferbert, and Budge (1994), who kindly provided their raw data. For those countries for which we

TABLE 4A.1   Governance Characteristics: Means and Standard Deviations by Country

	Number of municipalities	Group activity index		1party score (left to right) where + = right		Strong party organization		Percent Women Councilmbrs	
	N	Mean	Std Deviation	Mean	Std Deviation	Mean	Std Deviation	Mean	Std Deviation
U.S	1030	36	21	56	10	24	23	14	15
CANADA	100	36	18	59	10	13	13	17	12
FRANCE	176	36	18	48	27	80	27		
FINLAND	183	55	15	45	20	73	15	23	7
JAPAN	681	44	18	52	24	61	19	4	8
NORWAY	457			46	18	69	20	18	22
AUSTRALIA	241	30	16	52	22	24	24	19	11
DENMARK	275			55	15			26	10
SWEDEN	286			55	20			30	7
BELGIUM	646	37	15	51	22				
ARGENTINA	55			48	15				
CZECH REPUBLIC	135			69	12			24	17
HUNGARY	206			52	2			23	42
SLOVAKIA	167			47	18			18	16
GERMANY	146	59	14	45	18	68	13	28	6
ITALY	53	34	17	37	17	71	29	0	0
BRITAIN	593	35	19	55	23			16	34
POLAND, 1988	243			36	0	74	19		
POLAND, 1991	247			54	1			23	
ISRAEL	94	25	16	46	33	63	26	1	2

TABLE 4A.1 Governance Characteristics: Means and Standard Deviations by Country *(continued)*

	Percent Woman Mayors		Mayor's Age		Mayor's Years of Education		Media Importance	
	Mean	Std Deviation	Mean	Std Deviation	Mean	Std Deviation	Mean	Std Deviation
U.S.	13	33	51	10	16	2	50	27
CANADA	7	26	51	10	14	3	46	23
FRANCE	4	21	52	12	15	4		
FINLAND	9	29	51	8	17	1		
JAPAN	0	0	63	8	14	2	22	24
NORWAY	4	21	50	8	12	3		
AUSTRALIA			50	10	14	4	41	25
DENMARK								
SWEDEN								
BELGIUM	3	16	52	11				
ARGENTINA								
CZECH REPUBLIC	6	24	46	9	16	3	29	27
HUNGARY	9	28	45	9	14	3	29	27
SLOVAKIA	9	29	46	8	15	3	11	28
GERMANY	29	46	48	11	14	3		
ITALY	0	0	45	7	14	3		
BRITAIN	8	27			14	3	77	21
POLAND, 1988	9	29	45	7	17	1		
POLAND, 1991	10	30	41	8	15	2		
ISRAEL	4	20	53	10			59	33

Note: These means and standard deviations are based mainly on data from FAUI surveys. Means often differ little by country, and standard deviations are large. The N's listed are the highest for any single variable for that country, usually from Census data; for survey variables the Ns normally are lower as response rates were never 100%.

. = missing data

Source: FAUI Project.

TABLE 4A.2   Economic and Social Characteristics: Means and Standard Deviations by Country

	Number of Municipalities	% Blue Collar (Manual Occupations)		% Professional & Technical Occupations		Local Income		National Income	
	N	Mean	Std Deviation	Mean	Std Deviation	Mean	Std Deviation	Mean	Std Deviation
UNITED STATES	1,030	32	9	11	4	50	1	17480	0
CANADA	100					50	1	14120	0
FRANCE	176	32	9	4	2	50	1	10720	0
FINLAND	183	41	5			50	1	12160	0
JAPAN	681	51	10	8	2	50	1	12840	0
NORWAY	457	55	9			50	1	15400	0
AUSTRALIA	241	21	6	10	4	50	1	11920	0
DENMARK	275	33	5			50	1	12600	0
SWEDEN	286					50	1	13160	0
BELGIUM	646					50	1	9230	0
CZECH REPUBLIC	135								
HUNGARY	206								
SLOVAK REPUBLIC	167					50	1		
BRITAIN	593	41	7	5	2				
POLAND, 1988	243								
POLAND, 1991	247								

TABLE 4A.2 Economic and Social Characteristics: Means and Standard Deviations by Country *(continued)*

	% of population aged 35-44		Education (yrs of ed. of adults)		Population size		% Immigrants or foreign born persons		Inequality of education, Atkinson Index	
	Mean	Std Deviation	Mean	Std Deviation	Mean	Std Deviation	Mean	Std Deviation	Mean	Std Deviation
UNITED STATES	11	2	12	1	96810	290993	7	7	32	8
CANADA	15	2	12	1	92057	240868	17	8	32	3
FRANCE	12	1	10	0	63139	177550	9	5	15	5
FINLAND	14	2	10	1	39199	68203	.	.	26	1
JAPAN	15	2	11	0	132899	229589	.	.	25	2
NORWAY	13	2	10	0	9014	25388	0	0	21	3
AUSTRALIA	.	.	11	0	51835	55957	21	10	28	2
DENMARK	.	.	10	0	18615	36820	.	.	21	4
SWEDEN	.	.	10	1	29322	51380	4	3	17	4
BELGIUM	.	.	.	.	17253	28903	.	.	.	.
CZECH REPUBLIC	.	.	.	.	37084	116970	.	.	.	.
HUNGARY	.	.	.	.	14526	34753	.	.	.	.
SLOVAK REPUBLIC	.	.	.	.	8593	14472	.	.	.	.
BRITAIN	.	.	.	.	125404	91934	4	3	.	.
POLAND, 1988	14	1	9	0	10946	11555	.	.	6	1
POLAND, 1991	14	2	9	0	18648	62749	.	.	6	1

Note: These means and standard deviations are based mainly on data from national censuses. Means often differ little by country, and standard deviations are large. The N's listed are the highest for any single variable for that country, usually from Census data; for survey variables the Ns normally are lower as response rates were never 100%.

. = missing data

Source: FAUI Project.

TABLE 4A.3   Why Do Mayors Support Higher Spending? International Contrasts
A. Traditional Class Politics in France and Finland
B. Less Class Influence in Norway, Canada, Japan and Australia
C. Race Acts Like Class in the United States
Two Step Process:
Step 1 — Percent Blue Collar Residents leads to Traditional Left - Right Party Politics
Step 2 — Percent Blue Collar Residents and Left - Right Parties Influence Mayor's Spending
Preferences

A - Step 1. Two Countries Illustrate Traditional Class Politics:
Blue Collar Residents Vote Left, Betas are Significant

Dependent Variable: IPARTY

FRANCE	N = 80		FINLAND	N = 73	
Multiple R	.41		Multiple R	.35	
R Square	.17		R Square	.13	
Adj R Square	.06		Adj R Square	.06	
Variable	Beta	Sig T	Variable	Beta	Sig T
IPCTBLUE	-.39	.01***	IPCTBLUE	-.24	.04**
MAYED	.13	.27	IPOP3544	-.17	.14
FEMMAY	-.16	.16	MAYED	-.15	.20
IV144	.17	.19	IV144	.10	.41
FORNSTK	.17	.24	FEMMAY	.00	.97
IPOP3544	-.12	.44			
MAYYRS	-.02	.88			
IPCINCT	.23	.09			
LIPOPT	-.04	.77			

A - Step 2. Traditional Class/Party Politics: Party Drives Mayor's Preferences: Beta are Strong

Dependent Variable: PRFAVG

FRANCE	N = 80		FINLAND	N = 73	
Multiple R	.51		Multiple R	.50	
R Square	.23		R Square	.25	
Adj R Square	.15		Adj R Square	.17	
Variable	Beta	Sig T	Variable	Beta	Sig T
IPARTY	-.42	.00***	IPARTY	-.50	.00****
FEMMAY	.03	.79	IPCTBLUE	-.29	.04**
IV144	.18	.15	IMEANEDU	-.26	.06*
MAYYRS	-.12	.29	IV144	.18	.14
MAYED	-.11	.35	IPOP3544	.12	.30
IPOP3544	.11	.42	MAYED	-.08	.49
LIPOPT	.08	.50	FEMMAY	-.03	.81
FORNSTK	.11	.42			
IPCTBLUE	-.01	.92			
IPCINCT	.09	.50			

B - Step 1. Four Countries Illustrate Weak Class Politics: Betas Are Insignificant or Reversed for Blue Collar

Dependent Variable: IPARTY

NORWAY	N = 364			CANADA	N = 67			JAPAN	N = 70			AUSTRALIA	N = 37		
Multiple R	.34			Multiple R	.38			Multiple R	.45			Multiple R	.46		
R Square	.11			R Square	.15			R Square	.20			R Square	.21		
Adj R Square	.10			Adj R Square	.03			Adj R Square	.15			Adj R Square	.05		
Variable	Beta	Sig T		Variable	Beta	Sig T		Variable	Beta	Sig T		Variable	Beta	Sig T	
MAYED	27	.00***		CATHMY	-.26	.06*		IPCTBLUE a	.45*	.00***		IPCINCT	24	25	
IPCINCT	22	.00***		IPOP3544	.24	.06*		MAYYRS	13	28		FORNSTK	-.19	29	
IPCTBLUE	.05	.48		FEMMAY	-.19	13		MAYED	07	56		MAYED	-.19	31	
LIPOPT	-.02	.77		IV144	-.18	18		IV144	01	91		LIPOPT	-.17	35	
IV144	06	-.22		MAYYRS	16	22						IPCTBLUE	-.18	.38	
FEMMAY	06	20		FORNSTK	-.12	38						IV144	09	63	
				IPCTSEC	-.05	.84									
				MAYED	02	87									

B - Step 2. Four Countries Illustrate Less Class Influence on Spending Preferences:
Low or Insignificant Beta Coefficients for Blue Collar Variable, Although Party Is Strong in Norway, Japan, and Australia

Dependent Variable: PRFAVG

NORWAY	N = 362			CANADA	N = 66			JAPAN	N = 76			AUSTRALIA	N = 95 (34) c		
Multiple R	.34			Multiple R	.40			Multiple R	.27			Multiple R	.71		
R Square	.11			R Square	.16			R Square	.07			R Square	.50		
Adj R Square	.09			Adj R Square	.02			Adj R Square	.02			Adj R Square	.36		
Variable	Beta	Sig T		Variable	Beta	Sig T		Variable	Beta	Sig T		Variable	Beta	Sig T	
IPARTY	-.26	.00***		FORNSTK	28	.04***		IPARTY	.21	.05***		IPARTY	-.65	.00***	
FEMMAY	15	.00***		IPOP3544	18	20		IPCTBLUE	.21	15		IV144	27	11	
LIPOPT	-.04	53		CATHMY	-.15	30		MAYYRS	18	16		LIPOPT	-.23	14	
IPCINCT	-.12	04		IPARTY	-.09	52		MAYED	03	78		FORNSTK	-.19	24	
MAYED	00	88		MAYED	-.07	59		IV144	01	91		IPCTBLUE	.14	.46	
IV144	00	99		FEMMAY	06	64						MAYED	-.05	76	
				IPCTSEC	-.05	.69						IPCINCT	05	77	
				IV144	05	72									
				MAYYRS	00	98									

TABLE 4A.3 Why Do Mayors Support Higher Spending? International Contrasts

C - Step 1. For the U.S. Percent Non-White Is Strong, Blue Collar Is Insignificant			C - Step 2. The US Falls in the Middle: Race Performs Like Party and Class in France and Finland, but With Less Powerful Effects		
Dependent Var: IPARTY			Dependent Var: PRFAVG		
UNITED STATES	N = 239		UNITED STATES	N = 239	
Multiple R	.35		Multiple R	.27	
R Square	.12		R Square	.07	
Adj R Square	.09		Adj R Square	.03	
Variable	Beta	Sig T	Variable	Beta	Sig T
CATHMY	-.23	.00***	XNWH80US	.18	.03
XNWH80US	-.15	.05**	IV144	-.11	.11
MAYYRS	-.10	.14	IPARTY	-.07	.33
LIPOPT	-.10	.15	FEMMAY	.06	.34
MAYED	.08	.23	FORNSTK	.07	.36
IPCTBLUE	-.04	.54	MAYYRS	.04	.57
FEMMAY	-.02	.70	CATHMY	.02	.74
FORNSTK	-.01	.85	MAYED	-.01	.85
IV144	.00	.96	LIPOPT	-.01	.90
			IPCINCT	.00	.95

PRFAVG — Average spending preference of mayor on 13 FAUI items

LIPOPT — Log of city population

IMEANEDU — Mean level of education for the city's population

IPCINCT — Mean level of income for the city's population

IPCTSEC — Percent of the population in manufacturing

IPOP3544 — Percent of the population 35 to 44 years old

IPCTBLUE — Percent of the population who are blue collar workers

IPARTY — Mayor's party position on 0-100 scale of left-right party ideology (low=left)

IV144 — Age of mayor

CATHMY — Dummy variable for Catholic mayors (1=Catholic, 0=not)

MAYED — Years of education for the mayor

MAYYRS — Years as mayor

FEMMAY — Dummy variable for female mayors (1=female, 0=male)

FORNSTK — Percent of the population who are foreigners and/or immigrants

XNWH80US — Percent non-white residents in city (US only)

Note: Table 4A.3 shows the detailed results summarized in Figure 4.5. Steps 1 and 2 refer to the paths in Figure 4.5. These are multiple regressions to explain in Step 1, IPARTY, mayor's party. Step 2 explains support by mayors for increased spending on an index of up to 13 municipal spending areas, PRFAVG. The Multiple R, R Square, and Adjusted R2 are for equations containing all independent variables reported here. Similar models were utilized in each country, however not all independent variables were completely identical; see discussion of each in Appendix. Key variables for class and race politics are bold throughout: percent Blue Collar, Left-Right partisanship, and for the U.S. percent non-white.

Beta = standardized regression coefficient; Sig. T = significance (probability) level for that independent variable. Variables are ranked by the significance of the T statistic. For Sig T *=significant at .10 level; **=significant at .05 level; ***=significant at .01 level.

[a] Blue collar is the "wrong" direction for Japan, indicating that blue collar voters elect more conservative candidates. This is the opposite of "normal" class politics, but consistent with Japanese voting research.

[b] Percent blue collar not included in this regression because of multi-collinearity with IPARTY

[c] The Australia N = 95 for survey variables, except for IPARTY for which N = 37.

Source: FAUI surveys of mayors in each country supplemented by census and similar data.

Comments on Table 4A.3: Findings are robust for blue collar and party for the two countries illustrating Type A Traditional Class Politics. Type B is intermediary. Canada shows no effect of either blue collar or party in Step 1 or 2, suggesting very little class politics. In two of the other countries, differences in reported partisanship complicate interpretation. To simplify we have generally analyzed in this table only those mayors who reported party membership. But for Australia, this is just thirty-seven of the ninety-five mayors, that is, most Australian mayors are officially independent. In Japan even fewer mayors report party affiliation, but as Japanese councils are usually highly partisan, we assign the mayor the average party affiliation of the council. In Australia and Japan, Step 1 indicates no significant impact of blue collar residents on mayor's party (or is reversed in sign in Japan), but in Step 2, party does affect mayor's ideology. We might thus designate Australia and Japan as party-politicized, but not class based. But "party politicized" is by comparison only with the United States and Canada, where similar methods (i.e., omitting nonparty affiliated mayors) generates no impact of either blue collar or party in Step 1 or 2. "Party-politicized" also overstates the party effects for Australian cities generally, since most mayors are nonpartisan. The United States is unusual, first in that race (and Catholic) overwhelm blue collar in explaining party affiliation of mayors in Step 1. In Step 2, party has no impact on ideology in the United States, in sharp contrast to five of the six other countries, where party is the leading variable explaining ideology. The Finnish sample is for the larger cities; class politics effects weaken if smaller towns are included—for which we had partial data.

The same model was initially specified for Steps 1 and 2 for all countries. However multicollinearity (r > .4) among some variables led us to omit them. Specifically:

Country	Associated Variable	Variable Omitted
Finland	IPCTBLUE	IMEANEDU
Norway	IV144	MAYYRS
"	IPCTBLUE	IPOP3544
Japan	IPCTBLUE	IPCINCT
"	IPCTBLUE	IPOP3544
"	IPCTBLUE	IMEANEDU
United States	IPCTBLUE	IPCINCT

FEMMAY was omitted in Japan as there were no female mayors.

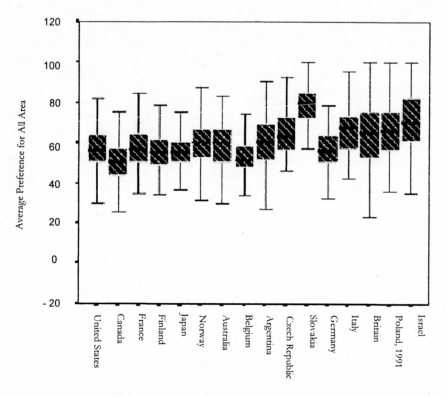

FIGURE 4.A1 High and Low Spending Mayors Vary Considerably Within Countries

Note: There are just a few national differences in spending preferences, but large differences among cities within counties. This is a standard boxplot of average spending preferences of the mayor for all areas, PRFAVG, by country. The dark line is the mean, the boxed image is a function of the standard deviation.

had data from two or three sources, intercorrelations of left-right rankings were nearly .9. We assigned the party of each mayor and council member in our survey an IPARTY score from these sources to permit analyzing, for instance, how strong the impact of blue-collar residents was on the mayor's party. Many analyses were replicated using individual parties as dummy variables for each party and logistic regression.

PRFAVG - Average spending preference of mayor on thirteen FAUI items. The key item was Mayor Q4: "Please indicate your own preferences about spending. Circle one of the six answers for each of the 13 policy areas. 1 Spend a lot less on services provided by the city 2 Spend somewhat less 3 Spend the same as is now spent 4 Spend somewhat more 5 Spend a lot more 6 DK Don't know/not applicable. Policy areas: All areas of city government, Primary and secondary education, Social welfare, Streets and parking, Mass transit, Public health and hospitals, Parks and recreation, Low income housing, Police protection, Fire protection, Capital stock (e.g., roads, sewers, etc.), Number of municipal employees, Salaries of municipal employees." The mean for a city was calculated if the mayor provided answers for a minimum of four policy areas, since some countries and mayors omitted items.

SOCCONS summed two social liberalism/conservatism items:

Q19 (V131) Would you be for or against sex education in public schools? (Circle one number) 1 For 2 Against 3 Don't Know/Not Applicable

Q20 (V132) Do you think abortion should be legal under any circumstance, legal only under certain circumstances, or never legal under any circumstances? (Circle one number) 1 Under any circumstances 2 Under certain circumstances 3 Never legal 4 Don't know/Not Applicable.

LIPOPT = Log of city population for a year near the time of the survey, often 1985 or 1990.

IMEANEDU = Mean level of education for the city's population, specifically the number of years of study was calculated from the categories (e.g. high school graduate) in which each national Census reported education. We consulted with education experts to ascertain the number of years of study that corresponded to each census category for each country.

IPCINCT = Mean level of income per capita for the city's population. In countries where this was not directly available, such as France, the best available measure of local wealth was used.

IPCTSEC = Percent of the local labor force working in manufacturing

IPOP3544 = Percent of the population 35 to 44 years old

IPCTBLUE = Percent of the local labor force who are blue-collar workers, i.e. who work as manual laborers or "production workers".

IPARTY Mayor's party position on 0–100 scale of left-right party ideology (low = left)

IV144 = Age of mayor in years

CATHMY = Dummy variable for Catholic mayors (1 = Catholic, 0 = not)

MAYED = Years of education for the mayor, calculated in similar manner to IMEANEDU above.

MAYYRS = Years served as mayor

FEMMAY = Dummy variable for female mayors (1 = female, 0 = male)

FORNSTK = Percent of population who are foreigners and/or immigrants

XNWH80US = Percent nonwhite residents in city (used only in US)

Split Halves Regression

The split halves regression near the end of Chapter 4 appears in Table 4A.4.

Questions About the NPC Approach

One reviewer asked if the NPC was "biased toward the industrialized world." This merits brief comment. The chapter 2 propositions suggest that the New Political Culture arises first in more affluent areas, with residents who are better educated, more often work in high-tech and service occupations, and are younger. Boulder, Colorado, is a strong illustrative case; so is Orange County, California. Examples of NPC issues in the politics of such places include (1) a sensitivity to social concerns and (2) the environment and growth management. Leadership in NPC places stresses more voluntary groups that focus on single issues. By contrast, in locations that have less-affluent, less-educated residents with stronger

TABLE 4A.4 SPD Analysis: Mayor's Policy Distance from the National Party

	Mayor's Policy Distance-SPD	Atkinson Ineq. of Education B	Atkinson Ineq. of Education t-statistic	Iparty score (Left-Right, Rights high) B	Iparty score (Left-Right, Rights high) t	Percent Blue Collar B	Percent Blue Collar t
UNITED STATES	Low	0.37	1.54	-0.19	-1.10	-0.31	-1.64
	High	0.61	1.78	0.24	1.00	-0.41	-1.45
CANADA	Low	1.64	1.17	-0.47	-1.33		
	High	1.25	0.81	0.43	0.58		
FRANCE	Low	-0.30	-0.34			0.35	0.69
	High	-2.23	-0.99			0.03	0.03
FINLAND	Low	-0.25	-0.29	-0.36	-7.55	-0.44	-2.63
	High	-0.17	-0.11	-0.51	-5.40	-0.71	-1.89
JAPAN	Low	-0.05	-0.04	-0.12	-1.81	-0.36	-1.39
	High	1.65	1.01	-0.14	-0.89	0.71	1.76
NORWAY	Low	0.01	0.02	-0.21	-5.49	-0.08	-0.66
	High	-1.74	-1.35	-0.03	-0.17	-0.43	-1.11
GERMANY	Low			-0.32	0.14		
	High			-0.35	-3.05		
ITALY	Low			-0.39	-2.32		
	High			-0.05	-1.23		

Note: This table splits the cities within each country into two halves, high and low on SPD. High SPD indicates more "independent" mayors in their ideology and party organization. The regression results show that they generally responded more to local social inequality (Atkinson index) in their policies concerning redistributive fiscal matters (public housing, welfare, etc.), indicated by higher b statistics. By contrast mayors with low SPD scores are closer to their national parties, responded less to Atkinson inequality (indicated by lower b statistics), and show more impact (higher b statistics) from their national party (IPARTY) and from percent blue collar residents on their fiscal policies.

The colums show the b and t statistics for three independent variables about which we had clear hypotheses. The full model was a multiple regression with redistributive fiscal policy (redistrx) as dependent variable and independent variables similar to those in regressions above: iatkedu5, iv130, spoix, media, iparty, iv144, mayed, mayyrs, femmay, ipctblue, ipop3544, fornstk, and cathmy.

We do not have a good measure of statistical significance of the differences in b's between high and low halves. Judging roughly from the t's, some differences are probably not significant, but others appear to be. Other more powerful statistical methods can assess the magnitude of these interactions more precisely and not loose data by splitting just at the mid-point (e.g. multiplicative interaction terms in OLS models, or various logistic models, such as those inspired by Leo Goodman). To keep the presentation simple, however, we only report split halves.

Source: International FAUI surveys.

manufacturing traditions, one finds not the NPC but more traditional politics. More salient are classic concerns of low-income persons for welfare and jobs, combined with political activism stressing ethnic groups, unions, and parties.

Does this formulation reflect a bias toward the industrialized world and less sensitivity to Third World countries? Yes and no. It is a theory that stresses characteristics more developed in places like Boulder rather than Newark or Calcutta. But insofar as the propositions identify characteristics (higher income, education, etc.) that distinguish locations, we test them mainly by comparing cities and countries. That is, to test our propositions, we need variation: both rich and poor cities with residents that vary on the dimensions the propositions identify. For most countries we have national populations of cities over a certain population size; for example, in the United States all 1,030 cities over 25,000; in Canada all cities over 20,000; and so on. We did not over sample rich or poor cities; we use the national population of cities over a certain size, which is ideal for testing such propositions. The countries included clearly over sample the Western postindustrial countries compared to the rest of the world. But these are the key countries where, in terms of the propositions, we should expect to find the NPC. This is not a bias in the sense that we ignore a key causal factor. It might be considered a bias in that we do not seek to model the details of non-NPC politics. That is simply the topic of another book.

Does multiple regression (OLS) bias results? Many analysts in the strong class politics tradition (e.g., Hout et al. 1994) stress the value of logistic regression over Ordinary Least Squares (OLS). The OLS regressions we computed for class politics in Table 4A3 were replicated by Ziad Munson (1995) using logistic regression. Results were very close to those using OLS.

Part 3

How Hierarchies and Parties Specifically Redirect Politics and Policy Priorities

5

Urban Political Parties: Role and Transformation

Vincent Hoffmann-Martinot

Introduction

This report presents a comparative study of the role of political parties in cities. This study uses data from the FAUI program of comparative research, especially the mayoral survey and municipal data on elections and citizens' characteristics. The FAUI program has analyzed local public policies by administering questionnaires to mayors, municipal councilors, and chief administrative officers and by studying interactions among political personnel, municipal employees, and interested groups. Although the FAUI survey has been conducted in thirty-five countries, this study concerns the FAUI surveys in the United States, Canada, Australia, Japan, Norway, Finland, Israel, and France. Table 5.1 presents characteristics of eight national samples of mayors who responded to FAUI surveys. Terry Nichols Clark is International and U.S. FAUI coordinator, but country experts directed surveys for each of the seven other nations.

These eight surveys were conducted between 1983 (United States and Canada) and 1989 (Israel). FAUI researchers administered the questionnaire to all mayors whose cities exceeded a certain population:

- in the United States, the 1,030 cities of more than 25,000 inhabitants
- in Canada, cities of more than 10,000 inhabitants of Ontario and the western states
- in France, the 382 cities of more than 20,000 inhabitants
- in Finland, the totality of the 445 communes
- in Japan, 674 cities (*sh*)

TABLE 5.1   Characteristics of Cities Sampled in Eight Countries

	USA	CANADA	FRANCE	FINLAND
Date	1983	1983	1985	1985
N	421	100	120	69
Minimal population	25,075 Winona (MN)		20,008 Hazebrouk	1,864 Kaskinen
Maximal population	7,071,637 New York (NY)		2,176,243 Paris	485,795 Helsinki
Median population	49,559 St. Cloud (MN)		33,622 Rezé	19,671 Raisio

	JAPAN	NORWAY	AUSTRALIA	ISRAEL
Date	1987	1986	1988	1989
N	101	380	150	19
Minimal population	20,120 Isikawa	269 Utsira	8,173	
Maximal population	539,842	447,257 Oslo	193,735	
Median population	65,308 Toki	4,323 Hareid	37,732	

- in Norway, 454 communes
- in Australia, 242 communes of more than 15,000 inhabitants
- in Israel, the 39 cities.

In most of the cases, the mayors were interviewed, but in Finland and Norway even officials of small communes were included.

The Roles of the Mayors

Mayors have different roles in different countries. In France, the mayor is the most powerful official. In Norway, the mayor is first among equals. In all nations except Finland, the mayor is above all a deputy of the people. In Finland, the title of mayor is borne by a clerk who directs the executive board and is nominated by the municipal council. The director of the Finnish FAUI study chose another official—the popularly elected president of the executive board—as the functional equivalent of mayor.

This report will successively concern the following: the theory of the New Political Culture (NPC); the present transformation of local partisan systems; the institutional and political role of parties in local political systems; and the variation of parties' organizational structure.

It draws on works that compare local politics cross-nationally.

The NPC Theory

Terry Nichols Clark developed the theory of the New Political Culture in several papers (e.g. Clark and Inglehart 1990, Clark and Lipset, 1991, Clark 1994a), in which he argues that "class analysis has grown increasingly inadequate in recent decades as traditional hierarchies have declined and new social differences have emerged" (Clark and Lipset, 1991: 397) and that "politics is organized less by class and more by other loyalties" (Clark and Lipset, 1991: 408). *"Political issues shift with more affluence: as wealth increases, people take the basics for granted; they grow more concerned with life-style and amenities.*

TABLE 5.2   An Overview of Intitutional Structures of Local Government in the Eight Countries

	USA	Canada	France	Finland	Japan	Norway	Australia	Israel
Electoral System								
Majority	x	x	x		x		x	
Proportional reprersentation				x		x	x	x
At large	x	x	x	x	x	x	x	x
Districts	x	x	x		x		x	
Preferential voting						x		
Opened lists				x		x		
Non-partisan elections	x	x						
Direct election of mayor	x	x			x		x	x
Mayor term length (years)	2–4	1–3	6	1	4	4	1–3	4
Municipal council term length	2–4	1–3	6	4	4	4	2–3	4
Modes of direct citizen participation								
Primaries	x							
Referendum	x	x		x				
Cities initiative	x	x			x			
Recall	x	x			x			
Internal distribution of power								
Parliamentary regime	x	x			x	x	x	
Presidential regime	x	x	x		x		x	x

Source: Assembled by V. Hoffmann-Martinot from sources such as works cited for this chapter.

Younger, more educated and more affluent persons in more affluent and less hierarchical societies should move farthest from traditional class politics" (Clark and Lipset, 1991: 403; emphasis in original). Parties have a distinctive causal role in the rise of the NPC. Closed parties (i.e., ones that ignore citizens' concerns or don't incorporate them into policies) tend to alienate citizenry. Closed parties usually are self-perpetuating, hierarchical, and oligarchical and often represent a particular class or social group. Citizens protest against closed parties by voting less frequently (declining turnout), becoming independent (partisan dealignment), and joining nonparty organized groups (e.g., ecological). The decline of absolute class voting demonstrates that traditional loyalties (class/party membership) explain less than previously; and that new parties and organizations emerged to fill the gap between oligarchical parties and citizens' preferences.

Closed parties are the mainstay of class politics, in which traditional stratification hierarchies generate vertically organized groups that are comprehensive in covering many issues (Clark and Inglehart, 1990, fig. 7). There are clear ideological cleavages, and high r's between fiscal and social issues. People who have higher income, occupation, education, and status tend to join social clubs, business organizations, and chambers of commerce and support traditional rightist parties that are fiscally and socially conservative (Clark and Inglehart, 1990, fig. 7). People who have lower income, occupation, education, and status tend to join trade unions and ethnic and neighborhood groups and support traditional left parties that are fiscally and socially liberal (Clark and Inglehart, 1990, fig. 7). Class politics is a contest between capitalists and workers over redistribution, workplace conditions, unemployment, and other materialistic issues.

The NPC is a reaction against class politics and hierarchically organized parties. The NPC is led by voluntary groups organized around social issues, like gender and the environment. Such groups partially supplant traditional political parties by incorporating social issues that traditional parties failed to address. Voluntary groups more often have a horizontal organizational structure as well as democratic decisionmaking, which differentiate them from most trade unions, business associations, and old parties. Such groups lobby elected officials and protest governmental actions that undermine individual or group rights. Such groups constitute the NPC "New Left," which grew out of protest movements led by peace, civil rights, and feminist advocates. NPC members of the New Left have changed traditional leftist parties by encouraging them to sponsor women's candidates; to organize caucuses for environmentalists, homosexuals, feminists, and ethnic minorities; and to listen to historically underrepresented groups like blacks, homosexuals, and women. Green or environmental parties have won seats in many European parliaments since 1980; such parties generally have democratic organizations that incorporate the preferences of local chapters. They are disproportionately supported by young people who have university degrees and high incomes. Most political parties now try to court environmentalist voters by proclaiming their commitment to conservation, reducing pollution, and so on.

New Politics and Political Parties

Growing Distance Between Citizens and Parties in Local Politics

During the 1980s, France and other European countries began institutional reforms of decentralization, which do not seem to have increased citizens' involvement in local politics. Electoral participation in municipal elections has declined, regardless of the orientation of institutional reforms (centralization in England, decentralization in France and the Scandinavian countries). Although the impact of local government on citizens has been increasing, citizens have been voting less frequently in local elections and disengaging from politics. Almost every new by-election witnesses an increased rate of poll strikes.

Since the 1960s, electoral participation has been decreasing in local elections in most Western countries.

- In the United States: The facts gathered with the help of the International City Management Association by Albert K. Karnig and Oliver B. Walter (Karnig and Walter, 1989: 20) reveal a constant increase in abstentionism in municipal elections in cities of more than 25,000 inhabitants.
- In France: About 6 percent fewer citizens voted in the first ballot of municipal elections held in 1989 than in those held in 1983. Also, 20 percent fewer citizens voted in the first ballot of the cantonal elections held in 1988 than in those held in 1982 (Hoffmann-Martinot, 1992).
- In Finland: Participation in municipal elections has been decreasing during the 1980s. The poorest rate of participation since the 1950s occurred in the municipal elections held in October 1988 (70 percent nationally and only 63 percent in Helsinki) (Heikki, 1989, Ståhlberg, 1990).
- In Norway: Participation in municipal elections held every fourth year has continuously decreased since 1963; it reached 65 percent in 1991, the lowest rate since 1947 (Bjørklund, 1988).
- In Israel: The decrease, of nearly 20 percent between 1950 and 1989, occurred mainly between 1978 and 1989—probably because national and local elections have not been simultaneous since 1978. In 1989, less than 50 percent of eligible voters voted in the local elections held in predominantly Jewish cities (42 percent in the three biggest cities: Jerusalem, Tel Aviv, and Haifa—45 percent in the other Jewish cities). Electoral participation averaged 76 percent in the predominantly Arabic cities (Kalchheim and Rosevitch, 1992).

Many of the nonvoters are interested in politics. They tend to be more "sophisticated" than other voters. They are unlikely to have a constant ideological and partisan affiliation yet are concerned about particular issues. This is the case in Finland. Quite recently the debate on discontent was fueled by some results from an opinion poll at the local government level. It was found that attitudes toward local government paralleled attitudes toward national government. Eight out of ten held that local politicians rapidly lose touch with their voters. The same share maintained that parties are interested in votes alone, not in the opinions of the voters. . . . At the same time, however, it has been noted that interest in politics has increased rather than decreased (Ståhlberg, 1990: 29).

Russell J. Dalton has developed a typology of partisan affiliation and political interest (Dalton, 1984): divide I (Interest in politics) by P (Proximity to parties). Dalton's typology indicates that there are four types of voters: the nonpolitical (I-/P-), the ritual partisans (I-/P+), the cognitive partisans (I+/P+), and the nonpartisans (I+/P-), whose numbers have been increasing. Members of the new middle classes, who fit the characteristics of the NPC, make up a disproportionate number of the nonpartisans—they are driving the shift from traditional loyalties (class and party) to loyalties based on personal values.

The transformation from class politics to NPC politics explains the decline of voting or party identification and the rise of individualized forms of citizens involvement in local politics. Associative renewal in France, Bürgerinitiativen in Germany, and the rising influence of Green parties are two examples. Norman H. Nie et al. have surveyed U.S. citizens and found that between 1967 and 1987 electoral participation has declined. However, membership in voluntary associations and in groups defending specific local interests has increased.

Split-ticket voting and preferential voting demonstrate the weakening of voters' traditional loyalties to class and party. Ticket splitting is voting for candidates belonging to different parties. Ticket splitting is impossible in countries like France that hold municipal, cantonal, and presidential elections on different days.[1] (The French regional elections have, however, been organized at the same time as the legislative elections of 1986 and the cantonal elections of 1992.) U.S. voters choose different types of representatives on the same day; ticket splitting in presidential-House, Senate-House, and state-local elections has continually increased since the 1960s. U.S. ticket splitting is highest in state-local elections, where it has increased from 28 percent in 1960 to 59 percent in the 1980s (Shaffer, 1992).

Ticket splitting has become increasingly common in Israel. In state-local elections held between 1955 to 1973, ticket splitting increased from 6 percent to 15.8 percent. Since 1978, the election of mayors and that of municipal councilors have been on the same day. Table 5.4 shows that split-ticket voting has increased since 1978 in Israeli local elections.

Decline of Political Parties?

Traditional political parties have been losing members and votes due to the decline of partisan identification and the weakening of partisan militancy; the fragmentation of partisan systems; and the marginalization of previously important parties, like communist parties (Franklin, Mackie, and Valen, 1992).[2]

Richard Katz and Peter Mair have gathered comparative data on party membership for Austria, Belgium, Denmark, Finland, West Germany, Italy, Netherlands, Norway, Sweden, and the United Kingdom. These data show that between the 1960s and the

TABLE 5.3   Evolution of Modes of Local Political Participation in the US

Mode of political participation	1967 (%)	1987 (%)	Evolution (%)
Regular vote at municipal elections	47	35	−12
Active membership in a local association	31	34	+3
Contacting a municipal official (issue)	14	24	+10
Contacting a municipal official (personal)	7	10	+3
Joining a group on a local specific issue	14	17	+3

Source: Norman H. Nie, Sydney Verba, Kay L. Schlozman, Henry E. Brady, and Jane Junn. 1989. *Participation in America: Continuity and Change.* Cambridge, Ma.: Harvard University, research report.

1980s party members have constituted a declining proportion of the electorate in all countries except Germany and Belgium. The rates in Finland and Norway are higher than the average but still have decreased from 18.9 percent to 12.9 percent in Finland and from 15.5 percent to 13.5 percent in Norway (Katz et al., 1992).

Still, party decline is not universal. In 1989–1990, Hans Geser administered a questionnaire to all 5,300 heads of the local Swiss parties, half of whom replied (Geser, 1991). He analyzed changes in the number, behavior, and methods of active militants; he did not analyze passive members and mere sympathizers. Geser concluded that between 1984 and 1989 the number of party militants increased in more than 50 percent of the cases. Since 1971, Swiss women have been able to vote. The entry of women could have increased the number of partisan militants in Swiss parties. Geser surveyed section leaders who perhaps tended to overestimate the weight and dynamism of their organizations (especially if we compare Geser's study to that conducted in 1981 by William Crotty, in which 72 percent of party officials in Chicago estimated that U.S. political parties had generally weakened between 1972 and 1981; only a minority of the party officials judged that this decline had affected their own section) (Crotty, 1986).

Samuel Eldersveld has argued that U.S. parties have not had progressively weaker local branches. Eldersveld studied the evolution of local partisan organizations from the 1950s to the 1980s in Detroit and Los Angeles (Eldersveld, 1986). Using, as measures of partisan activity, voters' registration, electoral canvassing, and activities of militants on election day, Elersveld did not note a clear decline of these indicators. He noted the rise in canvassing practices and the rise of black militant mobilization since the active local political involvement of the 1960s and 1970s, particularly in Detroit. The studies of Gibson et al. note the increasing number of local activists of U.S. parties from the 1960s to the 1980s. Gibson et al.: "Perhaps it is the very weakening of partisan attachments that has made it necessary for parties to become better organized, to become more effective at voter mobilization and persuasion" (Gibson et al., 1985).

Although parties may have strengthened their local organizations, citizens and even

TABLE 5.4 Difference in Percentage of Votes Received by Mayors and Votes Received by His Party's Municipal Councilors in Predominantly Jewish Cities in Israel

% of Votes for Mayor Above the Votes Received by His Party's Municipal Councilor	1989	1983	1978
Below 20%	21%	41%	40%
21–50%	38%	37%	30%
51–70%	12%	8%	9%
71–100%	9%	3%	5%
101% and over	5%	2%	1%

Source: Kalchheim and Rosevitch. 1992: 246.

many mayors have become increasingly distant from traditional parties. The increasing detachment of mayors from political parties demonstrates that a New Political Culture is emerging in our eight countries, especially in the United States, France, Japan, and Israel.

Since the 1970s, new popular mayors who distance themselves from traditional political parties have become common in U.S. local politics. Terry N. Clark and Lorna C. Ferguson (1983) have called such mayors "New Fiscal Populists" (NFPs), because they are fiscally conservative and socially liberal. Their increasing numbers have lessened the control of political parties over U.S. cities and have encouraged citizen input. NFP mayors resemble "urban populist" or "postmaterialist populist" mayors (Swanstrom, 1985, de Leon, 1991).

Many of the new mayors elected in France in 1983 and 1989 resemble the NFP mayors identified by Clark and Ferguson. Alain Carignon of Grenoble, Michel Noir of Lyon, or Noël Mamère of Bègles are NFP mayors who belong to rightist or leftist parties; they transcend traditional partisan divisions by disengaging themselves from partisan machines or even, as concerns Mamère, to struggle against them—"alone against all the others." This strategy is electorally beneficial because French voters are increasingly indifferent toward political parties. According to SOFRES polls held before the 1986 municipal elections, an increasing number of voters cast their vote based on the candidate's personality (50 percent in 1983, 58 percent in 1989) than on the political orientation of electoral lists (43 percent in 1983, 35 percent in 1989) (SOFRES, 1990). Despite local successes of NFP mayors, they must deal with existing local parties and their ramifications (in the sports and social-cultural sectors, for example). Candidates that totally break from existing parties have not succeeded. However, the breakup of the right-left continuum partially accounts for the electoral successes of NFP mayors in France—as does the disappearance, in the 1970s, of third-force alliances among the Right, the Center, and socialists. The rising numbers of postmaterialists weakened traditional leftist parties as well as the association between fiscal and social conservatism or liberalism. Factional dissidents transformed the French Communist Party by challenging its doctrinaire adherence to Stalinism. The Socialist Party was threatened by the "Big Bang," and the RPR was deeply divided on the European question. All of these developments favored the career of the "new independent" mayors.

The declining influence of urban partisan machines in Israel has disproportionately benefited independent mayors. This localization movement started in small communes and in large cities during the municipal election campaigns of 1973, during which local sections rebelled against central parties. Local sections hoped to affect the campaign strategies and selection of candidates; they clashed with central parties during the postelectoral negotiations on the formation of coalition municipal governments. Similar conflicts occurred following municipal elections in 1978 and 1983, in which mayors and national partisan organizations clashed. "Even though many people treat local government as unimportant, when looking at the future generation of leadership in Israel, they point with pride to the new crop of successful mayors, most of whom are not former generals brought in from outside the political process but truly local products who have come up from within their local communities" (Kalchheim and Rosevitch, 1992). Nonpartisan lists or new parties have been competing against traditional parties like the Likud and the Labor Party. The nonpartisan lists have multiplied since the 1970s and have been generally predominant in upper-middle-class suburbs like Kfar Shmaryahu, Kiryat Tivon, and Ramat Hasharon; this concentration shows that members of the new middle classes are protesting against local political clientelism and hope to improve the efficiency of services. A similar orientation in favor of a "good government" has also characterized many developing cities (in Kiryat Ono, we thus have the *Hakiryah Shelanu* [Our Town] list, in Kiryat Shmona, the *Hatnua Lizechuyot Haezrach* [Movement of Civic Rights] list). In 1983, these nonpartisan parties constituted 25 of the 96 mayors elected, and they received at least 17 percent of the votes in the elections for municipal councils (Goldberg, 1984). These nonpartisan parties received the most votes among the new parties that made a breakthrough in the 1989 elections. Other new parties included the "Zionist left," the Citizens Rights Movement (CRM), the Mapam, and the Centrist Shinui. The new parties do best in the suburbs and have an upper-middle-class majority. These new environmentalist, reformist, and progressive parties disregard the left-right demarcation and attract voters based on issues; they are close to the European Greens. According to Daniel Elazar and Shmuel Sandler (1992: 13-41, 32), "CRM is an Israeli-style Green party; and Shinui is what Terry Clark has described as Neo-Populist—fiscally conservative and liberal on life-style issues."

We know that most Japanese mayors are independent. The proportion of mayors who are not affiliated to a party increased from 74 percent in 1970 to 97 percent in 1987. As in other countries, this increase shows the rise of "new independent voters." Such voters are disproportionately new-middle-class people who have gradually abandoned left-wing parties, especially the Socialist Party, which the new middle classes supported in the 1960s (Steiner et al., 1980). In 1987, there was only one socialist mayor in Japanese cities (shi), compared to 24 in 1970. The new middle classes have transferred their votes from the socialists to independent candidates or to candidates belonging to new parties like the New Party of Japan.

Parties and Citizens

In strongly partisan local systems citizens have little control over municipal administration; political parties control elections and do not allow direct democracy. The parties stifle citizen input by choosing the candidates and by blocking citizens from choosing other candidates. Parties thus block participatory democracy and encourage alienated citizens to join new parties and voluntary groups that represent their interests.

Table 2 indicates that the United States, Canada, and Japan have referenda and citizen initiatives. Direct local democracy is part of the North American political culture. Fried and Rabinovitz estimate in their international comparative study that "only Swiss cities accord similar authority on voters to decide municipal policy and structure" (Steiner et al., 1980).

The town meeting is the oldest form of self-government in the former British colonies of North America. Inspired by the democratic practice of ancient Greece, it has been common in New England and persists today in thirteen northeastern states, particularly Vermont, Massachusetts, and Connecticut. About 1,000 U.S. towns hold regular town meetings. In New England, the town meeting is held annually; each citizen has the right to take part. Popularly elected selectmen choose the subjects of the meeting. The town meeting was suited for small rural communities that faced local problems. As the size and heterogeneity of towns increased, town meetings became less capable of managing increasingly complex local problems. Certain New England towns created "representative town meetings," conducted by popularly elected members.

Since the 1970s, initiatives and local referenda have become more common in U.S. cities. Recall elections are frequently held. Referenda and recall elections are also common in Canada, where early reformers privileged citizen participation. In Ontario and many western provinces, the Municipal Act provided for referenda on new municipal loans. Between 1955 and 1965, 168 Canadian municipalities held referenda; between 1964 and 1968, 109 local referenda were held in British Columbia alone, according to Higgins (1986).

Following World War II, occupying U.S. forces introduced local democracy into Japan and South Germany to check the excessive power of municipal bureaucracies. The U.S. forces strengthened local democracy by allowing:[3]

- Two percent of the municipal electorate to ask the mayor to consider, amend, or cancel a decision made by the municipal council;
- Two percent of the municipal electorate to submit proposals on municipal enterprises or local expenditure;
- One-third of the electorate to propose the dissolution of the municipal council; and
- One-third of the electorate to initiate a recall election on a municipal councilor or an administrative officer. Recalling a representative requires majority support of voters.

Direct democracy is uncommon in the other five countries considered in our research. Finnish and Norwegian municipal legislation permits local referenda, which have never been held. Norwegian law requires referenda on linguistic and temperance issues. French municipal referenda are purely consultative; the municipal council can ignore the results of a referendum. Municipal laws adopted since the Third Republic have vitiated direct or representative local democracy. The stand of the mayor of Auxerre, expressed at the beginning of this century, still reflects that of a great majority of elected municipal representatives in France: "We do not understand that an elected municipal council should ask a population what it should do. At this rate, anyone could act as a municipal councilor. The best referendum consists of repeating discussions in public at the municipal council, of debates in newspapers, and renewed contact with the public. This is to extract what is profitable from all propositions" (Legendre, 1969:74).

Parties limit citizen input by imposing their candidates upon voters. Spanish political parties pressured the Spanish Parliament to adopt municipal electoral legislation that allows blocked lists. The 19 November 1992 French law pertains to communes of more than 3,500 inhabitants; it allows parties to submit complete lists to voters. French voters cannot add, suppress, or modify any of the lists' names. Israeli parties can also prevent citizens from modifying the structure of candidate lists. In 1950, an alliance composed of deputies of the Mapai, Mapam, and a member of Palei Agudat in Israel brought down the General Zionists' attempt to allow voters to strike off certain names (Goldberg, 1988).

France and Israel differ from the Scandinavian countries, where voters can write in candidates or vote preferentially. Finnish and Norwegian communes are small and have close relations between citizens and municipal politicians. The Norwegian political system attempts to balance the respective influences of parties and citizens; the parties can force the opinion of voters by putting twice on their lists as much as one-quarter of their candidates. Norwegian voters can (Henriksen, 1991):

- Replace as many as one quarter of the names on a list by those from another one (thus, new names cannot be freely chosen);
- suppress a name; and
- give an additional vote to one or more candidates.

The selection of candidates in municipal elections by intrapartisan authorities constitutes a third mechanism that can prevent the direct intervention of citizens. This is the case in all eight countries—except for the United States, where there are primaries in all states (including Rhode Island and Connecticut, which originally opposed primaries) (Mayhew, 1986). Primaries are elections by citizens to choose the party candidates. They are open to all citizens who declare their partisan affiliation, which they do not have to prove. Primaries are one of the main foundations of direct democracy.

Anti- or Pro-Partisan Local Political Culture

Late-nineteenth-century reformers in the United States hoped to reduce the role of local parties. Their motto was: "There is no Democratic or Republican way to pave a street." Local government was weak then because of the fragmentation of municipal institutions (e.g., two-chamber systems, mayors elected for short-term mandates with limited power, local administrations virtually submerged by the flux of demands from the new Central and Southern European immigrants). Partisan machines ran most cities and gave public jobs to immigrants. Immigrants reciprocated by voting for the machine's candidates and becoming loyal members of the party. Each ward had an agent who doled out favors to the immigrants. The machines had a vertical organization in which precinct captains were subordinate to ward committeemen; municipal councilors were subordinate to the party boss. The system depended on mutually reciprocated favors, which created obligations between patrons (political officials) and clients (voters).

Robert Merton and Raymond Wolfinger have argued that the machines integrated immigrants into local politics and provided otherwise unavailable social services. The service exchange relations with the private sector were often excellent. Despite the absence of sufficiently solid governmental structures, the machines guaranteed a regular running of cities. However, the machines did not generally alleviate poverty; they gave favors and help to individuals but were conservative in resisting economic and social reforms. Cases of corruption by enterprises were common. How much they aided social integration of different immigrant and minority groups remains disputed. Some recent work suggests that in many cities, one group, often Irish, dominated and marginalized the others (Gosnell 1937, 1969; Clark 1975).

The reformers included social reformers, who wished to end the ghettos and the obvious social inequalities, and the "structural" reformers, who only wanted to modify the institutions to end the corruption. Both groups saw the machine as the main source of urban crisis. The National Municipal League campaigned against the machine and for "good government." These reformers mainly issued from the upper middle class and business. They wished a new mode of government: clean, industrious, inspired by the management system of the private sector, and suspicious of lower classes, which were the most active support basis of machines. They proposed two major institutional changes:

1. Non-partisan elections. Excluding parties from local elections should privilege general interests over partisan interests and "depoliticize" local elections.

2. Substituting districts for at-large elections. This would break up the whole organizational logic of the machine: wards, precincts, and so on. Elections by districts allowed minorities and ethnic groups to elect their own representatives. One of the most active reformers wrote: "Districts populated by bandits and thieves can choose the latter as municipal councilors." Reformers thought that candidates for an at-large election should address themselves to the electorate rather than to the inhabitants of one area. This reform would also allow the election of more qualified, competent, rational, and disinterested persons. Such elitism would give more power to the upper classes as well as to industrial and commercial groups—to the detriment of underprivileged social groups and machines.

The reform movement rapidly spread to small cities with few recent immigrant ethnic groups and to regions in the West and Midwest, that is, where machines were the least powerful. Between 1910 and 1930, the nonpartisan system of election spread to half of the towns of more than 30,000 inhabitants. Today, 75 percent of U.S. cities whose population exceeds 25,000 inhabitants have nonpartisan elections. A shift away from at-large to district elections occurred with black ethnic mobilization and the voting-rights acts from the 1960s. During the 1970s, 63 percent of cities had at-large elections; in 1986, only 50 percent of them did (Welch, 1990).

All U.S. cities do not share the same antipartisan political culture. William Crotty (1986) noted the big differences in the role and organization of parties that persist within the United States. Chicago (Crotty, 1986) and Detroit were long ruled by a hierarchic, authoritarian, and clientelistic Democratic Party. Los Angeles (Marvick, 1986)[4] and Houston (even Nashville) represent the voluntary organizational model and are open and decentralized. Still, legal structures do not operate deterministically. Chicago long had a nominally nonpartisan municipal government in which candidates who parties officially supported were most likely to win elections. This led to the humorous quotation of Banfield and Wilson: "As a wit remarked, the [city] council [of Chicago] is composed of 47 nonpartisan Democrats and three nonpartisan Republicans" (Marvick, 1986). Nonpartisan cities can correspond to one of these three principal profiles:

- Parties exist, without necessarily playing a very active role; in most of the cases, according to Charles Adrian (1959), their impact is strongly limited.
- Parties are largely absent from the electoral game, where only interest coalitions supported by business groups or press bodies intervene; parties are "purely local" organizations that not only elect candidates but also exert some control on the activity of the elected officials_"slate-making associations," that is, organizations that only intervene in the selection and nomination of candidates.
- There are no parties or other replacing organizations, the electoral campaigns being centered on individuals, as is the case in numerous small cities.

The reformist conceptions also influenced the evolution of local government in Canada. In the late 1800s, Canadian cities introduced nonpartisan, at-large elections; cities reduced parties' power by separating decisions between an elected body and a strong managerial administration (in Edmonton, a board composed of two professional commissioners).[5] Canadian parties were less strong than U.S. parties (excluding cities like Toronto).[6] Consequently, parties are nearly absent in local elections. As James Lightbody underlines in his analysis of sociopolitical transformation in Edmonton, "Non-partisanship is very much a part of the ethos of Canadian local politics in general, and Western Canadian practices in particular. This local system coexists with an intensely partisan federal and provincial political process" (Lightbody, 1984) Thus, according to the results of a study in Alberta in 1983, competition was structured by political parties only in seven cities (Naßmacher, 1992). However, in Canada and in the United States, parties sometimes act behind the scenes. The Citizens' Committee of Winnipeg and its successors and the Civic Non-Partisan Association of Vancouver were actually Liberal/Conservative coalitions.

Australia has never had an antimachine reform movement. Parties have rarely played a significant role in cities. U.S.-style machines did not develop in Australian cities, which have generally had homogenous populations (the Labor Party in Richmond, Victoria, was quite rare in having had a strong organization). The local government has had little legitimacy and weak institutional and political resources; the national government and especially state governments had much more power and legitimacy than local governments. Australian local governments have a narrow range of responsibilities—states control education and police, unlike North American cities. They are also extremely fragmented in all cities except Brisbane: In 1966, there were 43 units of local government in Melbourne and 35 in Sydney. "Under such conditions, it is difficult to speak confidently of a 'city government,' or to expect much real authority and political muscle being exercised" (Albinski, 1973).

Thus, parties are nearly absent from the Australian local political scene. According to the results of the survey research led in the 1970s by Margaret Bowman (1976), they are not represented in the municipal councils of South Australia, West Australia, and Tasmania; they have representatives in only a few cities. The elected officials belonging to a party frequently hide their affiliation because, according to John R. Robbins, "they would usually maintain that their party affiliation is irrelevant to their role in local government, many of them rejecting the notion of party involvement" (Robbins, 1990: 7).

Antipartisan or nonpartisan ideology is present in French, Finnish, Japanese, Norwegian, and Israeli cities; it is generally less important than in the United States, Canada, and Australia—probably because national parties successfully consolidated their territorial implantation during the twentieth century. French political analysts like Jean-Luc Parodi (1983) and Albert Mabileau (1991) insist that this happened during the Fifth Republic. Stein Rokkan (in particular in Rokkan 1970) argues that Norwegian parties became territorially established as municipalities introduced proportional representation. In 1937, the Labor Party of Norway presented candidates in 92 percent of the rural communes and in all but one urban commune. Conservative parties in Norway were slower in establishing themselves because they allowed local *Honoratioren* groups to present independent lists, or *Borgerlige felleslister*; since 1945, the conservative parties have formed local organization to counteract the Labor Party. The general evolution is the same in Finnish municipalities, where the proportion of lists presented by the political parties at the municipal elections has continuously risen from 1945 (62 percent) to 1976 (98 percent) (Sundberg, 1988).

Organizational Strength and Ideology

The FAUI survey of mayors allows one to rigorously compare the mayors' partisanship and parties' organization.

North Americans view partisanship as a simple feeling of proximity to a given party; Europeans see it as party membership.[7] The formulation of the question has therefore varied according to the countries; it is deliberately open in the United States: Although many cities have nonpartisan elections, parties still are sometimes important. *What political party, if any, do you identify with?*. The question is precise in France: *To which political party do you belong?*. The Japanese FAUI survey did not ask mayors about their partisan affiliation but rather asked about the names and number of parties supporting the mayors.

Figure 5.1 presents the partisanship rate of mayors. We grouped the data into three categories: affiliation to a national party, independence, and no answer. Some independents belong to local parties, especially in North American cities. Figure 1 presents no answers because mayors answered most of the other questions of the FAUI questionnaire. No answers show an unquestionable distance from parties, though they do not clearly denote independence.[8] The numbers inside the bars correspond to the number of answers for each category; thus, in the United States, 301 mayors were close to a party

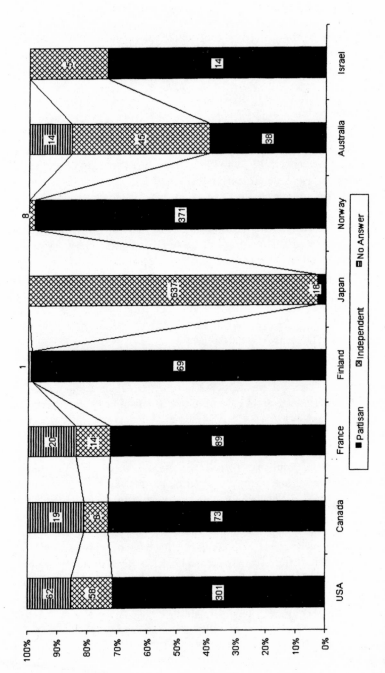

FIGURE 5.1 Percent Mayors Who Are Party Members

Source: For Japan, official statistics for 1987 published in Statistics Bureau, *Japan Statistical Yearbook,* Tokyo, 1988; other countries: FAUI surveys.

(so a bit more than 70 percent of all the answers); 58 claim their independence; we note 62 no answers.

This chart delineates three groups of countries: those in which most mayors are independent(Japan and Australia); those in which most mayors are partisan (United States, Canada, France, and Israel); and those in which virtually all mayors are partisan (Finland and Norway).

Japan is an odd case. Nearly all Japanese mayors are independent and have become more so since the 1970s. Twenty-six percent of Japanese mayors were partisan in 1970, 17 percent in 1984, 7 percent in 1979, 5 percent in 1984, and 3 percent in 1987. But Japanese parties are not absent from municipal politics. About 43 percent of municipal councilors were partisan between 1970 and 1987. Most Japanese mayors are supported by one or more parties. The Liberal Democratic Party (LDP) supported 86 of the 102 Japanese mayors who responded to the FAUI questions on partisan support.

Political parties play a small role in elections for mayor but have a large role in elections for Parliament and governor. Mayors' legitimacy results from direct election by the population and from maintaining a dense and personalized network of supporters (*koenkai*) founded on the reciprocal exchange of services.[9] Mayors attempt to portray themselves as a unifiers whose position and function are above partisan divisions. In 90 percent of the towns where the LDP is present, a heterogeneous coalition of parties supports the mayor. Thirty-one percent of mayors obtain one party's support (the LDP in 28 cases of 29), 12 percent of two, 12 percent of three, 30 percent of four, and 15 percent of five parties or more.

Japanese mayors try to break free from particular partisan interests, even if they have to hide partisan preferences or affiliation: "Many conservative candidates ... avoid the LPD's endorsement.... They believe that the LPD's party label is not only useless but also detrimental to their image as the representative of a neighborhood or a certain local community"(Wakata, 1986: 63).[10] Australia and Japan are the only countries where only a minority of mayors are affiliated to a party. Thus, the proportions in Figure 5.1 confirm the results of previous studies.

The data present an incomplete picture of Japanese and Australian local politics. Nominally independent mayors can be very close to a particular party. An Australian municipal representative said, "There's no politics in this council, we're all members of the National Party" (cited in Bowman, 1983). The Liberal Party of Australia has indirectly supported candidates like those of the Civic Reform Association in Sydney, whereas the Labor Party has tried to solidify its existing bases of support.

About 70 percent of U.S., Canadian, Israeli, and French mayors consider themselves close to a national party. Widespread institutional reforms did not suppress traditional parties in Canada and the United States. Certain mayors, who constitute 3 percent of the U.S. cities of the FAUI survey[11] claim affiliation to a "local party." The Berkeley Citizens Action is a local coalition heir to protest movements of the 1960s; it opposes the Democrats. Civic parties stand in municipal elections in one city. Canadian civic parties include the Independent Citizens Election Committee of Winnipeg, the Voters Association of Edmonton, and the Civic Non-Partisan Association of Vancouver.

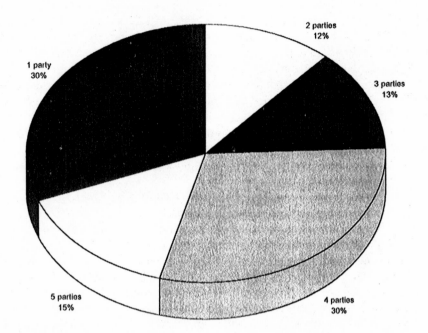

FIGURE 5.2 Distribution of Japanese Mayors according to their Partisan Support

Source: FAUI data (N = 94).

The first wave of civic parties resulted from the late-nineteenth-century reform movement, which was animated by a conservative and pro-business laissez-faire doctrine. The second wave of civic parties wanted to implement neighborhood assemblies and growth limit propositions to increase citizen input; they emerged during the late 1960s and included the French Groupes d'Action Municipaux. They can be considered as the precursors of the new politics of the 1980s and 1990s. In Edmonton, groups of citizens opposed the bureaucratic procedure of highway building and formed a local party called the Urban Reform Group of Edmonton. Once new civic parties become directly linked to the municipal administration, they will become less innovative.[12]

Local partisan organizations can be intimately linked to big parties. Teddy Kollek stands in the municipal elections as the leader to the "One Jerusalem Teddy's List," but everyone knows that the local section of the Labor Party supports him.

All Finnish mayors and 98 percent of Norwegian mayors consider themselves close to a national party. Official statistics concerning the partisan affiliation of municipal councilors confirm that nearly all Scandinavian municipal politicians are partisan. There were no abstentions in Finland and just one in Norway—but nearly 20 percent of U.S., Canadian, and Israeli mayors did not answer the FAUI question about partisan affiliation.

Secondly, it appears necessary, beyond the simple partisan affiliation of mayors, to try to compare the organizational force of local parties. In one of the rare comparative studies of political parties, William Crotty (1985: 52) distinguishes among decentralized, disorganized, noncohesive, elitist, and activist-based U.S. parties; and between highly centralized and organized and mass membership–based West European parties. This is a generalization on a national and international scale. There are important variations among the municipal organizations of U.S. parties; the variations depends on:

- Population: According to Mayhew (1986), large cities are most likely to have active and structure partisan organizations.
- Regional differences: The strongest parties are those of the old Northeast and Midwest cities.
- Level of education: As educational levels increase, the electorate becomes more critical and distant from parties; this weakens parties' organizations.
- Reformed institutions: At-large elections, council-manager government, and nonpartisan ballots reduce the influence of parties.

Strong local parties have not disappeared in the United States and are in fact common in cities marked by a clientelist political culture. Similar clientelist parties are found in France, especially in Mediterranean cities located in the regions of Corsica, Provence-Alpes-Côtes d'Azur, and Languedoc-Roussillon. Such parties are also dominant in the cities of Marseille, Nice, Corsica, and Perpignan. They function through clans and networks that are basically personalized, particularist, and non-ideological; they control whole sectors of the city. Structured by the "party of the mayor"—medecinist in Nice, defferrist in Marseilles, leotardist in Fréjus, soldanist in Draguignan—they are based on specific cultural codes (honor, generosity, and omerta or pride). French clientelistic parties are excellent at mobilizing voters, especially in local elections that determine municipal majorities.

Many questions of the FAUI study measure the degree of organization of parties' municipal organizations. Our main measure is a standard scale from 0 to 100, called Strong Party Organization Index (SPOIX). SPOIX was built from the mayors' answers to the three following questions:

IV137. How often did you mention your party affiliation in your last campaign? 1. Almost always 2. Frequently 3. Seldom 4. Almost never 5. Never 6. Missing.

IV138. How active was your party in your last election?

1. Party helped select and endorse me and was active in campaign 2. Party active in campaign 3. Party occasionally participated 4. Party not active in campaign 9. Missing.

IV139. Approximately how often do you meet with local party officials? 1. Several times a month 2. Once a month 3. Several times a year 4. Seldom 5. Never 9. Missing.

Figure 5.3 is a scatterplot in which we represented political parties according to their ideological orientation (International Party Measure).[13]

Leftist parties have higher SPOIX than rightist parties, within and across countries. Maurice Duverger also noted that Israel's Labor Party is more organized than Likud and that the Democrats are more organized than the Republicans. However, the Democrats have stronger municipal organizations than they do state organizations, whereas

Republicans, according to Gibson et al. (1983, 1985), have progressively consolidated their organizations—especially in the 1970s. The Democratic Party has become a serious rival of the Republican Party in northern New England and the Plains states. The Republicans have been increasing their implantation in the "modern South," in which factions and personalities had been dominant.

In Finland, the number of local sections of Centrist and Conservative Parties increased during the 1970s and 1980s, whereas the number of local organizations of left parties was stable, even decreasing. According to official statistics gathered by Sundberg (1983: 14), the average number of local sections by Finnish communes was 2.6 for the Communist Party, 3.3 for the Social-Democratic Party, 2.9 for the Swedish People Party, 8.8 for the Center Party, and 2.5 for the Conservatives. Finnish parties are also involved in the Lutheran Church, to which 90 percent of the population belongs. Parties presented more than 70 percent of candidates elected to the 600 Lutheran parish councils. Since 1970, parties have been authorized to present their own lists for those elections.

"Japanese parties are like ghosts, they have heads but no feet." This statement, by a former Japanese education minister, mostly applies to right-wing parties—especially the LDP, which has generally weak municipal organizations. James J. Foster analyzed parties of the Hyogo district (Foster 1982)[14] and found that the LDP had weak municipal organizations dominated by the mayor's personal characteristics. Kyoji Wakata's research (1986) confirmed the weakness of the LDP: "The LDP's official endorsements in city or town council elections means nothing but a nominal label. No other substantial aid, either in the form of funds or campaign workers, would come from party organs of the LDP.... Thus, the party does almost nothing for campaigns of official party candidates running for the city council."

The Japanese Communist Party is the only Japanese party that has strong municipal organizations; it has an important cadre of militants and proper financial resources. The Japanese Socialist Party is intimately linked to the Sohyo federal union, and the Democratic Socialist Party is linked to the Domei federation.

Conclusion

A New Political Culture is emerging throughout the world—especially in cities where citizens can use referenda, recall elections, and citizens' initiatives to express their preferences. The U.S. occupying forces implanted such institutions into Japan. Partisanship is less likely in the Anglophone countries and Japan (occupied from 1945 to 1952) because they generally share a common belief that local government should be democratic and efficient. This is similar to what NPC people believe: They want local governments to fulfill such ideals—but without the traditional bureaucratic structure that distances leaders from their constituents.

The increasing prevalence of nonpartisan citizens and voters demonstrates that an NPC is emerging where parties are weakest and where citizens can exercise the most control over local politics. NPC people hope to revive the nonpartisan tradition of

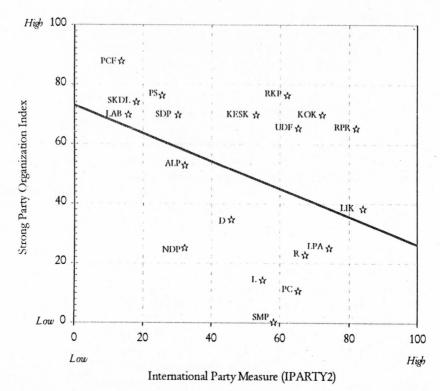

FIGURE 5.3   Left Parties Are Stronger than Right Parties

Note: The line clearly separates two groups of parties:

—US, Canadian, and Australian parties, which have a low SPOIX score. Such parties are: D: Democrats and R: Republicans—United States; PC: Conservative Party, L: Liberal Party, and NDP: New Democratic Party—Canada; and the ALP: Australian Labor Party and the LPD: Liberal Party.

—Finnish, Swedish, French, and Israeli parties, which have high SPOIX scores. Such parties include: SKDL: Finnish People Democratic League, SDP: Social Democratic Party, KESK: Center Party, RKP: Center Party, and KOK: National Coalition Party; PCF: French Communist Party, PS: Socialist Party, UDF: Union for French Democracy, and RPR: Rally for The Republic; and LAB Labor Party and LIK: Likud—Israel. The 0 score of the SMP (Finnish Rural Party) is for only one commune.

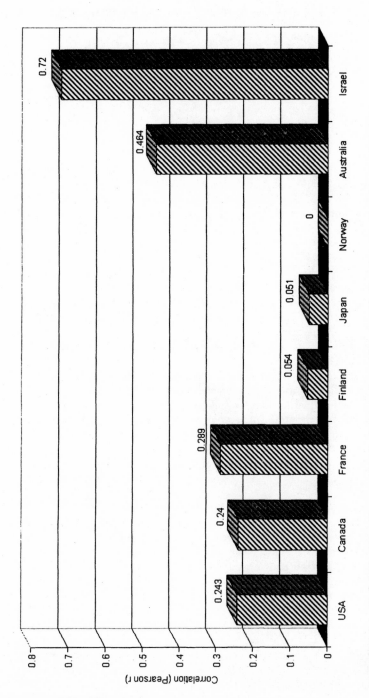

FIGURE 5.4 Left Cities Have Stronger Parties, in Most Countries: Correlations Between IPARTY2 and SPOIX

Note: The sign of the correlation is reversed to simplify interpretation.
Source: FAUI Project.

efficient, democratic local government by electing NFP and NPC mayors whose preferences resemble theirs.

Parties can choke off NPC movements through restrictive electoral systems found in much of Continental Europe—but then NPC people can join voluntary associations that directly lobby officials. NPC is a revolt against hierarchical arrangements that constrain popular input and is a demand for effective and democratic municipal administration.

Notes

[1] The French regional elections, however, were organized at the same time as the legislative elections of 1986 and the cantonal elections of 1992.

[2] See the various countries reports and analyses (in particular Australia, Canada, France, Norway, and the United States) in Franklin, Mackie, and Valen (1992).

[3] For more details on the introduction and use conditions of these new institutional mechanisms, see Steiner (1965).

[4] "The pervasiveness of its organization and the year-round services it provides to constituents take it beyond the range of the sporadically organized and intermittently active party organizations, with their amateur leadership, found in other areas. The Chicago machine is both rare and impressive in the range of services offered, the cohesiveness and permanence of its structure, the professionalism and experience of its members at all levels, and, of course, its electoral successes" Crotty. (1986: 190).

[5] On the historical evolution of parties' role in Canadian urban political systems, see Quesnel and Belley (1991).

[6] For Warren Magnusson, "The political, social, and economic life of the community was structured by a complicated pattern of clientelist relations.... Relations were structured by ethnic, religious, and fraternal loyalties." Magnusson (1983: 97).

[7] In the United States, the notion of party membership may have three meanings: (1) voting for a party in an election, (2) voting for a party in a primary, and (3) identifying with a party. (Eldersveld, 1982: esp. ch. 7, Crotty, 1985: 52).

[8] The treatment of no answers raises highly complex methodological problems that Terry Clark and his associates in Chicago have courageously tried to face for years in the realm of the FAUI program.

[9] In a thorough comparative analysis of the local political mobilization processes in Japan and the United States, Kyoji Wakata presents in particular one of the main integration means used by Japanese elected officials: "A very popular constituency service among local politicians in Kansai, and perhaps in all of Japan as well, is attending the funerals of residents in the community. One of our Kansai interviewees said that he attended funeral services usually twice or three times every week.... Another interviewee told us that he often helped family members of the deceased prepare the funeral rites, and often assumed the function of the chief of a funeral committee. As another example, it was reported that the mayor of a middle-sized city, who was particularly keen about citizens' funerals, attended two to three hundred funerals each year. Funerals are considered by many Kansai politicians to be an appropriate occasion for them to establish personal and emotional ties with family members of the deceased, gaining a reputation as a community leader who cares and who really understands *ninjo* (human feelings)." Wakata (1986: 73).

[10] For similar reasons such a distancing from political parties is cultivated by the "strong mayor" of Baden-Wurttemberg, who is also directly elected by citizens. See Wehling, 1992: 144).

[11] A similar proportion is reported in the survey *Form of Government* conducted in 1981 by the International City Management Association; see, for more details, Cassel (1986).

[12] See in particular the examples analyzed by Magnusson (1983).

[13] IPARTY 2 is a standardized measure of each party position on an international left-right scale from 0 to 100; the construction of this variable derived from the estimations of Derbeyshire and Derbeyshire (1989) and Castles and Mair (1984).

[14] Analyzing results from a 1980 survey of 940 municipal councillors in 24 Japanese communes, Moriwaki (1984) also underlines the central role not of parties but of candidate support organizations in electoral and political processes.

6

Transformations in Policy Preferences of Local Officials

Oscar W. Gabriel, Katja Ahlstich,
Frank Brettschneider, Volker Kunz *

Research Program

Local governments in Germany traditionally have played an important role in providing collective goods. Article 28 (2) of the German basic law charges them with the autonomous regulation of all local affairs within the established legal framework. Local governments not only fulfill their own administrative tasks but also implement about 80 percent of the federal and state laws. For example, about two-thirds of all public capital spending comes from local communities (for details see Gunlicks 1986:4, 137ff). Since local political decisions greatly affect a society's infrastructure, the study of the determinants, structure, and evolution of local administrative responsibilities is valuable not only to scientific research but also to political practice.

One of the most vigorously debated questions in current social research is whether new political priorities have arisen from the progression of Western societies, over the past fifty years, from an industrial stage to a postindustrial stage. According to some observers, attendant changes in the social structure—the rise of mass communication, the spread of modern technology, the reorganization of the labor market, and, finally, the attainment of unprecedented levels of wealth and security by general citizenries—have led to changes in value orientations and in preferences on related issues. Alongside a shift from traditional (conventional, conformist, materialist) to modern (unconventional, nonconformist, post-materialist) values (for details see Inglehart 1990; Klages

* The authors are grateful to Scott Cobb and Frank DeCabo for revising the manuscript. The manuscript was completed in December 1992 and revised in November 1994. The authors regret that they have not been able to include data from surveys conducted in Ulm, Heilbronn, and Stuttgart.

1984), traditional "bread and butter" issues (e.g., social security, economic growth) have lost salience in favor of new politics issues (e.g., environmental protection, political participation, and minority rights) (for details see Baker, Dalton, and Hildebrandt 1981:136ff; Kunz, Gabriel, and Brettschneider 1993).

As Terry Nichols Clark and Ronald Inglehart state in their introductory chapter, we may classify these various changes of values, political attitudes, and behavior under the heading of an emerging "New Political Culture" characterized by the following attributes, among others: "1. The classic left-right dimension has been transformed.... 2. Social and fiscal/economic issues are explicitly distinguished.... 3. Social issues have risen in salience relative to fiscal/economic issues.... 5. Questioning the welfare state" (see Chapter 2).

The emergence of a New Political Culture is supposed to have a strong impact on various aspects of political life. One probable consequence of change in peoples' value orientations would be a reshaping of political agendas at the various levels of the political system. In the next section we shall analyze some implications of the emergence of a New Political Culture in West German local communities. At the core of the analysis are the Clark-Inglehart assumptions on the changing role of the left-right dimension as a determinant of political life in Western democracies and the hypothesis of a shift in social issues versus fiscal and economic issues. This article focuses on the relation between new and old elements of the structure of political conflicts, on the one hand, and the spending preferences of local German decision-makers on the other. We should not take the validity of the Clark-Inglehart propositions as given, however; it must be established by empirical analysis.

Until now there has been little empirical evidence on how social, economic, and political changes affect local policymaking. There is even less information on whether local decision-makers are aware of changing social conditions, how they may become aware of these changing social conditions, and whether they react to them by adapting local administration to new political demands (among the rare exceptions are Arzberger 1980; Arzberger, Murck, and Schumacher 1979).

This chapter analyzes how local council members perceive the salience of several political issues at the local level. Four county-free cities from different parts of Germany (Bamberg, Bonn, Ludwigshafen, and Wiesbaden) were chosen for this purpose. In the German administrative structure, the status of county-free city has been given to 115 local communities. Because of their special position in the system of public administration (for details see Gunlicks 1986:36ff), we may regard them as "city counties" combining all of the administrative functions normally divided between the county and the local community.

This chapter will address the following questions:

(1) Which issues appear urgent enough to local decision-makers to affect their decisions on spending?

(2) Have there been changes in the perception of previous, current, and future local priorities, and are there particular areas of policy in which priorities have changed significantly?

(3) Do the differing ideological dispositions and value orientations of local deci-sion-makers lead them to have different (i.e., traditional versus new politics) spending preferences?

(4) Is party affiliation an important determinant of local spending preferences?

(5) How responsive are local politicians to their own perceptions of the preferences of the majority of the electorate?

The data used in this article were collected by a mailed questionnaire sent to 258 council members of the respective cities. The survey was conducted between February and April 1991. The response rate was 54 percent (144 respondents) and varied consid-erably from one city to another and between parties.[1]

The main part of the questionnaire concerned the most important economic, social, and cultural responsibilities of local government (for details see Table 6.1). Respon-dents were asked to evaluate these issues along several dimensions. The first question discussed here is whether the relative importance of these issues have changed over the years and are likely to change in the future. We also look at local council members' preferences for increased or reduced spending in each policy area.

Structure and Change of Local Priorities

Several surveys at the national level have demonstrated a shift from traditional to new political issues (see Baker, Dalton, and Hildebrandt 1981:136ff; Dalton 1986). Regarding local communities' position as important suppliers of collective goods, we shall seek first to determine whether there has been a corresponding change in priorities at the local level. This is not easy, since it is by no means clear what the notions of "new" and "traditional" politics really mean at the local level. Surely, the satisfaction of the most elementary needs with regard to safety and sustenance (e.g., law and order, housing, social security) is at the core of "old" politics, but local communities have also supplied public services in the areas of sports, public health, and so on, which may be seen as "new" policy concerns. Accordingly, we must examine empirically whether the concept of "new" versus "old" political issues has any relevance at all for local political systems.

The theoretical assumptions underlying the following empirical analyses can easily be related to the Clark-Inglehart concept of the New Political Culture. First, we hypoth-esize that the local decision-makers' spending preferences have been changing over the years and will continue to do so. But we deviate from the Clark-Inglehart assumption in postulating that the New Political Culture may have a particular meaning in the German local political system.

The problem lies in the ambiguous term *social issues*. In Germany, social issues are equated with welfare issues, which have been viewed as a core responsibility of state and local authorities since the last century (see Gunlicks 1986:84ff). From this point of view the question is not so much whether social issues have been rising on the local political agenda while economic ones have been falling, since both categories are tradi-tional responsibilities of the local political system or representatives of "old" politics.

More relevant in Germany is the position of traditional social and economic issues as compared to new lifestyle-related issues, particularly the amount and quality of state and local services in the areas of culture, leisure time, and environmental protection. According to the theory of the New Political Culture, economic and welfare issues should lose importance while lifestyle issues gain it.

Yet if we define social issues as cultural issues, such as abortion and homosexuality, the vision of Clark and Inglehart will hold. Welfare policies, then, will encompass traditional welfare issues as well as economic ones and will rank lower on the local agenda than they did several decades ago. The issues ranking higher in people's preference order are socio-cultural ones, as well as those of lifestyle and the environment. Since our survey did not address issues in the first category, we shall focus on the latter two categories.

Our second hypothesis concerns the basic political beliefs influencing people's issue orientations. According to Clark and Inglehart, the meaning of the left-right dimension is changing in the Western world. Although there seems to be a broad consensus in empirical research that this assumption is correct in principle, the particular pattern of change is a matter of debate. From our point of view, the most important change in people's conception of a good society is this: The traditional left-right dimension persists as a principle giving structure and meaning to political conflict, but it is no longer the only line of conflict relevant to political processes, particularly party competition. Further, a new value—conflict, described by Inglehart (1990) as materialism-post-materialism and by Klages (1984; 1988) as the KON–non–KON dimension, has emerged and shaped people's issue orientations. Typical of the traditional left-right dimension is a conflict of views on the role of state and local authorities in the production of social and economic goods. Simply speaking, leftists favor big government, whereas rightists favor small government except in the area of public order. However, the traditional left-right cleavage has been complemented by a new materialism-post-materialism conflict, leading to a differentiation between a traditional left and a new left. Whereas the former continues to put a strong emphasis on welfare policies and on economic interventions by government, the latter favors new lifestyle issues (for a more detailed description of these assumptions see Kunz, Gabriel, and Brettschneider 1993).

To summarize, we may derive the following expectations from the concept of the New Political Culture:

(1) Over the years, welfare and economic issues will lose importance while lifestyle issues become more prominent.

(2) Support for traditional rightist positions will be positively related to preferences for high spending on public order and on economic capital investments that might improve conditions for private economic activity.

(3) Support for traditional leftist positions will be positively related to preferences for high spending on welfare policies and economic capital investment (the latter mainly because of the preference for big government and the wish to avert unemployment).

(4) New left supporters will emphasize environmental protection, antigrowth mea-

sures, and cultural issues. Support of welfare expenditure cannot be excluded, since the concept of the New Political Culture comprehends a desire to help disadvantaged social groups.

Local Priorities of the Day

As the data in Table 6.1 as regards concerning shifts in the local agenda show, the issues most important to council members are public housing and the prevention and cleanup of street litter, closely followed by garbage disposal, public transportation, and urban development and renewal. At least 80 percent of respondents identified these issues as important local matters. The traditionally salient problem of local economic development ranked only seventh. In comparison, construction of streets and parking lots and construction of parks and recreation areas were given low priorities. In a comparison with a survey of CDU/CSU council members taken in 1987, we see a considerable shift of priorities in several areas. Public housing, which ranked lowest in the 1987 survey, was the most important issue in 1991. Conversely, economic development and public security were clearly given lower levels of priority in 1991 than four years earlier (similarly Gabriel 1992).

Apart from the relative importance of the issues, respondents were asked to assess their spending priorities: whether they favored cutting expenditures, maintaining current levels of spending, or spending more money for the respective policies. For all issues that ranked high on the local agenda, increased expenditures were supported (not surprisingly) by a large majority of local council members; respondents favored unchanged, or even lower, expenditures in all policy areas that ranked low (see Table 6.1).

An Assessment of the Change of Local Priorities

By comparing the current order of priority of local issues to the order given the same issues ten years ago, we can gain a useful impression of whether there has been a change in the local political agenda in Germany. Ten years ago the top three issues were (1) economic development, (2) street construction, and (3) public order. In contrast, garbage avoidance (prevention and cleanup of street litter), garbage disposal, and public transportation ranked very low and were called important by fewer than one-third of respondents. There has been a large increase in the rated importance of issues of environmental policy (for details see Zapf-Schramm 1989; Hahn 1991).

Instead of scrutinizing every issue reported in Table 6.1, focusing on broader policy areas seems an adequate strategy for assessing the change in the local agenda. The results are quite clear and in most instances confirm the Clark-Inglehart assumptions: Over recent years the percentage of local representatives favoring higher spending on public security has decreased; that favoring higher spending on economic infrastructure has held constant; and that favoring higher spending on welfare, lifestyle, and environmental issues has more or less strongly increased. The strongest shift regards environmental protection. We also see a marked increase with respect to social welfare issues; even in the case of lifestyle issues the change is substantial. With regard to our respondents' spending preferences, the period 1981 to 1991 was one of rising expectations, particularly in the fields of social welfare and environmental protection. Whereas the former field is part of the old politics complex, we must regard the latter as representing new politics. The remaining policy areas fit the expected pattern even better:

TABLE 6.1　Council Members' Policy and Spending Preferences in Bamberg, Bonn, Ludwigshafen and Wiesbaden

	Policy preferences (issues estimated as important/very important						Spending preferences		
	1981		1991		2001		Increase	Decrease	Difference
	%	Rank	%	Rank	%	Rank	%	%	
Public Security (1)	51.4		41.9		52.2				
Public order and security	51.4	3	41.9	17	52.2	15	25.0	12.3	12.7
Economic Infrastructure (1)	51.8		51.9		51.8				
Street construction	58.1	2	24.0	21	28.8	20	19.3	38.6	−19.3
Parking lot construction	49.8	8	35.8	20	28.0	21	34.4	39.5	−5.1
Local economic	59.7	1	76.0	7	70.0	11	50.2	8.2	42.0
Energy supply	39.7	(14)	71.6	10	76.7	7	32.2	6.5	25.7
Social Welfare (1)	37.9		67.8		67.8				
General welfare	29.8	13	75.1	8	74.9	9	28.7	12.6	16.1
Youth welfare	34.6	11	70.0	9	75.0	8	49.6	2.1	47.5
Social services	41.7	9	70.2	11	75.1	10	53.1	3.8	49.3
Public health	46.0	4	56.5	12	55.9	13	41.4	2.1	39.3
Public housing	31.8	16	92.1	1	83.7	5	83.8	0.4	83.4
Elementary schools	43.5	9	43.9	16	43.2	19	47.5	1.2	46.3
Lifestyle (1)	40.8		52.5		58.1				
Urban development/renewal	48.4	4	80.0	5	81.3	6	55.7	5.2	50.5
Sports and leisure facilities	42.1	12	43.1	18	44.7	18	31.9	13.7	18.2
Higher education	46.0	6	48.9	14	49.2	16	48.7	2.6	46.1
Culture	29.6	19	51.9	13	60.1	14	45.6	18.5	27.1
Sciences	45.0	7	52.4	15	67.3	12	44.3	6.5	37.8
Parks and recreation areas	34.2	15	38.7	19	46.2	17	39.0	7.7	31.3
Environmental Protection (1)	25.8		85.8		91.3				
Sewage disposal	29.7	17	78.3	6	87.4	4	40.1	1.6	38.5
Garbage disposal	27.0	20	88.4	3	92.0	2	66.7	3.8	62.9
Garbage avoidance (prevention and cleanup of street litter)	21.1	21	90.8	2	94.5	1	83.6	0.8	82.8
Public transportation	25.5	17	85.6	4	91.4	3	89.5	1.5	88.0

Old political issues have been downgraded and new ones have been upgraded.

According to our respondents, this trend will continue over the next ten years. Except in the area of public order and security, which has received lower rankings during the past ten years but will may have a revival in future, the recent trend should continue. The ranking of economic infrastructure will be more or less stable; that of welfare and environmental issues will rise further—but gradually; and lifestyle issues will show the most marked shift in the rankings.

Nevertheless, to assess the relevance of particular issues wholly on the basis of a comparison of marginal distributions would be a mistake. Respondents generally assigned the political system more responsibility for solving problems than they had done ten years before. There is some empirical evidence that Germans now expect more from their national government, in the way of attention to individual and collective well-being, than they used to. Some studies have identified a shift in value orientations as an important cause of this "spiral of rising expectations" (see Klages 1984; Roller 1992). Since most people do not differentiate between the goods and services they receive from the various branches of the public sector, it seems reasonable to assume that the growing demand for public goods applies both to national as well as local government. Hence the proportion of respondents naming particular local issues as important has clearly increased over the past decade. This is reflected in the changing proportion of respondents who see economic development as a salient issue. Ten years ago the figure was 60 percent; today it is 76 percent. One might think, from these data, that local economic development holds a higher priority today. Only when we compare the *rankings* of this issue over the years do we see just how misleading such a conclusion is. Ten years ago economic development ranked first on the list of issues; today it ranks seventh. This perspective shows that new politics issues have become more important over the past decade. Traditional local tasks such as street and parking lot construction, maintenance of public order, and economic development have lost importance, whereas environmental protection and public housing have gained it. This shift in the local political agenda shows that the new politics is not only a national phenomenon but also a local one.

Despite the considerable shifting of local priorities over the past decade, it appears likely that the rankings will be fairly stable over the next decade (see Table 6.1). Our findings predict only two movements in the rankings over that period. According to the respondents, garbage disposal and garbage avoidance (prevention and cleanup of street litter) will become more important, whereas economic development will continue to lose importance. In general, the first hypothesis derived from the Clark-Inglehart concept of the New Political Culture is confirmed by our analysis of local representatives' spending preferences: Lifestyle and environmental issues have become more important during the past decade and will continue to do so, whereas demand for higher spending on economic infrastructure and public security will be more or less stable. Only in the field of social welfare policies do the data fail to fit the assumptions; this discrepancy may arise from the ambiguity of the phrase *social issues*.

Determinants of Local Spending Priorities

The Explanatory Power of Particular Variables

Multivariate statistics is a useful tool in examining the factors that determine council members' spending preferences. Since several variables included in our model did not allow regression analysis, we decided to use multiple analysis of variance. The dependent variables are the council members' spending preferences over the twenty-one important policy areas. Two explanatory variables used in the analyses can be derived from the concept of the New Political Culture: self-placement on a left-right scale, and support of traditional (non-KON) versus modern (KON) values. We also need to consider council members' party memberships, because party affiliation and left-right position are expected to have different impacts on several policy preferences. We included a city variable as a global indicator of a local community's (objective) structure of needs and resources. Since objective conditions must be translated into *perceptions* in order to become factors in a person's preferences and behavior, we included three more needs-resources indicators as explanatory variables: the perceived life conditions in the respective communities, the perceived financial situation, and the citizens' preferences. In order to test the empirical relevance of the incrementalism hypotheses, we had to regard the spending preferences *as perceived* ten years ago as important determinants of the *actual* spending preferences. Finally, we considered a party's position in the local power structure, because nongoverning parties may be more apt to support high spending than governing parties.

On most of the issues under scrutiny, the respondents' spending preferences differ greatly (see Table 6.2). The only exceptions are a few issues on which almost every council member favored higher spending. The question whether the differences in priorities are systematically related to the variables included in the model is one that we can answer only by empirical analysis.

Excepting public health and elementary education, left-right orientation is an important determinant of every political issue under scrutiny. Nevertheless, the percentage of variance attributable to ideology ranges from 5.3 (sewage disposal) to 33.6 (parking lot construction).

As predicted, the respondents placing themselves on the right are most strongly in favor of more spending on street and parking lot construction and on economic development. This is not a surprising result, since these policies directly improve the conditions for private economic activities. Further, they do not imply direct intervention in the economic process, so we may regard them as parts of a conservative economic doctrine. Likewise, higher spending on public order is most strongly supported by rightist council members.

TABLE 6.2 Determinants of Local Spending Preferences (Explanatory Power of Single Variables in Percent of Total Variation)

	City	Ideology	Values	Party	Public's Preferences	Explanatory Power of Model
Street construction	–	26.3	7.1	7.9	5.8	53.9
Parking lot construction	14.3	33.6	–	5.1	–	59.0
Public order and security	–	24.3	–	–	–	37.3
Local economic development	10.1	8.2	–	14.1	14.0	51.9
Urban development/renewal	6.0	–	5.0	–	13.9	32.8
Sports and leisure facilities	7.5	–	–	13.4	–	30.8
General welfare	–	16.6	5.6	10.3	–	38.0
Youth welfare	–	14.3	5.0	–	–	28.0
Social services	–	28.7	6.7	6.4	–	47.2
Elementary schools	6.6	–	–	–	23.0	44.0
Higher education	9.8	–	–	–	17.9	42.7
Culture	18.4	–	–	–	8.4	41.7
Sciences	–	–	–	–	11.4	33.1
Public health	9.0	–	7.3	–	12.7	36.1
Parks and recreation areas	17.6	–	–	–	6.4	34.2
Public housing	7.1	14.7	–	13.0	18.0	53.7
Sewage disposal	–	5.3	–	–	12.3	36.9
Garbage disposal	–	–	–	5.3	23.2	41.5
Garbage avoidance (Prevention and cleanup of street litter)	–	25.9	–	8.1	8.3	48.0
Public transportation	–	23.5	–	–	10.8	40.7
Energy supply	–	–	10.5	–	–	25.3

TABLE 6.3 Ideology as a Determinant of Issue Preferences (Means of Spending Preferences of Different Groups)

	Left	Moderate	Right
Street construction	2.4	2.84	2.93
Parking lot construction	2.31	3.02	3.62
Public order and security	2.83	3.27	3.48
Local economic development	3.44	3.44	3.61
General welfare	3.22	3.12	3.32
Youth welfare	3.56	3.45	3.48
Social services	3.72	3.58	3.48
Public housing	4.49	4.19	4.43
Sewage disposal	3.55	3.5	3.43
Garbage avoidance (Prevention and cleanup of street litter)	4.47	4.21	4.01
Public transportation	4.68	4.66	4.02

The opposite is true in matters of welfare policy. People placing themselves on the left are most strongly in favor of higher spending in the areas of youth welfare, general welfare, and social services. Nevertheless, the mean differences between the three groups are less marked than in the policy areas discussed above, and in one instance they do not conform to the expected pattern. With respect to most social welfare issues, people placing themselves in the center of the left-right continuum are least apt to favor higher spending.

The third policy area largely influenced by left-right self-placement is environmental protection. Except with regard to garbage disposal and energy supply, ideological orientation is an important explanatory variable. Generally, leftists favor higher spending more than rightists.

As the data show, left-right orientation, an important determinant of opinion on the national political agenda, also affects opinion on local political issues. Besides social welfare issues, environmental issues too are elements of a leftist policy profile. In Germany it has often been said that local politics is not strongly influenced by ideological factors (for details and further references see Gabriel 1984; Lehmbruch 1979). Our data do not support this assertion.

New and Old Values

Hypotheses on the impact of values on policy preferences have been stated—and investigated empirically—by several researchers. According to Inglehart (1977, 1990), a shift from materialist to post-materialist values is taking place in advanced industrial societies. Conditions of life in such societies have improved markedly since the end of World War II; values linked with participation, equality, self-fulfillment, and quality of life have become more important to their citizenries, whereas traditional values related to social and physical security, economic growth, and maintenance of favorable economic conditions have become less so. Klages and others (Klages 1984, 1988; Klages and Herbert 1983) have made similar assumptions, differentiating between traditional KON and modern non-KON dispositions. KON dispositions are defined by items such as self-control, fulfillment of one's duties, adaptation to the expectations of the social environment, and security. Participation, emancipation, and an idealistic way of life are elements of non-KON dispositions. In addition to the pure KON and non-KON value orientations, Helmut Klages et al. introduced two mixed types of value orientation: one defined by a combination of weak KON and strong non-KON dispositions, the other defined by the opposite combination. From our point of view, the instrument used by Klages et al. is theoretically more appropriate to the measurement of value orientations than is Inglehart's, since Klages's measurement items refer more directly to abstract conceptions of a desirable society.

According to the theory of value change, post-materialist and non-KON dispositions affect people's ranking of "important" issues. With respect to the issues studied here, these dispositions incline people to support higher spending on matters of environmental protection (garbage avoidance, garbage disposal, en-

TABLE 6.4 Value Orientation as a Determinant of Issue Preferences (Means of Spending Preferences of Different Groups)

	KON	none	both	non-KON
Street construction	2.88	2.4	2.7	2.51
Urban development/renewal	3.8	3.96	3.9	3.38
General welfare	3.18	3.36	3.13	3.39
Youth welfare	3.34	3.93	3.47	3.61
Social services	3.42	4.14	3.48	3.81
Public health	3.39	3.22	3.71	3.34
Energy supply	3.05	2.99	3.39	3.5

ergy supply, public transportation, parks and recreation areas) as well as on culture and higher education. Our data give at least partial support to this assumption. Although the threshold of 5 percent of explained variance is reached only in the case of energy supply, people also favor higher spending on culture and garbage disposal.

The traditional KON disposition presumably entails a strong emphasis on economic growth, public order, and social welfare. Street and parking lot construction, economic development, public security, social security, public health, and public housing belong to this cluster of traditional issues. As Tables 6.2 and 6.4 show, our hypothesis is confirmed with respect to street construction, public order, and economic development but not with respect to welfare issues. Contrary to our expectation, people with non-KON dispositions support government's taking an active role in matters of social welfare. As mentioned above, support of new values does not preclude a welfare policy orientation in the traditional sense. It is not big government, as such, that supporters of new values oppose; whether post-materialists and non-KON people demand more or less government intervention depends on what type of government activity is in question.

In general, the impact of value orientation on spending preferences is weaker and less consistent than that of left-right orientation. It seems reasonable to assume that the conflict of old versus new values is less central to people's belief systems than traditional left-right orientation.

We may summarize the state of research on the issue of parties and policies thus: Whether leftist parties control government has an impact on policy output. We must not overestimate that impact, however; it varies substantially from one policy area to another. We may assume that there is a similar relation between party affiliation and spending preferences at the local level (for details see Grüner, Jaedicke, and Ruhland 1988; Gabriel, Kunz, and Zapf-Schramm 1990). This hypothesis is supported by the role that political parties play in the processes of interest articulation and aggregation.

TABLE 6.5   Party Affiliation as a Determinant of Issue Preferences (Means of Spending Preferences of Different Groups)

	CDU/CSU	FDP	SPD	Greens
Street construction	2.70	3.76	2.74	1.59
Parking lot construction	2.99	3.61	2.87	1.93
Local economic development	3.71	3.52	3.54	2.07
Sports and leisure facilities	3.05	2.50	3.54	2.87
General welfare	2.90	3.13	3.26	4.34
Social services	3.40	3.38	3.67	4.21
Public housing	3.99	3.65	4.70	4.99
Garbage disposal	3.79	3.29	3.99	3.67
Garbage avoidance (prevention and cleanup of street litter)	4.08	3.32	4.48	4.81

Note: Table shows only policy areas in which party affiliation explains at least 5 percent of variation. Party abbreviations: CDU/CSU, Christian Democrats (most rightist on left-right scale); FDP, Liberal party (nearest to CDU/CSU on left-right scale); SPD, Social Democrats (moderately leftist). The Greens are the new post-materialist left (most leftist on left-right scale).

Programs and platforms offered to the electorate by political parties vary considerably according to the parties' particular traditions, the composition of their memberships and electorates, and their ideologies. Consequently, people with different political demands support different parties according to their own values and interests. The core of a social-democratic policy profile is made up of social welfare issues; conservative parties are preoccupied with the issue of public order. Concerns about economic and technological development do not go along with any particular party affiliation. On the one hand, we may see them as instrumental to social welfare policies; on the other, we may see them as highly relevant to the interests of rightist voters. Since new politics issues were not central parts of the policy profiles of rightist and social-democratic parties, a new political cleavage has arisen in West European societies with the emergence of green/alternative parties. These new parties not only are critical of concentration on economic growth and public order but also strongly favor expansion of the welfare state (see also Kunz, Gabriel, and Brettschneider 1993).

Contrary to the crucial role attributed to party affiliation in the policy output literature, we find party impacts varying by issue. The party affiliation variable has its greatest explanatory power in the area of economic development. Further, party affiliation has a statistical impact on opinion in the areas of sports and leisure facilities, public housing, social aid, street and parking lot construction, garbage disposal, garbage avoidance (prevention and cleanup of street litter), and social services (for details see Table 6.5). In matters of economic infrastructure, social welfare policy, and environmental protection, the most marked differences are between the liberal FDP and the Green Party. Unlike the Liberals, who favor higher spending for street and parking lot construction and for economic development, the Greens support the cutting of spending in these areas. New value orientations lead to a strong and consistent antigrowth orientation only when they are translated into a party preference—that is, affiliation with the Green Party. The preferences on spending for social welfare issues largely match our expectations: Green council members call for higher spending on several social welfare issues, whereas Liberals oppose it. Social Democrats are on the side of the Greens; conservative CDU/CSU council members at least partly share the spending preferences of the Liberals.

Generally, opinion on environmental protection is not strongly influenced by party affiliation. The observed pattern largely resembles that seen in the areas discussed above: Greens favor higher spending, whereas Liberals oppose it.

Party does not matter for most of the remaining issues. In the areas of public security, youth welfare, schools, parks and recreation areas, culture and sciences, public health, sewage disposal, public transportation, and energy supply, the explanatory power of the party variable amounts to less than 5 percent.

Past researchers' assumptions on the impacts of party affiliation, value orientation, and ideological disposition are not consistently supported by the empirical evidence presented here. Our results match past assumptions in some policy areas (economic development, social security) and defy them in some others (public order). There is considerable multi-colinearity in the particular variables included in the models. Hence, we cannot say unreservedly that party affiliation matters.

The Responsiveness of Local Council Members to the Perceived Demands of the Majority of the Electorate

According to normative democratic theory, there is one factor that should influence the spending preferences of local council members more than any other: the demands of the majority of the electorate. The responsiveness of decision-makers to the electorate's preferences has always been seen as an essential element of democratic government. Since Warren E. Miller and Donald E. Stokes's (1969) important study, there have been several attempts to analyze the impact of the electorate's preferences on decision-makers' legislative behavior. Although studies of this type usually run into considerable theoretical and methodological difficulties, it is one of the most important tasks of empirical democratic theory to define the linkage between the elected and the electorate. Since the local political system seems particularly open to citizen participation, it is an interesting arena in which to analyze patterns of political representation; we may expect the demands of the electorate to have more impact on politicians' behavior than at the national level (for details see Dahl 1971:1ff).

Our research design refers only to a small segment of the opinion/policy nexus: the impact of the preferences of the majority of the electorate, *as perceived by local council members* (independent variables), on the council members' preferences (dependent variables). Miller and Stokes have assumed that this relation is a particularly important part of the process of representation, since voters' opinions are thought to be directly related to the decision-making behavior of council members. We shall analyze the relation between the council members' preferences and the perceived demands of the electorate in two steps: First, we assess the overall congruence of the spending preferences of both groups; second, we assess the congruence in particular areas of policy.

Since our survey included no items measuring the policy preferences of the general public, direct comparison of the preferences of council members and voters is impossible (for this possibility see Arzberger 1980:137ff). Instead, we asked council members for their own assessments of the spending preferences of the majority of voters. This is not a true measure of the preferences of the electorate; still, it is an interesting question how much the local council members' perceptions of public opinion influence their spending preferences.

We measured the strength of the representational linkage with a simple procedure developed by Russell J. Dalton (1985). The percentage of voters favoring higher spending on a given issue is represented on the x axis; the percentage of politicians, on the y axis. If the preferences of the two groups were identical, all points of the scatter plot would fall on the diagonal. The more marked the differences between the groups, the more scattered would be the points over the sector between the x and y axes. If we represented this with a regression equation, the value of the constant a would be 0, the regression coefficient b would be 1.0, and the R^2 would be 1.0.

A common feature of responsive political systems is strong correspondence between the spending preferences of decision-makers and their own perceptions of prevailing opinion among the electorate. As the data in Figure 6.1 show, empirical data only partly match the ideal of responsiveness found in the normative theory of democracy. There is a positive relation between the preferences of the two groups under observation, but it turns out to be weak ($r = .30$). A similar picture emerges from a comparison of the two groups' rankings of the items (rho = .21). To some degree, these results agree with an analysis presented by Klaus Arzberger (1980:147) stating that the priorities of local representatives are not always similar to the wants of average people.

When we look at various policy areas the situation becomes somewhat more complicated. We can discern a strong impact of perceived preferences of voters in matters of public housing, public health, school construction, and sewage disposal. Interestingly, all these issues rank relatively low on the decision-makers' agenda. Yet the respective groups differ considerably on street and parking lot construction, public security, sports, and leisure facilities. In these areas voters favor higher spending more than do politicians. On several other issues local politicians think of themselves as more conservative than the electorate; they show more support for higher spending on economic development and scientific research. Several studies conducted in the United States and Switzerland produced similar conclusions (see Windhoff-Heritier 1981; Verba and Nie 1972:299ff; Hoffmann-Lange 1991:280ff).

Because of the small numbers of respondents, we must take care in interpreting any breakdown of the spending data by cities and parties. Although the impact of the majority's demands on the preferences of local decision-makers is far from strong in general, the representational systems of the four cities differ greatly. The same holds true for political parties as intermediary agents. More recent analyses conducted with a larger set of local communities and correspondingly larger numbers of respondents (see Ahlstich and Kunz 1994; Gabriel and Brettschneider 1994) are in line with the results presented here.

The correlation coefficients between the spending preferences of local decision-makers and the perceived preferences of the electorate indicate that local politicians are most strongly influenced by the majority of the electorate in Ludwigshafen (Pearson's $r = .39$), closely followed by Wiesbaden (.31). In Bamberg (.17) and Bonn (.14) the results are at the opposite end of the scale. Party affiliation is another variable affecting the responsiveness of local decision-makers. With respect to their self-evaluation, members of the CDU/CSU are most responsive to the electorate (Pearson's $r = .43$), the Greens least so (.26), and the Social Democrats (.33) in-between. Again, similar results were presented by Arzberger (1980:147ff), who compared preferences of the electorate and local elites. Presumably these data mirror the fact that while the large parties seek support from broad coalitions of various groups, small parties, such as the Greens, see themselves as representing the demands of particular minorities among the electorate—*not* the preferences of the majority of the entire electorate (for details see Herzog et al., 1990).

Concluding Remarks

At the beginning of our analysis we asked whether there are new spending priorities in German local politics. Insofar as this question can be answered by the results of our survey of local council members in four cities, the answer is yes. Traditional issues like economic development, street construction, and public order have clearly lost importance over the past decade; environmental issues and public housing rank higher on the local agenda than before. These findings conform to some evidence, from national surveys, of an increase in the importance of new politics issues and a decrease in the importance of traditional ones.

Like the parties working at the national level (see Herzog et al. 1990; Hoffmann-Lange 1986; Schmitt 1987), party representatives at the local level have become sensitive to new politics issues. This goes along with particular ideological positions, value orientations, and party affiliations, however; we may characterize demands in the new politics area as arising chiefly from leftist and nonconformist concerns. Social Democrats and Greens are particularly open to these concerns and are willing to take them into account when reshaping local spending. Contrary to the original expectation, in the case of the Greens this is complemented by a strong concern for social welfare issues. This pattern stands in sharp contrast to the preference for economy-related spending found on the right, or materialist, end of the ideological spectrum. The CDU/CSU and FDP parties represent the latter position. Obviously, we found no ideologically neutral, nonpartisan style of local politics in any of the four cities that we studied.

Notes

[1] The response rates in the cities under observation: Bamberg: 19 of 45 council members (CSU 12 of 21, SPD 3 of 13, FDP 0 of 2, Greens 3 of 4, others 1 of 5), Bonn: 27 of 73 (CDU 7 of 32, SPD 7 of 24, FDP 6 of 8, Greens 7 of 9), Ludwigshafen: 39 of 59 (CDU 8 of 18, SPD 17 of 33, FDP 1 of 2, Greens 1 of 2, other 2 of 4), Wiesbaden: 55 of 81 (CDU 18 of 27, SPD 28 of 41, FDP 2 of 6, Greens 7 of 7. To correct for bias of the data only weighted data are used in the descriptive parts of this article. Weights are computed according to the true proportions of the parties in the local councils.

7

Toward a One-Dimensional Ideological Culture?
Evidence from Swiss Local Parties

Hans Geser

Theoretical considerations

In all Western democracies, the landscape of political cleavages, ideological polarizations and controversial political issues looks quite different now than thirty years ago. In the first decades after World War II, most domestic political conflicts crystallized along the neatly defined dimension of "left" and "right." In its classical connotation, molded by the traditional labor movement and by socialist parties, "leftism" implied a commitment for stronger governmental control and intervention.

As the major conflicts focused on the distribution of quantitative resources (e.g., income, leisure time, etc.), theorists expected that they could be gradually softened or even solved by sophisticated negotiation procedures and by continuous economic growth.

In the late 1960s, the civil rights movements and the student revolts gave rise to a novel, encompassing understanding of leftism (or "radicalism"), including the perspective of extending basic standards of human rights and welfare to all kinds of discriminated population segments (e.g., people of color, females, gays and lesbians, starving poor in underdeveloped nations, etc.) and extending principles of democratic decisionmaking into all societal spheres (like universities, firms and even prisons).

There emerged potent movements directed against all traditional values and habits that sought to prevent full individual self-determination (e.g., the feminist and "pro-choice" movement). All this gave rise to a countervailing wave of "neo-conservatism" articulating the need for upholding basic social bonds and values and a profound skepticism toward all endeavors for far-reaching sociocultural change. Compared with "classical" distributive issues, these new problems were far more linked to irreconcilable divergencies of fundamental values and, sometimes, systems of religious and metaphysical belief. In the 1970s, political controversies crystallized around an additional dimension: the "ecology question." Ecologism and social liberalism share at least the following characteristics:

1. Both ideologies start from the basic premise that processes of socioeconomic development have resulted in a neglect of other important values, in enormous negative consequences that call for compensatory corrective actions (through governmental legislation as well as in everyday life).

2. In both cases, political activism did not emerge from groups fighting for their own material interests but from "advocacy groups" acting in the name of oppressed populations(e.g., the civil rights movement), of animals or plants, or of humanity (e.g., the pacifist movement and the anti-atomic energy movement).

3. Both ideologies gave rise to "new social movements" very similar in terms of membership composition, rhetoric, tactical behavior and internal organization (Kriesi 1989). Among other similarities, these movements relied on informal network structures, recruited members mainly from younger and more educated strata (particularly from social and cultural occupations) ready to engage in "unconventional political action" and cultivated a generalized skepticism (and diffidence) toward a wide variety of established elites, conventional belief systems and hierarchical institutions.

Since about 1985, manifest "new social movement activities" have been less frequent (Kriesi 1989) while the issues evoked by them nourish public discussion, intraparty quarrels and parliamentary deliberations. There are various theories that emphasize the communalities of "new politics." New politics issues were too heterogeneous (and too variable) to be part of a consistent ideological belief system. Thus, the notion of "post-materialism" (Inglehart 1984) reflects the fact that the new issues are not primarily related to vital interests of specific societal groups, whereas the "new liberalism" focuses on a generalized attitude of "cosmopolitanism" and "anti-institutionalism" particularly prominent among highly educated younger cohorts (Bell 1979, Brint 1984).

Despite extensive cross-national research on the matter, there are still many unresolved questions concerning the total impact of new politics on the ideological, institutional and behavioral aspects of Western political systems. In particular, two central questions have not been sufficiently clarified:

1. How are class politics and the different dimensions of new politics related to each other? In what sense are social liberalism and ecologism manifestations of a "new political culture" (Clark/Quillian 1993) no longer linked to classical understandings of "left" and "right"?

2. How do "old politics" and "new politics" differ in the way they are anchored in society? Are social liberalism and ecology attitudes still shaped by

class position and occupation or predominantly determined by age and education?

Concerning the first issue, several authors argue that social liberalism and
ecologism define a "new political culture" that differs from traditional leftist
stands and ideologies. Thus, Inglehart presented convincing empirical data showing that attitudes of the general electorates of seven European countries toward
"materialist" issues and toward "post-materialist" issues are rather weakly correlated with each other. As correlations are particularly low among younger age
cohorts, he concluded that intergenerational change contributed to a growing
independence of these two dimensions (Inglehart 1984, 25ff; Inglehart 1989:
372ff).

Following a similar argument, Clark and Inglehart, in chapter 2 of this book,
and Clark, Lipset, and Rempel (1993: 305) suggest that rising affluence and
intergenerational change contribute to a growing salience of "social value issues" that constitute "a distinct political dimension from more traditional economic or fiscal issues." They present survey data that show that among citizens
in Western Europe and in the United States correlations between attitudes of
fiscal liberalism and social liberalism are extremely low.

In addition, they cite a cross-national study of mayors that shows that the
younger the mayor, the less interrelated the fiscal and social liberalism. They
conclude that "a declining impact of traditional left-right cleavages in the political socialization of the young ... takes place in these several countries" (Clark/
Lipset/Rempel 1993: 308). Consistent with this view, many American cities
have seen the rise of "new fiscal populists" since the mid-1970s: Mayors who
combined pronounced leftist stands on "post-materialist" issues with rather
conservative fiscal positions (Clark/Ferguson 1983).

Although Lipset maintains that the superposition of post-materialist issues
on older materialist issues has lead to an uneasy coexistence of "two lefts" (Lipset
1981), Clark and Quillian hold that the meaning of "leftism" is changing by
becoming more and more linked to social issues while loosening its traditional
association with class issues (Clark/Quillian 1993: 2). This accords at least partially with Bürklin's findings that younger German respondents showed higher
correlations between left-right self-placement and new politics issues. Yet he
reports that the relationship between left-right orientation and traditional economic issues seems stable with diminishing age (Bürklin 1982).

Besides social liberalism, *ecologism* is also said to constitute a new ideological
dimension, less and less associated with conventional radicalism. Thus, a cross-
national study (comparing the populations of England, Germany and the United
States) found that ecology attitudes are not correlated to stands on traditional
left-right issues (like governmental control) (Kessel/Tischler 1984).

Yet there is also evidence that attitudes toward "old" and "new" political
issues are significantly interrelated and that this linkage has not been eroded by
either socioeconomic development or intergenerational change. It cannot be

denied that during the last twenty years many Western countries (particularly in Europe) have seen the emergence of "red-green parties," which combine ecological and socially liberal stands with pronounced leftist positions in all traditional domains (e.g., in economic and social policy) (Poguntke 1987). In a sophisticated empirical study, Weakliem (1991) has shown that the "materialist" and the "post-materialist" dimension of political ideology show considerable interfactor correlations (between .40 and .60). This is consistent with Inglehart's findings that—at least for political elites—materialist and post-materialist issue positions appear more closely linked and to be components of an overarching left-right dimension encompassing economic as well as non-economic issues (Inglehart 1984: 33). According to Inglehart, the functional needs for organizing politics along a single "left-right" dimension are so imperative that—in the long run at least—post-materialist issues will become assimilated to this dimension rather than evolving to an independent second ideological axis (Inglehart 1984: 37). This contrasts with Clark and Lipset's contention—based on newer evidence—that the significance of the left-right continuum is in a secular decline (Clark/Lipset/Rempel 1993: 300).

To conclude, five major questions are still open to debate:

1. How are attitudes on materialist issues and post-materialist issues interrelated?

2. How do old issues and new issues differ in their relationship with the general dimension of "left" Versus "right"?

3. Is "new politics" a unidimensional phenomenon or instead a conglomerate of several separate components (e.g., "social liberalism" and "ecologism")?

4. How do all these relationships change across time as a consequence of (a) socioeconomic development and (b) intergenerational change?

5. Are these correlations and developments the same across all Western countries, or are they conditioned by particular cultural factors?

This paper addresses the first four questions. A second, unsolved controversy concerns the question of whether "new politics" differ from "old politics" by being anchored in different social strata or by being less conditioned by any structural factors. An extreme position is marked by Clark and Lipset, who maintain that with rising affluence and increasing diversification of the occupational structure class factors begin to lose their impact on all kinds of political preferences (Clark/Lipset 1991). They find this hypothesis corroborated by the regularity that in several Western nations the degree of "class voting" has generally declined (Clark/Lipset 1991). However, such evidence seems to be rather weak because there are also some countries (e.g., Belgium, Sweden and France) in which class voting has increased (Przeworski/Sprague 1986) or (like Denmark) remained invariant across time (Andersen 1984).

Inglehart, advocating a moderate position, maintains that the weakening of class impacts is confined to non-economic (post-materialistic) issues. Such issues are far more related to general value positions than they are to the interests of particular social classes (Inglehart 1984). According to Inglehart, increasing societal affluence and higher education pave the way for a spread of post-materialist attitudes among extensive segments of the population, particularly younger cohorts less socialized into the older patterns of class-related ideologies (Inglehart 1984: passim; 1989: 399).

In his survey of candidates for the European Parliament (1979), Inglehart also shows that inter-correlations of different issue positions with each other and with left-right self-placement are much stronger on the level of political elites than they are within the general population (Inglehart 1984:passim; 1989: 368). This is consistent with the general regularity that politically inactive citizens often lack the cognitive capacities to organize their specific political attitudes and to relate them to a framework of more abstract values and ideologies (Converse 1964; Pierce/Rose 1974; Achen 1975). In addition, non-elites seem to relate notions of "left" and "right" more to changing issues of short-term salience (like terrorism), whereas elites maintain more stable semantic connotations associated with invariant issues (like governmental economic control) (Inglehart 1989: 370ff.). Thus, he maintains that the rise of post-materialism means something much more fundamental than a mere change in the contents of salient political issues: namely, *a change from a class-based to a value-based system of political preferences* (Inglehart 1984: 26).

Similar empirical results are reported by Brinkmann, who maintains: (1)that all segments of affluent "new middle classes" have shifted toward the left and toward a higher acceptance of post-materialist values; and (2)that in younger age cohorts, occupation loses its impact on political values, whereas education becomes a more powerful predictor (Brinkmann 1989). Yet such dramatic conclusions are contradicted by several thorough empirical studies in which more precise measures of socioeconomic status. They consistently show that occupational status and situs are powerful predictors of social liberalism and ecology attitudes and that such influences are unlikely to diminish with socioeconomic development and/or intergenerational change. However, it seems that traditional vertical class cleavages (between workers and employers) have lost significance in favor of new functional divisions between different kinds of occupations. Thus, Weakliem finds that the classical "materialist" dimension polarizes manual workers and the petty bourgeoisie, whereas the second "post-materialist" axis opposes professionals, nonmanual employees and managers to the petty bourgeoisie and the farmers. Comparing age cohorts, he finds that although the whole population may shift leftwards (particularly on the second dimension) and although the causal impact of education is growing there is no evidence that such status factors are weakening due to intergenerational change (Weakliem 1991).

Other studies have found remarkably clear ideological antagonism within the highly salaried, upper-white-collar classes separating the liberal professionals (mainly social and cultural occupations within the public sector) from conservative economic elites. For instance, Lamont (1987) and Alber (1985) argue that this ideological opposition stems from a basic new societal class cleavage between "tax producing" occupations in the private economy and "tax consuming" public employees. For objective reasons, public employees tend to be "fiscal liberals" because their material subsistence is based on public revenues. Favoring a general increase in the public sector, they may also support many "new politics" issues that often imply government control over private activities (e.g., by prescribing measures of environmental protection or more equal treatment of women). Using impressive empirical evidence, Brint (1984) concludes that sympathy for "new liberalism issues" is only fostered within a narrow range of social and cultural professions whose incumbents have become socialized into a framework of cultural values and goals. Similarly, Kriesi found that sympathizers and active adherents of "new social movements" originate predominantly in occupations far from the sphere of economic production and large formal organizations (e.g., teachers, artists, social workers, etc.), whereas the participation rate of employers and unskilled workers is almost nil (Kriesi 1989a, 1989b). Similar regularities are reported by Cotgrave and Duff concerning adherents of environmental movements in Great Britain (Cotgrave/Duff 1980). Following Freidson (1986), Kriesi argues that openness to social liberalism and ecology issues is fostered by occupations where a "substantive rationality" (oriented toward the cultivation of knowledge or the personal well-being of clients) prevails, whereas elites concerned with efficient functioning of organizations follow a "formal rationality" more consistent with conservative and "materialist" political views. He concludes that such divergencies stemming from occupational *situs* are likely to increase (and override *status*-related differences), as suggested by strong mobilization differentials between economic and sociocultural elites among younger respondents (Kriesi 1989a; 1989b).

This abstract argumentation is also consistent with the hypothesis that on higher status levels the same occupational groups favor or oppose materialist fiscal issues as well as post-materialist social and ecological issues. Workers and lower employees, however, are expected to support fiscal liberalism much more than social liberalism or ecological issues, because they may agree with the employers that economic efficiency should not be hampered (and jobs not be threatened) by too many governmental regulations.

The Study

Local Parties as a Field for Studying "Ideological Cultures"

The following empirical study seeks to shed light on the ideological culture in Swiss communal politics and how it relates to the status characteristics of the politically active. It explores the multilinguistic composition of Swiss society by showing how ideological patterns covary with underlying regional cultures. In contrast to the "political culture" that encompasses more basic "rules of the game," ideological cultures may be seen as more variable pattern covarying with long-term changes of societal value systems as well as more short-term developments on the level of social movements, salient issues or attitudinal "fashions." The concept of "ideological culture" implies the existence of collective political perspectives—values and goals governing the behavior of individuals and organizations transmitted by regular processes of socialization. In general, average individual citizens are poor informants of "culture" because their thinking is heavily shaped by psychological idiosyncrasies and because they often lack the cognitive and intellectual capacities to perceive and interpret these collective patterns adequately. Studying *politically active elites* may be a better approach, but it still assumes that cultural patterns are mirrored in the subjective consciousness of their minds. By studying *groups* and *organizations* more justice can be done to the basic fact that culture is primarily expressed in the outcomes of collective communications and activities: for example, in the explicit results of discussions, negotiations and deliberative procedures, in formally stated decisions and action programs or, at least, in mutually recognized "majority opinions." *Political parties* have particularly strong links to ideological culture because it is their job to contribute to the aggregation and articulation of collectively shared opinions, values and goals. Local party sections have the additional virtues of being so numerous that rigorous multivariate methods of comparative analysis can be applied and of being so low in organizational complexity that a single central member is capable of delivering all relevant information.

Switzerland is outstanding because formalized party groupings are so widespread, being found even in tiny communities (500 or fewer inhabitants). They essentially control all major political processes on the communal level (Geser et al. 1994: passim). Given the mix between direct and representative democracy typical of Swiss politics, most of these local parties have the dual function of influencing elections on the one hand and decisions about specific political issues on the other. With a total number of about 200,000 participating members (about 5 percent of Swiss voters), these groupings encompass the bulk of politically active citizens.

The Survey

The data presented in this study are based on an extensive survey including all formalized party groupings regularly active in any of the 3,022 Swiss communities in the late 1980s. Based on information stemming from community administrations and from the secretariats of cantonal parties, a list of about 5,500 groups fulfilling these criteria was established. More than 80 percent of all local groupings are sections of the four big nationwide parties (Social Democrats, Radicals, Christian Democrats and Populists); the others are extensions of minor national or regional parties or autonomous groupings not affiliated to any supralocal organization.

In the fall of 1989, a questionnaire was mailed to the current chairpersons ("presidents") of all these groupings, in which they were asked to provide standardized information about the membership, internal structure, external activities and political goals and preferences of their section. Within four months, 2,638 usable responses were received. A multidimensional analysis (by type of party, geographic region and size of community), showed that the universe was mirrored in the sample without major biases, indicating that results could be generalized to all Swiss communities.

The Dependent Variables

To assess the stands of party sections on the three ideological dimensions, the presidents were asked: "Political parties differ in the way they relate to salient political issues of our time. We would like to know which opinion prevails among the active adherents of your grouping on the following issues (majority supporting (1), majority opposed (–1), divided opinions (0))."

1. *Fiscal liberalism*
   1.1 *The general tax burden should be lowered (-)*
   1.2 *Community tax rates should be lowered (-)*
   1.3 *Governmental spending for social welfare should be increased (+)*
   1.4 *Governmental spending for cultural matters should be increased (+)*
2. *Social liberalism*
   2.1 *It is very important to establish full equality of men and women (+)*
   2.2 *More should be done in favor of immigrant refugees and applicants of asylum (+)*
   2.3 *The legal protection of tenants should be improved (+)*
   2.4 *In neighbourhood areas, traffic speed should be lowered and traffic-free streets should be created. (+)*
3. *Ecologism*
   3.1 *There should be no environmental protection measures if they hamper further economic growth (-)*
   3.2 *Nuclear power plants should cease operations. (+)*
   3.3 *More restrictive construction laws should be enacted to improve the protection of natural landscapes and historical buildings (+)*
   3.4 *Garbage bags should be charged a public fee. (+)*

The more *general ideological stand* of the party was assessed by asking the president to locate his grouping on a scale from 1 (extreme left) to 10 (extreme right).

Table 7.1 shows the frequency distributions of local parties on all these variables.

About 80 percent of all respondents (1,599 in German-speaking Switzerland and 417 in French- and Italian-speaking regions) have answered the whole set of questions completely. The response rate was about equal in all three regions.

TABLE 7.1 Issue Positions and Ideological Positions of Local Parties
1. Issue Positions

	Majority opinion of active members (% of sections)			
	Support	*Divided opinions*	*Opposition*	*(N=)*
1. Fiscal liberalism				
1.1 General tax reduction	63.0	27.3	9.7	(2,451)
1.2 Communal tax rate reduction	56.2	28.5	15.3	(2,516)
1.3 More public spending for social welfare	51.9	33.1	15.0	(2,480)
1.4 More public spending for cultural matters	49.5	38.3	12.2	(2,455)
2. Social liberalism				
2.1 Equality of men and women	76.8	20.3	2.9	(2,487)
2.2 More support for refugees	19.5	50.5	30.0	(2,444)
2.3 More protection for tenants	51.6	33.2	15.2	(2,407)
2.4 More traffic restrictions	65.5	26.0	9.0	(2,423)
3. Ecologism				
3.1 Avoiding obstacles to economic growth	36.2	44.6	19.2	(2,426)
3.2 Shut down nuclear power plants	24.4	40.7	34.9	(2,459)
3.3 More protection of landscapes and historic buildings	60.1	31.9	8.0	(2,536)
3.4 Charges for garbage bags	46.7	30.0	23.3	(2,373)

2. Ideological Positions

Position on the left-right - scale (% of sections)

1	2	3	4	5	6	7	8	9	10	(N=)
1.3	5.4	12.2	10.5	13.8	19.5	16.3	14.6	3.6	1.8	
(33)	(134)	(303)	(260)	(344)	(486)	(394)	(362)	(89)	(38)	(2487)

TABLE 7.2 Political Orientations of Leftist, Centrist and Rightist Local Parties: According to Wealth Level of Community and Age of Membership: German-Speaking Communities

1. Leftist parties (scale values 1-4)

Level of Community Affluence *	Fiscal Liberalism		Social Liberalism		Ecologism	
	Older members**	*Younger members***	*Older members*	*Younger members*	*Older members*	*Younger members*
Low	0.31	1.09	2.00	2.96	1.00	2.06
	16	53	14	57	15	54
Medium	1.42	2.05	2.95	3.41	2.10	2.60
	24	97	24	103	20	97
High	2.46	2.61	3.04	3.64	2.58	3.08
	26	72	24	84	24	75

2. Centrist parties (scale values 5-6)

Level of Community Affluence *	Fiscal Liberalism		Social Liberalism		Ecologism	
	Older members	*Younger members*	*Older members*	*Younger members*	*Older members*	*Younger members*
Low	-1.27	-1.11	1.09	.65	.25	-.55
	11	35	11	34	8	33
Medium	-1.17	-.83	1.48	1.00	.21	.35
	29	30	29	30	28	34
High	-1.22	-.81	1.30	.75	.00	-.39
	23	21	23	20	23	18

3. Rightist parties (scale values 7-10)

Level of Community Affluence *	Fiscal Liberalism		Social Liberalism		Ecologism	
	Older members	*Younger members*	*Older members*	*Younger members*	*Older members*	*Younger members*
Low	-1.70	-1.45	-.20	0.42	-.72	-.39
	33	66	30	60	29	64
Medium	-1.79	-1.60	0.12	.09	-.86	-.68
	63	81	59	74	65	80
High	-1.61	-1.61	0.42	0.36	-.90	-1.00
	54	31	48	28	51	31

* "Low": Less than SFr. 250.- federal income tax per capita (1980). "Medium": Between SF4. 251 and 450 federal income tax per capita (1980). "High": More than SF4. 450.- federal income tax per cpaita (1980).

** "Older members": Less than 40% of active members below 45. "Younger members": More than 60% of active members below 45.

Because the percentage refusing self-placement on the left-right scale was particularly low (less than 3 percent), it may be safely concluded that concepts of "left" and "right" are widely understood by party activists in the Swiss political system.

Empirical Results

Interrelationships Among Fiscal, Social and Ecological Liberalism

Inglehart's theory of post-materialism and Clark's "new political culture" suggest that parties with younger members and in highly developed communities (e.g., urban or suburban communities with highly educated populations) are most affected by political value changes. Such groupings should show the following characteristics: (1) Leftist and rightist parties are primarily polarized on "new politics" dimensions while correlations with fiscal liberalism tend to be weak; and (2) social liberalism and ecology attitudes may also spread to many nonleftist (e.g., centrist) parties that remain irreconcilable on classical fiscal issues.

For groupings in less developed (rural) areas and with older members, inverse conditions would hold. Their self-placement on the left-right scale would be determined predominantly by their fiscal liberalism attitudes while correlations with social and ecological liberalism would be low.

TABLE 7.3 Intercorrelations Between Different Dimensions of Political Orientation: According to Wealth Level of Community, and Age Structure of Membership: German-Speaking Communities (Pearson coefficients; $p < .01$ for all coefficients)

	Level of Community Affluence			
	Low		High	
	Older members	Younger members	Older members	Younger members
Leftism*/fiscal lib.	.37	.53	.67	.72
Leftism/social lib.	.47	.53	.54	.70
Leftism/ecologism	.43	.51	.64	.77
Fiscal lib./social lib.	.64	.64	.67	.79
Fiscal lib./ecologism	.36	.44	.62	.78
Social lib./ecologism	.37	.53	.66	.78
(N =)	(66)	(165)	(110)	(138)

*Self-rating of local parties (by the president) on a left-right scale ranging from 1 to 10 (signs reversed).

German-speaking communities

Looking at local party sections in the German-speaking (northern and east-ern) parts of Switzerland, most of the predictions are *not* borne out (see Table 7.2). In accordance with the hypotheses, community affluence and young mem-bership are two cumulative factors causing leftist parties to rank higher on so-cial liberalism and ecology attitudes. But, unexpectedly, these same variables have similar positive effects on *fiscal liberalism*, thus reinforcing the relation-ship among leftism and *all three* ideological dimensions. The symmetrical hy-pothesis that rightist parties are shifting their opposition focus from "antifiscalism" to "anti–social liberalism" and "antiecologism" is also not cor-roborated. These groupings don't seem to be consistently affected by socioeco-nomic development and intergenerational change (as measured by age). Finally, there is no evidence that support for social liberalism and ecology issues is spread-ing to nonleftist parties. To the contrary, centrist parties show more sympathy for "new politics issues" when most of their members are older than forty-five.

Table 7.3 shows that the correlations of all three political dimensions with each other and with left-right self-placement are tightest when party member-ship is young *and* community affluence is high. One must conclude that in German-speaking Switzerland socioeconomic development and intergenerational change tend to generate a more unified and one-dimensional ideological culture in which "old" and "new" issues are more thoroughly linked to each other as subcomponents of an overarching general dimension of "left" and "right."

On the theoretical level, these results are in sharp disaccord with the assump-tion that a new "multidimensional" political culture is emerging or that "new politics" is becoming more and more independent from conventional notions of "left" and "right." Yet they are consistent with Inglehart's assumption that modern political systems tend to organize preferences along a single dimension of ideological preferences (Inglehart 1964: 37). And on the empirical level, they confirm Poguntke's impressionistic analysis of "new green parties," which are found to maintain a "syncretistic" version of progressivism in which old social-ist and modern post-materialist stands are combined (Poguntke 1987). The find-ings also fit with Bürklin's diagnosis that younger age cohorts are more "ideo-logical" in the sense that they derive their specific issue attitudes from more abstract levels of political values and goals, whereas older generations show more "pragmatic" attitudes (related to concrete issue characteristics and situational conditions) (Bürklin 1984).

Although all four ideological variables are highly interrelated, this may be because active party members generally have more consistent ideological views than inactive citizens (Inglehart 1984: 33). In comparison with single individu-als, party groupings may be even more disposed to organize their views in a coherent fashion and to relate specific issue positions to more general ideologi-cal levels because they are under pressure to make their views explicit, to work

TABLE 7.4   Political Orientations of Leftist, Centrist and Rightist Local Parties: According to Wealth Level of Community and Age of Membership: French- and Italian-Speaking Communities.

1. Leftist parties (scale values 1-4)

Level of Community Wealth	Fiscal Liberalism		Social Liberalism		Ecologism	
	Older members	Younger members	Older members	Younger members	Older members	Younger members
Low	1.11	.73	2.82	2.81	.43	1.47
	17	22	17	22	30	19
Medium	-.16	1.37	1.83	3.37	.55	1.81
	12	30	12	32	11	27
High	.67	1.36	2.33	2.92	1.57	1.42
	6	11	6	13	7	12

2. Centrist parties (scale values 5-6)

Level of Community Wealth	Fiscal Liberalism		Social Liberalism		Ecologism	
	Older members	Younger members	Older members	Younger members	Older members	Younger members
Low	.67	-.21	2.00	1.58	-.67	.00
	3.00	14	4	12	3	13
Medium	-.40	.46	3.00	1.00	.00	-.09
	5	13	5	10	6	11
High	-.50	-.38	2.80	2.00	.80	.40
	6	8	5	8	5	5

3. Rightist parties (scale values 7-10)

Level of Community Wealth	Fiscal Liberalism		Social Liberalism		Ecologism	
	Older members	Younger members	Older members	Younger members	Older members	Younger members
Low	-.50	-.68	1.30	.81	-.45	-.65
	12	19	10	16	11	17
Medium	-1.18	-.31	1.11	.76	-.11	-.86
	11	16	9	17	9	14
High	.00	-1.67	1.60	.40	-.40	-1.00
	7	9	5	5	5	4

TABLE 7.5   Intercorrelations Between Different Dimensions of Political Orientation: According to Wealth Level of Community, and Age Structure of Membership: French- and Italian-Speaking Communities (Pearson coefficients; p < .01 for all significant coefficients)

	Level of Community Affluence			
	Low		High	
	Older members	Younger members	Older members	Younger members
Leftism*/fiscal lib.	.55	.32 (n.s.)	.67 (n.s.)	.76
Leftism/social lib.	.51	.50	.54 (n.s.)	.64
Leftism/ecologism	.50	.46	.64 (n.s.)	.52
Fiscal lib./social lib.	.50	.36 (n.s.)	.67 (n.s.)	.63
Fiscal lib./ecologism	.51	.48	.62 (n.s.)	.58
Social lib./ecologism	.47	.46	.66 (n.s.)	.62
(N =)	(28)	(57)	(18)	(27)

*See note to Table 7.3

out internal consensus and to present consistent doctrines and action programs to the outside world.

Although cross-sectional data never provide conclusive evidence on diachronic developments, these findings nevertheless suggest that in German-speaking regions intergenerational change as well as processes of modernization may be contributing to a rise (or at least not to a decline) of ideological thinking, because young modern party adherents are most prone to relate specific issue attitudes to the general categories of "left" versus "right."

French- and Italian-speaking communities

In the French- and Italian-speaking regions, quite different conclusions seem to be warranted (see Table 7.4). Looking at the leftist parties, it is evident that none of the three dimensions is consistently affected by community affluence and that only ecologism gains somewhat from having younger members. Although ecologism seems to be much less an ingredient of leftist political culture than in German-speaking regions, "social liberalism" is much more prevalent across the whole spectrum of political parties. Insofar as socioeconomic and intergenerational change promote political polarization, this is caused mainly by the rightist parties, which have more extreme attitudes when community affluence is high and membership is young. The intercorrelations (see Table 7.5) add insights into the political culture in Western and Southern Switzerland:

(1) Intergenerational change (age) raises interrelations only when community affluence is high. Thus, in contrast to the German-speaking regions, the increase in "ideological thinking" is restricted to nonrural regions. (2) Contrary to post-materialist theory, it is primarily the relationship between leftism and *fiscal liberalism* that is gaining strength. (3) Social liberalism and (particularly) ecologism remain rather loosely linked to leftism and fiscal liberalism.

Thus this conclusion: In the French- and Italian-speaking cantons, the trend toward a one-dimensional "red-green" political ideology is much less pronounced than in the German-speaking regions. Yet both regions are similar in showing no evidence of an emerging "new political culture" because all recognizable trends indicate a closer linkage of classical materialist attitudes with left-right self-placement as well as with post-materialist issue positions.

Nevertheless, the coupling between specific issues and general left-right orientations seems to remain consistently lower, because leftist parties show less "ecologism" (and centrist and rightist parties more "social liberalism").

Of course, these divergences between the regions permit divergent causal interpretations. On the one hand, they may reflect basic differences in regional ethnic cultures that give rise to stable (and even growing) divergences in ideological culture. More specifically, the German-speaking regions are mainly affected by the ideological culture in Germany, where the "greens" are quite leftist (and the Social Democrats rather green) (Poguntke 1987). Similarly, the other two regions reflect patterns reigning in France and Italy, where the ecological movements have remained so insignificant that a more conventional (materialist) leftism has been preserved.

On the other hand, one could suggest that the regions are in different stages of a common evolutionary process that may lead to a convergence sometime in the future. In this second perspective, the German-speaking regions may be more advanced in the trend toward a more highly ideologized political culture, whereas the French- and Italian-speaking communities still reflect more traditional stages where community politics were less ideological.

Relationships Between Political Ideologies and Occupational Structure

Impressed by the parallel decline of "class voting" in several Western nations, some adherents of "new politics theory" boldly conclude that all kinds of liberal, leftist or "socialist" attitudes are losing their traditional foothold in social classes and occupational structures. Adding the perspective of "post-materialism," more cautious researchers readily assume that such developments take place at least in social liberalism and ecology issues, because these issues lack any intrinsic relationship with the interests of specific class or occupational segments of the population. But if we consider our Swiss findings above—that interrelations between fiscal, social and ecological liberalism increase with socioeconomic progress and younger age—we might expect these three ideological dimensions to show increasing convergences in their causal relationships to class and occupation. Given that we are analyzing social aggregates (party sections), and not single individuals, there is no direct way to assess relationships between *individual* status characteristics and *individual* political opinions. I thus draw inferences indirectly from correlations between the social composition of the membership and political stands of local political parties.[1] Occupation effects can be observed with the regression results.

German-speaking communities

At least for the eastern, German-speaking region of Switzerland, the "new politics" hypothesis is refuted (see Table 7.6): (1) All three ideological orientations of local parties are determined to a similar (and quite considerable) degree by the class and occupation of their members. (2) The coefficients for occupa-

TABLE 7.6   Composition of Membership and Political Orientations of Local Parties in German-Speaking Switzerland: According to the Wealth Level of the Community (Multivariate regressions: unstandardized B-coefficients)

Percentage of member category	Fiscal Liberalism Level of Wealth		Social Liberalism Level of Wealth		Ecologism Level of Wealth	
	Low	High	Low	High	Low	High
Farmers	-1.254 *	-3.324 **	-2.563 ***	-5.872 ***	-2.732 ***	-4.268 ***
Employers	-2.591 ***	-5.818 ***	-3.528 ***	-6.715 ***	-4.067 ***	-5.691 ***
Managerial employees	-0.124	-4.238 ***	0.048	-3.508 ***	-1.839 *	-4.054 ***
Lower employees	+1.389 *	2.43 **	0.202	0.675	-1.173	1.097
Workers	+1.308	2.292	0.724	1.01	0.672	-0.229
Public officials	+3.690 ***	0.535	+3.34 ***	-0.628	0.859	-2.102
Teachers	+7.578 ***	5.422 ***	+5.045 ***	+3.938 **	+7.578 ***	+6.273 ***
below 45	+.059	1.164	+.897 *	0.996	0.597	+1.410 **
with university degree	0.207	-0.361	-0.315	-0.617	-1.623	-0.857
Constant	-1.046 **	-0.073	+.888 **	+2.348 ***	0.653	+.912 **
R^2	.204	.352	.261	.440	.240	.355
(N=)	(381)	(386)	(374)	(386)	(369)	(386)

$^* p < .05;$ $^{**} p < .01;$ $^{***} p < .001.$

tion, as well as the cumulated percentages of variance explained, show these structural factors are not less but more decisive when community affluence is high. (3) Contrary to Inglehart, Clark, and Lipset, almost no independent effects from younger age or higher education of party adherents are observed. Only for ecologism do parties in affluent communities appear somewhat more liberal when the majority of their active members are younger than forty-five.

Inspecting the occupational effects more closely, further astonishing regularities for all three dimensions can be identified: (1) Farmers and employers are the most consistent conservatives in all respects and under any socioeconomic conditions. Although both segments shrink in size in higher developed (nonrural) communities, their antiliberal political preferences seem accentuated in such modernized settings. (2) Only in more affluent communities do higher employees join farmers and the self-employed in their opposition to liberal issue positions. Thus, modern economic elites seem far more inclined to ally with the traditional petty bourgeois (and to substitute their declining influence in industrialized settings) than to coalesce with their lower-ranking colleagues in the

TABLE 7.7 Composition of Membership and Political Orientations of Local Parties in German-Speaking Switzerland: According to the Age Structure of Party Members (Multivariate regressions: unstandardized B-coefficients)

Percentage of member category:	Fiscal liberalism		Social liberalism		Ecologism	
	Age of members+		Age of members		Age of members	
	older	younger	older	younger	older	younger
Farmers	-2.018 *	-3.811 ***	-3.024 ***	-4.328 ***	-2.732 ***	-3.598 ***
Employers	-5.199 ***	-4.128 ***	-5.243 ***	-5.933 ***	-4.965 ***	-5.509 ***
Managerial employees	-1.883	-3.432 ***	-2.438 **	-2.232 **	-4.089 ***	-3.856 ***
Lower employees	+1.876 *	+1.384 *	+1.253	-.496	+.767	-.950
Workers	+1.573	-.054	+1.646	-1.448	+1.914	-1.674 *
Public officials	+2.041	+.456	+2.533 *	-.048	-0.005	-.553
Teachers	+7.306 **	+6.765 ***	+6.710 **	+4.830 ***	+6.150 **	+6.847 ***
below 45	-2.420 *	+.667	-1.648	.725	+.738	+.725
with university degree	+.182	+1.118	-.216	.250	-.853	+.462
Constant	+.100	-.127	+2.052 ***	+2.377 ***	+.793	+1.373 **
R2	.232	.348	.323	.429	.271	.391
(N=)	(306)	(505)	(297)	(506)	(291)	(504)

* $p < .05$; ** $p < .01$; *** $p < .001$.

same private firms. (3) Compared with the quite decisive political preferences of the economic elites, the ideological profiles of the lower classes and the public officials are rather weakly articulated.

Although the lower-white-collar employees seem to support at least fiscal liberalism issues, workers are conspicuous by their complete lack of influence on any of the three political dimensions. In accordance with theories about their objective interest in a large scope of the public sector (see Alber 1987, Kriesi 1989), public officials support fiscal and social liberalism—but surprisingly only in less developed communities. Thus, the only confirmation of the "new politics" theory is that the lower classes show no preference for liberalism (or leftist) attitudes. But this is evidently the same for all levels of socioeconomic development and seems to represent a long-term invariant of the Swiss political system (Kerr 1987). (4) Teachers are evidently the only occupational group consistently and strongly supporting all three strains of ideological liberalism. Their influence appears attenuated in wealthier communities but still remains strong. This regularity may indicate that political liberalism in Switzerland is primarily based on social and cultural elites who fill the vacuum created by the low ideological commitment of workers and lower-level employees.

In summary, ideological polarizations on "old politics" and "new politics" both are anchored in class and occupation, and processes of socioeconomic development seem more likely to strengthen than attenuate such linkages. Although traditional economic elites seem to develop a "generalized conservatism" encompassing social and ecological issues not directly in their material interests, localities with more teachers show the opposite: "generalized liberalism," including support for "classical" socialist issues (e.g., about fiscal policy).

However, for workers, lower employees and public officials the contention may be valid that their occupational status is not linked to specific ideological views. Thus, these lower strata at least may be disposed to fix their political stands in accordance with subjective value standards (or other variable not included here) rather than with their structural-occupational condition.

Although German-speaking Switzerland may be too homogeneous to contain any causally relevant differences in socioeconomic development, it might still be argued that linkages between class/occupation and political ideology are gradually eroding due to intergenerational change. Driven by a conventional work ethic, older age cohorts may shape their political views from their occupational status and roles, whereas younger party adherents—being more affected by post-materialist values—may feel freer to follow subjective value standards or current ideological trends. If this is the case, the causal weight of occupational factors should be higher in parties where the overwhelming majority of adherents is older than forty-five. The results show exactly the opposite (see Table 7.7). In groups with younger members, occupational factors display much greater explanatory power, particularly for social and ecological liberalism. This tight-

TABLE 7.8 Composition of Membership and Political Orientations of Local Parties in French- and Italian-Speaking Switzerland: According to theWwealth Level of the Community (multivariate regressions: unstandardized B-coefficients)

Percentage of member category:	Fiscal liberalism		Social liberalism		Ecologism	
	Level of wealth		Level of wealth		Level of wealth	
	low	high	low	high	low	high
Farmers	-2.033	-1.502	-.236	-1.17	-429	-3.258
Employers	-5.229 ***	-5.039 *	-3.754 *	-5.268 **	-3.214	-3.118
Managerial employees	+.703	-1.818	-.060	-.345	-.472	-2.377
Lower employees	-.558 *	-1.131	-1.164	+598	-1.435	+.058
Workers	-.398	+.002	+.391	-2.233	+.959	-.427
Public officials	-.010	-.794	-.997	-2.032	+1.378	+.791
Teachers	+.887	+5.670 *	+2.729	+3.729	+2.275	+5.211
below 45	-.171	-2.74	+.087	-.018	+.437	+.146
with university degree	+2.354	-1.632	-.913	-.560	+.455	+2.256
Constant	+.542	+1.234	+2.195 ***	+2.623 ***	+.245	+.453
R2	.077	.088	.014	.429	.010	.177
(N=)	(143)	(78)	(131)	(73)	(130)	(69)

$* p < .05; ** p < .01; *** p < .001.$

ened relationship is mainly caused by the farmers and the employers who are more likely to be antiliberal and antiecological if young. Younger managerial employees also show more resistance to fiscal liberalism, not differing much from their older colleagues in the other two dimensions.

Again, there is no evidence that higher education is gaining strength as an independent determinant of liberalism. Instead, *teachers* are the only liberalizing factor irrespective of age. One might conclude that processes of structural (socioeconomic) change and processes of cultural (intergenerational) change synthetically strengthen the relationship between occupation and political ideology and that in both cases the same few occupational categories (farmers, employers, managerial employers and teachers) are responsible for this trend. Particularly for social liberalism and ecologism, the other categories do not consistently contribute to ideological participation, so their political attitudes may be

TABLE 7.9 Composition of Membership and Political Orientations of Local Parties in French- and Italian-Speaking Switzerland: According to the Age Structure of Membership (multivariate regressions: unstandardized B-coefficients)

Percentage of member category:	Fiscal liberalism		Social liberalism		Ecologism	
	Age of members +		Age of members		Age of members	
	older	younger	older	younger	older	younger
Farmers	-1.293	-1.734	-2.732	-2.056	-2.758	-1.972
Employers	-1.767	-4.423 **	-2.571	-4.878 ***	-.598	-5.842 ***
Managerial employees	-4.802 ***	-1.584	-1.938	-3.938 **	-3.061	-2.483
Lower employees	-1.699	-.672	-1.693	-1.949 *	+.036	-1.719
Workers	-.6176	-1.168	+.304	+.830	+.960	-.899
Public officials	-1.766	-.378	-.088	-.458	+.961	+.590
Teachers	+.604	+4.585 *	+2.412	+5.180 **	+4.974	+3.655
below 45	-1.712	-.084	-.491	-.292	+.484	+.882
with university degree	-1.040	-.104	+.926	+1.230	-.446	+1.766
Constant	+.704	+.878	+2.808 ***	+2.446 ***	+.321	+.682
R2	.067	.090	.058	.303	.010	.200
(N=)	(77)	(151)	(72)	(142)	(130)	(133)

* $p < .05$; ** $p < .01$; *** $p < .001$.

predominantly shaped by *nonoccupational factors*. Although the overall validity of these findings may be questioned because of the methodological weaknesses indicated above, they at least make it extremely hard to contend that exactly the opposite (that is, an attenuation of occupational impacts) is taking place.

French- and Italian-speaking communities

Looking at the western and southern regions of Switzerland, a completely different picture emerges (see Table 7.8). In less affluent communities, the cumulative explanatory power of all predictors on social liberalism and ecologism is almost nil and very modest (less than 8 percent) in the classical field of fiscal policy. In wealthier settings, the impact of occupational variables on "new politics" issues is significantly increased due to the more pronounced conservatism of farmers and employers and the liberalism of teachers. Still, the causal effects of both categories often remains below statistical significance. In remarkable contrast to German-speaking regions, the managerial employees do not show signs of any significant antiliberal tendencies; they differ little from lower employees, workers and public officials.

These findings suggest different class structures in the more developed settings of each region. In German-speaking regions, higher employees join employers in their antiliberal and antiecological stands, whereas in the other two regions employers alone defend such conservative views. The same causal irrelevance of age and education holds in all regions.

Thus these conclusions: The linguistic regions are *similar* in that (1) the main impacts on party ideology stem from occupational factors; and (2)the relevance of these factors increases with higher socioeconomic development. Yet the regions are extremely different in that: (1) the causal impact of occupational factors varies, being much lower in French and Italian regions; and (2) modern economic elites (managerial employees) do not contribute to ideological polarization. Comparing the constants of the equations, it is evident that when all status effects are controlled parties in French- and Italian-speaking communities show considerably higher levels of fiscal and social liberalism, whereas ecologism is somewhat lower. On all three dimensions, differences stemming from community affluence are also lower than in German-speaking communities.

As in German-speaking Switzerland, parties with younger members show considerably stronger linkages between ideology and occupational structure, particularly in social liberalism, where cumulative predictive power reaches 30 percent (see Table 7.9). This is mainly because younger employers seem to assume a more antiliberal profile, whereas younger teachers are more progressive.

Thus, these two groups are evidently becoming more similar to their counterparts in the German-speaking regions. Again, there are no indications that higher education moves young voters toward liberal or proecological preferences.

Conclusions

Disregarding the (quite substantial) interregional divergences, the following results stand out: (1) Issue positions in the realm of "old politics" (fiscal liberalism) and "new politics" (social and ecological liberalism) are strongly interrelated; these positive correlations are consistently highest when community affluence is high and party members are young. (2) Party positions on all three ideological scales are mainly determined by class and occupational characteristics of their members (not by education or age); these relationships are strengthened (not weakened) in the course of socioeconomic development and intergenerational change (although we infer change patterns by comparing differences across communities at one time point.)

Both these major findings are starkly inconsistent with the "new politics" thesis that predicts that classical-materialist and new-post-materialist strands of leftism will grow distinct from one another as well as distinct from structural antecedents like social class and occupation. Rather, the results support the conclusion that a single-dimensional, highly generalized new ideological polarization is emerging in Switzerland. It is based on the old opposition between "left" and "right," but these two terms are associated with a richer corona of connotations than in the past, because many new political issues are readily "coded" into the traditional paradigm. It is not likely that this process of ideological concrescence is a temporary "fashion," because it is anchored in structural realities: the generalized liberalism of social occupations (teachers) as well as the increased antiliberalism of economic elites. It is still important that in all Swiss regions lower employees, workers and public officials do not contribute significantly to ideological polarization. Thus, broad strata of citizens feel free to define their political stands unimpeded by considerations of class or occupation_supporting the hypothesis that at least within lower classes status impacts on politics have vanished. Still, there are no indications that this lack of linkage is recent, because the same noncorrelations hold in less developed communities and in parties dominated by the older generation.

Comparing the regions, all regularities are far more pronounced in the German-speaking communities. In the French- and Italian-speaking cantons, correlations between different ideological dimensions (particularly between leftism and ecologism) remain low, managerial employees show no ideological commitment and significant impacts of occupation (particularly on social liberalism and ecologism) are only found when community affluence is high and/or most of party members are younger than forty-five.

These last regularities encourage the speculation that interregional differences may be due to the asynchronism of historical developments. With a delay of two decades or more, the French and Italian regions may experience the same increases in "ideological coherence" that have begun earlier in the German parts of the country.

Yet it is equally likely that the results mirror stable cultural differences not significantly affected by either socioeconomic development or intergenerational change. Paradoxically, such cultural peculiarities are most vivid on classic socialist issues (fiscal liberalism) where French- and Italian-speaking regions show linkages to occupational factors under all conditions of statistical control. This would be consistent with the assumption that eastern Switzerland is heavily influenced by the ideological culture in Germany, distinguished by early emergence of "green parties" that join traditional leftist attitudes with progressive stands on social liberalism and ecology issues (see Poguntke 1987). Likewise, the two other regions are more affected by the ideological cultures in neighboring France and Italy, where leftism remains more separate from ecologism.

Thus, it might be concluded that studies in political and ideological change

may be inconclusive if they omit intercultural comparisons. When such significant interregional divergences are observed even within a single nation (characterized by an overarching political culture), they may be much more pronounced
between different countries with quite distinct ideological and institutional traditions.

It is not enough to think of regional (or ethnic) culture as a mere residual
variable explaining some variance not grasped by structural factors. Culture
may instead be a first-order variable conditioning interrelations between different components of ideology and their linkages to social structure.

Consider the following implications for international comparative research:

1. The inconsistencies with other studies may be due to the basic methodological fact that local party sections, not individuals, are studied. Thus, any
decisive conclusions about the singularity (versus generalizability) of the findings would require parallel studies of *party officials* in other national settings
(not currently available). In general, party staff hold more consistent and integrated ideological stands than individuals because (a) it is their job to aggregate
the attitudes of their divergent members and factions into explicit action programs and specific political decisions, and (b) their visible public status sets
them under high pressure to be consistent so as to appeal to potential voters or
adherents.

This means that high intercorrelations between different ideological strands
(like "socialism" and "ecologism") in the case of urban parties may not at all
reflect a similar covariance by individual citizens. It shows instead their success
in aggregating "socialist factions" and "ecological factions" into an overarching
party platform (e.g., for simple tactical reasons of winning elections). Exactly
this must be expected in the case of Swiss local parties, because their highly
democratic (nonhierarchical) internal structure makes them prone to assimilate
new values, trends and social movements. Thus, younger cohorts supporting
socially liberal and ecologist positions are likely to be welcomed in leftist (i.e.,
traditionally "socialist") parties, particularly in wealthier and more urban settings where traditional supporters (e.g., unionized workers) are no longer in a
dominant position. As a consequence, much higher covariances between socialist, social liberalism and ecology attitudes are generated *on the party level* than in
other countries where parties are more hierarchical and conservative—forcing
the adherents of new political values to articulate their views though other channels (e.g., interest groups or social movement organizations).

2. The higher ideological consistency found in more urban and wealthier
contexts may reflect the regularity that higher educated social strata and political elites are more prone to organize their political attitudes in more coherent
fashion (e.g., to show higher correlations between general position on the left-
right scale and specific positions on political issues [see Inglehart 1990]). Likewise, it has been noted that such deficiencies in "ideological consciousness" are
particularly great in community politics, because there issues are often defined

as nonpolitical problems to be solved by mere common sense or technical expertise (Wurzbacher/Pflaum 1954; Vidich/Bensman 1968 etc.)

3. By combining these two regularities, we may well hypothesize that the lower ideological coherence shown by parties with less modern and older membership does not reflect the presence of any "new political culture" but instead the contrary: the persistence of a traditional culture inimical to any kind of ideological thinking. This accords with the historical fact that until recently many of these communities have been dominated by somewhat apolitical, strictly local associations before they were "colonized" and "ideologized" by branches of supralocal parties. Further, these regularities are quite consistent with Inglehart's hypothesis that it is in highly complex and volatile political contexts where the left-right continuum gains maximum functional importance (to reduce complexity and facilitate political decisions) (Inglehart/Klingemann 1976: 243ff).

4. Thus, the findings would not contradict the NPC hypothesis if it could be verified that two contradicting developments may go on at the same time: (a) a "modernizing" trend leading to an upward shift in ideological consistency—by raising educational levels as well as the average levels of political information; and (b) a "postmodernizing" trend that lowers ideological consistency by promoting a less coherent system of political values and orientations. The theoretical discussion above shows that when the modernization trend is quite strong an increase in ideological consistency may result despite the simultaneous increase of a post-materialist (or post-socialist) political culture. Of course, it is not possible to separate these two countervailing vectors in cross-sectional studies. Only longitudinal studies can identify their presence and their relative strength (under varying contextual conditions).

5. Finally, it is significant that the rather high correlations among classical leftism, ecologism and social liberalism are asymmetrically caused by the tendency of leftist parties to syncretize these three aspects into an overarching value system. In other words, Swiss leftist parties have proven to be quite receptive to new post-materialist values without discarding their more traditional class-related stances. It is this assimilative capacity of leftist groupings that seems to be more pronounced in the German-speaking and the more urbanized parts of the country. We may speculate that this openness toward new value systems is related to the highly democratic, nonhierarchical internal structure of Swiss local parties. The absence of a controlling elite of elderly unionists may also be effective in preventing the intrusion of newer values in many other Western countries (e.g., in France). The differences between the linguistic regions may then well be explained by the fact that plebiscitarian democratic traditions are more pronounced in German-speaking communities than in the western parts of the country (where cantonal centralism and institutions of representative democracy prevail). In addition, the lower ideological intercorrelations in less affluent communities may be explained by the fact that most of these settings are char-

acterized by a high predominance of traditional industrial sectors, which may be associated with the presence of "classic socialist elites" (e.g., union functionaries) exercising control within the more leftist parties. By contrast, leftist parties in the more affluent communities are mostly dominated by adherents from the tertiary sectors (e.g., teachers, social workers, etc.) who are likely to import new post-materialist values (while still clinging to classical social-democratic positions).

These old socialist allegiances may not endure in the future, because the new leftist strata do not share the objective class characteristics of traditional unionized workers. Thus, the high syncretism between traditional and modern aspects of leftist ideology may well represent a transitory condition characterized by a certain equilibrium of power between "classical" and "modern" leftist elites.

Notes

[1] Such inferences are risky for at least two methodological reasons:

(1) Ambiguity of causal interpretations. When a specific relationship—for example, a positive correlation between liberalism and the percentage of public officials—is observed, at least three competing interpretations must be considered: a) public officials are influencing parties to conform better to their own (pre-existing) liberalism opinions, b) public officials are selectively attracted by parties with (pre-existing) liberalism stands. c) public officials are more disposed to let themselves socialize by liberal parties (whenever they have entered them for any (non ideological) reason).

Although hypothesis (c) is improbable in the case of genuinely *voluntary* associations like local parties, hypothesis (b) is plausible when the absolute percentage of an occupational category is so low that it may not be able to exert active influence within the party. Nevertheless, the difficulty of deciding between (a) and (b) is not substantial since in both cases, public officials show *an affinity to liberal political party activity.* To show this may even be considerably more useful than to prove that public officials hold "liberal political attitudes"—because it may well be that many of these are politically irrelevant because they are only displayed in privacy, not in the context of active political roles.

(2) Ecological fallacies. Inferences from the aggregate level to the individual level are plagued with risks of spuriousness stemming from the interrelationships among different variables. For instance, when it is found that parties with high percentages of farmers are more conservative, this correlation may not at all be caused by the farmers, but by the fact that such parties are in rural areas where many other categories of adherents (e.g., the self-employed) lean to the conservative side. Although ecological fallacies can never be ruled out because of the large number of potential "disturbing" variables, they can be significantly reduced by eliminating some possible sources of spuriousness by multiple statistical controls. For these reasons, multivariate regression analysis helps separate "spurious" from "genuine" relationships and for make different impacts comparable on a quantitative level.

8

Citizen Preferences for
Local Growth Controls:
Trends in U.S. Suburban Support for a
New Political Culture Movement

Mark Baldassare

Introduction

U.S. suburbs can no longer be described as communities situated in a residential "zone of commuters" outside of the central cities (Burgess, 1925). Today's suburbs are found in large, dense, and diverse regions where most Americans live and work (Kasarda, 1978; Pisarki, 1987; Schneider, 1991). As the urbanization of the suburbs has continued, urban problems have surfaced, and the quiet, residential suburban way of life has been vanishing (Baldassare, 1986; Cervero, 1986; Dowall, 1984; Fischer, 1984; Fishman, 1987; Garreau, 1991; Jackson, 1985; Popenoe, 1985). Responding to the urbanization of the surrounding region, suburban residents in a wide variety of community settings have placed political pressures on their local governments to control local growth and development.

The political mobilization against local growth in U.S. suburban communities has taken many different forms. There has been a rise in local ballot measures to control local growth. County and municipal elections have been defined along the lines of "pro-growth" and "anti-growth" political candidates. In addition, municipal governments have adopted stricter land use regulations (Baldassare, 1992; Glickfeld and Levine, 1990; Clark and Goetz, 1994; Logan and Zhou, 1989).

This chapter examines the trend of U.S. suburban residents mobilizing to enact local growth controls. I seek to delineate the factors that explain why a large number of suburban residents support local growth controls. My data sources are public opinion surveys in Orange County, California.

I shall study the extent to which suburban support for growth controls is consistent with the New Political Culture (NPC) model described by Terry Nichols Clark and Ronald Inglehart (Chapter 2). The recent emergence of suburban support for limiting growth seems to be an ideal example of a "post-materialist" citizen movement. First, the anti-growth movement is a lifestyle or environmental issue. In addition, anti-growth movements are found in the context of the U.S. suburbs, which fit the NPC profile of a youthful, affluent, and highly educated group with rising incomes.

I derive the following hypotheses about trends in suburban support for local growth controls, and the predictors of support for growth controls, from Clark and Inglehart (Chapter 2) and Clark and Quillian (1993).

• *Hypothesis 1.* Public support for local growth controls is found in significant levels in Orange County, California, a suburban region with the NPC profile of an affluent, educated, and youthful public with rising incomes.

• *Hypothesis 2.* Public support for local growth controls will increase in good economic times, since rising incomes provide the conditions for the NPC; public support declines during economic recession.

• *Hypothesis 3.* The antigrowth coalition in the suburbs is an "issue-oriented" citizen movement, since it is based on the NPC. Thus, public support for local growth controls is predicted by community attitudes, such as perceived local problems and the quality of life.

• *Hypothesis 4.* Public support for local growth controls, since it is based upon the NPC, is not predicted by political party or general political orientation.

• *Hypothesis 5.* Public support for local growth controls, since it is based upon the NPC, is predicted by youth, higher income, and higher education.

Previous Research on Local Growth Controls

There is sufficient data from both the United States and other nations to indicate that many municipalities are not only encountering antigrowth citizen movements but are responding to them by adopting local growth controls (Mouritzen and Nielsen, 1988; Clark and Goetz, 1994; Glickfeld and Levine, 1990; Logan and Zhou, 1989). Limiting growth is sometimes used by municipalities as a strategy for coping with fiscal austerity (Mouritzen and Nielsen, 1988) or to ensure the high socioeconomic status of the community through exclusionary zoning practices (Logan, 1978; Logan and Schneider, 1981; Logan and Semyonov, 1980; Logan and Molotch, 1992). Local growth controls in U.S. suburbs, however, are frequently examples of local government responding to citizen mobilization against growth (Clark and Goetz, 1994); they might also be local governments' reactions to problems, such as traffic congestion, perceived to be a result of growth.

Many different sources have reported that U.S. suburban residents support stricter controls on local development. National surveys find that residents of growing suburbs oppose new development (Baldassare, 1981). Local elections and community surveys have found large majorities of suburban residents favoring local growth limitations (Baldassare, 1992; Glickfeld and Levine, 1990). Scholarly reports from a wide range of suburban communities—from older, affluent suburbs to recently built developments on the metropolitan fringe—provide examples of residents who are pressuring their local governments to control growth (Danielson, 1976; Dowall, 1980; Morrison, 1977).

The predictors of suburban support for local growth controls have been studied by many urban scholars. There has never been a strong link between actual local population growth rates and either public support for local growth controls or the presence of local growth controls (Baldassare, 1986; Glickfeld and Levine, 1990). Thus, studies have considered other explanations, such as demographic factors, political attitudes, and community attitudes.

The best predictor of support for local growth controls in previous public opinion studies has been community attitudes and residents' perceptions of local population growth. Residents who perceive rapid growth in the locality, who complain about local government services, or who are dissatisfied with the quality of community life are more supportive of local growth controls (Anglin, 1990; Baldassare, 1986, 1990, 1992; Bollens, 1990; Gottdiener and Neiman, 1981; Johnston, 1980). These findings provide strong evidence that the antigrowth movement is an NPC citizen movement that is based on issue-oriented politics.

No studies to date have found that support for local growth controls varies with political attitudes. There are no differences across political parties or in regard to liberal versus conservative politics (Baldassare, 1986, 1992). Nor is there a connection between political support for the antitax movement and favor or opposition toward local growth controls. The supporters of local growth controls, then, are similar to the "New Fiscal Populists" (NFPs) (Clark and Ferguson, 1983) or the NPC model of citizen movements. They are brought together by issue-specific political attitudes and policy preferences rather than by political party membership or political orientation.

Demographic variables have had ambiguous effects on support for local growth controls. There is no consistent evidence that younger adults, college graduates, or higher-income residents are more likely than other residents to support local growth controls (Albrecht et al., 1986; Baldassare, 1986; 1992; Bollens, 1990; Connerly and Frank, 1986; Gottdiener and Neiman, 1981). Some report that the suburbs with local growth controls have higher socioeconomic status—for example, more homeowners and white-collar workers—and that development is discouraged in affluent suburbs (Green and Fleischmann, 1991). However, local growth controls are also found in suburbs that are less affluent (Baldassare and Protash, 1982; Protash and Baldassare, 1983).

Finally, there are some examples pointing to the fact that support for local growth controls is contingent upon a sense of economic well-being. This would seem to indicate that the NPC context of rising incomes is significant to this citizen movement. Most suburban residents are staunchly opposed to local no-growth policies, even as they support stricter controls on local development (Baldassare, 1990). Support for local-growth-control ballot measures declines, particularly among less affluent residents, when the economic costs of such policies or the threat of job losses due to growth controls are discussed (Connerly, 1986; Neiman and Loveridge, 1981).

In sum, previous studies provide some support for predicting suburban support for growth controls with the NPC model. Resident attitudes are the most important factor in predicting support for local growth controls, pointing to the fact that it is an issue-specific political coalition. There is no indication that support for local growth controls differs among liberals and conservatives or by political party. However, there is only contradictory evidence that the young, affluent, and better-educated suburban residents are more likely than others to support limits on growth. Support for local growth controls also seems to be contingent upon economic security, and favor for this policy decreases under the threat of economic losses.

The current study seeks to test the NPC model by examining public support for local growth controls during a special period in the history of Orange County, California. This is a suburban region that experienced rapid population growth and economic expansion followed by a serious economic recession. But I also examine the predictors of the effects of resident attitudes on support for local growth controls over time in an effort to determine if the NPC model applies during periods of economic growth and recession.

Orange County: Growth and the New Political Culture

Orange County is an ideal location to study trends over time in regard to suburban support for local growth controls. It experienced rapid population growth and economic expansion in the 1980s, followed by an economic recession in the early 1990s.

Some may question the generalizability of studies of a new political movement in a suburban region. However, research conducted in suburban regions is extremely relevant today because the biggest part of the U.S. population lives in the suburbs and because the fastest-growing places are in suburban regions (Frey, 1993). Orange County is a setting that will provide relevant findings since suburban regions throughout the United States have gone through similar transformations from residential communities to centers of economic activities (Baldassare, 1992; Muller, 1989). Indeed, Orange County has been previously studied as the location of the new urban-industrial economy, with emerging high-technology industries and employment (Scott, 1988) and "edge cities" and other new forms of communities (Garreau, 1991). Other researchers have compared Orange County to twenty other leading suburban counties in other regions of the United States, including places such as Suffolk, New York, DuPage, Illinois, Gwinnett, Goergia, and Santa Clara, California, and have found similar population and employment characteristics. (Kling et al., 1991).

Orange County is a suburban region south of Los Angeles and had a population of about 2.5 million in 1990. It experienced two consecutive decades of rapid population growth. For instance, between 1970 and 1980, Orange County's population grew by about 500,000, more than any other county in California. Between 1980 and 1990, Orange County gained an additional 478,000 residents—for an overall increase in county population of 25 percent.

The demographic characteristics of Orange County fit the NPC profile. The residents are more affluent, more educated, and younger compared to the rest of the United States, and households experienced rising incomes in the 1980s.

According to the 1990 census, the median household income was $46,000 in Orange County and $30,000 in the United States. Twenty-eight percent of Orange County residents who are twenty-five and older have college degrees, compared to 20 percent in the United States. The median age of the adult population in Orange County is 31 and in the United States it is thirty-three; in particular, Orange County has more residents in the eighteen-to–forty-four category than the United States as a whole (73 percent to 68 percent).[1]

There is also evidence of rising incomes in the 1980s in Orange County that far outpaced the nation. Adjusting for local inflation, median household income increased in constant 1990 dollars from $36,625 in 1980 to $45,922 in 1990, a 25 percent gain. In the nation, meanwhile, median household income increased in constant 1990 dollars from $28,090 in 1980 to $29,943 in 1990, a 6 percent gain. Housing prices also reflect growing affluence among the six in ten Orange County residents who are homeowners. Adjusting for local inflation, median home value increased in constant 1990 dollars from $166,023 in 1980 to $252,700 in 1990, a 52 percent increase. In the nation, median home value increased in constant 1990 dollars from $69,147 in 1980 to $79,100 in 1990, a 14 percent increase.[2]

However, the era of rising incomes in Orange County came to an end in 1990 with an economic recession. There was a net loss of about 55,000 jobs. The median annual household income stopped growing. Consumer confidence fell sharply from the mid-1980s to the early 1990s, indicating a growing pessimism among local residents about personal finances as well as the regional economy. Orange County population continued to grow (150,000 new residents in the early 1990s), although building permits for residential construction slowed considerably.

The political context of Orange County clearly fits the NPC model. This is because large, hierarchical political organizations are absent or have limited power. The political fragmentation of local government found in other suburban regions is evident in Orange County. The county government has no mayor and is run by a five-member Board of Supervisors that is elected by local district. There are thirty-one municipalities and an unincorporated area under county government authority. There are numerous special districts and local agencies with jurisdiction over school, water, sanitation, environmental, and transportation issues. In sum, large governments do not dominate the political decision-making in Orange County.

Orange County politics have also been defined as "issue-oriented" politics, another component of the NPC model. For instance, traffic congestion was a major issue in the early 1980s. The public was divided about the need for a local sales tax increase for transportation improvements. After failing twice, a half-cent sales tax measure passed in 1990. Population growth then emerged as a major political issue. In June 1988, a countywide ballot measure that sought to slow growth was narrowly defeated. However, many voters continued to support local candidates and municipal ballot measures that would limit growth in their own municipalities. In sum, Orange County voters have focused on candidates and ballot measures that support their positions on local issues and have not relied on political parties and political ideologies to set their political agendas.

Further, Orange County residents fit the New Fiscal Populist label associated with the NPC, that is, they are liberal on social issues and conservative on fiscal issues. Republicans outnumbered Democrats (53 percent to 34 percent) in the early 1990s. However, six in ten voters describe themselves as moderate to somewhat conservative, and only 12 percent say they are "very" conservative (Baldassare and Katz, 1992). In previous surveys, voters have consistently supported "personal choice" issues, such as legal abortion, while opposing new taxes (Parsons, 1988; Scheer, 1989).

The Orange County Annual Survey

The data source for this chapter is the Orange County Annual Survey, which I have conducted since 1982 while at the University of California, Irvine. Each year, about 1,000 Orange County adult residents are randomly selected to participate in a twenty-minute telephone interview on a wide range of political, social, and economic issues.

The interviewing for the annual survey is conducted during a two-week period each year on weekend days and weekday nights, using a random sample of listed and unlisted telephone numbers. These telephone numbers are generated by computer from a list of working blocks of existing telephone exchanges. Working blocks are the groupings of telephone numbers in an exchange that are currently in use. The numbers from the existing exchanges are randomly selected in direct proportion to the number of residential numbers currently in use within each working block.

Within a household, survey respondents are randomly chosen for interviewing, so that adult men and adult women (18 years and older) of different ages are equally likely to be interviewed. The 1992 survey includes English and Spanish interviewing, since the 1990 census indicated a significant proportion of Latino residents.

The survey data were compared to U.S. Census figures on population and housing characteristics such as age, income, education, and homeownership. The survey sample reflects the demographic profile of adult residents in Orange County.

I will first examine the changes in residents' attitudes toward the community and then discuss trends over time in citizen's policy preferences for local growth controls. Some of the questions have been asked every year since the survey began in 1982; others were not included until later. I will then analyze the predictors of support for growth controls, using the 1989 and 1992 surveys. Those two surveys were chosen because they include similar questions on demographics, political attitudes, and community attitudes and thus allow one to compare trends in the predictors of citizen support for local growth controls.

Trends in Community Attitudes

In the 1980s, there were significant shifts in residents' attitudes toward Orange County and its localities as the county experienced population and economic growth.

The survey asked the following question beginning in 1985: "Considering all the issues in Orange County, which of these is the most serious problem?" Traffic and growth were mentioned by 46 percent of residents in the 1985 survey. By the 1989 survey, 57 percent thought that traffic and growth were the top county issues. Thus, there was an increase of 11 points in the mention of traffic and growth problems.

The survey asked the following question beginning in 1983: "In the future, do you think Orange County will be a better place to live than it is now, or a worse place to live than it is now, or will there be no change?" In 1983, 40 percent believed that Orange County would become a better place; 35 percent believed it would be a worse place to live. By 1989, 28 percent thought it would be a better place to live; 47 percent thought that it would be a worse place to live. That means that between 1983 and 1989 the number of pessimists grew by 12 points.

The survey asked the following question beginning in 1982: "In the last three years, do you think the population in your city or community is growing rapidly, growing slowly, staying about the same or losing population?" In the 1982 survey, 57 percent reported that their city or community was growing rapidly.

In the 1988 survey (the last time the question was asked in the 1980s), 72 percent said it was growing rapidly. Thus, between 1982 and 1988 there was a 15-point increase in the perception of rapid population growth in the locality.

The survey asked the following question about residential satisfaction beginning in 1987: "Thinking about the quality of life in Orange County, how would you say things are going—very well, somewhat well, somewhat badly or very badly?" In 1987, 87 percent said things in Orange County were going well and 13 percent said badly. When the question was repeated in the 1989 survey, 77 percent said things were going well and 23 percent said badly. Thus, there was a 10-point increase in negative quality of life ratings.

In the 1990s, there were shifts in several measures of community attitudes as Orange County entered an economic recession. However, the trend toward negative ratings of the quality of community life continued.

Twenty-five percent of residents rated traffic and growth as the county's biggest problems in the 1992 survey, a 32-point drop from the 1989 survey. The 1992 survey indicated that 43 percent viewed crime and the economy as the biggest issues.

In 1992, 54 percent reported that their cities and communities had been experiencing rapid growth. Thus, the number perceiving rapid local growth had declined by 18 percentage points between 1988 and 1992.

In the 1992 survey, 32 percent said that Orange County would be a better place to live in the future, whereas 32 percent said it would be worse. Since 1989, the number saying things will get worse dropped by 15 points. This was mostly because of an 11-point increase in the number of residents saying things will be the same in the future.

Meanwhile, the perceptions of the quality of community life continued to decline. In the 1992 survey, 60 percent thought that things were going well in Orange County, whereas 40 percent thought things were going badly. Since the 1989 survey, then, those saying that things were going badly had increased by another 17 percentage points.

Examining responses to several other survey questions provides further evidence of the increasing significance placed on economic issues in the 1990s. In the 1992 survey, fewer than one in five residents rated the county economy as "excellent" or "good"; when asked to forecast the county's economy in two years, fewer than half thought conditions would be in better shape. As for consumer confidence, the number forecasting good economic times for the nation in the next year dropped from 68 percent in 1989 to 28 percent in 1992. The number who expected personally to be better off financially in the next year dropped from 56 percent in 1989 to 44 percent in 1992. Clearly, economic worries among residents in the 1990s had risen sharply.

Citizen Support for Local Growth Controls

In the 1982 survey, 40 percent thought that local growth restrictions were not strict enough, 51 percent reported that local growth regulations were about right, and 9 percent viewed them as too strict. In the 1989 survey, 59 percent found current local growth restrictions inadequate, 35 percent found local controls about right, and 6 percent said they were too strict. There was a large increase in public support for stricter local growth controls in the 1980s, as fewer described local policies as about right.

However, there was a significant decline in public support evident in the 1992 survey. Fifty percent said that local controls were not strict enough, 40 percent thought they were about right, and 10 percent said they were too strict. This represented a 9-point decline in support from 1989. This shift was a result of a 5-point increase in those saying controls were about right and a 4-point increase in those saying controls were too strict (see Table 8.1).

In sum, a significant number of suburban residents favored stricter local growth regulations at all times. Further, support increased by 19 points in the 1980s, then declined by 9 points in the 1990s. The increase in public support did generally correspond to the era of rising incomes and economic expansion, whereas the decline in favor for local growth controls occurred when there was an economic recession.

Next, I examine the predictors of support for local growth controls in 1989 and 1992. I consider the effects of three demographic factors that are discussed in the NPC model: age, income, and education. I also examine two political factors— party registration (i.e., Democrats and Republicans) and orientation (i.e., liberal-conservative)—to determine if supporters of local growth controls have a particular political profile. Finally, I analyze three community attitudes— quality of life ratings, perceptions of the county's future, and ratings of traffic and growth as the biggest county problems—to test the notion that citizen support for growth controls is an issue-oriented movement.

TABLE 8.1   Public Support for Local Growth Controls: Trends Over Time

"Do you think that government regulations in your city or community aimed at controlling growth are . . ."

	Not Strict Enough	*About right*	*Too Strict*
1982	40%	51%	9%
1989	59	35	6
1992	50	40	10

Source: Orange County Annual Surveys, University of California, Irvine.

TABLE 8.2   Predictors of Public Support for Local Growth Controls in 1989

UNIQUE EFFECTS — MULTIPLE R	
Demographics Only	.04
Politics Only	.10 **
Community Attitudes Only	.20 ***
All Factors	.23 ***
BETA WEIGHTS FROM FINAL EQUATION	
Age	.01
Income	.00
Education	-.06
Conservative	-.06
Republican	-.06
Quality of life ratings	.09 **
County's future "worse"	.13 **
Traffic/growth problems	.09 **

Note: Stepwise regression equations. Significant at ** $p < .01$; *** $p < .001$.

Table 8.2 summarizes a regression analysis in which demographics, politics, and community attitudes are first each separately entered into an equation to determine the unique effects of these factors on public support for local growth regulations. Community attitudes contribute the most to predicting support for local growth restrictions. For example, the multiple R for the community attitudes is .20, whereas the multiple R for the final regression equation is .23. In comparison, demographics and politics have much lower multiple R's than community attitudes.

Table 8.2 also presents the beta weights and significance levels from the final regression equations that included all independent variables. The three measures of community attitudes are each significantly related to support for local growth controls. No demographic variables and no political factors are statistically significant.

Next, I consider the predictors of support for local growth controls in the 1992 survey. I use the same factors as in the 1989 survey: three demographics (age, income, education), two political variables (Republican, conservative) and three measures of community attitudes (quality-of-life ratings, traffic and growth problems, county's future).

Table 8.3 reports the unique effects of demographics, political attitudes, and community attitudes derived from separate regression equations. Community attitudes have the strongest association with public support for local growth controls. The multiple R for community attitudes is .22, compared to the overall multiple R in the final regression equation of .24. Demographics and politics are insignificant factors in predicting support for local growth controls.

TABLE 8.3 Predictors of Public Support for Local Growth Controls in 1992

UNIQUE EFFECTS — MULTIPLE R	
Demographics Only	.04
Politics Only	.08
Community Attitudes Only	.22 ***
All Factors	.24 ***
BETA WEIGHTS FROM FINAL EQUATION	
Age	.03
Income	-.03
Education	.00
Conservative	-.07
Republican	.00
Quality of life ratings	.08 *
County's future "worse"	.16 ***
Traffic/growth problems	.11 ***

Note: Stepwise regression equations. Significant at * $p < .05$; ** $p < .01$; *** $p < .001$.

In Table 8.3, I present the beta weights and significance levels from the final regression equation that included all of the predictor variables. Each of the three measures of community attitudes is significantly related to support for local growth controls. No demographic factors and no political variables are significant. Thus, the 1992 survey results are similar to the 1989 survey findings.

Using the 1992 surveys, I shall next consider the extent to which economic and growth perceptions explain declining support for local growth controls. I add three factors to the analysis: (1) the overall ratings of the county's current economy (from excellent to poor); (2) residents' perceptions of the county's economy in two years (from much better to much worse); and (3) residents' perceptions of local population growth in the past three years (from loss to rapid growth).

Table 8.4 indicates that economic and growth perceptions do have important effects on public support for local growth controls. The multiple R for economics and growth perceptions is similar to that noted for community attitudes. The overall multiple R for the equation with economics and growth perceptions included is .30, compared to .24 without this factor. Thus, adding economics and growth perceptions modestly improves the ability to predict support for local growth controls.

The final regression equation including all variables indicates that it is the perception of rapid growth, rather than economic attitudes, that is most significantly related to support for local growth controls. Perceptions of the county's future and traffic and growth problems are still significantly related to support

TABLE 8.4 Predictors of Public Support for Local Growth Controls in 1992: Including Economics and Growth Perceptions as Factors

UNIQUE EFFECTS — MULTIPLE R	
Demographics Only	.04
Politics Only	.08
Community Attitudes Only	.22 ***
Economics/Growth Perceptions Only	.23 ***
All Factors	.30 ***
BETA WEIGHTS FROM FINAL EQUATION	
Age	.04
Income	-.02
Education	.00
Conservative	-.06
Republican	.00
Quality of life ratings	.06
County's future "worse"	.15 ***
Traffic/growth problems	.09 ***
Perception of rapid growth	.19 ***
County's current economy	.02
County's future economy	-.01

Note: Stepwise regression equations. Significant at * $p < .05$; ** $p < .01$; *** $p < .001$.

for local growth regulations. No demographic variables and political factors are significant. Importantly, none of the economic perceptions is significant.[3]

What explains the decline in favor for local growth controls? Table 8.5 suggests that decreases in the perceptions of community problems that predict support probably played a role. {Those who agree that traffic and growth are the biggest county problems dropped by 32 points between 1989 and 1992 (57 percent to 25 percent). Those who say the county will be a worse place to live in the future declined by 15 points between 1989 and 1992 (47 percent to 32 percent). Indeed, the drop in favor for growth controls may have been more dramatic had it not been for the fact that negative quality of life ratings, which also predict support, increased between 1989 and 1992 (23 percent to 40 percent).

Conclusions

This chapter examines trends in public support for local growth controls, a new U.S. political movement. I considered a number of hypotheses based upon the New Political Culture model, which were tested using the Orange County

TABLE 8.5 Changing Community Attitudes and Public Support for Stricter Local Growth Controls: Trends Over Time

	1989	1992	Change
Favor stricter growth controls	59%	50%	-9
Traffic/growth biggest problems	57	25	-32
County's future "worse"	47	32	-15
Quality of life going "badly"	23	40	+ 17

Source: Orange County Annual Surveys, University of California, Irvine.

(California) Annual Survey. I first examined support for growth controls over time and then the predictors of public support for local growth controls. The results clearly suggest that the NPC is a useful framework for understanding this new political movement.

With regard to the first hypothesis: As expected, a significant level of public support for local growth controls is found throughout the 1982–1992 period. Between 40 percent and 59 percent support stricter local growth regulations in a suburban region with an NPC profile of affluence, high education, and youth.

The NPC hypothesis that public support for local growth controls would increase in times of economic growth and decrease in times of economic recession was confirmed. Support for local growth controls rose from 40 percent in 1982 to 59 percent in 1989. The 1980s were an era in which Orange County's population, employment, and personal income all increased at a rapid rate. Then, public favor for local growth controls dropped from 59 percent in 1989 to 50 percent in 1992. The early 1990s was a time of decline for employment, personal income, and new construction.

The fact that public support for local growth controls is tied to the context of rising incomes and economic growth replicates previous research. Suburban residents may prefer "slow growth," but they are strongly opposed to "no-growth" policies for their communities. In addition, suburban residents are less interested in restricting local growth and development if they are told that such policies will have negative impacts on jobs and the local economy.

The NPC hypothesis that support for growth controls is driven by issue-oriented politics was also confirmed. Community attitudes were the best predictors of support for local growth controls. Specifically, the identification of traffic and growth as the biggest county problems, negative quality-of-life ratings, and pessimism about the region's future were all factors in predicting this new political movement.

In fact, this study found similarity over time in the community attitudes that predict support for local growth controls. This consistency in sources of support seems to indicate that the NPC model can be a powerful predictor in explaining new political movements. Both the 1989 and 1992 surveys find certain kinds of community attitudes, rather than demographics and politics, to best explain this policy preference. These findings replicate the results from the 1982 survey, which found that the perception of rapid growth and declining community quality distinguished those who favored limiting development (Baldassare, 1986). What is most noteworthy is that levels of support ranged widely in the three surveys without any change in the issue-oriented factors predicting preferences for local growth controls. The surveys were also taken at times when levels of population, employment, and income growth were different.

The NPC hypothesis that support for growth controls is not related to membership in political parties or to traditional measures of political ideology was also confirmed. There was no evidence that being a Republican or a Democrat or a liberal or a conservative helped explain support for local growth controls.

The hypothesis that youth, higher incomes, and more education are associated with support for local growth controls was not confirmed. One possibility is that the dimensions of age, income, and education may be more useful in explaining differences between societies or between regions than within one suburban region. For instance, Terry Clark and Edward Goetz (1994) find that antigrowth movements are more common in U.S. cities with more young and highly educated residents.

Future studies should examine the demographic characteristics of antigrowth movement leaders and political activists as well as the predictors of citizen support for growth controls. It will be important to know, for instance, whether the leaders and political activists fit the NPC profile of youth, affluence, and high education. In addition, it would be important to know whether leaders and activists are best described as belonging to an "issue-oriented" political movement in which the members have certain community attitudes in common as opposed to having similar party membership and political orientations.

This study indicates that changes in community conditions lead to changes in community perceptions and then to shifts in policy preferences. For instance, as the size of key attitude groups grew and shrank, local support for growth controls increased and decreased. The findings point to several areas for future research.

First, we need to know about the causal links between actual community conditions and community perceptions. How do residents learn about their community's conditions, when do changes become critical, and how do they reach a decision about their impacts? What is the role of the media, local government, opinion leaders, and social networks?

We also need to understand the causal mechanism that turns community perceptions into policy preferences. At what point do residents believe that policy action is needed? Is it when they perceive agreement with others that certain problems are serious? How do residents come to realize and evaluate the local policy options that are available? Does confidence in local government officials encourage or discourage residents to seek action?

This study suggests there are unique political advantages to NPC citizen movements such as the antigrowth coalition because they are issue-specific in nature. First, the absolute size of the group in favor of policy change is not limited by the membership in any given demographic or political group. Instead, antigrowth coalitions can draw supporters who have reached a common view about community problems. Further, supporters do not have to take their case through normal political channels, such as political parties or interest groups, and thus can appeal their case quickly and directly to local government.

The fact that support for local growth controls is not dependent upon the presence of certain political and demographic factors also means that the antigrowth citizen coalitions can develop in many different kinds of communities. Growth revolts are thus not confined to high-status suburbs, or family-oriented suburbs, or liberal communities, or Republican-controlled cities. Any community can reach consensus on supporting local growth controls—irrespective of its politics and social character—if there is agreement on perceptions of community conditions.

In sum, the strengths of a political movement based on the NPC foundation point to reasons why growth controls were adopted in many U.S. suburbs in the 1980s. Large citizen groups are mobilized through attitude change to pressure local officials for new growth policies.

A political movement such as the antigrowth coalition, however, also has some inherent weaknesses. A change in community attitudes can reduce the size of the group supporting growth controls. As this study has shown, community perceptions can, and often do, shift quickly and dramatically. If the local economy is in a recession, public support could significantly erode. When progrowth advocates bring up fears of employment or income loss, the option of local growth controls may become much less appealing to residents. And if residents turn their focus from traffic and growth toward protecting their jobs and economic prosperity, the preference for stricter local growth controls could also fade.

The example of suburban support for local growth controls raises more general questions about the stability of new political movements based upon the New Political Culture. It will be important to learn whether a wide range of new movements that were formed during an era of economic growth will remain active during economic reversals. This will depend upon, among other things, the abilities of supporters to form active organizations and to institutionalize their "issue-oriented" coalitions. Time-series analyses of data from the 1980s and the 1990s on a variety of movements in Western Europe and North America could answer important questions about the turbulence of the New Political Culture.

Notes

[1] As for race and ethnicity in 1990, Orange County residents compared to the United States are as likely to be Caucasian (79 percent to 80 percent), more likely to be Hispanic (23 percent to 9 percent) and Asian (10 percent to 3 percent), and less likely to be Black (2 percent to 12 percent).

[2] Sources are Baldassare and Katz (1992, 1993); California Department of Finance (1992, 1993); County of Orange (1991); O'Dell (1994); Real Estate Research Council (1992); U.S. Bureau of the Census (1988, 1990, 1991, 1992a, 1992b, 1992c).

[3] Questions in the 1992 survey that measure consumer confidence, such as forecasts for the U.S. economy and personal finances in the next year, were also not significantly related to support for local growth controls.

Bibliography

Achen, Christopher H. 1975. "Mass Political Attitudes and the Survey Response." *American Political Science Review* 69: 1218-1231.

———. 1977. "Measuring Representation: Perils of the Correlation Coefficient." *American Journal of Political Science* 21 (November): 805-815.

Acs, Z., and D. Audretsch. 1993. *Small Firms and Entrepreneurship*. Cambridge: Cambridge University Press.

Adrian, Charles. 1959. "A Typology for Non-Partisan Elections." *Western Political Quarterly* 12: 449-458.

Aglietta, Michel. 1987. *A Theory of Capitalist Regulation: The U.S. Experience*. New York: Verso.

Ahlstich, Katja, and Volker Kunz. 1994. "Die Entwicklung kommunaler aufgaben in zeiten des wertewandels," in Oscar W. Gabriel and Ruediger Voigt, eds., *Kommunalwissenschaftliche Analysen*. Pp. 167-210. Bochum.

Alber, Jens. 1985. "Modernisierung, neue spannungslinien und die politischen chancen der grünen." *Politische Vierteljahresschrift* 26: 211-226.

Albinski, Henry S. 1973. *Canadian and Australian Politics in Comparative Perspective*. New York: Oxford University Press.

Albrecht, Don, Gordon Bultena, and Eric Hoiberg. 1986. "Constituency of the Anti-Growth Movement." *Urban Affairs Quarterly* 21: 607-616.

Allum, P. 1973. *Italy*. London: Wiedenfeld and Nicolson.

Almond, Gabriel A., and James S. Coleman, eds. 1960. *The Politics of the Developing Areas*. Princeton, N.J.: Princeton University Press.

Andersen, Jorgen Goul. 1984. "Decline of Class Voting or Change in Class Voting? Social Classes and Party Vote in Denmark in the 1970s." *European Journal of Political Research* 12: 243-259.

Anglin, Ronald. 1990. "Diminishing Utility: The Effects on Citizen Preferences for Local Growth." *Urban Affairs Quarterly* 24: 684-696.

Arzberger, Klaus, Manfred Murck, Jürgen Schumacher, 1979. *Die Bürger*. Königstein.

———. 1980. *Bürger und Eliten in der Kommunalpolitik*. Stuttgart.

Atkinson, A. B. 1975. *The Economics of Inequality*. London: Oxford University Press.

---. 1995. Incomes and the Welfare State. Cambridge: Cambridge University Press.

Bachelor, L. 1994. "Regime Maintenance, Solution Sets, and Urban Economic Development." *Urban Affairs Quarterly* 29 (4): 596–616.

Bagnasco, A. 1977. *Tre Italie*. Bologna: Il Mulino.

Bainbridge, William Sims. 1989. "The Religious Ecology of Deviance," *American Sociological Review* 54 (2): 288–296.

Baker, Kendall L., Russell J. Dalton, Kai Hildebrandt. 1981. *Germany Transformed*. Cambridge and London.

Baldassare, Mark. 1981. *The Growth Dilemma: Residents' Views and Local Population Change in the United States*. Berkeley: University of California Press.

---. 1986. *Trouble in Paradise: The Suburban Transformation in America*. New York: Columbia University Press.

---. 1990. "Suburban Support for No-Growth Policies." *Journal of Urban Affairs* 12: 197–206.

---. 1992. "Suburban Communities." *Annual Review of Sociology* 18: 475-494.

---. 1992. *Orange County Annual Survey: Final Report*. Irvine: University of California.

Baldassare, Mark, and Cheryl Katz. 1993. *Orange County Annual Survey*. Irvine: University of California.

Baldassare, Mark, and William Protash. 1982. "Growth Controls, Population Growth and Community Satisfaction." *American Sociological Review* 47: 339–346.

Baldersheim, Harald, Richard Balme, Terry Nichols Clark, Vincent Hoffman-Martinot, and Hakkan Magnusson, eds. 1989. *New Leaders, Parties, and Groups: Comparative Tendencies in Local Leadership*. Paris and Bordeaux: CERVEL.

Baldersheim, Harald, et al., eds. 1996. *Local Democracy and the Processes of Transformation in East-Central Europe*, Boulder, Colo.: Westview Press, Urban Policy Challenges Series, 1996.

Baldridge, J. 1991. "New Social Movements and the Emergence of a New Political Culture." Presented at Workshop in Urban Policy, University of Chicago, Winter.

Balme, Richard, Jeanne Becquart-Leclercq, Terry Nichols Clark, Vincent Hoffmann-Martinot, and Jean-Yves Nevers. 1986–1987. "New Mayors." *The Tocqueville Review* 8: 263–278.

Banfield, Edward C. 1961. *Political Influence*, New York: Free Press.

Barnes, Samuel H., Max Kaase et al. 1979. *Political Action*. Beverly Hills, Calif.: Sage.

Baron, James N. 1984. "Organizational Perspectives on Stratification." *Annual Review of Sociology* 10: 37–69.

Bartels, C. A., and P. Nijcamp. 1976. "An Empirical Welfare Approach to Regional Income Distributions." *Socioeconomic Planning Sciences* 10: 244–263.

Beck, E. M., Patrick M. Horan, and Charles M. Tolbert II. 1978. "Stratification in a Dual Economy." *American Sociological Review* 43: 704-720.

Becker, Gary. 1982. "A Positive Theory of the Redistribution of Income and Political Behavior." Presented to Industrial Organization Workshop, University of Chicago.

Becquart-Leclercq, Jeanne, Vincent Hoffman-Martinot, and Jean-Yves Nevers. 1987. *Austerite et innovation locale, les strategies politico-financiers des municipalities urbaines dans la crise*. Volumes 1 and 2. Paris: Compte Rendu Au Ministere De La Technologie.

Bell, Daniel. 1973. *The Coming of Post-Industrial Society*. New York: Basic Books.

---. 1976. *The Cultural Contradictions of Capitalism*. New York: Basic Books.

Benoit-Smullyan, Emile. 1944. "Status, Status Types and Status Interrelationships." *American Sociological Review* 9: 151–161.

Bentley, A. F. 1908. *The Process of Government*. Chicago: University of Chicago Press.

Berger, Peter L. 1987. *Moral Judgment and Political Action*. Boston: Trustees of Boston University.

Bernier, Lynne Louise. 1989. "Political Consequences of Change in the French Intergovernmental System." Presented to American Political Science Association Annual Meeting.

———. 1992. "Socialist Intergovernmental Policy During the Mitterand Era." *Publius* 22 (Fall): 47–66.

Bettin, Gianfranco, and Annick Magnier. 1991. *Chi governa la citta?* Padova: CEDAM.

Birch, D. L. 1979. *The Job Generation Process*. Cambridge: Massachusetts Institute of Technology Program on Neighborhood Change.

Bjørklund, Tor. 1988. "The 1987 Norwegian Local Elections: A Protest Election with a Swing to the Right." *Scandinavian Political Studies* 11 (3): 211–234.

Block, J. 1981. "Some Enduring and Consequential Structures of Personality," in Albert Rabin et al., eds., *Further Explorations in Personality*. Pp. 27–43. New York: Wiley.

Boaz, David, ed. 1986. *Left, Right and Baby Boom*. Washington, D.C.: Cato Institute.

Bobo, L., and F. D. Gilliam. 1990. "Race, Socio-Political Participation, and Black Empowerment." *American Political Science Review* 84: 344–93.

Bollens, Scott. 1990. "Constituencies for Limitation and Regionalism." *Urban Affairs Quarterly* 26: 46–67.

Boudon, Raymond. 1974. *Education, Opportunity, and Social Inequality*. New York: John Wiley.

Bourdieu, Pierre. 1984. *Distinction*. Cambridge, Mass.: Harvard University Press.

Bowles, Samuel, and Herbert Gintis. 1987. *Democracy and Capitalism*. New York: Basic Books.

Bowman, Margaret. 1976. *Local Government in the Australian States*. Canberra: Australian Government Publishing Service.

———. 1983. "Local Government in Australia," in Margaret Bowman and William Hampton, eds., *Local Democracies*. Pp. 165–184. Melbourne: Longman.

Brady, Henry, Norman Nie, Sydney Verba. N.D. "Tables for Study in Progress on Citizen Participation." Manuscript. University of Chicago.

Brand, Karl Werner, Büsser Detlef, and Rucht Dieter. 1984. "Bilanz und perspektiven der neuen sozialen bewegungen," in *Aufbruch in eine andere gesellschaft*. Pp. 241–271. Frankfurt and New York: Campus.

Brim, Orville G., Jr. 1966. "Socialization Through the Life Cycle," in Orville G. Brim, Jr., and Stanton Wheeler, eds., *Socialization After Childhood*. Pp. 368–388. New York: Wiley.

Brim, Orville G., and Jerome Kagan, eds. 1980. *Constancy and Change in Human Development*. Cambridge, Mass.: Harvard University Press.

Brinkmann, Heinz Ulrich. "Neue schicht_neue werte?" *Zeitschrift für umweltpolitik und umweltrecht* 2 (1989): 159–183.

Brint, Steven. 1994a. "Sociocultural Analysis of Political Culture." *Research on Democracy and Society* 2: 3–41.

———. 1994. *In an Age of Experts*. Princeton, N.J.: Princeton University Press.

Brint, Steven, and Susan Kelley. 1993. "The Social Bases of Political Beliefs in the United States." *Research in Political Sociology* 6: 277–317.

Brint, Steven, William L. Cunningham, and Rebecca S. K. Lee. 1997. "The Politics of Professionals in Five Advanced Industrial Societies," in Terry Nichols Clark and Michael Rempel, eds., *Citizen Politics in Post-Industrial Societies.* Pp. 113–142. Boulder, Colo.: Westview Press.

Brint, Steven. 1984."'New-Class' and Cumulative Trend Explanations of the Liberal Political Attitudes of Professionals." *American Journal of Sociology* 90: 30–71.

Brooks, Clem, and Jeff Manza. 1997. "Partisan Alignment of the 'Old' and 'New' Middle Class in Post-Industrial America," in Terry Nichols Clark and Michael Rempel, eds., *Citizen Politics in Post-Industrial Societies.* Pp. 137-151. Boulder, Colo.: Westview Press.

Brown, William. 1990. "Class and Industrial Relations: Sociological Bricks Without Institutional Straw," in *John Goldthorpe.* Jon Clark, Celia Modgil, and Sohan Modgil, eds. New York: Falmer Press.

Bruce-Briggs, B. 1979. *The New Class?* New Brunswick, N.J.: Transaction Books.

Brunell, Anthony R. 1986. "Parliaments and Eurocommunism: The Italian Case." *Parliamentary Affairs* 39 (July): 368-85.

Budge, Ian, and Hans Keman. 1990. *Parties and Democracy.* Oxford: Oxford University Press.

Burgess, Ernest. (1925) 1967. "The Growth of the City," in R. Park, E. Burgess, and R. D. McKenzie, eds., *The City.* Pp. 47–62. Chicago: University of Chicago Press,

Bürklin, Wilhelm P. 1982 "Die grünen und die 'neue politik.'" *Politische vierteljahresschrift* 23: 339–345.

———. 1984. *Grüne politik.* Opladen: Westdeutscher Verlag.

Butts, P. M. 1992. "Feminist Attitudes and Political Involvement: A Cross National Analysis." Paper Presented to Workshop in Urban Policy, University of Chicago, Winter.

———. 1997. "The Social Origins of Feminism and Political Activism," in Terry Nichols Clark and Michael Rempel, eds., *Citizen Politics in Post-Industrial Societies.* Pp. 209–244. Boulder, Colo.: Westview Press.

California Department of Finance. 1993. *Orange County Population and Housing Estimates, January 1, 1993.* Sacramento: State of California.

———. 1992. *California Statistical Abstract.* Sacramento: State of California.

Cameron, David R. 1978. "The Expansion of the Public Economy: A Comparative Analysis." *American Political Science Review* 71: 1243-1261.

Cassel, Carol A. 1986. "The Nonpartisan Ballot in the U.S.," in Bernard Grofman and Arend Lijphart, eds., *Electoral Laws and Their Political Consequences.* Pp. 226–241. New York: Agathon Press.

Castles, F., and P. Mair. 1984. "Left-Right Political Scales: Some 'Expert' Judgments." *European Journal of Political Research* 12: 73–88.

Cavalli, A., and A. De Lillo. 1988. *Giovani anni 80,* Bologna: Il Mulino.

Cervero, Robert. 1986. *Suburban Gridlock.* New Brunswick: Center for Urban Policy Research.

Chandler, J. A., and T. N. Clark. 1995. "Local Government (Around the World)," in Seymour Martin Lipset, ed., *The Encyclopedia of Democracy.* Pp. 767-773. Washington, D.C.: Congressional Quarterly.

Cherlin, Andrew J. 1981. *Marriage, Divorce, Remarriage.* Cambridge, Mass.: Harvard University Press.

Chicago Tribune. 1995. Quotes of the Day. Evening Update Edition, 8 November. P. A2.

Clark, Terry Nichols, ed., 1968. *Community Structure and Decision-Making.* New York: Thomas Y. Crowell.

———. 1972. "Structural Functionalism, Exchange Theory, and the New Political Economy" and "Institutions and an Exchange with Professor Parsons." *Sociological Inquiry* 42(3–4): 275–311.

———. 1973. *Prophets and Patrons.* Cambridge, Mass.: Harvard University Press.

———. 1974. "Community Autonomy in the National System," in Terry Nichols Clark, ed., *Comparative Community Politics.* Pp. 21-51. Beverly Hills, Calif.: Sage Publications.

———. 1975. "Community Power," in Alex Inkeles, James Coleman, and Neil Smelser, eds., *Annual Review of Sociology* 1: 271–296 .

———. 1975. "The Irish Ethic and the Spirit of Patronage." *Ethnicity* 2: 305–359.

———. 1985–86. "The Dynamics of Political Culture." *The Tocqueville Review* 7: 174–190.

———. 1993. "Local Democracy and Innovation in Eastern Europe." *Government and Policy* 11: 171-198.

———, ed. 1981. *Urban Policy Analysis, Urban Affairs Annual Reviews,* vol. 21 Beverly Hills, Calif.: Sage.

———, ed. 1985, 1986, 1987, 1988, 1992, 1994, 1996. *Research in Urban Policy.* Greenwich, Conn.: Jai Press.

———, ed. 1994a. *Urban Innovation.* Thousand Oaks, Calif.: Sage.

———. 1994b. "Program for a New Public Choice," in J. L. Chan, ed., *Governmental and Nonprofit Accounting,* vol. 8. Pp. 3–28. Greenwich, Conn.: JAI.

———. 1994c. "Clientelism, USA," in L. Roniger and A. Gunes-Ayata, eds., *Democracy, Clientelism, and Civil Society.* Pp. 121–144. Boulder: Lynne Rienner.

———. N.D. "Does Globalization Limit Urban Leadership?" Presented to annual meeting American Political Science Association, San Francisco, August.

———. 1995. "Who Cares If Social Class Is Dying, or Not? Being an Effort to Articulate a Framework to Deepen the Meaning of Such Questions." Prepared for Conference on Social Class, Nuffield College, Oxford, February.

———. 1996. "Structural Realignments in American City Politics: Less Class, More Race, and a New Political Culture." *Urban Affairs Review* 31 (January): 367-403.

———. 1997a. "Clientelism and the University." *The Tocqueville Review,* pp. 183-205.

Clark, Terry Nichols, Jerzy Bartkowski, Lincoln Quillian, and Doug B. Huffer. 1994. "The New Political Culture: An International Shift in Urban Rules of the Game." Presented to RC03, World Congress of Sociology, Bielefeld, Germany.

Clark, T. N., and L. C. Ferguson. 1983. *City Money: Political Processes, Fiscal Strain and Retrenchment.* New York: Columbia University Press.

Clark, T. N., and E. G. Goetz. 1994. "The Anti-Growth Machine," in T. N. Clark, ed., *Urban Innovation.* Pp. 105–145. Newbury Park, Calif.: Sage.

Clark, Terry Nichols, Vincent Hoffman-Martinot, and Jean-Yves Nevers. 1987. *L'innovation Municipale a L'epreuve De L'austerite Budgetaire.* Bordeaux: Cervel, Institut D'etudes Politiques.

Clark, T. N., and Ronald Inglehart. 1989. "The New Political Culture." Presented for session of the Fiscal Austerity and Urban Innovation Project, annual meeting American Political Science Association, Atlanta, Georgia, August 31-September 3. Revised version presented to Research Committee 03 sessions, International Sociological Association, Madrid, Spain, July 1990.

Clark, Terry Nichols, and Claude Jeanrenaud. 1989. "Why Are (Most) Swiss Leaders Invisible? The Swiss Communal Ethic," in Harald Baldersheim, R. Balme, T. N. Clark, V. Hoffman-Martinot, and H. Magnusson, eds., *New Leaders, Parties, and Groups*. Pp. 114–132. Paris and Bordeaux: Cervel.

Clark, T. N., and S. M. Lipset. 1991. "Are Social Classes Dying?" *International Sociology* 4: 397–410.

Clark, T. N., S. M. Lipset, and M. Rempel. 1993. "The Declining Political Significance of Social Class." *International Sociology* 8 (3): 293–316.

Clark, T. N., and June Pallet. 1994. "Commentary on Terry Nichols Clark," in James L. Chan, ed., *Governmental Accounting and Nonprofit Accounting*, vol. 8. Pp. 29–38. Greenwich, Conn.: Jai Press.

Clark, Terry Nichols, and Lincoln Quillian. 1993. "The New Political Culture Emerges: Sources and Dynamics Among Citizens and Others." Presented to Annual Meeting of the European Consortium for Political Research (ECPR), Leiden, Holland.

Clark, T. N., and M. Rempel, eds. 1997. *Citizen Politics in Post-Industrial Societies*. Boulder, Colo.: Westview Press.

Clark, T. N., and Clarence Stone. 1994. "Nationalism, Globalism and Urban Regimes." Manuscript, University of Bristol, U.K.

Clarke, Susan. E., ed. 1989. *Urban Innovation and Autonomy*. Newbury Park, Calif.: Sage, Sage Urban Innovation Series.

Coleman, James S. 1957. *Community Conflict*. New York: Free Press.

———. 1974. *Power and the Structure of Society*. New York: W. W. Norton,

Coleman, R. P., and L. Rainwater with K. A. McClelland. 1978. *Social Standing in America*. New York: Basic Books.

Connerly, Charles, and James E. Frank. 1986. "Predicting Support for Local Growth Controls." *Social Science Quarterly* 67: 572–585.

Connerly, Charles. 1986. "Growth Management Concern." *Environment and Behavior* 18: 707–32.

Converse, P. E. 1964. "The Nature of Belief Systems in Mass Publics," in David Apter, ed., *Ideology and Discontent*. Pp. 206–261. New York: Free Press.

———. 1972. "Change in the American Electorate," in Campbell, A. E., and Philip E. Converse, eds., *The Human Meaning of Social Change*. New York: Russell Sage.

———. 1975. "Public Opinion and Voting Behavior," in Fred I. Greenstein and Nelson W. Polsby, *Handbook of Political Science*. Pp. 75–170. Reading, Mass.: Addison-Wesley.

Costa, Paul T., Jr., and Robert McCrae. 1980. "Still Stable After All These Years," in Paul B. Baites and Orville G. Brim, eds., *Life-Span Development and Behavior*, vol. 3. Pp. 65–102. New York: Academic Press.

Cotgrove, Stephen, and Andrew Duff. 1980. "Environmentalism, Middle Class Radicalism, and Politics." *Sociological Review* 28.

Coulter, P. B. 1989. *Measuring Inequality*. Boulder, Colo.: Westview Press.

County of Orange. 1991. *Orange County Progress Report*. Santa Ana, Calif.: County of Orange.

Cowell, Alan. 1997. "A Neo-Nazi 'Time-Bomb.'" *International Herald Tribune.* June 19, p. 6.

Crotty, William. 1985. *Comparative Political Parties.* Washington, D.C.: American Political Science Association. Annenberg/CPB Project.

———. 1986. "An Agenda for Studying Local Parties Comparatively," in William Crotty, ed., *Political Parties in Local Areas.* Pp. 1–38. Knoxville: University of Tennessee Press.

———. 1986. "Local Parties in Chicago," in William Crotty, ed., *Political Parties in Local Areas.* Pp. 157–195, 190. Knoxville: University of Tennessee Press.

Crozier, Michel. 1964. *The Bureaucratic Phenomenon.* Chicago: University of Chicago Press.

Dahl, R. A. 1961. *Who Governs?* New Haven, Conn.: Yale University Press.

———. 1971. *Polyarchy.* New Haven/London.

Dahrendorf, R. 1959. *Class and Class Conflict in Industrial Society.* Stanford, Calif.: Stanford University Press.

Dalton, Russell J. 1984. "Cognitive Mobilization and Partisan Dealignment in Advanced Industrial Democracies," *Journal of Politics* 46 (February): 264–284.

———. 1984. "The West German Party System Between Two Ages," in Dalton, Russell J., Flanagan, Scott C., and P. A. Beck, eds., *Electoral Change in Advanced Industrial Democracies.* Pp. 104–133. Princeton: Princeton University Press.

———. "Political Parties and Political Representation." *Comparative Political Studies* 18: 267-299.

———. 1985. "Wertwandel oder Wertwende," in Hans-Dieter Klingemann and Max Kaase, eds., *Wahlen und politischer Prozeß.* Pp. 427-454. Opladen.

Danielson, Michael. 1976. *The Politics of Exclusion.* New York: Columbia University Press.

David J. Lee, and Bryan S. Turner, eds., 1996. *Conflicts About Class.* London and New York: Longman.

Davis, J. A. 1989. "Attitudes Toward Free Speech in Six Countries in the Mid 1980s," in *NORC-GSS Cross National Report 9.* Chicago: National Opinion Research Center.

De Swaan, Abraham. 1973. *Coalition Theories and Cabinet Formations.* San Francisco: Jossey-Bass.

Degraff, Paul M., and Harry B. G. Ganzeboom. 1993. "Family Background and Educational Attainment in the Netherlands for the 1891-1960 Birth Cohorts," in Shavit and Blossfeld, pp. 75–100.

Denters, Bas, and Peter Geurts. 1992. "Aspects of Political Alienation and Voting Behavior in Dutch Local Elections." Prepared for European Consortium for Political Research, Limerick, Ireland, April.

Derbeyshire, J. Dennis, and Ian Derbeyshire. 1989. *Political Systems of the World.* Edinborough: W and R Chambers.

Deutsch, Karl W. 1964. "Social Mobilization and Political Development." *American Political Science Review* 55 (September): 493–514.

———. 1966. *Nationalism and Social Communication.* Cambridge, Mass.: MIT Press.

Di Palma, G. 1977. *Surviving Without Governing: The Italian Parties in Parliament.* Berkeley and Los Angeles: University of California Press.

Dietrich Herzog et al., 1990. *Abgeordnete und Bürger.* Appleton. Opland.

Dionne, E. J. 1991. *Why Americans Hate Politics.* New York: Simon & Schuster.

Dirn, Louis. 1992. "Chroniques Des Tendences De La Societe Francaise," *Observations Et Diagnostiques Economiques* 39 (January): 75-91.

———. 1993. *Observations Et Diagnostiques Economiques.* 46 July.

Donovan, M. 1994. "The 1994 Election in Italy: Normalisation or Continuing Exceptionalism?" *West European Politics* 17 (4).

Dowall, David. 1984. *The Suburban Squeeze.* Berkeley: University of California Press.

———. 1980. "An Examination of Population Growth-Managing Communities." *Policy Studies Journal* 9: 414-27.

Downs, Anthony. 1957. *An Economic Theory of Democracy.* New York.

Dunleavy, Patrick. 1987. "Class Dealignment in Britain Revisited." *West European Politics* 10: 400-419.

Dunleavy, Patrick, and C. Husbands. 1985. *British Democracy at the Crossroads.* London: Allen and Unwin.

Durant, Robert R., William Lyons, and Michael R. Fitzgerald. 1989. "Urban Culture, Service Provision, and Fiscal Strain," in Terry Nichols Clark, William Lyons and Michael Fitzgerald, eds., *Research in Urban Policy.* Greenwich, Conn.: Jai Press.

Dye, Thomas R. 1996. *Politics, Economics, and the Public.* Chicago.

Ekhart, Hahn, 1991. "Lokale Umweltpolitik," in Bernhard Blanke, ed., *Staat und Stadt.* Pp. 477-499. Opladen.

Elazar, D. 1984. *American Federalism.* New York: Harper and Row.

———. 1987. *Exploring Federalism.* Tuscaloosa, AL: University of Alabama Press.

Elazar, Daniel J., and Joseph Zikmund, eds. 1975. *The Ecology of American Political Culture.* New York: Crowell.

Elazar, Daniel, and Shmuel Sandler. "Forging a New Political Center," in Daniel J. Elazar and Shmuel Sandler eds., *Who's the Boss in Israel: Israel at the Polls, 1988.* 1990. Pp. 13-41. Detroit: Wayne State University Press.

Eldersveld, Samuel J. 1982. *Political Parties in American Society.* New York: Basic Books.

———. 1986. "The Party Activist in Detroit and Los Angeles: A Longitudinal View, 1956-1980," in ibid., pp. 89-119.

Eldserveld, Samuel J. 1995. *Party Conflict and Community Development: Postwar Politics in Ann Arbor.* Ann Arbor, Michigan: University of Michigan Press.

Ercole E. 1989. "New Trends in Local Politics in Italy," in H. Baldersheim, R. Balme, T. N. Clark, V. Hoffmann-Martinot, and H. Magnusson, eds., *New Leaders, Parties and Groups: Comparative Tendencies in Local Leadership.* Bordeaux and Paris: CERVEL-IEP.

Ercole, E., P. Lange, and S. Tarrow. 1985. "Gli Amministratori Comunali, 1975-1987: Composizione Sociale E Reclutamento Territoriale." *Amministrare* 18 (3).

———. 1985. "I movimenti nel PCI", *Politica et Economia* 16 (12).

Ercole, Enrico, and Guido Martinotti. 1989. "New Parties and Local Dynamics in Italy." Presented to Fiscal Austerity and Urban Innovation Project, Conference on New Leaders, New Parties, New Groups in Local Politics, Paris, April.

Erikson, Robert, and John Goldthorpe. 1992. *The Constant Flux.* Oxford: Clarendon Press.

Ericson, R., J. H. Goldthorpe, and L. Portocarero. 1979. "Intergenerational Class Mobility in Three West European Societies." *British Journal of Sociology* 30: 415-441.

Erikson, Robert S., Norman G. Luttbeg, Kent L. Tedin. 1988. *American Public Opinion.* New York/London.

Esping-Andersen, Goesta. 1994. "Postindustrial Cleavage Structures," in David B. Grusky, ed., *Social Stratification.* Pp. 697-707. Boulder: Westview Press.

Evans, Geoffrey. 1993a. "Is Gender on the 'New Agenda'?" *European Journal of Political Research* 24: 135-158.

———. 1993b. "Class, Prospects, and the Life-Cycle." *Acta Sociologica* 36: 263-276.

———, ed. Forthcoming. Book in Progress from Conference on Social Class at Nuffield College, Oxford in 1995.

Evans, Mariah D., and Edward O. Laumann. 1983. "Professional Commitment," in Donald J. Treiman and Robert B. Robinson, eds., *Research in Stratification and Mobility*, pp. 3-40.

Farnham, Alan. 1989. "The Trust Gap." *Fortune*, December 4, pp. 56-78.

Featherman, David L., and Robert M. Hauser. 1978. *Opportunity and Change.* New York: Academic.

Ferman, Barbara. 1996. *Challenging the Growth Machine.* Lawrence: University Press of Kansas.

Fischer, Claude. 1984. *The Urban Experience.* New York: Harcourt, Brace, and Jovanovich.

Fishman, Robert. 1987. *Bourgeois Utopias.* New York: Basic Books.

Flynn, Kevin. 1994. "Weaving the Intricate Webb," *Public Issues* (Summer): 2-5.

Foreman, Dave. 1991. *Confessions of an Eco-Warrier.* New York: Harmony Books.

Forse, Michel. 1986. "La Diversification De La Societe Francaise Vue a Travers La Marriage Et L'ideologie." *The Tocqueville Review* 7: 223-33.

———. 1993. "Les Creations D'associations Progressent Selon Un Rythme Ralenti" *Chronique Des Tendences De La Societe Francaise* 46 (July): 272-274.

Foster, James J. 1982. "Ghost-Hunting." *Asian Survey* 22 (9): 843-857.

Fox, Karl A. 1974. *Social Indicators and Social Theory.* New York: Wiley-Interscience.

Fox, Stephen. 1981. *John Muir and His Legacy.* Boston: Little-Brown.

Franklin, M., T. T. Mackie, and H. Valen. 1992. *Electoral Change.* New York: Cambridge University Press.

Franklin, Mark. 1985. *The Decline of Class Voting in Britain.* Oxford: Oxford University Press.

Freidson, Eliot. 1986. *The Professional Powers.* Chicago: University of Chicago Press.

Frey, William H. 1993. "The New Urban Revival in the United States." *Urban Studies* 30: 741-74.

Friedman, Philip S. 1995. "The Democrats' Quota System." *Wall Street Journal*, 19 April, p. A14.

Fuchs, Ester. 1992. *Mayors and Money.* Chicago: University of Chicago Press.

Gabriel, Oscar W. 1992. "Wertewandel" in Franz Schuster and Günter W. Dill, ed., *Kommunale Aufgaben im Wandel*, Berlin, Pp. 149-235.

Gabriel, Oscar W., Volker Kunz, and Thomas Zapf-Schramm. 1990. *Bestimmungsfaktoren des kommunalen Investitionsverhaltenpp.* München.

Gabriel, Oscar W., Frank Brettschneider, 1994. "Die Kommunen und die Neue Politik." Presented at CNRS Conference, Paris, April.

Galli, G., and A. Prandi. 1970. *Patterns of Political Participation in Italy.* New Haven: Yale University Press.

Gans, H. 1962. *The Urban Villagers.* Glencoe, Ill.: Free Press.

Garreau, Joel. 1991. *Edge City.* New York: Doubleday.

Geser, H., et al. 1994. *Lokalparteien in Der Schweiz.* Zürich: Seismo.

Geser, Hans. "The Local Party as an Object of Interdisciplinary Comparative Study," in Hans Geser and Martin Saiz, eds., *Local Parties in Political and Organizational Perspective*. Unpublished Manuscript. Notre Dame: Department of Political Science.

Geser, Hans. 1991. "Dealignment Oder Neue Integrationsbereitschaft?" *Schweizerische Zeitschrift Für Soziologie* 17 (2): 233–272.

Gibson, James L., Cornelius P. Cotter, and John F. Bibby. 1983. "Assessing Party Organizational Strength." *American Journal of Political Science* 27 (2): 193–222.

Gibson, James L., Cornelius P. Cotter, John F. Bibby, and Robert J. Huckshorn. 1985. "Whither the Local Parties? A Cross-Sectional and Longitudinal Analysis of the Strength of Party Organizations." *American Journal of Political Science* 29 (1): 139–160.

Giddens, A. 1980. *The Class Structure of the Advanced Societies*. New York: Harper and Row.

Ginsborg, P. 1990. *A History of Contemporary Italy*. London: Penguin Books.

Giurickovic, Cinzia Dato. 1996. *Il sindaco taumaturgo e il governo delle citta*. Milan: FrancoAngeli.

Glenn, Norval D. 1974. "Aging and Conservatism." *Annals of the American Academy of Political and Social Science* 415: 176–186.

———. 1980. "Values, Attitudes, and Beliefs," in Orville G. Brim Jr. and Jerome Kagan, eds., *Constancy and Change in Human Development*. Pp. 596–640. Cambridge: Harvard University Press,

Glickfeld, Madelyn, and Ned Levine. 1990. "The New Land Use Regulation 'Revolution'." University of California, Los Angeles, Mimeo.

Goldberg, Giora. 1984. "The Local Elections in Israel—1983," *Electoral Studies* 3 (August): 203–206.

Goldberg, Giora. 1988. "Local Elections," in Daniel Elazar and Chaim Kalchheim, eds., *Local Government in Israel*. Pp. 129–163. Lanham, MD: University Press of America.

Goldsmith, Michael J., and Edward C. Page. 1987. *Central and Local Government Relations*. London: Sage.

Goldthorpe, John H. 1994. "Modelling the Pattern of Class Voting in British Elections, 1964–1992." Presented to Bielefeld Conference ISA.

———. 1996. "Class and Politics in Advanced Industrial Society," in Lee and Turner, pp. 196–208.

Gosnell, Harold F. 1937. *Machine Politics: Chicago Model*. New York: AMS Press (1969 Reprint).

Gottdiener, Mark, and Max Neiman. 1981. "Characteristics of Support for Local Growth Controls." *Urban Affairs Quarterly* 17: 55–73.

Gouldner, Alvin W. 1979. *The Future of Intellectuals and the Rise of the New Class*. New York: Seabury.

Green, Gary, and Arnold Fleischmann. 1991. "Promoting Economic Development." *Urban Affairs Quarterly* 27: 145–154.

Greenberg, Stanley B. 1995. *Middle Class Dreams*. New York: Times Books.

Grüner, Hans, Wolfgang Jaedicke, Kurt Ruhland. 1988. Rote Politik im schwarzen Rathaus? in *Politische Vierteljahresschrift* 29: 42–57.

Grusky, David B. 1986. "American Social Mobility in the Nineteenth and Twentieth Century." Ph.D. Dissertation. University of Wisconsin-Madison, Department of Sociology.

———. 1994. *Social Stratification.* Boulder, Colorado: Westview Press.

Gunlicks, Arthur B. *Local Government in the German Federal System*, Durkham.

Hardiman, Niamh. 1990. "Capitalism and Corporatism," in John Clark, Celia Modgil, and Sohan Modgil, eds., *John Goldthorpe.* New York: Falmer Press.

Hardt, Ulrike, Rolf-Dieter Postlep, Horst Zimmermann. 1987. Bestimmungsgründe der kommunalen Finanzsituation. *Schriftenreihe der Gesellschaft für Regionale Strukturentwicklung*, Vol. 15, Bonn.

Harrington, Michael. 1989. "Toward a New Socialism." *Dissent* (Spring): 3–13.

Harrison, B. 1994. *Lean and Mean.* New York: Basic Books.

Harrison, Bennett, and Barry Bluestone. 1988. *The Great U-Turn.* New York: Basic Books.

Hauser, Robert M. 1972. *Socioeconomic Background and Educational Performance.* Washington, D.C.: Rose Monograph Series, American Sociological Association.

Hauser, Robert M., and David B. Grusky. 1984. "Comparative Social Mobility Revisited." *American Sociological Review* 49: 19–38.

———. 1987. "Cross-National Variation in Occupational Distributions, Relative Mobility Chances and Intergenerational Shifts in Occupational Distributions." Draft Paper.

Heath, Anthony, Robert Jowell, and John Curdice. 1985. *How Britain Votes.* Oxford: Pergamon Press.

Heath, A., M. Yang, and H. Goldstein. N.D. "Multilevel Analysis of the Changing Relationship Between Class and Party in Britain 1964–1992." Nuffield College.

Heath, Anthony, et al. 1991. *Understanding Political Change: The British Voter 1964–1987.* Pergamon.

Heckman, James J. 1979. "Sample Selection Bias as a Specification Error." *Econometrica* 45: 153–161.

Heikki, Paloheimo. 1989. "Puolueuskillisten Kunnallisvaalit 1988," *Politiikka* 31 (1): 23–33.

Henderson, Mark. 1997. "Minorities Join Record Numbers of Women MPs," *The Times* (London), Saturday, May 3, p. 2.

Henriksen, Joan Felicia. 1991. *Norwegian Politics.* Oslo: Aschehoug.

Hernandez, Donald J. 1986. "Childhood in Socio-Demographic Perspective." *Annual Review of Sociology* 12: 159–180.

Higgins, Donald J. H. 1986. *Local and Urban Politics in Canada.* Toronto: Gage.

Hine D. 1993. *Governing Italy. The Politics of Bargained Pluralism*, Oxford: Clarendon Press.

Hirshman A. 1970. *Exit, Voice and Loyalty. Responses to Decline of Firms, Organizations and States.* Cambridge: Harvard University Press.

Hoffman, Wayne Lee, and Terry Nichols Clark. 1979. "Citizen Preferences and Urban Policy Types," in John P. Blair and David Nachmias, eds., *Urban Affairs Annual Reviews*, vol. 17: *Fiscal Retrenchment and Urban Policy.* Beverly Hills: Sage. Pp. 85–106.

Hoffmann-Lange, Ursula. 1983. Eliten Zwischen Alter und Neuer Politik in Hans-Dieter Klingemann and Max Kaase, ed., Wahlen Und Politischer Prozeß. Analysen Aus Anlaß Der Bundestagswahl, Opladen, pp. 108–150.

———. 1991. Kongruenzen in den politischen einstellungen von eliten und bevölkerung als indikator für politische repräsentation, in Hans-Dieter Klingemann and Richard Stöss/Bernhard W Eßels, ed., *Politische klasse und politische institutionen.* Opladen, pp. 259–274.

Hoffmann-Martinot, Vincent. 1989 "Municipal Employees and Personnel Policies" in Poul-Erik Mouritzen, ed., *Defending City Welfare*. Odense: University of Odense. Pp. 317–368.

———. 1992. "La Participation aux Élections Municipales Dans Les Villes Françaises." *Revue Française De Science Politique* 42 (Février): 3–35.

Hoffmann, Paul. 1990. *That Fine Italian Hand*. New York: Henry Holt.

Hoge, Warren. 1997. "The Hard Times of a Coal Town, Ignored in Booming Britain's Vote." *New York Times*, April 22, pp. 1, A6.

Hollander, E. L. 1986. "The Administration of New Fiscal Populism," in T. N. Clark, ed., *Research in Urban Policy* 2b. Pp. 177–184. Greenwich, CT: JAI.

Hout, M., C. Brooks, and J. Manza. 1993. "The Persistence of Classes in Post-Industrial Societies." *International Sociology* 8 (3): 259–77.

Hout, Michael. 1988. "More Universalism, Less Structural Mobility." *American Journal of Sociology* 93: 1358–1400.

Hout, Michael, Clem Brooks, and Jeff Manza. 1995. "The Democratic Class Struggle in the United States, 1948–1992." *American Sociological Review*, 60, 6 (December): 805–828.

Hunter, F. 1953. *Community Power Structure*. New York: Doubleday.

Inglehart, R. 1971. "The Silent Revolution in Europe: Intergenerational Change in Post-Industrial Societies." *American Political Science Review* 65, 4: 991–1017.

———. 1977. *The Silent Revolution*. Princeton, NJ: Princeton University Press.

———. 1990. *Culture Shift*. Princeton: Princeton University Press.

———. 1984. "The Changing Structure of Political Cleavages in Western Society," in R. J. Dalton, S. C. Flanagan, and Allen, eds., *Electoral Change in Advanced Industrial Democracies*. Princeton: Princeton University Press. Pp. 25–69.

———. 1985. "New Perspectives on Value Changes." *Comparative Political Studies* 17, 4 (January), pp. 485–532.

———. 1987. "Value Change in Industrial Societies." *American Political Science Review* 18: 1289–1303.

———. 1989. *Kultureller Umbruch. Wertwandel in Der Westlichen Welt*. New York and Frankfurt: Campus.

———. 1997. "The Trend Toward Post-Materialist Values Continues," in Michael Rempel and Terry Nichols Clark, Eds., *Citizen Politics in Post-Industrial Societies*. Boulder: Westview Press, pp. 57–66.

Inglehart, R., and H. D. Klingemann. 1976. "Party Identification, Ideological Preference and the Left-Right Dimension Among Western Publics," in I. Budge, I. Crewe, and D. Farlie, eds., *Party Identification and Beyond* New York: John Wiley. Pp. 243–273.

Jackson, Kenneth. 1985. *Crabgrass Frontier*. New York: Oxford University Press.

Jambrek, Peter. 1986. "Socialism Without Welfare?" in *Research in Urban Policy*, Volume 2a, pp. 219–226.

Jang, Wonho. 1996. *The New Political Culture in Japan*. Ph.D. Thesis, Department of Sociology, University of Chicago.

Jencks, Christopher, et al. 1979. *Who Gets Ahead?* New York: Basic Books.

Jennings, M. K., and J. W. V. Deth, eds. 1989. *Continuities in Political Action*. New York: Walter De Gruyter.

Jennings, M. Kent, and Gregory B. Markus. 1984. "Partisan Orientations over the Long Haul." *American Political Science Review* 78: 1000–1018.

Jennings, M. Kent, and Richard Niemi. 1981. *Generations and Politics*. Princeton: Princeton University Press.

Johnson, Norman. 1987. *The Welfare State in Transition*. Amherst: University of Massachusetts Press.

Johnston, Robert. 1980. "The Politics of Local Growth Control." *Policy Studies Journal* 9: 427–439.

Judd, J., and M. Parkinson, eds. 1990. *Leadership and Urban Regeneration*. Newbury Park, CA: Sage.

Kalchheim, Chaim, and Shimon Rosevitch. 1992. "The 1989 Local Elections," in Elazar and Sandler, pp. 233–250.

Karnig, Albert K., and Oliver B. Walter. 1989. "Municipal Voter Turnout During the 1980s: Continued Decline." Paper presented at the Midwest Political Science Association Congress, Chicago, April 13–15.

Kasarda, John. 1978. "Urbanization, Community and the Metropolitan Problem," in D. Street (Ed.) *Handbook of Contemporary Urban Life*. San Francisco: Jossey Bass. Pp. 27–57.

Kaase, Max, and Kenneth Newton. 1995 *Beliefs in Government*. Oxford: Oxford University Press.

Katja Ahlstich and Volker Kunz. "Die Entwicklung Kommunaler Aufgaben in Zeiten Des Wertewandels," in Oscar W. Gabriel/Rüdiger Voigt (Ed.) Kommunalwissenschaftliche Analysen, Bochum. Pp.167–210

Katz, Richard S., et al. 1992. "The Membership of Political Parties in European Democracies, 1960–1990," *European Journal of Political Research* 22 (October): 329–345.

Kerr, Henry H. 1987. "The Swiss Party System," in Hans Daalder, ed., *Party Systems in Denmark, Austria, Switzerland, the Netherlands and Belgium*. London: Francis and Pinter. Pp.109–191.

Kessel, Hans, and Wolfgang Tischler. 1984. *Umweltbewusstsein. Oekologische Wertvorstellungen in Westlichen Industrienationen*. Berlin Sigma Verlag.

Kiechel, Walter. 1993. "How We Will Work in the Year 2000," *Fortune*, May 17, pp. 37–52.

Kilson, M. 1989. "Problems of Black Politics," *Dissent* 36, 4: 526–34.

Kinder, Donald. 1988. Paper on Sociotropic Voting, *American Journal of Political Science*.

Kitschelt, H. 1990. "New Social Movements and the Decline of Party Organization," in *Challenging the Political Order*, ed. R. J. Dalton and M. Kuechler. New York: Oxford University Press.

Klages, Helmut. 1984. *Wertorientierungen im Wandel*. Frankfurt,New York.

———. 1988. *Wertedynamik*. Zürich.

Klages, Helmut, and Willi Herbert. 1983. *Wertorientierungen und Staatsbezug*. Frankfurt, New York.

Kling, Robert, Spencer Olin, and Mark Poster. 1991. *Postsuburban California*. Berkeley: University of California Press.

Klingemann, Hans-Dieter, Richard I. Hofferbert, and Ian Budge. 1994. *Parties Politics, and Democracy*. Boulder, CO: Westview.

Knoke, David. 1981. "Urban Political Cultures," in T. N. Clark, ed., *Urban Policy Analysis, Urban Affairs Annual Reviews:* 21. Beverly Hills: Sage. Pp. 203–226.

Knutsen, Oddbjorn. 1990. "The Materialist/Post-Materialist Value Dimension as a Party Cleavage in the Nordic Countries." *West European Politics* 13, 2 (April): 258–273.

Kobayashi, Yoshiaki, and Yasukuni Iwagami. 1989. "National-Local Relations, Party Clientelism, and Policy." Presented to Annual Meeting of American Political Science Association.

Kriesi, H. 1989. "New Social Movements and the New Class in the Netherlands." *American Journal of Sociology* 94 (5): 1078–1116.

———. 1989b. "The Mobilization Potential of the New Social Movements in the Netherlands in 1986 and 1987," in *New Social Movements and Value Change,* Ed. Harry B. G. Ganzeboom and Henk Flap. Amsterdam: Siswo Publications. Pp.51–88.

———. 1989a. "New Social Movements and the New Class in the Netherlands." *American Journal of Sociology* 94: 1078–1116.

Kristof., Nicholas D. 1995. "TV Stars Defeat Politicians in Tokyo and Osaka Governor Races." *The New York Times,* 10 April.

Kristol, Irving. "About Equality." *Commentary* 54 (1972): 41–47.

———. 1978. *Two Cheers for Capitalism.* New York: Basic Books.

Kuhn, Thomas. 1996. *Structure of Scientific Revolution* (3rd Edition). Chicago: University of Chicago Press.

Kunz, Volker, Oscar W. Gabriel, Frank Brettschneider, 1993. Wertorientierungen, Ideologien und Policy-Präferenzen in der Bundesrepublik Deutschland, in: Oscar W. Gabriel,Klaus G. Troitzsch (ed.), *Wahlen in Zeiten des Umbruchs,* Frankfurt,Bern, Pp. 203-240

Ladd, H. F., and J. B. Wilson. 1985. Proposition 2 ½, in *Research in Urban Policy* 1. Ed. T. N. Clark. Pp. 199–244. Greenwich, CT: JAI.

Lamont, Michele. 1987. "Cultural Capital and the Liberal Political Attitudes of Professionals: Comment on Brint." *American Journal of Sociology* 92: 1501–1505.

Landa, Martha Diaz de. 1995. "Tendencias en el liderazgo local y el Nuevo Populismo Fiscal."*Annuario del Centro de Investigaciones Juridicas y Sociales,* Universidad Nacional de Cordoba: 199-205.

———. 1996. "Culturas politicas locales: diversadad y emergincia de la Nueva Cultura o del Nuevo Populismo Fiscal." *Revista El Principe,* vol. 4, forthcoming.

Lange, Peter Michael, Cynthia Irvin, and Sydney Tarrow. 1990. "Mobilization, Social Movements, and Party Recruitment: The Italian Communist Party Since the 1960s." *British Journal of Political Science.* 20 (January): 15-42.

Laponce, J. A. *Left and Right.* Toronto: University of Toronto Press, 1981.

Lee, David J., and Bryan S. Turner. 1996. *Conflicts About Class.* London and New York: Longman.

Legendre, Pierre. 1969. *L'administration Du XVIIIème Siècle À Nos Jours.* Paris: Puf (Thémis), p. 74.

Lehmbruch, Gerhard. 1979. Der Januskopf der Ortsparteien. Kommunalpolitik und das lokale Parteiensystem, in: Helmut Köser (ed.), *Der Bürger in der Gemeinde.* Bonn, Pp. 320-334

Leighley, Jan E., and Jonathan Naglet. 1992 "Socioeconomic Class and Bias in Turnout, 1964–1988" *American Political Science Review* 86: 725-736.

Leon, Richard E. de. 1991. "San Francisco: Postmaterialist Populism in a Global City," in H. V. Savitch and John Clayton Thomas (Eds.), *Big City Politics in Transition.* Newbury Park, CA: Sage, Urban Affairs Annual Reviews 38: 202–215.

Lerner, Daniel. 1958. *The Passing of Traditional Society.* Glencoe, IL: Free Press.

Lichbach, M. I. 1985. "An Evaluation of 'Does Economic Inequality Breed Political Conflict?' Studies." *World Politics* (1985): 431–469.

Lieberson, S. 1969. "Measuring Population Diversity." *American Sociological Review* 34 (December): 850–862.

Liesner, Thelma. 1985. *Economic Statistics, 1900–1983.* New York: Facts on File.

Lightbody, James. "The Political Tradition of a Prairie Canadian City," *Local Government Studies* 10, 4 (July/August 1984): 11–24, 18.

Lijphart, A. 1977. *Democracy in Plural Societies.* New Haven: Yale University Press.

Lipset, Seymour M. 1981 (1959). *Political Man: The Social Bases of Politics,* 2d ed. Baltimore: Johns Hopkins University Press.

–––. 1991. "No Third Way: A Comparative Perspective on the Left," in Daniel Chirot, Ed., *the Crisis of Leninism and the Decline of the Left.* Seattle and London: University of Washington Press, pp. 183–232.

–––. 1995. "Malaise and Resilience in America." *Journal of Democracy* 6, 3 (July): 4-15.

–––. 1996. *American Exceptionalism: A Double-Edged Sword.* New York: W.W. Norton.

Lipset, Seymour Martin and William Schneider. 1983. *The Confidence Gap.* New York: Free Press.

Logan, John, and Harvey Molotch. 1987. *Urban Fortunes.* Berkeley: University of California Press.

Logan, John, and Mark Schneider. 1981. "The Stratification of Metropolitan Suburbs: 1950 to 1970." *American Sociological Review* 46:175–186.

Logan, John, and Min Zhou. 1989. "Do Suburban Growth Controls Control Growth?" *American Sociological Review* 54:461–471.

Logan, John, and Moishe Semyonov. 1980. "Growth and Succession in Suburban Communities." *Sociological Quarterly* 21:93–105.

Logan, John. 1978. "Growth, Politics, and the Stratification of Places." *American Journal of Sociology* 84: 404–416.

Longoria, T. Jr. 1994. "Empirical Analysis of the City Limits Typology." *Urban Affairs Quarterly*, 30, 1: 102–113.

Lydon, Christopher. 1992. "William Floyd Weld," *New York Times Magazine,* August 2, pp. 33, 52-53.

Mabileau, Albert. 1991. *Le Système Local.* Paris: Montchrestien.

Magnusson, Warren. 1983. "Introduction: The Development of Canadian Urban Government," in Warren Magnusson and Andrew Sancton (Eds.). *City Politics in Canada.* Toronto: University of Toronto Press, pp. 3–57.

–––. 1983. "Toronto," in Warren Magnusson and Andrew Sancton (Eds.). *City Politics in Canada.* Toronto: University of Toronto Press, pp. 94–139.

Manza, Jeff, Michael Hout, and Clem Brooks. 1994. "Class Voting in Capitalist Democracies Since World War II." *Annual Review of Sociology,* Forthcoming.

Marsaud, Jacques. 1995. "Recul, Redeploiement Ou Deploiement Du Management Dans Les Communes?" *Politique et Management Public* 13, 3 (September): 225-248.

Marvick, Dwaine. 1986. "Stability and Change in the Views of Los Angeles Party Activists, 1968–1980," in Crotty, *Political Parties in Local Areas*, pp. 121–155.

Mayhew, David R. 1986. *Placing Parties in American Politics.* Princeton: Princeton University Press.

Mcadam, Doug. 1988. *Freedom Summer.* New York: Oxford University Press.

Melis A. and Martinotti G. 1988. "Gli amministratori comunali, 1975-1987: composizione sociale e reclutamento territoriale," *Amministrare*, v.18, no.3.

Mendras, Henri. 1980. *La Sagesse Et Le Desordre: France 1980.* Paris: Gallimard.

———. 1997. *L'europe Des Europeens.* Paris: Gallimard.

Meyer, John. 1994. "The Evolution of Modern Stratification Systems, " in Grusky, Ed., pp. 730–737.

Milbrath, Lester W., M. and Goel. 1977. *Political Participation,* 2d ed. Chicago: Rand McNally, pp. 114–128.

Miller, Warren E., and Teresa E. Levitin. 1976. *Leadership and Change.* Cambridge: Winthrop.

Miller, Warren E. Donald E. Stokes. 1969. Constituency Influence in Congress, in: Charles F. Cnudde, Deane E. Neubauer (ed.), *Empirical Democratic Theory,* Chicago, Pp. 388-407.

Miranda, Rowan . 1994. "Containing Cleavages: Parties and Other Hierarchies." Pp. 79-103 in Clark 1994a.

Moore, Barrington. 1966. *Social Origins of Dictatorship and Democracy.* Boston: Beacon Press.

Moriwaki, Toshimasa. "Election and Daily Activities of Local Assemblymen in Japan." *Kwansei Gakuin Law Review* (1984): 7–31.

Morrison, Peter. 1977. "Migration and Rights of Access." Rand Series P-5785 (March), Santa Monica, CA.

Mouritzen, Poul-Erik, and K. Nielsen. 1988. *Handbook of Urban Fiscal Data.* Denmark: Fiscal Austerity and Urban Innovation Project.

Mouritzen, Poul Erik. ed., *Managing Cities in Austerity: Urban Fiscal Stress in Ten Western Countries.* London, Newbury Park, New Delhi: Sage Urban Innovation Series, Vol 2, 1992.

Muller, Peter. 1989. "The Transformation of Bedroom Suburbia into the Outer City," in Barbara M. Kelly (Ed.) *Suburbia Re-Examined.* New York: Greenwood Press, pp. 39–44.

Munson, Ziad. 1995. "Social Class and Logistic Regression." Presented to Annual Meeting of Social Science-History Association, Chicago, November.

Nasar, S. 1994. "Myth: Small Business as Mighty Job Engine." *New York Times*, March 25, p. C1–2.

Naßmacher, Hiltrud. "Parteien in Nordamerika?" *Zeitschrift Für Parlamentsfragen* 1 (März 1992): 110–130.

National Commission on the State and Local Public Service. 1993. *Hard Truths/Tough Choices: An Agenda for State and Local Reform.* Albany, NY: Nelson A. Rockefeller Institute for Government, State University of New York.

National Performance Review. 1993. *From Red Tape to Results: Creating a Government That Works Better &Costs Less.* Washington, D.C.: U.S. Government Printing Office.

Neiman, Max, and Ronald Loveridge. 1981. "Environmentalism and Local Growth Control: A Probe into the Class Bias Thesis." *Environment and Behavior* 13: 759–772.

Nevers, Jean-Yves. 1989. "Changements Politiques et Nouveaux Modeles De Gestion Municipale Dans Les Villes Francaises." Presented to Fiscal Austerity and Urban

Innovation Project, Conference on New Leaders, Parties, and Groups in Local Politics, Paris, April 8–9.

Nieuwbeerta, Paul, and Nan Dirk De Graaf. 1995. "Traditional Class Voting and the Influence of Varying Class Structures in 16 Western Countries: 1956–1990." In Evans, forthcoming.

Nieuwbeerta, Paul. 1995. *The Democratic Class Struggle.* Amsterdam: Thesis Publishers.

Novack, Janet. 1993. "William Floyd Weld," *Forbes Magazine,* December 20, vol. 52, no. 14, p.144.

Nove, Alec. 1985. "Feasible Socialism?" *Dissent* (Summer): 14–37.

O'Dell, John. 1994. "Orange County Jobs Recount Makes Recession Less Depressing." *Los Angeles Times,* March 18.

Offe, C. 1987. "Challenging the Boundaries of Institutional Politics: Social Movements Since the 1960s," in *The Changing Boundaries of the Political,* Ed. C. S. Maier. New York: Cambridge University Press, pp. 63–106.

Olsen, Randall. 1980. "A Least Squares Correlation for Selectivity Bias." *Econometrica* 48: 1815-20.

Orr, M. E., and G. Stoker. 1994. "Urban Regimes and Leadership in Detroit," *Urban Affairs Quarterly* 30, 1 (September): 48–73.

Oyen, Else, ed. 1990. *Comparative Methodology.* Newbury Park, CA: Sage.

Pacelle, Richard L. 1991. *The Transformation of the Supreme Court's Agenda.* Boulder: Westview Press.

Paddock, Joel. 1990. "Beyond the New Deal." *Western Political Quarterly,* 43, 1 (March): 181-190.

Pakulski, J. 1993. "The Dying of Class or Marxist Class Theory." *International Sociology* 8 (3): 279–292.

Parodi, Jean-Luc. "Dans La Logique Des Élections Intermédiaires." *Revue Politique Et Parlementaire,* 903 (Avril 1983): 42–70.

Parsons, Dana. 1988. "County's Image Is the Right of Voters." *Los Angeles Times,* October 30.

Parsons, T. 1937. *The Structure of Social Action.* Glencoe, IL: Free Press.

Parsons, Talcott, and Gerald M. Platt. 1973. *The American University.* Cambridge: Harvard University Press.

Patterson, O. 1977. *Ethnic Chauvinism.* New York: Stein and Day.

Pawel Swianiewicz and Terry Nichols Clark. 1996. "The New Local Parties," in Baldersheim et al, pp. 141-159.

Pempel, T. J. ed. 1990. *Uncommon Democracies.* Ithaca and London: Cornell University Press.

Perry, H. L. 1991. "Deracialization as an Analytical Construct in American Urban Politics." *Urban Affairs Quarterly* 27, 2: 181–191.

Peteri, Gabor ed. 1991. *Events and Changes: The First Steps of Local Transition in East-Central Europe.* Budapest: Local Democracy and Innovation Project.

Peters, T. J., and R. H. Waterman. 1982. *In Search of Excellence.* New York: Warner Books.

Peterson, P. E. 1981. *City Limits.* Chicago: University of Chicago Press.

Pierannunzi, C. A., and J. D. Hutcheson Jr. 1991. "Deracialization in the Deep South." *Urban Affairs Quarterly* 27: 192-201.

Pierce, J. C., and D. Rose. 1974. "Non-Attitudes and American Public Opinion: The Examination of a Thesis." *American Political Science Review* 68: 626–649.

Pisarki, Alan. 1987. *Commuting in America*. Westport, CT: Eno Foundation.

Poguntke, Thomas. 1987. "Grün-Alternative Parteien." *Zeitschrift Für Parlamentsfragen* 3: 369–382.

Popenoe, David. 1985. *Private Pleasure, Public Plight*. New Brunswick: Transaction Press.

Protash, William, and Mark Baldassare. 1983. "Growth Policies and Community Status." *Urban Affairs Quarterly* 18: 397–412.

Przeworski, A., and J. Sprague *Paper Stones*. Chicago: University of Chicago Press, 1986.

Przeworski, Adam, and Henry Teune. 1970. *The Logic of Comparative Social Inquiry*. New York: Wiley Interscience.

Putnam, R. 1993. *Making Democracy Work*. Princeton: Princeton University Press.

———. 1995. "Bowling Alone," *Journal of Democracy* 6, 1 (January): 65-78.

Quesnel, Louise, and Serge Belley. 1991. *Partis Politiques Municipaux*. Montréal: Editions Agence D'arc.

Quillian, Lincoln. 1990. "Political Parties, Interest Groups, and the SPO Thesis," B.A. thesis, University of Chicago.

Ragin, Charles. 1987. *The Comparative Method*. Berkeley: University of California Press.

Real Estate Research Council. 1992. *Real Estate and Construction*. Pomona: California State University.

Reich, Charles A. 1970. *The Greening of America*. New York: Random House.

Reid, Gary J. 1987. "Logrolling and the Median Voter." School of Public Administration, University of Southern California, Unpublished.

Rempel, M. 1992. "Social and Fiscal Liberalism in the U.S." Paper Presented to Workshop in Urban Policy, University of Chicago, Winter.

Rempel, Michael, and Terry Nichols Clark, "Post-Industrial Politics: A Framework for Interpreting Citizen Politics Since the 1960s." in Clark and Rempel, Eds., pp. 9–56 .

Riker, William and Peter Ordeshook. 1973. *An Introduction to Positive Political Theory*. Englewood Cliffs, N.J.: Prentice-Hall.

Riley, Matilda, and Kathleen Bond. 1983. "Beyond Ageism" in Matilda Riley, Beth B. Hess and Kathleen Bond (Eds.), *Aging in Society*. Hillsdale, NJ: Lawrence Erlbaum, pp. 243–52.

Robbins, John R. 1990. "Perceptions of Financial Management in Australian Local Government." Paper presented to the World Congress of the International Sociological Association, Madrid, July 9–13.

Rojo, Teresa. 1990. "Austerity and Urban Innovation in Spain." Presented to RC03 Sessions of World Congress, Interantional Sociological Association, Madrid, published in Spanish.

Rokkan, Stein. 1967. "Geography, Religion, and Social Class." *Party Systems and Voter Alignments*, Ed. S.M. Lipset and Stein Rokkan. New York: Free Press, pp. 67-444.

———. 1970. *Citizens, Elections, Parties*. Oslo: Universitetsforlaget.

Roller, Edeltraud. 1992. *Einstellungen der Bürger zum Wohlfahrtsstaat der Bundesrepublik Deutschland*. Opladen

Rowan Miranda, George Boyne, Terry Nichols Clark. 1994.,Party dynamics and growth of government. Presented to RC03 World Congress of Sociology, Bielefeld, Germany.

Samuelson, Paul A. 1969. "Pure Theory of Public Expenditure and Taxation," in Julius

Margolis and H. Guitton, Eds., *Public Economics.* New York: St. Martin's Press, pp. 28–123.

Sani, G., and G. Sartori. 1983. "Polarization, Fragmentation, and Competition in Western Democracies," in H. Daalder and P. Mair, Eds., *Western European Party Systems.* Beverly Hills: Sage, pp. 307–340.

Sassen, Saskia. 1991. *The Global City.* Princeton: Princeton University Press.

Sassoon D. (1986) *Contemporary Italy.* London and New York: Longman.

Schain, Martin. 1988. "On Changes in French Communism." Presented to Annual Meeting American Political Science Association.

Scheer, Robert. 1989. "Survey Shows Change in Cold War Thinking." *Los Angeles Times,* January 24.

Schmidt, Manfred G. 1982. *Wohlfahrtsstaatliche Politik unter bürgerlichen und sozialdemokratischen Regierungen.* Frankfurt,New York.

Schmitt, Hermann. 1987. *Neue Politik in alten Parteien.* Opladen.

Schneider, William. 1991. "Rule Suburbia." *National Journal* 39: 2335–2336.

Schumaker, Paul, Allan Cigler, Howard Faye. 1989. "Bureaucratic Perceptions of the Municipal Group Universe." Presented to Fiscal Austerity and Urban Innovation Project, Conference on New Leaders, New Parties, New Groups in Local Politics. Paris. April.

Schuman, H., C. G. Steeh, and L. Bobo. 1988. *Racial Attitudes in America.* Cambridge: Harvard University Press.

Schwartz, J., and C. Winship. 1979. "The Welfare Approach to Measuring Inequality," in *Sociological Methodology*, Ed. K. F. Scheussler. San Francisco: Jossey-Bass.

Schweisguth, Etienne. 1988. "La Dimension Gauche-Droite En France," Draft Paper, Centre D'etude De La Vie Politique Francaise, Paris, France.

Schweisguth, Etienne. N.D. "Le Dissensus Nouveau Est Arrive," Centre D'etude De La Vie Politique Francaise, Paris, France.

Scott, Allen J. 1988. *Metropolis.* Berkeley: University of California Press.

Sears, David O. 1981. "Life-Stage Effects on Attitude Change." in S. B. Diesler et al. (Eds.), *Aging.* New York: Academic Press.

———. 1983. "On the Persistence of Early Political Predispositions," in L. Wheeler (Ed.), *Review of Personality and Social Psychology*, vol. 4. Beverly Hills: Sage.

Shaffer, Stephen D. "A Multivariate Explanation of Rising Ticket Splitting." Paper Presented at the Meeting of the Southern Political Science Association, Atlanta, 1992.

Shavit, Yossi, and Hans-Peter Blossfeld, Eds., 1993. *Persistent Inequality.* Boulder: Westview Press.

Skocpol, Theda. 1979. *State and Social Revolution.* Cambridge: Cambridge University Press.

Smith, T. W. 1985. "Atop a Liberal Plateau?" in *Research in Urban Policy* 1. Ed. T. N. Clark. Greenwich, CT: JAI, 245–58.

Sofres. 1985. *Opinion Publique 1985.* Paris: Gallimard.

———. *L'état De L'opinion 1990* (Paris: Seuil, 1990), p. 174.

Ståhlberg, Krister. 1990. *Finnish Local Government in the Postwar Period.* Åbo: Meddelanden Från Ekonomisk-Statsvetenskapliga Fakulteten Vid Åbo Akademi.

Starks, R. T. 1991. "A Commentary and Response to 'Exploring the Meaning and Implications of Deracialization in African-American Urban Politics.'" *Urban Affairs Quarterly* 27 (2): 216–21.

Steiner, Kurt, Ellis S. Krauss, and Scott C. Flanagan, eds. 1980. *Political Opposition and Local Politics in Japan.* Princeton: Princeton University Press.

Steiner, Kurt. 1965. *Local Government in Japan.* Stanford: Stanford University Press.

Stone, C. N. *Regime Politics.* 1989. Lawrence: University Press of Kansas, 1989.

Summers, M. E., and P. A. Klinker. 1991. "The Daniels Election in New Haven and the Failure of the Deracialization Hypothesis." *Urban Affairs Quarterly* 27 (2): 202–15.

Sundberg, Jan. 1988. "The Role of Party Organizations in the Electoral Process: Membership Activity in National and Local Elections in Finland." Prepared for Presentation at the XIVth World Congress of the International Political Science Association, August 28–September 1, Washington.

Surazaska, Wisla. 1995. "Local Revolutions in Central Europe: 1990-1994." Presented to Conference on Political Culture, September, Chicago.

Swanstrom, Todd. 1985. *The Crisis of Growth Politics.* Philadelphia: Temple University Press.

Swianiewicz, Pawel, and Andrew Kowalczyk. 1989. "Grass Roots Movements and Local Leaders in Poland." Presented to Fiscal Austerity and Urban Innovation Project, Conference on New Leaders, New Parties, New Groups in Local Politics. Paris. April.

Szalai, Alex et al, ed. 1973. *The use of time.* Series: Publication of the European Coordination Centre for Research and Documentation in the Social Sciences, V. 5.

Tarrow, S. 1977. *Between Center and Periphery: Grassroots Politicians in Italy and France.* New Haven and London: Yale University Press.

Tarrow, S. 1989. *Democracy and Disorder.* Oxford: Claredon Press.

The Economist. 1994. "A Nation of Groupies," (August 13th), pp. 49-51.

Theil, H. 1967. *Economics and Information Theory.* Amsterdam: New Holland.

Thoenig, Jean-Claude. 1986. "Master Plan and System Effects," in Clark 1986, pp. 77–88.

Thompson, Michael, Richard Ellis, and Aaron Wildavsky. 1990. *Cultural Theory.* Boulder: Westview.

Tillman, D. 1986. "Movement Activism from Martin Luther King to Harold Washington," in *Research in Urban Policy* 2b. Ed. T. N. Clark. Greenwich, CT: JAI, pp. 155–158.

Topf, Richard. 1989. "Political Change and Political Culture in Britain, 1959-1987," in John R. Gibbins, Ed., *Contemporary Political Culture.* London and Newbury Park, Ca: Sage, pp. 52-79.

Tramier, Sylvanie. 1994. "Un Maire Ecologiste a Ete Elu a Montreal." *Le Monde,* November 9, p. 2.

Treiman, Donald J., and Kazuo Yamaguchi. 1993. "Trends in Educational Attainment in Japan," in Shavit and Blossfeld, 1993, pp. 229–250.

Truman, D. B. 1951. *The Governmental Process.* New York: Alfred Knopf.

U.S. Bureau of the Census. 1990. *Census of Population and Housing.* Washington, DC: U.S. Government Printing Office.

––––. 1988. *City and County Data Book.* Washington, DC: U.S. Government Printing Office.

––––. 1991. *State and Metropolitan Area Data Book.* Washington, DC: U.S. Government Printing Office.

––––. 1992a. *Statistical Abstract of the United States.* Washington, DC: U.S. Government Printing Office.

---. 1992b. *Summary Social, Economic and Housing Characteristics U.S.: 1990 U.S. Census of Population and Housing.* Washington, DC: U.S. Government Printing Office.

---. 1992c. *General Population Characteristics: U.S. Census of Population and Housing.* Washington, DC: U.S. Government Printing Office.

Vanneman, R., and L. Weber. 1987. *The American Perception of Class.* Philadelphia: Temple University Press.

Verba, S., and N. H. Nie. 1972. *Participation in America.* New York: Harper and Row.

Verba, Sidney, Norman H. Nie, and Jae-on Kim. 1978. *Participation and Political Equality.* Cambridge and New York: Cambridge University Press.

Vidich, A. J., and J. Bensman. 1968. *Small Town in Mass Society.* Princeton: Princeton University Press.

Wakata, Kyoji. 1986. "Electoral Mobilization in Kansai and California," *Kansai University Review of Law and Politics* 7 March: 31–104.

Walder, Andrew G. 1986. *Communist Neo-Traditionalism.* Berkeley: University of California Press.

Ward, C., and A. Greeley. 1989. "'Development' and Tolerance." Draft Paper. Chicago: National Opinion Research Center.

Waters, S. 1994. "Tangentopoli and the Emergence of a New Political Order in Italy," *West European Politics* 17, 1.

Weakliem, D. 1991. "The Two Lefts? Occupation and Party Choice in France, Italy and the Netherlands." *American Journal of Sociology* 96 (May): 1327–1361.

Weakliem, David L., and Anthony F. Heath. 1995. "Class Voting in Britain and the United States." In Evans, Forthcoming.

---. Undated Draft. "Regional Differences in Class Dealignment." Submitted to *Political Geography.*

Webber, Carolyn, and Aaron Wildavsky. 1986. *A History of Taxation and Expenditure in the Western World.* New York: Simon and Schuster.

Wehling, Hans-Georg. 1992. "Politische beteiligung und kommunale demokratie," in Karl Starzacher, Konrad Schacht, Bernd Friedrich, Und Thomas Leif (Hrsg.). *Protestwähler und wahlverweigerer. krise der demokratie?* Köln: Bund-Verlag, pp. 131–145.

Weil, F. 1985. "The Variable Effects of Education on Liberal Attitudes." *American Sociological Review* 50: 458–474.

Welch, Susan. "The Impact of at-Large Elections on the Representation of Blacks and Hispanics." Journal of Politics 52, 4 (November 1990): 1050–1076.

Wilensky, Harold I. 1976. *The "New Corporatism".* London: Sage Publications.

Wilson, James Q. 1973/1974. *Political Organizations.* New York: Basic Books.

Wilson, James Q., and Edward C. Banfield. 1971. "Politial Ethos Revisited," *American Political Science Review* 65 (December): 1048–1062.

Wilson, W. J. 1978. *The Declining Significance of Race.* Chicago: University of Chicago Press.

Windhoff-Héritier, Adrienne. 1983. "Partizipation und Politikinhalte," in Oscar W. Gabriel (ed.), *Bürgerbeteiligung und kommunale Demokratie,* München, Pp. 305-337.

Wolman, H. 1992. "Mental Maps of Mayors." Presented to ECPR Conference, Limerick, Ireland.

Wolman, Harold, and Michael Goldsmith. 1987. "Local Government Fiscal Behavior and Intergovernmental Finance in a Period of Slow National Growth," in *Environment and Planning C: Government and Policy,* pp. 171–182.

World Bank. 1988 and other years. *World Development Report.* Oxford: Oxford University Press.

Wright, Erik Olin. 1985. *Classes.* London: Verso.

———. In Draft. *Class Counts.*

Wurzbacher, G., and R. Pflaum. 1954. *Das Dorf Im Spannungsfeld Industrieller Entwicklung.* Stuttgart: Enke.

Yankelovich, Daniel. 1981. *New Rules.* New York: Random House.

Yi, Joseph. 1997. "What I Found So Far: Atkinson National and FAUI Inequality Indices Compared," FAUI Project memo, University of Chicago.

Ysmal, Colette. 1990. "The Browning of Europe: Right Wing Extremism in European Elections." Draft Paper, Fondation National Des Sciences Politiques, Paris.

Zapf-Schramm, Thomas. 1989. Kommunale Umweltpolitik, in: Oscar W. Gabriel (ed.), *Kommunale Demokratie zwischen Politik und Verwaltung,* München, Pp. 299-336.

Zijderfeld, Anton. 1986. "The Ethos of the Welfare State," *International Sociology* 1: 443–458.